THE TORY CRISIS
IN CHURCH AND STATE
1688-1730

Francis Atterbury

The Tory Crisis
in Church and State
1688 – 1730

The career of Francis Atterbury
Bishop of Rochester

G. V. BENNETT

Clarendon Press · Oxford
1975

Oxford University Press, Ely House, London W.1

GLASGOW NEW YORK TORONTO MELBOURNE WELLINGTON
CAPE TOWN IBADAN NAIROBI DAR ES SALAAM LUSAKA ADDIS ABABA
DELHI BOMBAY CALCUTTA MADRAS KARACHI LAHORE DACCA
KUALA LUMPUR SINGAPORE HONG KONG TOKYO

ISBN 0 19 822444 3

© *Oxford University Press* 1975

*Printed in Great Britain
by W & J Mackay Limited, Chatham*

To

ERIC SYMES ABBOTT

Dean of Westminster

1959–1974

Preface

In the generation after the Revolution of 1688 the Church of England had to face the harsh fact that its status and authority had been severely diminished. At the Restoration the clergy as a class had become deeply committed to a high religious theory of kingship; they had supported the use of a revived and strengthened royal prerogative in the expectation that by its aid the Church's control over the morals and religious duties of the nation might be enforced and extended. Tory landowners had employed religious tests to secure for themselves a monopoly in municipal government and the administration of local justice. The Revolution was thus a shattering blow to the whole Anglican alliance of Church and State, and it ushered in an era of bitter grievance and furious agitation. Soon the ecclesiastical establishment was torn apart by a great clash of parties and it was clear, even to the most detached observer, that clergy and laity were engaged in a radical re-appraisal of the whole role of the national Church in English society.

Their discontents, anxieties and confusion of purposes went far to provide the very stuff of conflict in the party politics of the age of Anne; and indeed many of the great issues which agitated the statesmen and members of Parliament and sharpened the pens of the newsmen and pamphleteers were, or purported to be, religious in character. Tory politicians thought of themselves as engaged in a rearguard defence of a traditional way of life, but of all the causes which they pursued so passionately that of the Church of England was indisputably pre-eminent. The political crisis sprang in large measure from the fact that a vast majority of churchmen were prepared to join in an angry campaign for a return to the past when Church and State had conjoined in a single authoritarian regime. Indeed, even in the defeat of the High Church cause after 1714, when the iron bands of political patronage descended upon them, there were still men of character and intelligence who sought to restore the old order by the desperate expedient of plotting to bring back the exiled Stuart dynasty. This book is primarily an attempt to penetrate behind the slogans of Tory and Whig, High and Low Church, to discover the real nature of the great Anglican crisis after 1688.

It was necessary that this study should take the form of a biography, for at every step the story of Anglican Toryism marches parallel with the career of the most remarkable churchman of his day: Francis Atterbury, Bishop of Rochester. I am aware that in recent years there has developed a minor industry in the production of biographies of Augustan ecclesiastics, and I had no wish to add yet one more name to the roll-call of such worthies. There is, however, ample justification for offering a modern life of Francis Atterbury. First, his career is of a political importance equalled by that of no other Anglican divine with the possible exception of Jonathan Swift. For thirty years he was the prime mover and champion of the High Church cause and was closely involved in many of the major political events of the era. His life and ideas impinged on those of some of the outstanding men of his day: Harley, Bolingbroke, Walpole, Swift, and Alexander Pope. And, secondly, the colourfulness of his personality, with its many flaws as well as gifts, imparts to the story not only pace and excitement but also humour and something of the bizarre.

During his lifetime there were various attempts to portray Atterbury's career, but even the most competent of these was little more than a journalistic sketch. The difficulty for would-be biographers was that there was a total lack of basic evidence. The British Government, the Jacobites, and the families of those who had been closely involved with the Bishop in his trial and exile had all good reason for refusing to disclose information. It was only in 1783 that John Nichols began to publish some papers in private possession and not until 1847 that J. H. Glover printed the earlier Atterbury letters in the Stuart papers, by then at Windsor. Macaulay's famous essay in the *Encyclopaedia Britannica* was based only on these printed materials. In 1869 a journalist, Mr. Folkestone Williams, put out an imposing two-volume *Memoirs and Correspondence*, which contained virtually nothing not already in print and a narrative which joined wild surmise to gross error. In 1909 Canon H. C. Beeching published a brief and judicious biography which made use of the reports of the Historical Manuscripts Commission to that date; he was given access to the unsorted Stuart papers but appears to have flinched before the prospect of working systematically through them.

It is in the sixty years since Beeching wrote that the materials for a modern historical study have become available. The Stuart papers have been put into immaculate order, and a vast quantity of Atterbury correspondence has come to light. The Harley papers in the Portland loan at the British Museum have proved a far richer source than could have been suspected by those who had only the printed reports on them. The archive of Robert Walpole in the Cholmondeley (Houghton) deposit in the Cambridge University Library has made possible for the first time an informed assessment of the Atterbury plot and trial. And the heroic work of numerous local record offices since 1945 has revealed a host of new manuscript sources of first importance for Atterbury's career.

I have incurred many obligations in the course of writing this book. It is an honour to be able to head my list of acknowledgements with the name of Her Majesty Queen Elizabeth II by whose gracious permission I was allowed to use the Stuart papers and to quote freely from them. The Royal Librarian, Sir Robert Mackworth-Young, and his staff showed me every kindness. The owners of many other private collections permitted me to consult their manuscripts and, in particular, I acknowledge my debt to the Duke of Marlborough, the Duke of Portland, the Marquess of Bath, the Marquess of Cholmondeley, the Marquess of Downshire, the Earl of Harrowby, the Earl Waldegrave, Mrs. O. R. Bagot, Miss Olive Lloyd-Baker, Professor P. N. S. Mansergh, Mr. Francis Williams, and the Wake Trustees. The Deans and Chapters of Carlisle, Westminster, and York allowed me to consult their records. I am grateful for the courtesy and assistance of the library staffs of many public institutions in Britain and the United States.

Since I have taught at Oxford I have been especially fortunate in my research pupils, and I am sure that Robert Beddard, Henry Horwitz, and Bill Speck will recognize in these pages many matters which we have discussed together; I am grateful to them for their help. Geoffrey Holmes, John Walsh and Dame Lucy Sutherland have read my drafts and afforded me invaluable criticism and encouragement.

New College,
Oxford.   G. V. BENNETT

Contents

List of Illustrations

Abbreviations

All the printed sources cited in the footnotes were published in London, unless it is stated otherwise.

Add. MSS.   Additional Manuscripts.

Arch. Aff. Etr.   Archives du Ministère des Affaires Etrangères, Quai d'Orsay, Paris: Correspondance Politique, Angleterre.

Beeching   H. C. Beeching, *Francis Atterbury* (1909).

B.M.   Department of Manuscripts, the British Museum, London.

Bodl.   Department of Western Manuscripts, Bodleian Library, Oxford.

Bolingbroke Corr.   *Letters and Correspondence of Henry St. John, Viscount Bolingbroke,* ed. Gilbert Parke (2 vols., 1798).

C(H) MSS.   The Cholmondeley (Houghton) papers, deposited in the Cambridge University Library.

Coll. Trelawn.   Collectanea Trelawniana: a volume of transcripts from the papers once at Trelawne, Cornwall, the property of Mr. Francis Williams.

Coxe, M.   William Coxe, *Memoirs of John, Duke of Marlborough* (3 vols., 1818-19).

Coxe, W.   William Coxe, *Memoirs of the Life and Administration of Sir Robert Walpole* (3 vols., 1798).

C.R.   *Reports from Committees of the House of Commons,* Vol. I: *1715-1735* (1803), pp. 99-350: 1 March 1722 [i.e. 1723]: 'report from the committee appointed to examine Christopher Layer and others.'

E.C.   *The Epistolary Correspondence of the Right Reverend Francis Atterbury, D.D., Lord Bishop of Rochester,* ed. J. Nichols (4 vols., second edn, 1789-90; the fifth vol., first edn, 1798).

E.H.R.   *The English Historical Review.*

FA	Francis Atterbury.
FR	Atterbury as Bishop of Rochester.
Glover	*Letters of Francis Atterbury, Bishop of Rochester, to the Chevalier de St. George*, Vol. I [all published], ed. J. H. Glover (1847).
H.M.C.	The Historical Manuscripts Commission.
H.O.T.	*Bishop Burnet's History of His Own Time*, ed. M. J. Routh (6 vols., Oxford, 1823).
Kennett's diary	British Museum, Lansdowne MS. 1023: the diary of White Kennett, 1710-1714.
LCM	British Museum, Additional MS. 34713: Lord Chancellor Macclesfield's notes on Atterbury's trial.
L.J.	*Journals of the House of Lords.*
L.R.	*A Report from the Lords Committees empowered by the House of Lords to examine C. Layer, etc., 23 April 1723* (1723).
Nicolson's diary	'The diaries of William Nicolson', ed. Bishop Ware, *Transactions of the Cumberland and Westmorland Antiquarian and Archæological Society*, new series, vols. 1-6 (1901-1906); vol. 35, ed. R. G. Collingwood (1935); vols. 46, 50, ed. T. Gray and E. Birley (1946, 1950).
N.L.W.	Department of Manuscripts, National Library of Wales, Aberystwyth.
Parl. Hist.	*The Parliamentary History of England, 1066-1803*, ed. William Cobbett (36 vols., 1806-20).
Pol. Annals	Abel Boyer, *History of the Reign of Queen Anne*, digested into Annals (11 vols., 1703-13).
Pol. State	Abel Boyer, *The Political State of Great Britain, 1711-40* (60 vols., 1711-40).
Pope Corr.	*The Correspondence of Alexander Pope*, ed. George Sherburn (5 vols., Oxford, 1956).
Prussian MSS.	Deutsches Zentralarchiv, Merseburg, East Germany, Rep. XI (England), Frederick Bonet's dispatches.
R.A.	The Royal Archives, Windsor Castle.
R.O.	Record Office.

Sharp	Thomas Sharp, *The Life of John Sharp, Archbishop of York, collected from his diary, letters,* ed. T. Newcome (2 vols., 1825).
Sharp MSS.	Hardwicke Court, Gloucester, the Lloyd-Baker-Sharp papers.
S.P.	The Public Record Office, Chancery Lane, London, W.C.2: State Papers, Foreign and Domestic.
Stella	Jonathan Swift, *Journal to Stella,* ed. Harold Williams (2 vols., Oxford, 1948).
Swift Corr.	*The Correspondence of Jonathan Swift,* ed. Harold Williams (5 vols., Oxford, 1963-5).
Timberland	Ebenezer Timberland, *The History and Proceedings of the House of Lords from 1660 to the present time* (8 vols., 1741-2).
Wake's diary	Lambeth Palace Library MS. 1770: the diary of Archbishop Wake, 1705-1725.
Wake MSS.	Christ Church, Oxford: the papers of William Wake as Bishop of Lincoln and Archbishop of Canterbury

In passages quoted from manuscripts abbreviations have been extended and spelling has been modernized, unless this would interfere with the essential character of the text. Punctuation has been conformed to modern usage in cases where the meaning would otherwise be obscured.

A NOTE ON DATING

During Atterbury's lifetime Britain used the 'Old Style' dating of the Julian calendar while Western European countries used the 'New Style' of the Gregorian calendar. In this book Old Style is used for the years when Atterbury lived in England and New Style for the period of his residence in Belgium and France. Where there is possibility of confusion, as when letters pass between France and England, the dates are given in both styles. It is assumed that the new year begins on 1 January rather than on 25 March.

PART ONE

THE HIGH CHURCH CHAMPION

CHAPTER ONE

The Anglican Crisis

I

F O R the greater part of the seventeenth century religion held a place of unrivalled importance in men's lives. Belief in God and his providential ordering of human affairs was so universally embraced that by most thinkers it could be taken as intuitive. Christian faith provided a framework of ideas about kingship, law, society and the family. Political debate was conducted by appeals to Scripture, and the vexed questions of true religion and the purity of the Church were the very stuff of civil conflict. Religion was the atmosphere in which men felt most at home, its characteristic explanations those which came most readily to the mind. In England the Church remained what it had been since medieval times: the most important institution in the land. It was intimately bound up with government, landownership, and the social hierarchy. In the county palatine of Durham the Bishop still exercised a princely function; he appointed the officials of local administration and justice was administered in his name. Great sees like those of London and Winchester had rent-rolls equal to those of a duke. Tenants and farmers depended on the clergy for favourable leases and moderate fines, and with such economic dependence went social and political influence. The arrival of a new bishop in his cathedral city was an occasion of splendour, with the gentry riding out to meet him, the city fathers in their formalities, bells pealing, soldiers parading, and guns saluting. Deans and chapters, with the officials and lawyers who did the Church's business, could dominate the life of the provincial towns in which they were set. And in numberless parishes, lost in the deep obscurity of English rural life, the parson, poor and neglected though he might be, was often the only literate person in a community of farmers and simple rustics. He supplied their news, controlled their charities, collected their tithes, and censored their morals. It was impossible to ignore the influence of the Church or avoid its authority. Lawyers, administrators and agriculturalists met it in their daily work; and lovers, fornicators, neglected spouses and the bodies of the dead were involved in its jurisdiction.

That the Church was a divinely commissioned body few would have ventured to deny, perhaps because on the English scene this meant in practical terms very little. If men thought of the authority of the Church of England they thought primarily in terms of law. The ecclesiastical establishment as such had no central government. It consisted of a series of legal 'corporations', the character of which was defined by a complex of statutes, canons, past judicial decisions, and customary practice. A bishopric, an archdeaconry, a cathedral prebend, a rectory, and even a humble vicarage: each was, in the lawyers' language, a 'corporation sole'. When once their 'incumbents' had been duly confirmed, collated or instituted they possessed a freehold for life: they had a right to gather the income and an obligation to carry out the prescribed duties. In such a world precedent was immensely important, and ancient charters, founders' statutes, and dusty minute-books were cherished and studied with loving care. Even clergymen who were otherwise of exemplary piety showed a tendency to regard their function in terms of what the law required. Only the unbeneficed, the clerical proletariate of mere curates, lacked security. Everyone else, including ecclesiastical officials such as chancellors of dioceses, registrars and chapter-clerks, held their offices for life and were (except in cases of quite flagrant misbehaviour) irremovable. Only an Act of Parliament could change or reshape any part of this complex ecclesiastical establishment: those who lived in it and did its work had to abide by its conditions and limitations. It was widely recognized that all this was a grave obstacle in the way of any coherent policy or reform. Successive Archbishops of Canterbury felt their powerlessness, and sought by dint of careful scholarship and close application to business to make themselves experts in the history and law of the Church. The official papers of Archbishops Sancroft, Tenison and Wake bristle with rare points of law and antiquarian treatises. Only by the manipulation of such dry matter could their pastoral oversight be made effective.

Preaching in 1661 at the consecration of a new bishop, Dr. Robert

South expressed succinctly the political faith of the Restoration Church:

The Church of England glories in nothing more than that she is the truest friend of kings and kingly government, of any other church in the world; that they were the same hands that took the crown from the king's head and the mitre from the bishops.[1]

After all the disasters of the Civil War and the Commonwealth, as by a miracle, the hereditary monarchy and the Anglican order of the Church had been re-established. Few doubted that in the future they would stand or fall together. The divines accepted without hesitation their role as servants of a regime of personal monarchy and as advocates of an authoritarian view of society. The national Church was cherished as a bulwark against civil strife and religious anarchy. As a class the clergy became committed to a high religious theory of kingship. Each 30 January, the anniversary of the execution of Charles I, and each 29 May, the day of his son's return, the pulpits thundered forth the doctrines of the divine hereditary right of kings and the utter sinfulness of resistance to their commands. The bishops of Charles II were considered as great officers of state, and the ordinary diocesans were expected to report on the political condition of the counties in their pastoral charge and 'promote good elections'. In the great struggle between the King and those who sought to exclude from the succession his Roman Catholic brother, James, Duke of York, the episcopate was immovable in the Duke's cause. So eminent were their services that in February 1681 the bishops of Scotland were moved to send their congratulations. They were

verie sensible of the great right your lordships have done to the Protestant principles, and the interest of both churches, by your unshakable loyaltie to the king, and by your steddie and resolut appearing for his royall Highness's just right.[2]

The most single-minded of the servants of the House of Stuart was

[1] R. South, *A Sermon preached at Lambeth Chapel upon the Consecration of the Lord Bishop of Rochester, Nov. 25 1661*. I am grateful to Macmillan & Co. for allowing me to use in the following paragraphs material which appeared in my essay 'Conflict in the Church' in *Britain after the Glorious Revolution 1689-1714*, ed. G. Holmes (1969).

[2] Bodl. MS. Tanner 37, fo. 245.

undoubtedly William Sancroft, Archbishop of Canterbury from 1677 to 1691, a man who combined an almost mystical reverence for monarchy with a passion that the influence of his Church should be extended. After 1681 he united with Court politicians, and especially with the Hyde brothers, the Earls of Clarendon and Rochester, to build up a strong Yorkist party. When the King created an Ecclesiastical Commission to advise him on all senior appointments in the Church the Archbishop used it as an instrument to promote only those of proven loyalist opinions. During his primacy no fewer than twenty-two of the twenty-seven dioceses received a new and royalist Father-in-God.[1]

In return for so energetic a contribution to the Stuart cause, Sancroft hoped that a revived and strengthened prerogative might be put to work to serve the Church. Closely associated with a religious theory of kingship was a religious interpretation of human society and social obligation. With obedience to kings went reverence and submission to parsons and squires, to fathers and employers. Indeed loyalist doctrines tended to the position that all rightful authority was a reflection of God's providential rule of the world and that disobedience was sinful in character. Sancroft's voluminous papers reveal how thoroughgoing were his efforts to refurbish Anglican discipline over the nation. Many of his projects were reminiscent of those of Laud; and he was anxious to increase the reputation, learning and income of the parish priests who were to be the agents of this policy. His greatest concern was with the Church courts. It is commonly stated by historians that after 1660 the ecclesiastical courts were never able to recover the vigour of their jurisdiction, but the evidence is quite otherwise. Perhaps a few technical questions they did yield to Chancery, but Restoration common-law judges showed a far greater readiness to lend their assistance to the ecclesiastical jurisdiction than had their earlier seventeenth-century predecessors. The consistory court of a bishop or the court of an archdeacon dealt with a wide range of matters which would now be considered wholly civil: matrimonial causes,

---

[1] See the excellent article by R. A. Beddard, 'The Commission for Ecclesiastical Promotions, 1681-84: an instrument of Tory reaction', *The Historical Journal*, x (1967), 11. Dr. Beddard's forthcoming book on Sancroft will illuminate the problems of the Restoration Church.

probate, tithe, and even cases of brawling and unseemly conduct. They also exercised a comprehensive control over the morals and religious duties of the laity. Once a year the churchwardens of every parish had to 'present' to the archdeacon all moral offences and all cases of ecclesiastical neglect. It was open to any private person to 'promote the office of the judge' and accuse his neighbours of similar defects. In fact the records of the Church courts after 1661 abound in the moral offences of the laity: adultery, fornication, begetting bastard children, and blasphemy. Ecclesiastical offences were even more frequent: not coming to church on Sundays, working on holy days and fast days, not receiving the sacrament at Easter, not sending children or servants to be catechized, and acting as schoolmaster, physician or midwife without proper episcopal licence.[1]

It is important not to underestimate the effectiveness of this Anglican discipline. Doubtless there were abuses, and an obdurate offender well provided with time and money could involve his prosecutor in grievous costs. A continual pressure had to be kept on local officials to make them work the system. As the Bishop of Peterborough explained to Sancroft in 1680:

> The defects can never be known by the presentments of the churchwardens when they shall be hastily demanded to give an account of them. They will forswear themselves over and over rather than bring expense on themselves and their neighbours, epecially when they have to do with men whom they never saw before and shall never see again, who cannot tell whether they speak true or false.[2]

But, in spite of difficulties, the profession of an ecclesiastical lawyer flourished, and careful manuals were written of their practice. The courts were certainly not without sharp teeth; and their chief sanction, the excommunication of an offender, had serious consequences for any man of position. An excommunicate could neither make a will nor bring an action in a civil court, and he could not qualify himself for public office under the Test and Corporation

[1] See M. G. Smith, 'The administration of the diocese of Exeter during the episcopate of Sir Jonathan Trelawny, 1689-1707' (Oxford unpublished B.D. thesis, 1964); and Bodl. MS. Tanner 300, fo. 143 for a paper in Sancroft's handwriting, 'for the regulation of ecclesiastical affairs'.

[2] Bodl. MS. Tanner 31, fo. 277, White to Sancroft, 1 Mar. 1680.

Acts by receiving the sacrament of Holy Communion. If the ecclesiastical judge 'signified' him to the secular authority he could be imprisoned until submission. What Sancroft's policy achieved, when the Government lent its aid, was impressive. In 1676 two country parsons recorded their figures of Easter communicants. William Sampson, Rector of Clayworth, Nottinghamshire, was a grasping, ungenerous man for whom his parishioners can have felt little affection, yet he noted the names of no less than 200 communicants where only 236 persons were of an age and qualified to receive the sacrament. Between 1676 and 1686 his numbers remained constant at this high level. In the Kentish village of Goodnestone the curate, Francis Nicholson, recorded 128 persons who communicated out of a possible 144.[1] The year 1676 was, of course, a time when the Government of Danby was lending its full support to Anglican efforts, but the fact remains that when virtually the whole population of a village from the squire down to the labourers and their wives knelt at the altar rails, the power of the Church, at least in the countryside, was still strong.

2

The Anglican scheme possessed one fatal flaw. Both Charles II and his brother were earnest in their endeavours for a general toleration, and influential Anglicans always recognized that this royal desire posed a serious threat to their whole ecclesiastical polity. The position was especially difficult at a time when educated opinion was hardening against the coercion of respected and peaceable Dissenters. It thus became their tactic to counter every suggestion of a 'toleration' with an offer to consider a 'comprehension'. A toleration would obviously shatter the whole disciplinary machinery of the national Church, but a comprehension would at least preserve the theory that all citizens came under the aegis of ecclesiastical authority. Thus at all moments of political crisis discussions were held with leading Dissenters with a view to relaxing the stricter terms of membership of the Anglican Church: ceremonies were to be optional, oaths and subscriptions attenuated, and easy conditions

---

[1] *The Rector's Book, Clayworth, Notts.*, ed. H. Gill and E. L. Guilford (1910); Peter Laslett, *The World we have lost* (1965), p. 71.

laid down by which Nonconformist ministers might receive preferments and benefices.[1] Comprehension was always the policy of
avowed High Churchmen such as Daniel Finch, Earl of Nottingham; and Sancroft lent the notion his full support. Its underlying
aim was to comprehend all moderate Dissenters into the Church of
England, but then to continue the persecution of obdurate sectaries
or admit them to only the barest form of a toleration.

The blow which ruined everything was struck by King James II.
When the Duke succeeded to the throne in 1685 Sancroft and his
friends staked their future on his willingness to work with and
through Anglicans, and they were not without reason for their
hopes. Although an emphatic and devout Roman Catholic, James
had repeatedly promised his many Anglican allies that he would
always 'support and defend' their Church. During the time of his
personal rule in Scotland he had associated himself firmly with the
episcopalian party. But from 1686 the King reversed his whole
policy and attacked the Anglican regime in Church and State with
the utmost vehemence. In April 1687 his Declaration of Indulgence
decreed that 'all and all manner of penal laws in matters ecclesiastical for not coming to Church or not receiving the sacrament, or
for any other nonconformity . . . be immediately suspended.'
Whatever the legality of such a declaration, its effect on the Church
of England was immediate and catastrophic. From the summer of
1687 the whole class of business in the Church courts concerning
attendance at church drops away, and the number of moral cases
against the laity perceptibly diminish.[2] Amid the collapse of their
cherished order of things, Sancroft and his brethren hoped desperately that the King might come to his senses and return to his
Anglican alliance. As reports came up to them from the dioceses of
the full extent of the ecclesiastical revolution, they found themselves
moved, however unwillingly, to protest. The famous petition of the
Seven Bishops was an uneasy bid by a group of Court loyalists to
save the authority of their Church by warning the King and calling
him back to the path of Anglican-Tory authoritarianism. Yet, even

[1] R. Thomas, 'Comprehension and Indulgence', in *From Uniformity to
Unity, 1662-1962*, eds. G. F. Nuttall and O. Chadwick (1962).
[2] See M. G. Smith, op. cit., p. 89, for the immediate effect on the business
of the courts at Exeter.

when their master had them publicly prosecuted and tried for sedition, they prayed and looked for a reconciliation with him. The invasion of William of Orange and James's flight to France brought them no joy; it was the final stroke which laid in ruins their whole concept of the alliance of Church and State.

The events of the Revolution put the clergy under the severest strain. Although the Tory lay politicians did their best to secure some formula which would satisfy the old beliefs about kingship, the outcome was stark. In March 1689 the throne was declared vacant, and a resolution of both Houses of the Convention Parliament offered the Crown jointly to William and Mary. New oaths were prescribed by statute to be sworn by all office-holders and beneficed clergy. Private diaries and surviving correspondence attest the agony of spirit endured by those faced with the oaths to the new rulers. Could Anglican divines disavow their preaching for a generation? Was not James II rightful king still, and was not the Revolution a prime example of that rebellion and resistance against which they had so often inveighed? If they thus shifted their allegiance, where stood now the religious view of society and social obligation? For some their course was quite clear. Archbishop Sancroft refused by word or action to acknowledge the new regime; five of his episcopal brethren followed him into the wilderness of deprivation and poverty, and just over four hundred of the lower clergy. These Nonjurors were few in number, but their effect on the great body of conforming Anglicans was profound: they were like a ghost of the past, confessors who stood in the ancient ways, devout, logical and insistent. For the Nonjurors the conforming Church of England was no Church at all; it had apostatized from its distinctive doctrines by adhesion to a usurper. Men such as George Hickes or Henry Dodwell, who had given up everything in the cause of loyalty, treated conformists with an angry contempt. The majority of the clergy took the oaths, usually on the casuistical argument that they would obey William as *de facto* king but continue to honour James as their *de jure* prince. Most went into the new era with deeply uneasy consciences. They sought around for some formula or theory by which they could preserve as much as possible of the old ways of thought in the conditions of a changed age.

The most delicate question of the 1689 was that of the degree of toleration to be allowed to the Dissenters. Its solution was strangely unsatisfactory. On 27 February Lord Nottingham introduced two bills into the House of Lords: one for a comprehension, the other for a toleration. The two were designed to go together. The first laid down generous terms by which Dissenters might be admitted to the Church of England, while the second provided carefully limited terms for the toleration of the relatively small number who could be expected to refuse to be so comprehended. On 14 March both bills received a second reading. But two days later King William made a grievous personal error. Without testing the opinion of his Ministers, he appeared in the House of Lords and from the throne proposed the abolition of the Test and Corporation Acts. Anglican alarm and anger were difficult to keep within bounds. Not only was the King's proposal overwhelmingly defeated, but the Comprehension Bill itself was lost, and the Toleration Bill alone went on to become law. The result was that the new act, which had been designed to deal with a small number of intransigent Nonconformists, now had to apply to nearly half a million sober and respectable citizens. It was a modest document. Dissenters who took the oaths of Supremacy and Allegiance and made the Declaration against Transubstantiation were allowed to worship separately in their own meeting-houses. Ministers had to subscribe to such of the Thirty-Nine Articles as did not directly concern church-government, and all places of worship had to be registered with a bishop or at the Quarter Sessions. Services had to be conducted with the doors unlocked. No mention was made of permission for Dissenting education, and Non-conformists still laboured under the disabilities of the Test and Corporation Acts. The Toleration Act specifically laid it down that the old laws about attendance at church on a Sunday still applied to those who did not resort to a meeting-house. But it was soon clear that such stringent provisions could not stand. Although the clergy professed to stand by its strict terms, it was interpreted quite differently by the Government and by the great majority of ordinary lay-people. Churchwardens and others insisted on regarding the act as a statutory continuation of the state of affairs which had existed since James II's Declaration of Indulgence. The wardens of Ditton in Surrey may be taken as typical. When chided by the archdeacon in 1690 as to why they had not presented absentees from church, they replied defiantly: 'liberty of conscience being allowed by the supreme authority, we have nothing of neglect or defect to present.'[1] Another archdeacon, that of Norwich, complained bitterly that the Toleration Act had not so much given a liberty to Dissenters as destroyed any control he could exercise over churchgoing:

> The mischief is, a liberty being granted, more lay hold of it to separate from all manner of worship to perfect irreligion than go to the meeting-houses; and although the act allows no such liberty, the people will understand it so, and, say what the judges can at the assizes, or the justices of the peace at their sessions, or we at our visitations, no churchwarden or constable will present any for not going to church, though they go nowhere else but to the ale-house, for this liberty they will have.[2]

Obviously where squire and parson united to bring social pressure to bear on a rural community something of the old order remained, but in the absence of a Sir Roger de Coverley congregations decreased year by year. After 1689 Parson Sampson's Easter communicants diminished remorselessly; and in 1701, the last year of his records, they had fallen to 126 souls. At Bucknell in Oxfordshire they crept down from 55 in 1699 to 32 in 1709. By the 1740s the process had completed itself, and with increasing population numbers even began to rise again. But between 1732 and 1742 a young and energetic vicar, such as Thomas Leigh of Lower Heyford, Oxfordshire, had to rest content with an average of only twenty of his parishioners at the Easter sacrament, out of a qualified population of 220.[3]

The evidence is clear that the middle years of King William's reign proved deeply unhappy for the parochial clergy. In particular there was much grievance over the relationship of the Church to the newly legitimized Dissenting bodies. The number of licences taken out under the Toleration Act was a great surprise. In the first year

---

[1] Greater London Council Archives Office, AB 1-3: churchwardens' presentments, 1664-1927.

[2] *Letters of Humphrey Prideaux to John Ellis, 1674-1722*, ed. E. M. Thompson (1875), p. 154. For an account of Prideaux, see R. W. Ketton-Cremer, *Norfolk Assembly* (1957), pp. 65-91.

[3] Bodl. MS. Top. Oxon. e. 11, 'communicants at Bucknell, 1699-1723'; MS. Top. Oxon. f. 50, 'incumbent's book of Lower Heyford.'

of its operation 796 temporary and 143 permanent meeting-houses were licensed, and the Quakers set up an additional 239. In the years from 1691 to 1710 no less than 2,536 places were licensed.[1] Many of these would have been private houses or even barns, and the number of specifically constructed chapels was still small, but up and down the land parsons were facing a new and disturbing phenomenon: a local Dissenting congregation meeting openly for worship and competing with them for the hearts and minds of their parishioners. Especially vexed was the issue of Nonconformist education. Most churchmen made a clear distinction between Dissenting 'academies' and ordinary grammar schools. On the whole they were prepared to turn a blind eye on the activities of the former, which were institutions of university standard where students were trained for the ministry and a higher education was available for those who would not take the religious tests imposed at Oxford and Cambridge. In the years after the Revolution these academies underwent an extraordinary expansion and were even popular with some Anglican parents who hesitated to entrust their offspring to the right-wing politics and conspicuous expenditure of the universities. In 1690 some Yorkshire clergymen prosecuted Richard Frankland, the distinguished principal of the academy at Rathmell, and secured his excommunication in the consistory court. The result, however, was an order from the King himself requiring his immediate absolution, and on three similar occasions the Archbishop of York also quashed proceedings against him.[2] But most bishops drew the line at Dissenting participation in public elementary or grammar school education, and they made great efforts to compel schoolmasters to take out licences. By the Act of Uniformity of 1662 such an episcopal licensing authority was specifically provided for, but at the end of William's reign a judicial decision in the civil courts threw the whole matter into confusion and made prosecutions difficult and expensive.

An even greater grievance was the practice known as Occasional Conformity. Under the Test and Corporation Acts any person appointed to an office of profit under the Crown or to any municipal

---

[1] E. D. Bebb, *Nonconformity and Social and Economic Life, 1660-1800* (1935), pp. 45, 174.
[2] A. Tindal Hart, *John Sharp* (1949), pp. 136-38.

office had to receive the Holy Communion according to the Anglican rite and obtain from the officiating minister a qualifying certificate. On any re-election or re-appointment another certificate had to be acquired. The device was plainly intended to exclude all non-Anglicans from public office, and it did effectively so exclude Roman Catholics, but it became a widespread practice that Dissenters should pay a single visit to their parish church, receive the sacrament and their certificate, and thereafter go regularly and cheerfully to a meeting-house. Some borough corporations, and notably the great cities of London and Bristol, were heavily stocked with such 'occasional conformists'. And as the Anglican squirearchy saw their monopoly invaded, their anger knew no bounds. To William Bromley, one of the most able and respected Tory politicians, it was 'that abominable hypocrisy, that inexcusable immorality of occasional conformity'.[1] A few clergy went so far as to refuse the sacrament to Dissenters, though this could legally be done only on the grounds that the intending communicant was 'an open and notorious evil-liver'. The truth was, however, that occasional conformity had a long and respectable history. After the great ejectment of 1662 many ministers, such as a Richard Baxter and William Bates, had continued to communicate in their parish churches as an occasional act of charity; and at a time when it was customary for the sacrament to be celebrated only three or four times in the year many Dissenters received Holy Communion only in Anglican churches. At no time was the line between churchman and Dissenter closely drawn, and many families went to both church and the meeting-house.

The effect of the Toleration on the church courts was marked. Occasionally after 1689 offenders were put to penance in the old style, but this kind of moral oversight became increasingly harder to enforce. The poorer classes might submit for a while, but in 1718 Bishop Blackburne of Exeter freely admitted that most of the correction business in his courts had failed because neither he nor his archdeacons were prepared to meet the financial outlay involved.[2] The attitude of the Government tended to reflect the popular determination. In the years 1689, 1694 and 1708 Whig

[1] Bodl. MS. Ballard 38, fo. 137, Bromley to Charlett, 22 Oct. 1702.
[2] Wake MSS. 21, fo. 27, Blackburne to Wake, 23 Aug. 1718.

administrations secured the passing of Acts of General Pardon which at a stroke brought proceedings in the church courts to a standstill and annulled the temporal penalties of excommunication. Occasionally a zealous churchwarden tried to reactivate the old system. In 1693 a warden at Plymouth presented a shipwright for working on a naval vessel on a fast-day, and at once a letter was sent down from no less exalted a personage than the Secretary of State himself directing that the Bishop should put a stop to this interference with the war-effort.[1] Thus by the beginning of the eighteenth century a great change had come over the ecclesiastical jurisdiction, and the bulk of its business, apart from routine procedure in matrimonial and probate causes, came to consist of tithe cases and trivial matters relating to the parish church and its furnishings. In only one respect did their business actually increase, and that was in cases involving the clergy themselves. Energetic and reforming diocesans like Tenison, Sharp, Burnet and Trelawny turned their attention to the disciplining of parsons who neglected their duties, allowed their chancels to fall into disrepair or brought disgrace upon their cloth by scandalous or dishonest behaviour. There is little doubt that part of the mood of bitterness which characterized the ordinary clergy after the Revolution lay in the sense of betrayal which they felt when the courts, which had once been their own instrument against recalcitrant parishioners, were turned against themselves.

The problem of clerical poverty was a familiar theme during the seventeenth century, and it was a recognized fact that a poor parson who could not buy books, distribute charity or keep his family above servile labour could not command the respect of rustics nor do effective work among them. On the whole those who had the status of 'rector' and thus the right to collect all the tithes of the parish were in reasonable circumstances. 'Vicars', who could claim only the lesser tithes, were usually poorer; and could be very poor. Throughout the Restoration era great endeavours had been made to raise and augment the incomes of benefices by a host of sympathetic patrons and benefactors, but this work was now undone.[2] During

---

[1] *Calendar of State Papers Domestic, 1693*, p. 260, Nottingham to Trelawny, 10 Aug. 1693.
[2] See the many examples quoted by White Kennett in *The Case of Impropriations* (1704).

the period from 1689 to 1702 no less than £58 millions were raised in taxation, mostly through the Land Tax. The parson who lived mostly off the profits of land, by his tithes and glebe, had to pay on the major part of his income. In addition tithes were assessed to the poor-rate, and the various attempts during the 1690s at a poll-tax gave clergymen a high rate of payment.[1] By 1697 beneficed clergy were often paying between a quarter and a third of their income in some kind of tax or levy. Writing in 1704 of the bitterness of party conflict, Charles Davenant remarked shrewdly that 'the scandalous poverty of the clergy has very ill effects'.[2]

3

Material poverty was, however, as nothing compared with the un-nerving experience of living in the ferment of a theological revolution. Seventeenth century divinity had been massively learned. Today its great tomes lie heavily on the shelves of old libraries and surprise the casual reader with closely printed columns, an array of ancient languages, and intricate reference to the authority of the traditional past. Theological argument was won or lost by appeal to the writings of the Fathers of the Early Church. But after 1660 men became tired of endless disputes over church-government or the nature of justification, and turned with relief to a plainer teaching. Increasingly they became fascinated by science and mathematics, and the new view of the world which these seemed to open up. Many of the natural scientists, such as Robert Boyle and John Ray, were convinced Christians who protested piously that their methods could only support a sense of awe before God's mighty and intricate wisdom in creation. They argued modestly for a diligent collection of plants and fossils, and for drawing reasonable general conclusions from their study. But it was from their colleagues, the mathematicians, that a veritable revolution was to come; and soon Sir Isaac Newton's famous law of gravity came to supply the norm by which

[1] See *The Parson's Case under the present Land Tax* (1689), p. 5, et seq. The author argues that the clergy were paying a quarter more tax than their neighbours if rectors and a third more if vicars. In the Bodleian copy [Pamph. 191] there are contemporary MS. additions which seek to show that the clergy's assessment to the poor-rate was correspondingly too high.

[2] B.M. Add. MSS. 773, fo. 17.

all other kinds of truth were to be judged. Newton showed men that, no matter how vast or complex the universe might be, it was still governed by a single uniform mathematical order, the principles of which could be stated simply and clearly. The natural order was indeed like a mechanism and beautiful in the utter regularity of its working. After this it was not easy to find a place for that sovereign working of God's providence in which the seventeenth century had believed with such passionate intensity.

As Newton gave his contemporaries a new universe so John Locke gave them a new picture of the working of the human mind. His writings provided exactly that blend of reason and simplicity which was coming to be expected and admired. Locke himself was a humble and genuinely devout man. He wrote with penetrating argument and a graceful style, and his works achieved a European reputation. No one so clearly embodied the eighteenth century impatience with revered and traditional authority. 'Reason', he declared, 'must be our best judge and guide in all things.' Repeatedly he castigated those who would 'take men off from the use of their own reason and judgement, and put them upon believing and taking upon trust without further examination'. If one desired true knowledge one must begin with 'self-evident facts and self-evident propositions, and proceed by mathematically correct deductions'. He believed that by his own methods he could prove that it was 'as clear as demonstration can make it that there must be an eternal Being', and he was prepared to claim that this rational argument for God's existence was 'equal to mathematical certainty'. But when so exalted a place was given to human reason in the discovery of religious truth, some account had to be given of the place of divine revelation in the scheme. What of the Bible and its authority? What of the person of Jesus Christ and the miracles recorded in the Gospels? To such difficult questions Locke turned in 1695 when he published a momentous book, *The Reasonableness of Christianity*. His position was carefully stated. Though he could never accept that there could be anything in religion contrary to reason, yet there were some matters *above* it, and these were the sphere of revelation. But this revelation was simple in content. He had found, he said, 'little satisfaction and consistency in most of the systems of divinity', and he had resolved 'to betake myself to the sole reading of the Scripture'.

For contemporaries, brought up in the old ways, there was something immensely exciting as a distinguished philosopher cast aside traditional theology and went to Scripture, insisting that it should be 'understood in the plain, direct meaning of the words and phrases'. And Locke professed himself amazed by what he found. All that was necessary to be believed on the strength of revelation was that Jesus was the 'Messiah' and that he pointed the way to a good life. 'Salvation or perdition', he concluded, 'depends upon believing or rejecting this one proposition.' It was true that a place had been preserved for divine revelation, but the Christ whom Locke now presented was a pale shadow of the powerful Saviour of the seventeenth century preachers.

Thoughtful churchmen knew that Locke's theories, taken to their logical conclusion, left no place either for traditional orthodoxy or for the authority and discipline of the Church of England. But the attraction of the new notions was strong, and many followed Locke discreetly in preaching a Christianity which was reasonable and which consisted above all in living well. John Tillotson, with his beautifully phrased and prudential discourses, revolutionized preaching style; and soon a host of his imitators were attracting large audiences to prosperous City churches. These prominent Anglican exponents of the new religion of 'reason and natural religion' usually left much unsaid and tended to avoid pronouncements on the nature of the Church or the person of Christ. But where they were silent, it was too much to expect that the lesser fry would similarly hold their peace. In 1695 the Licensing Act expired, by which the Archbishop of Canterbury and the Bishop of London had censored theological books. Pamphleteers still had to walk circumspectly when writing on political questions, and until well into the eighteenth century it was a hazardous business to defame ministers of the Crown, but heresy and attacks on the ministers of God now became virtually unpunishable and a flood of heterodox and anti-clerical literature poured on to the popular bookmarket. Among the most notorious of the new writers was John Toland, who in 1696 published a small book which set the clerical world in a fury. In this *Christianity Not Mysterious* he professed to write as a candid friend, a loyal member of the Church of England who was disquieted that the clergy should continue so besotted with antiquated divinity:

How many voluminous systems, infinitely more difficult than the scriptures, must be read by him that would be a master of the present theology? What prodigious number of barbarous words (mysterious no doubt), what tedious and immethodical directions, what ridiculous and discrepant interpretations must you patiently learn and observe, before you can begin to understand a professor of that faculty.[1]

In place of this 'scholastic jargon' he proposed a Christianity which was not only reasonable but which rigorously excluded everything not immediately intelligible to an ordinary man. God, opined Toland, would not have communicated himself to human beings 'if what he said did not agree with their common notions'. Revelation's function was to confirm what reason discovered for itself, and he was firmly against so-called 'mysteries' or any doctrine which went beyond man's usual comprehension. Toland's treatise was presented as a common nuisance by the Grand Jury of Middlesex and the Irish Parliament ordered it to be burnt by the public hangman, but the very fury which followed it showed the intense interest aroused. The letters of country clergymen at this period are a study in the shock and anger which a class of men, naturally conservative, feel when their accustomed ways of thought are suddenly questioned and derided. Socinians such as the indefatigable Thomas Firmin or plain anti-clericals like Anthony Collins, Matthew Tindal or Charles Blount had been given their freedom. The Blasphemy Act of 1697 was passed as some defence against the new writings but proved a dead letter from the start. Bishop Burnet described how

it became a common topic of discourse to treat all mysteries in religion as the contrivances of priests to bring the world into a blind submission to them; *priestcraft* grew to be another word in fashion, and the enemies of religion vented all their impieties under the cover of these words.[2]

Certainly none can doubt the anti-clerical animus of the writers who followed Toland. Indeed Alexander Pope was not unjust when he pointed to a constant denigration of the clergy as the distinguishing

---

[1] The edition of 1696, p. xxiv, quoted by G. R. Cragg, *From Puritanism to the Age of Reason* (Cambridge, 1950). Dr. Cragg has a useful discussion of Toland.

[2] *H.O.T.*, iv. 378.

mark of the new theologians, and wrote of 'Toland and Tindal, prompt at priests to jeer'.[1]

4

By the end of William's reign it was clear that the great body of the clergy, dismayed and resentful at the changes which had come upon them, longed for a return to the past. The Stuart era became invested with the character of a golden age in which the Church of England had stood secure, before the Toleration had shattered her discipline, and taxes and infidels had begun to oppress her ministers. Around the person of the last monarch of the old House, that devoted churchwoman, Queen Anne, they hoped to revive the doctrines of divine right and passive obedience, and stop the gradual seeping away of a religious basis to social and political obligation. At the heart of the High Church movement was a simple belief that the conditions of the old establishment could be restored by firm political action. If a majority of Anglican loyalists could be returned to the House of Commons then they could press for legislation which would define the Toleration Act as a bare permission for separate Nonconformist worship. Parliament alone, with the advice and assistance of Convocation, could put an end to the continual decay in the status and authority of the clergy. But for all this they needed the support of influential politicians, and those who had survived from the days of the Anglican Court party of Sancroft and the Hydes exercised a special attraction for the country parsons. When Rochester or Nottingham beckoned, many were eager to follow. They represented hope for a return out of captivity, and the majority of the Anglican priesthood looked to them to provide a way by which the Temple of the Lord might be rebuilt in Sion.

An alternative policy was that adopted by Thomas Tenison who in 1695 succeeded John Tillotson as Archbishop of Canterbury.[2] Tenison was a dull and prosaic man, and yet by any account he was a great primate. He realized plainly that the Church of England could now expect little from the Government and that any increase

---

[1] *The Poems of Alexander Pope*, iv. *The Dunciad*, ed. J. Sutherland (1963), p. 144. For an especially insulting work, see C. Blount, *Great is Diana of the Ephesians* (1695).

[2] E. F. Carpenter, *Thomas Tenison, Archbishop of Canterbury* (1948) has a useful but somewhat ill-digested account.

in spiritual effectiveness would have to come from voluntary action. Thus the Williamite bishops made great efforts to turn their clergy's attention to pastoral concerns. A new vigour came into the episcopal office. Archbishop Sharp of York and Bishops Burnet, Stillingfleet, Patrick and Kidder travelled out into remote corners of their dioceses which had scarcely ever before seen a confirmation service; episcopal visitations inquired into negligent incumbents; and unauthorized pluralists and absentees were called to account.[1] The process was not always a popular one. Burnet in particular handled his diocesan clergy with less than tact and earned a deep and lasting dislike for his attempts to change their ways. But the rise in standards was perceptible.

In the midst of political conflict the 1690s saw the beginnings of a spiritual revival. As Vicar of St. Martin's-in-the-Fields, Tenison had shown an immense compassion for the poor and unchurched of his vast parish, and he had been a pioneer in voluntary relief work. People as diverse as the fastidious diarist John Evelyn or the astute courtier Lord Sunderland had sought his spiritual advice, which was kindly, practical and unexciting. But passion touched his stolid nature when he contemplated the face of his parish. With so much ostentatious wealth in evidence, the poor lived crowded into tenements and basements amid squalor, stench and filth. The death-rate, and especially the infant mortality, was appalling. Around his church, to which the fashionable came in great numbers, were brothels, ginshops and gambling houses. One bitter November night in 1687 he sat by the bedside of Nell Gwyn as she lay dying in her lodgings in Pall Mall; and, perhaps troubled by the thought of many sins, she accepted his suggestion for a public bequest: not to the church but for 'clothes for the winter and such other necessaries as he shall think fit' for the very poorest of his parishioners. With the aid of a group of earnest laymen he was able to found on land beside the church a parochial school where the children of the indigent could be clothed, fed and educated. When they were ready to leave, the foundation would pay for them to be entered as apprentices. They were to be taught the elements of literacy and to cast simple

---

[1] For a valuable review of the problems and achievements of the early eighteenth century episcopate, see Norman Sykes, *Church and State in England in the XVIII Century* (Cambridge, 1934), chapter 3.

accounts, but the whole education was to be on the strictest Anglican principles. The masters had to be regular communicants and bring their charges regularly to church; the children had to learn the catechism and recite from the Bible and the Prayer Book. The sight of these clean and neatly dressed scholars, filling the galleries and sitting attentatively during service and sermon, had the power to move churchmen to tears, and funds for new schools were readily forthcoming.[1] Thus when Tenison became Archbishop he gave vigorous support to the whole voluntary movement. In the middle years of King William's reign a host of 'societies' sprang into existence, of which the Society for Promoting Christian Knowledge and the Society for the Propagation of the Gospel were to be the most notable. While they were under the patronage of the clergy, their real driving force came from the work of devout and purposeful laymen who collected the money, served on the committees, and acted as officers and local agents. Under Tenison's guidance some of the most vital work of the Church came to be done by voluntary associations outside the legal establishment. Missionaries were dispatched to the American colonies and the West Indian islands, and a network of Anglican 'charity schools' began to cover the country. Cheap religious tracts were printed and circulated, and 'societies for the Reformation of Manners' attempted to supply the place of the ecclesiastical courts by initiating prosecutions for immorality under existing statutes.[2] It was clear that a great and critical choice lay before Anglicans. Were they ready to accept the place in English society of a basically voluntary body working within the legal conditions of the establishment or were they going to agitate for a return to the past when Church and State had conjoined in a single authoritarian regime?

[1] See White Kennett, *The Charity of Schools for Poor Children Recommended* (1706), and M. G. Jones, *The Charity School Movement in the XVIII Century* (Cambridge, 1938).

[2] See Dudley W. R. Bahlman, *The Moral Revolution of 1688* (New Haven, 1957), and G. V. Portus, *Caritas Anglicana* (1912). H. P. Thompson, *Thomas Bray* (1954) is a valuable account of one of the most zealous promoters of the societies.

CHAPTER TWO

A Tory in the Making, 1663–1699

I

FRANCIS Atterbury was the son of an unhappy and neglected country parson. The hard fact was that his father had been a Cromwellian whose career had been shattered by the Restoration of Charles II. It had been only too easy for an able and ambitious young clergyman like Lewis Atterbury to make a grave miscalculation on the political future. He had been elected a Student of Christ Church in 1647, at a time when Oxford was in a state of confusion after the civil wars. In 1648 his own father, the Rector of Middleton-Malsor in Northamptonshire had seen fit to take the Solemn League and Covenant, and Lewis had followed his lead. When the Parliamentary visitors came to Oxford he accepted their tests and regulations, even though many of his contemporaries chose to suffer deprivation and ejection rather than submit. And for a few years, as one of the few young dons who had complied, Atterbury was in high favour with the regime. He had the M.A. degree conferred upon him by special mandate of the Lord Protector; in 1654 he was given the valuable rectory of Great Risington in Gloucestershire after a nomination by the lawful patron had been set aside; and three years later he was permitted to take the living of Milton Keynes in Buckinghamshire and hold it in plurality. The return of King Charles was thus a terrible blow which put his whole future into jeopardy. He did everything possible to transform his image into that of a fervently loyal Anglican divine. Without delay he secured himself a title as chaplain to Henry, Duke of Gloucester; and even persuaded the university to grant him a doctorate of divinity as a sign of his theological orthodoxy. He had already received episcopal ordination, and now hastened to take every oath or subscription required of him by the Act of Uniformity. But this sea-change had been effected somewhat too rapidly for the general conviction, and he was repeatedly challenged. He was accused of being 'one who had

served against his Majesty', and eventually found himself turned out
of Great Risington as an intruder. When his second son was born on
6 March 1663 Lewis Atterbury was a man under a cloud, living
frugally on his remaining country living in Buckinghamshire. In
spite of constant affirmations of loyalty to the House of Stuart and
support for Tory causes, he received no further promotion or
recognition. For one who had started out so well, it was a bitter
experience, and the home in which his children grew up was not an
easy one.

He was, at least, determined that his two sons, Lewis and
Francis, should have their chance for the distinguished career which
had been denied to him, and both were sent to the foremost school
of the day: to Westminster under the regime of the already legendary Dr. Busby. When in 1674 young Francis was elected one of the
forty King's Scholars he set his foot on an academic ladder which
could lead to remarkable heights. Westminster was geared to
success. Every May there came to the school the heads of the
two most magnificent societies in the English university world,
Christ Church, Oxford, and Trinity College, Cambridge; and their
purpose was to choose the most talented boys for places on their
respective foundations. At one time no less than half the twenty-six
bishops on the Bench were former pupils of Dr. Busby; and it was
even reported that Bishop Sprat of Rochester had been heard to
thank God that he had managed to obtain a bishopric 'although no
Westminster'. The great names of John Locke, Christopher Wren,
Robert Hooke, and John Dryden showed that old Westminsters
were as eminent in the world of the arts and sciences as they were in
the Church. The boys who were the heirs of this tradition had a
reputation for poise, self-confidence and sophistication. They lived
at the centre of national events, close to the monarch and Parliament,
and to the statesmen and bishops who lived in Dean's Yard and in
the new fashionable streets around. There was, of course, another,
less desirable, side to living in a crowded urban area. Busby's fero-
cious punishments were a byword, but apparently the whippings
were a less than successful attempt to impose order and decency in a
school which was beset by all the temptations which the back-
streets and criminal classes could offer. It took a strong-minded
and even aggressive boy to survive and make his way amid the

austerities and brutalities of a harsh and competitive institution.[1]

Richard Busby's genius as a teacher is not easy to describe. The learning he imparted was not so much rigorous or profound as wide and cultivated. He aimed to produce young scholars who could produce witty and elegant speeches, and who had the confidence to deliver them with ease before a large public audience. 'Election Day', when the Westminsters performed, was one of the events of the London season. Richard Steele once described the boys as having 'such a peculiar readiness of fancy and delicacy of taste, as is seldom found in those educated elsewhere, though of equal talents'. In such a milieu Francis Atterbury fulfilled all Busby's requirements for a favourite pupil. Many years later a school-fellow recalled an incident which illustrates something of the sympathy and affection which was established between the man and boy:

Atterbury used to steal his master Busby's peaches; he missing them, set his man to watch; and Atterbury coming pulled a peach and held it up and published the banns of marriage between his lips and it, and was there any that knew any impediment, etc. The man told Dr. Busby this—and he pulling down his briches published the banns of matrimony between the rod and his brich, etc. Atterbury forbid the banns. The doctor laughed and said 'hang him, an unlucky rogue', and so dismissed him.[2]

The mock severity, the pert witticism and the underlying sympathy: all these indicate that Busby was prepared to tolerate the spirit of mischief, if only it had style. It must have been by his master's assistance that in May 1680 Atterbury passed to a Christ Church studentship at the head of his election. During the first eighteen months at Oxford he wrote to Busby regularly, describing in detail his new life and studies; and even the formality of Ciceronian Latin could not disguise the warm attachment of a young man who 'has left behind your counsel, cautions, and gifts given to overflowing'. For a while he seemed quite unable to cut himself free from the distinctive influence of the teacher who had shaped him. In some ways he was never to do so.[3]

[1] See the fiercely critical account, written by FA's school-fellow, George Smalridge, to J. Harrington, B.M. Add. MSS. 36707, fo. 54: 27 Dec. 1688.

[2] *The Diary of the Rev. John Thomlinson*, The Surtees Society, vol. 118 (1910), p. 75.

[3] *E.C.*, i. 1-5.

The Oxford college which Atterbury joined at the end of 1680 was indisputably pre-eminent in the university. When in 1686 the Earl of Lindsey wrote to Archbishop Sancroft on academic matters a consideration of Christ Church moved him to a superlative. 'It is', he concluded, 'a most flourishing society; and hath bred vast numbers of worthy persons, fit for any station in the Church.'[1] Much of this prosperity in the Restoration era was due to the wise government of Dr. John Fell, who had been Dean since 1660, but in its very constitution Christ Church was made for greatness. It was a unique combination of cathedral foundation and large Oxford college; it possessed great wealth and the undoubted prestige of being exempt from any outside authority except that of the Crown. Within the walls the Bishop of Oxford had neither voice nor power to command. The Chapter, consisting of the Dean and eight Canons, managed the revenue, appointed all other members of the society, and enforced discipline. The 'Students', who ranged from the most senior tutors down to mere freshmen, numbered no less than one hundred, and made Christ Church by far the largest college. And to the rich income from its landed estates were added the fees from the ten noblemen and thirty-five gentleman-commoners usually in residence. There is ample evidence of the jealousy and resentment with which this powerful foundation was regarded by the rest of the university community.

On Atterbury's arrival the House—as Christ Church was always known—was a place of unyielding Stuart loyalism. Royal nominations under the influence of Sancroft and Rochester had produced a body of canons devoted to a high theory of monarchy. It was indeed on Christ Church insistence that in July 1683 the Convocation of the university voted the burning of the Solemn League and Covenant, the works of Thomas Hobbes, and other 'republican treatises'. At this bookburning in the Schools Quadrangle the Christ Church undergraduates pressed round and, under the direction of Canon William Jane, 'gave several hums whilst they were burning'.[2] Within this fiercely royalist and High Anglican society the Westminsters were an undoubted élite, a confident and

---

[1] Bodl. MS. Tanner 30, fo. 93: 29 July 1686.
[2] Anthony à Wood, *Life and Times*, iii: 1682–1695, ed. Andrew Clark (Oxford Historical Society, 1894), p. 63.

superior group of clever young men who kept their own select company. Atterbury came up with most of his friendships already cemented and spent his time with men he had already known at school: George Smalridge, diligent and mild-mannered; James Harrington, soon to be a prodigy among common-lawyers before his tragically early death; William King, voluble in argument and erratic in behaviour; and Francis Gastrell and Robert Freind. It was natural, too, that the Westminsters should gravitate into the circle of an older man who was himself the very ideal of an education under Busby; and indeed they all came powerfully under the influence of the sub-dean, Henry Aldrich. Aldrich was a middle-aged bachelor of great charm and vitality; he enjoyed entertaining and was a witty and expansive talker, always surrounded by clouds of tobacco-smoke. He was a man of rigidly conservative politics, but more remarkable was his quite extraordinary range of artistic talent. He was a gifted musician and composer, a skilled engraver, and an even more distinguished architect.[1] In the closing years of Dean Fell's long reign Aldrich had virtually taken over the day-to-day administration of the college, and he was naturally marked out as the old man's successor. Among his many occupations he took over the direction of the young Atterbury's studies, and quickly perceived that there was real literary talent there. In 1682 he encouraged him, while still an undergraduate, to publish a spirited translation into Latin of John Dryden's *Absalom and Achitophel*.[2] Two years later Atterbury issued an elegant little anthology of Latin verse, ancient and modern. In the same year 1684 he took his bachelor's degree and the sub-dean gave him his first pupils, an unusual honour for so junior a Student of the House.

In the summer of 1686, however, Christ Church was suddenly plunged into crisis. When Dr. Fell at last died King James II did not appoint Henry Aldrich to the deanery but a virtually unknown outsider named John Massey. And in December the new Dean arrived in the college, bearing his Letters Patent and a royal dispensation, releasing him 'from coming to prayers, receiving the sacrament, taking of all oaths, and other duties belonging to him

---

[1] See W. G. Hiscock, *Henry Aldrich of Christ Church, 1648–1710* (1960).
[2] See H.M.C., *Second Report* (1871), p. 69, FA to Jacob Tonson, bookseller, 15 Nov. 1681.

as Dean'. Massey was in fact a Roman Catholic. Though holding
the dignity of Dean of an Anglican cathedral he intended to set up
his own private chapel, in which Mass would be celebrated. For the
High Tories of Christ Church it was a most terrible dilemma.
Like other Anglicans they had put great trust in James's repeated
assurances that he would always 'support and defend' the Church
of England, but now on the very day the new Dean was installed
there were open signs that the loyalism of the college was near to
breaking. Anthony à Wood reported that the younger Students
'said what they pleased, but the Canons looked grave'. It was not
long before ordinary academic life was disrupted. The noblemen
and gentleman-commoners did not return at the beginning of the
new term and admissions fell away alarmingly. Undergraduates
attended Massey's chapel in Canterbury Quadrangle to mock and
interrupt, and all authority and discipline collapsed. One of
Atterbury's friends wrote of the 'grossest abuses that were ever
offered by anyone to an inferior much less a governor', and in after
years Atterbury himself was remembered as a leader of the muti-
neers.[1] It was only to be expected that the Westminsters would
rally behind the figure of Henry Aldrich, and he indeed became
the centre of resistance to the Roman Catholic campaign in
Oxford. There was soon ample work for him and his able young
men.

By the beginning of 1687 the Anglican interest in the university
found itself under vigorous attack. There began the long-drawn-
out struggle to force a Roman Catholic President on to the Fellows
of Magdalen College; and Obadiah Walker, Master of University
College, who had been converted to the King's religion, started to
issue out a stream of propaganda tracts. At first his pamphlets were
printed on the university press under the Sheldonian Theatre, but
when a loyal Anglican compositor undertook to supply Christ
Church with proof sheets, the Master was forced to retire back to
his own lodgings. The Roman tracts were badly produced and
poorly argued. Their crudity proved a mere foil to the flashing
display of Christ Church wit and acumen which Aldrich now organized. In May he himself published a reply to a pamphlet by Abraham
Woodhead on the eucharist and George Smalridge put out a clinic-

---

[1] B.M. Add. MSS. 36707, fo. 21, Newey to Harrington, 5 Apr. 1688.

ally exact answer to a wild piece on the English Reformation. But the reply which attracted most attention came from the pen of Francis Atterbury. In the summer Obadiah Walker's press had produced a work entitled *A Discourse concerning the Spirit of Martin Luther*. It was crude vilification, utterly confused in argument, and barely literate. Luther was accused of sexual indecency, abusing the primitive Fathers, and inventing new doctrines such as Justification by Faith. The writer endeavoured to prove that Luther had had personal communication with the Devil and had received his theology by direct diabolic revelation. Atterbury's reply was devastating. He began with some snide remarks about the 'peculiar beauties in the style' of his adversary, and then quickly changed the mood to one of systematic destruction. Quotations were shown to be false and references to learned works fraudulent. Writing in short, crisp sentences he scored point after point. Obviously during the summer of 1687 he had put a great deal of research into the Reformation writings of Martin Luther, and now he managed to produce in a brief space a remarkably clear picture of the doctrinal position of the Reformer.[1] Atterbury was not unsympathetic but as an Anglican he admitted to considerable reservations on some aspects of Luther's teaching, and he firmly denied that the theology of the Church of England was identical with that of the German Reformation, as the Roman writer seemed so readily to assume. 'How comes the Church of England to be so concerned in what Luther said or did?' he demanded. If Luther was to be defended it was as a skilled biblical commentator and a learned patristic scholar. No reliable evidence had been produced to show that he was a man of immoral life, and the nature of his home and family would seem to indicate that he was not. He was a man of conscience who thought of himself as reviving a biblical Christianity rather than consciously innovating. The polished style and deadly argument of Atterbury's work earned it a reputation quite beyond the immediate circumstances of the moment. Bishop Burnet thought it was the best short piece by an Anglican on Luther, and in 1690 there was even some talk of the young Christ Church don beginning his clerical career as domestic chaplain to the new Bishop of Salisbury,

---

[1] See Westminster Abbey MSS. 65022 for his careful notebook on Luther's writings.

astonishing as that suggestion may seem in the light of later events.

2

After the Revolution, when all James II's plans had collapsed in ruins, one of the first of King William's appointments was that of Henry Aldrich to the deanery of Christ Church. Few could have disputed his claim, and there was difficult work to be done in restoring the college's discipline and recouping its finances by enticing back the profitable noblemen and gentleman-commoners. All this Aldrich did with notable success. But in one sense Christ Church was deeply out of tune with the new order in Church and State. All the members of the Chapter, save William Wake, who succeeded to Aldrich's canonry, were imbued with the spirit of Anglican conservatism; and to contemporaries the college became a byword for old-fashioned Toryism. In 1690 the gentle Wake showed a distinct uneasiness at the thought of having to keep his periods of residence in Oxford: 'nor would I choose Christ Church for my retirement', he explained to a friend, 'had I espoused any party or interest opposite to that of those who must be my nearest companions in it.'[1] Archdeacon Humphrey Prideaux was horrified at the thought that he himself might be offered a canonry at his old college. 'I nauseate Christ Church;' he wrote, 'I have an unconquerable aversion to the place, and will never live more among such people who have the prevailing power there.'[2] After 1689 the deanery became almost a headquarters of Toryism, a meeting-place for the politicians and clergy of the now discarded Court party. Aldrich, with the backing of William Jane, Regius Professor of Divinity and Dean of Gloucester, did as much as anybody to organize the opposition to William III's cherished scheme for a comprehension. The Earls of Clarendon and Rochester were frequent guests, and contemporaries remarked on the continual plotting which seemed to be in progress. It was at the deanery that the editorial work was done on the first Earl of Clarendon's *History of the Great Rebellion*, which was intended to provide a standard for the

---

[1] Bodl. MS. Ballard 3, fo. 57, Wake to Charlett, 2 Apr. 1690.
[2] *Letters of Humphrey Prideaux to John Ellis, 1674-1722*, p. 150: 12 Oct. 1691.

new Tory party. The network of influence and patronage which centred in Christ Church obviously did much to sustain and make effective the High Church opposition to William's Government in the years after 1689.

Living in this milieu, Atterbury soon became one of the busiest younger tutors. In December 1687 he had been ordained deacon and, having taken his M.A. degree, he was ready to take a full part in college teaching.[1] When in the summer of 1688 it was announced that the Princess Anne was to pay a state visit to Oxford, he was charged with organizing her reception in the Great Quadrangle and composing the Latin and English verses to be recited in her honour. Increasingly Aldrich came to rely on him in the day-to-day administration, and in 1690 committed to his charge the Honourable Charles Boyle, son of Lord Orrery, who had just come up to the House as a nobleman. It was a full life, but he was restless and dissatisfied. The small, dark-haired young don with the expressive manner and witty conversation was emerging as a formidable personality. Letters from his friends speak of him with admiration and affection: he was amusing, vivacious, and a sought-after companion on social occasions.[2] But there was another side to him: an emotionalism, impatience and pugnacity, which could make life exceedingly difficult in the close society of an Oxford college. As tutor to idle aristocrats he was far less than a success. In 1688 an 'honourable parting' had to be arranged by the authorities between him and a gentleman-commoner, Christopher Codrington. When he was appointed one of the Censors, his reputation for irascibility with the young was sufficiently established for his friend, George Smalridge, to offer a gentle caution. 'You are resolved', he wrote in 1691, 'to bestir yourself, you say, in your office in the House, foresee some trouble and ill-will, and are yet resolved for the good of the House:—a hero!—I suppose you expect to do little good but upon the Westminsters. No gruffness, I beseech you. Use them civilly, and stick to your point.'[3] There was even some tension with the Dean and quarrels with colleagues. In 1691 we learned of the 'great

---

[1] Bodl. MS. Top. Oxon. c. 250: 'Clerus Dioc. Oxon., 1542–1908.' FA was made deacon, 18 Dec. 1687, and ordained priest, 8 Mar. 1691.

[2] *E.C.*, i. 28, Smalridge to Gough, 19 June [1690].

[3] Ibid., i. 24-26: 23 Feb. 1691.

controversy' between him and another don, James Cascoigne, which Drs. Jane and Smith had to be brought in to compose.[1]

It is true that conditions of life in college were austere and comfortless. Even George Smalridge complained of his rooms in Canterbury Quadrangle, plagued by rats and finally falling into such a state of disrepair that he was forced to camp out in another Student's sitting-room.[2] But with Atterbury it was something more. He was incurably ambitious and (as for Oxford dons of every age) the great world of London made his own round of tutorials and college business seem trivial and frustrating. In October 1690 he poured out his dissatisfaction in a letter to his father:

I am perfectly wearied with this nauseous circle of small affairs, that can neither divert nor instruct me. I was made, I am sure, for another scene and another sort of conversation, though it has been my hard luck to be pinned down to this. I have thought and thought again, Sir, and for some years: now I have never been able to think otherwise, than that I am losing time every minute I stay here. The only benefit I ever propose to myself by the place is studying, and that I am not able to compass. Mr. Boyle takes up half my time, and I grudge it him not; for he is a fine gentleman, and while I am with him I will do what I can to make him a man. College and university business take up a great deal more, and I am forced to be useful to the Dean in a thousand particulars; so I have little time.[3]

To Dr. Atterbury such a combination of excitability and restlessness was unaccountable, and distinctly alarming in a clergyman son. Amid his own law-suits he sat down to compose his reply:

I know not what to make of your uneasiness. It shews unlike a Christian, and savours neither of temper nor consideration. I am troubled to remember it is habitual. You used to say 'when you had your degrees, you should be able to swim without bladders'. You seemed to rejoice at your being moderator, and of your *quantum* and sublecturer; but neither of these pleased you; nor was you willing to take those pupils the House afforded you, when Master; nor doth your Lecture please you, or noblemen satisfy you. But you make yourself and friends uneasy, and cannot trust Providence.[4]

[1] B.M. Add. MSS. 36707, fo. 94, Newey to Harrington, 23 Apr. 1691.
[2] Ibid., fo. 70, Smalridge to Harrington, 10 Oct. 1689.
[3] *E.C.*, i. 15-16, FA to Lewis Atterbury, 24 Oct. 1690.
[4] B.M. Add. MSS. 5143, fo. 102, 1 Nov. 1690.

The poor man concluded on a pathetic note: he could wish his son 'all the great livings you are capable of, but I can never secure them to you nor myself.' He could think of no solution to his son's problem but that of making a rich marriage.

The opportunity of making a powerful patron was, in fact, at hand for in 1690 the Christ Church Tories found themselves involved in one of the most celebrated Oxford quarrels of the later seventeenth century: the case of Exeter College. Early in that year the Rector, Dr. Arthur Bury, published a work of radical theology with the intriguing title *The Naked Gospel*. Brief, provocative, pertly written, it was an attack on 'priestcraft' and proposed, in the interests of a 'New Reformation', to reduce Christianity to the two simple notions of Jesus as Messiah and the need for personal penitence before God. It was a theme which John Locke was soon to take up and expound in a magisterial way, but in 1690 it was still a novelty. And it seemed to conservatives immensely shocking that a priest of the Church of England who had the spiritual formation of candidates for ordination should conclude his work with a scornful attack on the Athanasian formula of the Trinity as the product of a crabbed and factious patristic age. Aldrich and Professor Jane were at once determined to root out this heresy in the university, and Sir Jonathan Trelawny, Bishop of Exeter and a former Student of the House, was persuaded to intervene in his capacity as Visitor of Exeter College. Trelawny was himself no theologian. His claim to fame was as one of the Seven Bishops and as a Cornish baronet who was the greatest boroughmonger in the West Country, but he was a determined opponent of any innovation which seemed to threaten authority in Church or State. In the summer he moved into Christ Church and lodged in Jane's house, and concerted with his allies a plan to conduct a formal visitation of Exeter College. There was some occasion for one in that Bury had recently expelled one of his Fellows on a charge of begetting a bastard child. And so, after some preliminaries, on 26 July the Bishop set out in solemn procession from the House. But at the front gate of Exeter the doors were slammed in his face and Bury shouted to him that he was denied entrance. For a man of uncertain temper this was too much and the Bishop ordered his servants to force a way in. The Rector put up a token resistance, but in the college hall he found himself not only deposed from office but actually excommunicated for his contumacy.[1]

It was the signal for a furious controversy in which the Rector derived much support from those in the university who bitterly resented this interference by Christ Church in the affairs of another college. The hostility grew to even greater proportions when Aldrich and Jane proposed and forced through the House of Convocation a resolution that Bury's book should be anathematized and publicly burnt in the Schools Quadrangle.[2] As the pamphlets began to fly thick and fast Trelawny leaned heavily on his Christ Church allies for comfort and support, and particularly on the younger ones who could devote time and effort to the research required in preparing his case. Thomas Newey and George Smalridge were diligent, but the main burden fell on Atterbury and James Harrington. Though only recently called to the Bar, Harrington managed the Bishop's case in London and briefed senior counsel. Atterbury at Christ Church spent hours in close study of the legal and historical niceties of the powers of a Visitor of a college, and acted as Trelawny's Oxford agent. At Christmas he travelled up to London and lodged in Chancery Lane so that he could concert matters with Harrington. Only the urgent need to return to fulfil his lecturing commitments brought him back to Oxford.[3] It was not until 1696 that the House of Lords reached a decision in Trelawny's favour, but he was already deeply grateful to his Christ Church helpers. Smalridge was offered a living in Exeter diocese and Thomas Newey was actually collated to a prebend in the cathedral. And it was by the Bishop's recommendation that Atterbury now obtained the removal from Oxford which he so much desired.

St. Bride's, Fleet Street, was 'the largest and most considerable parish' in the City of London, and had a great congregation of business and professional people. In the summer of 1691 their afternoon lectureship or preachership fell vacant, and the gentlemen of the Vestry to whom the appointment belonged decided to throw it open to general competition. On successive Sundays they sat and

---

[1] Bodl. MS. Smith 47, fo. 66, Bernard to Smith, 27 July 1690.

[2] Ibid., fo. 69, 14 Aug. 1690; *E.C.*, i. 12–14, Smalridge to FA, 1 Sept. 1690.

[3] *E.C.*, i. 22, FA to Arthur Charlett, [22] Nov. 1690; ibid., i. 23–24, [Dec. 1690]; ibid., i. 28, Smalridge to Gough, 8 Jan. [1691]; ibid., i. 24–27, Smalridge to FA, 23 Feb. 1691.

listened to no less than twelve clergymen preach trial sermons and, perhaps not surprisingly, they became thoroughly confused and unable to make up their minds. 'To preserve the peace and unity of the parish' it was resolved to ask the Bishop of London, Henry Compton, to make a choice on their behalf only so long as none of the divines whom they had heard was appointed. Compton, old Christ Church man and close ally of Trelawny, at once gave the post to Atterbury, and on 22 October the Vestry gladly accepted him.[1] It was a most desirable appointment. Since it was not a legal benefice he could retain his studentship as a non-resident but resign all his offices in the House and live in town. And it was an excellent opportunity to present himself before a large and important London congregation as a preacher. This was Atterbury's chance for public note, and he took it. There is no doubt that he was an instant success in the pulpit and that his reputation was almost immediately established. Within seven months he was invited to preach before Queen Mary in the Chapel Royal, and his sermon on that difficult holy-day, 29 May, was printed by royal command. In October 1693 an even greater post came to him when he was elected minister of the ancient Hospitals of Bridewell and Bethlehem. Technically this made him chaplain of a remarkable institution which was a combination of reformatory, poor house and lunatic asylum; but as far as the governors were concerned his sole task was to conduct Sunday service in the hospital chapel and keep up a large congregation whose offertories would go to swell the charity's coffers. They required not a pastor to the inmates so much as a preacher who could draw the crowds. And it is clear that this is what they obtained, for within a matter of days after his election it was announced that their new minister had been chosen as a Chaplain-in-Ordinary to the King and Queen. At the age of thirty he had arrived on the London scene. With the Bridewell appointment he achieved financial security and freedom from the enforced celibacy of college life. With a house in the precincts and sufficient income he could afford to resign his studentship. Accordingly in 1695 he married Miss Catherine Osborne, a distant relative of the Duke of Leeds and daughter of a country parson near Oxford. In the

[1] Ibid., i. 484, for extracts from vol. 10 of the St. Bride's vestry minute-book.

next few years Atterbury was to present all the appearance of a prosperous and successful young divine. After 1696 he rented a new house in a row facing the river at Chelsea, near to the Old Church, and here his children were born: Mary in October 1698, Elizabeth in March 1700, and Francis (who lived only a few months) in March 1701. At weekends he left his house, family and growing collection of books to travel into town, lodge at the Bridewell and preach his two Sunday sermons, there and at St. Bride's. It was a happy life with a growing reputation and acclaim.

A study of Atterbury's published sermons reveals the cause of their popularity: they provided a direct contrast to the current vogue for preaching in the style of Tillotson. The Archbishop's discourses, so extravagantly admired in their own day, were cool and systematic expositions of a rational and judicious Christianity; they were unadorned, instant appeals to virtue and charity, and an assurance of that divine favour and temporal reward which were laid up in heaven for the well-disposed. Atterbury, on the contrary, harked back to an older form of preaching, and his model was the venerable Dr. South rather than Tillotson. While he scrupulously avoided all the complexity and intricate allusion of the old method, he yet had more warmth, richer illustration, and a greater stress on the emotions of his hearers. His sermons were clearly exciting occasions. He took immense pains to commit them to memory lest the need to refer to notes should spoil the ease and flow of his delivery. 'He had a sweet voice', recalled one contemporary, 'a charming address and such a graceful appearance as engaged the attention of his audience at his first speaking.'[1] A gentle manner and youthful good looks, a quiet voice which could suddenly become touched with emotion and what was called 'elevation of style': all these won him many admirers, especially among women, for whom the Tillotsonian method was too dry and unexciting. In a famous description of Atterbury in the pulpit Richard Steele declared that 'he never attempts your passions until he has convinced your reason, but when he thinks he has your head, he very soon wins your heart.'[2] On the surface the sermons were attempts to deal

---

[1] Ibid., iii. 164 et seq. for a collection of admiring comments on FA's preaching.

[2] The *Tatler*, no. 66: 10 Sept. 1709.

with the intellectual problems and doubts of the day, but the arguments are rarely sustained or laborious. The effective part is rather a warm appeal which seeks to engage the sympathy and emotional response of the audience, but to do this within the limits of restraint and taste which the early eighteenth century Anglican pulpit prescribed.

A significant feature of these discourses is their stress on a personal religion: on the free and mysterious gift of salvation to individual men. Over against Tillotson's theme of a practical and prudential Christianity Atterbury pointed to a sinful and alienated state of man, and his dependence on the forgiveness and renewal which God alone could give. He tried to lead his hearers into realizing the wonder of finding oneself set in the world as 'a reflecting, thoughtful, inquisitive being', but this does not lead on to any consideration of man's power of reason. He continually contrasts the frailty of man and the awesome majesty of God. He speaks of the 'baseness of humane nature, its small regard to Truth and Justice, to Right and Wrong; to what is or is not to be praised. But he who hath a deep sense of the excellencies of God upon his heart, will make a God of nothing else besides.'[1] In his well-known sermon on *The Power of Charity to cover Sin* he was explicit in attacking the weaknesses of rational Christianity. By attempting to conform everything to the immediate understanding of man, and by stressing man's effort continually, it was striking at the very heart of the Christian faith. It was this 'very easy and comfortable divinity' which seemed 'to lessen the worth of that only true and proper satisfaction for sin, made by our Saviour on the Cross'.[2] Unlike so many of his contemporaries he was prepared to talk of the 'scandal' of Christian preaching, of Christ crucified for men and for their salvation. 'The Primitive Apostles', he told his audience, 'did not like those of a later date, preach up first a glorified and then a crucified Saviour; but bare the Scandal of the Cross wherever and to whomsoever they opened the doctrines of it: the *Slaying* of *Jesus*, and his being *hanged on a tree*, is mentioned in one of the first sermons

---

[1] *Sermons and Discourses on Several Subjects and Occasions* (1723): sermon on 'the duty of praise and thanksgiving', preached before Queen Mary on 29 May 1692.

[2] Ibid., p. 50.

of St. Peter. This (humanely speaking) was an unlikely way of gaining proselytes.'[1]

Characteristic of his preaching was its devotional emphasis: the need for prayer, sacrament, and times of quiet if a man (or woman) were to attain to a true knowledge of God. In one sermon, continually reprinted, he asked his hearers to consider their own lives, 'ever seemingly very busy, and ever really very idle'. Were they not 'tossed and disquieted in their minds during the intercourse we maintain with the world'? Let them by 'contrition, resolution and prayer' discover that inner frame of mind where 'the winds are presently laid' and 'there is a perfect calm'. He advised the frequent use of the sacraments, and in a striking phrase spoke of 'the lively image of a crucified Saviour' set forth in the Holy Communion. All this was, of course, quite different from the discourses of Tillotson and his many imitators, and those intrigued by the High Church background of so many of the later leaders of the Evangelical revival may look with profit at Atterbury's preaching which has such remarkable similarities with John Wesley's Arminianism.[2] That the preacher was admired and sought after in the 1690s was shown by the series of special sermons which he was asked to deliver and by the four times his discourses were printed by royal command. In 1698, at the invitation of the Tory lawyer, Sir John Trevor, Master of the Rolls, he became preacher at the Rolls Chapel, and resigned his post at St. Bride's for this more prestigious appointment. This was indeed a rapid mounting of the ladder of preferment.

3

The character of a Christ Church education was soon to be illustrated in a remarkable literary clash. It arose out of an academic exercise assigned by Dean Aldrich to the Honourable Charles Boyle, Atterbury's former pupil. From the time that he had first arrived in the college the young nobleman had received the most elaborate deference and attention. Indeed to assist in his education the Dean himself went to the trouble of composing a textbook of elementary

[1] Ibid., p. 105.
[2] See John Walsh, 'Origins of the Evangelical Revival' in *Essays in Modern English Church History in Memory of Norman Sykes*, eds. G. V. Bennett and J. D. Walsh (1966).

logic, which he dedicated fulsomely to 'the great ornament of our college'. From his letters to Atterbury, written soon after the latter had departed for London, Boyle emerges as a priggish and superior youth who took himself and his 'reputation' very seriously indeed. He worked hard at his books and covered a considerable amount of reading in the classics and modern authors, but he had no notion of the time and application which went into the making of a genuine scholar. Atterbury seems to have liked him and done his best to encourage his efforts, but he could barely conceal the fact that all this juvenile self-esteem irritated him almost beyond endurance. In 1693 the united persuasion of Boyle's mother and his tutor only just prevented him from throwing up his university career and joining the army in Flanders to acquire 'reputation'; and to encourage his flagging enthusiasm Aldrich proposed that he should prepare an edition of the Epistles of Phalaris.[1] The boy was promised that the result would then be printed and distributed to the members of the House as the Dean's New Year gift. The choice of the topic was not without its element of self-interest. Boyle at this time was hoping that the distinguished elder statesman, Sir William Temple, would act as his patron and recommend him at Court; and only the previous year Temple had published his *Essay on Ancient and Modern Learning*, in which he had extolled Phalaris as the very model of a letter-writer.[2] Living in retirement at Moor Park, with Jonathan Swift as his secretary, the former diplomat was setting himself up as an arbiter of taste in polite letters. And the excellence of Phalaris he took to prove his chief point: the indisputable superiority in sentiment and style of the ancient writers over the modern.

In the course of his work Boyle needed to collate the received text of the Epistles with a manuscript in the King's Library in St. James's Palace. It was thus that the youthful editor crossed swords with the Librarian, the formidable Dr. Richard Bentley, a man whose background, manners and learning were all in direct contrast with those of the gentlemen-wits of Christ Church.[3] Bentley was the product of a Yorkshire grammar school; he was rough-tongued and

---

[1] See *E.C.*, i. 29-42, for the series of letters from Boyle to FA, 1691-93.

[2] See J. Nichols, *Illustrations of Literary History*, iii (1818), 271: Smalridge to Gough, *circa* 1698.

[3] See R. J. White, *Dr. Bentley: a Study in Academic Scarlet* (1966).

self-opinionated, but his scholarship was massive and accurate. For the uncritical and lightly aesthetic approach to literature he had a contempt which he did not bother to disguise. Boyle did not approach the Librarian personally but sent along an amanuensis to do the work for him. To this humble figure Bentley expressed himself in no uncertain terms: the whole project of an edition was a waste of time; the so-called Epistles of Phalaris were forgeries composed hundreds of years later than the sixth-century tyrant who was supposed to be their author. When the collator proceeded to linger and procrastinate over the job, Bentley lost all patience. Without ceremony he took the manuscript back, closed the library and went off to Cambridge. He thought no more of the incident until January 1695 when Boyle's edition was published, and he was astonished to find it asserted in the preface that he, *pro singulari sua humanitate*, out of his characteristic humanity, had denied access to the manuscript. At once he wrote to Boyle to protest, but received a cool and lofty reply which indicated that he could do exactly what he liked about it.

Forbearance was not a marked feature of the Yorkshireman's character. He worked grimly and systematically at a riposte, which came out in 1697 under the title of *A Dissertation on the Epistles of Phalaris*. In a hundred trenchant pages he exposed the letters as patent forgeries. Deploying a detailed knowledge of ancient history and classical philology, he demonstrated that their chronology was absurd and their Greek quite dissimilar from that in use in the sixth century. They were 'a fardle of commonplaces without any life or spirit from action or circumstances'. So much for Sir William Temple. But what really caused offence was his undisguised contempt for Christ Church scholarship. Boyle he brushed aside as not worth serious consideration and treated the work as if it were a collective product of the Oxford classical luminaries. As he laid bare error upon error he referred heavily to 'our new editors', 'our annotators', and 'our great geniuses'. It was, tantamount to a declaration of literary war, and the reading public whetted its appetite for a clash of pundits and the prospect of the public humiliation of one or possibly both of the contestants.

The besmirched honour of the House had to be defended, and it was decided that Atterbury would have to come to the rescue of his former pupil. Smalridge, Anthony Alsop, and the brothers Freind, Robert and John, rallied to the cause, but the main burden had to be carried by a busy man who already had to write two sermons a week for demanding London congregations. The reply, of course, had to be in Boyle's name and he had to be consulted, but little aid could be expected from his amateur abilities. It was clear, too, as Atterbury began to examine Bentley's evidence, that this pretentious and vain young aristocrat was wholly in the wrong, and that his seniors had been put in the position of having to argue a virtually untenable case. There was nothing for it but to obscure the force of Bentley's scholarship by erecting a screen of mockery and satire, and somehow to imply that his literary critical methods were a menace to Christian faith. It was hard and unsatisfying work, and when Boyle ventured to criticize the proofs of the forthcoming book Atterbury exploded with justifiable wrath. It was bad enough, he wrote, having to slave away in a controversy which he had not begun, but it was intolerable to find oneself in the position of one

whose opinion all along in this controversy you have not seemed very willing to take, and whose pains in it, I find, have not pleased you. Some time and trouble this matter cost me. In laying the design of the book, in writing above half of it, in reviewing a good part of the rest, in transcribing the whole, and attending the press, half a year of my life went away.

'Hitherto', he concluded, 'I have endeavoured to serve your reputation, without your thanks and against your will. But it does not become me always to do it.'[1]

Dr. Bentley's Dissertation on the Epistles of Phalaris Examined appeared early in 1698, and was an instant publishing success. Almost immediately it went into a second printing, and was again sold out. For a few months it was the sole topic of conversation in the literary coffee-houses and at social gatherings. The work was academically unscrupulous, personally malicious, eminently readable, and very funny. It was essentially addressed to those who had just enough knowledge to be acquainted with the issues but insufficient expertise to form a worthwhile judgement on the evidence. For most

[1] *E.C.*, i. 46–7, FA to Boyle, *circa* Jan. 1698.

readers *Boyle's Examination* (as it came to be called) was the last word on both Phalaris and Bentley. George Smalridge indicated the tone of the book when he wrote of his confidence 'that all persons of quality and good breeding will declare against him, when it shall appear how clownishly and unlike either a gentleman or a scholar he has treated Mr. Boyle and Sir William Temple.'[1] Much play was made with Bentley's humble origin and rough manners. This 'library-keeper' was a mere pedant, a 'turner of lexicons', and he had attacked his betters: 'one would imagine that he had avowed hostility to all gentlemen pretending to letters'. There followed an ingenious re-arrangement of Bentley's own evidence and a cavalier dismissal of his critical method. It was implied that Cambridge men were dangerous. Was it not by the very techniques which he had adopted that atheists were denying Moses' authorship of the Pentateuch and the literal chronology of the Old Testament account of the Creation? The book culminated in a hilarious piece in which with much mock solemnity Atterbury sought to demonstrate that Dr. Bentley of Trinity College, Cambridge, could not possibly, on the basis of his own methods, be the author of the *Dissertation on the Epistles of Phalaris*.

To Bentley's dour mind all this was mere 'banter and grimace'. To the general public, however, it was quite otherwise. Jonathan Swift in his celebrated essay *The Battle of the Books*, written at this time, awarded Boyle the honours of the contest; and was still sufficiently of the same opinion in 1704 to let the work be published under his own name. Samuel Garth in his poem *The Dispensary* reported the verdict of the coffee-houses:

> So Diamonds take a lustre from their foil,
> And to a Bentley 'tis, we owe a Boyle.

In 1701 Atterbury followed up his triumph with a pamphlet, *A Short View of the Controversy*, which embroidered the points of Bentley's rudeness, ingratitude to Boyle's family, and dangerously critical use of evidence. Amid all this noise of conquest Bentley published in 1699 his monumental volume, entitled simply *Dissertation on Phalaris*. It received at the time comparatively little attention, and it was to be a later generation which recognized it for what it was:

[1] J. Nichols, op. cit., iii. 268, Smalridge to Gough, 22 Feb. 1698.

the destruction, scholarly annihilation and utter sinking out of sight for ever of Boyle, Atterbury and the rest of the Christ Church wits '*Immortalis ista dissertatio*' was the hushed comment of the great Porson upon it. But this was in the future. For the moment victory lay with ingenuity, and the ability to write wittily and persuasively.

CHAPTER THREE

The High Church Revolt, 1697–1702

I

IN the last years of King William's reign English political life was torn apart by a great conflict of parties. None could doubt that the root of all this bitterness lay in the strain produced in the structure of society by the great war with France. Just as the country clergy found their position eroded so country landowners came to believe that their own security was being threatened by new forms of executive government and by the power of high finance. It was a deeply depressing era for those who lived exclusively on an income from rents. In 1694 the Land Tax was fixed at four shillings in the pound and, with poor harvests and violent fluctuations in the price of corn, it began to bite deeply into landlords' incomes. By Anne's reign men were convinced that the bottom was falling out of the landmarket.[1] The aristocracy were often able to consolidate and extend their estates but many smaller gentlemen found it increasingly difficult to hold their own. Yet if the 'landed interest' was in difficulties, it was clear that the 'monied interest' was growing apace. To sustain the new machinery of public credit which had been created with the Bank of England the Government required the confidence of financiers and bankers, and these exerted an influence on public policy out of all proportion to their numbers. Toryism aimed simply to preserve the influence of landed property in English life and to maintain the traditional beliefs of a paternalistic society. It saw Whiggism as inextricably bound up with political oligarchy, 'monied men', and the liberal theories which were dissolving ecclesiastical order and social subordination. It was only natural that the country squires should see the discontents of the parish clergy as part of their own cause, and that the 'High Church' movement should have their ready sympathy and support.

[1] For a valuable survey, see W. A. Speck, 'Conflict in Society' in *Britain after the Glorious Revolution*, ed. Geoffrey Holmes (1969).

The origins of the revolt of the lower clergy went back to the year 1689 when for a moment it seemed possible that there might be a total rupture between the new King and the priesthood of the established Church.[1] William was a convinced Dutch Calvinist; on previous state visits to England he had joined in Anglican worship, but in Holland he had clearly resented the services in Mary's chapel and he had bullied and harassed her chaplains. Once in England he acted with great unwisdom: he received prominent Dissenting ministers with open cordiality and dropped them hints of a comprehension on the terms 'wherein all the Reformed churches do agree'. By the early summer churchmen were deeply suspicious and were already concerting defensive action in Parliament. But suspicion turned to grievance and anger when in July it became known that William had consented to an act of the Scottish Parliament which abolished prelacy and established a Presbyterian church-order. In fact the King had had little choice in the matter: episcopal authority in Scotland had always been much weaker than in England and almost to a man the Scottish bishops had refused to take the new oaths. But now the episcopalians went out, a tiny, persecuted Jacobite remnant, and it was inevitable that the King should receive the blame for their sufferings. Before 1688 there had at least been the appearance of ecclesiastical unity in the three kingdoms. Now Anglicans saw their church-order diminished to an establishment in England and Wales, with the precarious outpost of the Church of Ireland.

That the situation did not develop into an open clash with the clergy was due to the timely intervention of the Earl of Nottingham, who in the autumn of 1689 persuaded William to adopt a policy of compromise and conciliation, and to accept an alliance with a body of moderate Tory churchmen.[2] Nottingham was a politician of an impeccable Anglican and loyalist background. He had never been close to the Yorkist party of Sancroft and the Hydes, and his own

---

[1] See G. V. Bennett, 'Conflict in the Church', op. cit. I am grateful to Macmillan & Co. for allowing me to use some passages which appeared in that essay.

[2] See G. V. Bennett, 'King William III and the Episcopate' in *Essays in Modern English Church History*, eds. Bennett and Walsh (1966); Henry Horwitz, *Revolution Politicks: The Career of Daniel Finch, Second Earl of Nottingham, 1647-1730* (Cambridge, 1968).

particular brand of churchmanship laid more store by theology and
the laws of England than high-flying political theory. But a feature
of the Finch family had been the way by which they had built up a
connection of distinguished London clergymen who looked to the
Earl as their patron and mentor. As William's Secretary of State
Nottingham was able to offer the King a useful alliance with a set of
moderate-minded but indubitably Tory politicians and divines, and
it was this which William eventually had the wisdom to accept.
Bishop Burnet put the point clearly: 'I reckon that I do not exceed
the severe rules of history when I say that Nottingham's being in the
ministry, together with the effects which it had, first preserved
the Church and then the Crown.'[1] In the two years following the
Revolution there was an unprecedented series of vacancies in bishoprics and deaneries, by death and by a refusal of Nonjurors to take
the oaths, and the places were filled with men of real distinction and
learning. Pre-eminent among them was Nottingham's close friend
and ally, John Tillotson, who became Archbishop of Canterbury in
1691. It is often said that King William packed the episcopal Bench
with 'Whig Latitudinarians', but the evidence is quite otherwise.
The early appointments, after those of the first few months, were
made on the advice of a prominent Tory politician and were
intended to reconcile the clergy to the new regime.

The fragility of such a policy was shown in the autumn of 1689
when Nottingham attempted to revive his comprehension project.
A Royal Commission was set up to prepare a scheme which could be
laid before the Convocation of Canterbury. The commissioners
laboured hard and produced a carefully devised and generous set of
proposals which might have stood a fair chance of persuading
moderate Dissenting ministers to be included once again in the
national Church. Obviously for the Secretary of State and his clerical friends this recreation of ecclesiastical unity was an essential prelude to a reimposition of Anglican discipline. But when Convocation
met all their plans came to nothing. The ordinary parish clergy had
elected some of the most intransigent of their brethren to the
Lower House, and the word went forth that there was to be no
change in the formularies of the Church of England at the will of a

---

[1] *A Supplement to Burnet's History of My Own Time*, ed. H. C. Foxcroft
(Oxford, 1902), p. 314.

Calvinist foreigner. In opposition to Nottingham's candidate for the chair the lower clergy proceeded to elect Dr. William Jane, Canon of Christ Church. His forthright speech and his rousing cry of *Nolumus leges Angliae mutari* spelt the doom of comprehension. Without delay, and with his Ministers' ready consent, the King brought the sessions to an end. So truculent an assembly was clearly too dangerous in an ecclesiastical situation of such delicate balance.

In the following years Archbishop Tillotson and his successor, Thomas Tenison, endeavoured to preserve the peace of the Church. Convocation was given no further licence to sit and act, and it became customary to send down a schedule of prorogation immediately the formal opening ceremonies had taken place. The King made a point of keeping ecclesiastical promotions from becoming a matter of party competition and making sure that he personally was as little connected with the business as possible. While she lived Queen Mary dealt with all nominations to bishoprics and deaneries, and after her death in 1694 they were handed over to a standing Royal Commission. Ministers and aristocrats were forbidden to approach William directly for any piece of preferment, and the two Archbishops with a small group of their closest friends were given the task of choosing moderate and unexceptional men who would not meddle in politics.

In spite of all Tenison's precautions, however, the Church was drawn increasingly into the political conflict and into an increasingly fierce differentiation of parties. After the Election of 1695 the King reversed his former Tory policies and put himself into the hands of the Earl of Sunderland and the Junto group of Court Whigs; and there came into existence a powerful 'Country' party, consisting of a union of 'Country Whigs' and Tories. It was an opposition which thrived on discontent, and the grievances of the clergy were grist to to the political mill. Thus from about 1697 there may be seen the formation of a 'new High Church party' as an aspect of that 'new Tory party' which attacked King William's Ministers so remorselessly. The recruitment of clerical propagandists for the cause was no haphazard affair, and all was done under the supervision of the Earl of Rochester, now a leading opposition figure. He was aided and abetted by Bishops Compton of London, Trelawny of Exeter and Sprat of Rochester, three survivors of the pre-Revolution regime;

and Dean Aldrich of Christ Church supplied to the fight a number of energetic and eminently literate young divines. It was by this 'old Tory' connection that Francis Atterbury was drawn into the national political conflict and quickly emerged as the stormy petrel of the High Church revolt.

2

At the end of 1696, with the verve of the born journalist that he was, Atterbury launched on its way the pamphlet which began the famous Convocation controversy, and from which so much political division was to flow. The initial idea came from Sir Bartholemew Shower, an able Tory lawyer and a close associate of both Rochester and Sir Edward Seymour. He discussed his theories with clerical friends in Oxford and they advised that Atterbury should be called in to write up a tract and present the arguments in as vigorous and challenging a way as possible.[1] The theme of *A Letter to a Convocation Man* was ingenious and in Atterbury's hands it was cleverly aimed to fit in with the mood of the ordinary clergy. It re-hearsed all the grievances of the Church, not least the growth of heresy and blasphemy, and it demanded as the only remedy a sitting and acting Convocation. This was called for not as an act of grace on the part of the King but as a constitutional right of the clergy of England. What Atterbury challenged was the royal legal power to silence and ignore the Church's own deliberative assembly. He did not rely on any theoretical notion of ecclesiastical independence of the civil authority, but based his case on an elaborate review of English constitutional history and legal precedent. He was attempt-ing to invoke the Church's 'rights, powers and privileges' under the legal terms of her establishment.

It was not difficult for a writer of Atterbury's incendiary talent to make out a case that the condition of religion in England required an urgent remedy. There was 'a open looseness in men's principles and practices, and a settled contempt of religion and the priesthood have prevailed everywhere'; it was clear that a massive campaign had been organized by 'a sort of men, under the style of Deists, Socinians, Latitudinarians, Denyers of Mysteries and pretended

---

[1] *Hearne's Collections*, Oxford Historical Society, iii. 279: 16 Dec. 1711.

Explainers of them, to undermine and overthrow the Catholick Faith'. It was useless to think that the defence of the Church could be left to individuals or even the church courts in their present weakened condition. Only one bishop, Trelawny of Exeter, had had the courage to prosecute flagrant heresy and he had been subjected to intolerable insult and involved in grievous expense. The only effective action would be that taken at a national level by Parliament and Convocation. Time was short. Even loyal subjects and conformable members of an established Church could not lay aside indefinitely their right to assemble as 'a spiritual society, of which Jesus Christ is the Head, who has also given our laws and appointed a standing succession of officers under himself for the government of this society'. It was at this point that Atterbury introduced the startling novelty of his pamphlet: his assertion that the English Reformation had in no way diminished or abridged the right of the clergy of the Church of England to sit and debate as they would the urgent affairs of their Church.

There followed a dazzling survey of the history and nature of an English Convocation. Until this time it had been accepted legal doctrine that the great Act of Submission of the Clergy in 1534 had placed the two Convocations of Canterbury and York entirely under the royal authority: that they could not meet except by the King's initiative and that they could neither debate nor enact canons without his licence and assent. Atterbury, on the contrary, stressed the similarity of Parliament and Convocation. As one was the King's highest temporal court, so the other was the highest spiritual court. In fact, the two were different aspects of one and the same parliamentary occasion. He pointed out that when a bishop was summoned to take his place in the House of Lords his writ contained a clause, known as the *Praemunientes*, which required him to bring up to Parliament his dean, his archdeacons, and proctors or representatives of his cathedral and diocesan clergy. This, Atterbury claimed, proved that the lower clergy were an essential part of a Parliament. And it was a complete misunderstanding of the Act of Submission to imagine that a Convocation, attending on Parliament as one always did, was unable to sit, debate and do business without a licence. The act had only made it necessary that canons should receive the royal assent before they became the law of the land, but this itself made their likeness to statutes even more remarkable. Now, he concluded, there must be a loud and widespread demand for a sitting and acting Convocation. The law prescribed it and urgent business could be delayed no longer.

The pamphlet caused an immediate sensation. Interest was aroused as soon as the first copies came off the press in November 1696 and soon the publisher was steadily reprinting. It was read and discussed in common-rooms and coffee-houses, in episcopal palaces and county assizes: but the principal excitement was among the parish clergy. They were delighted, not only by its brevity and wit but by its vigorous espousal of the cause of doctrinal orthodoxy and a revived discipline. There was intense speculation on the identity of the anonymous author, and George Smalridge reported from Oxford the reaction at Christ Church. 'The *Letter to a Convocation Man*', he wrote to a friend, 'will be well worth your reading. It is much talked of and much liked here. We are not able to guess at the author. Some will have it to be our Dean's, but I am certain they are in the wrong. Some have done me the honour to father it on me, but they compliment me too highly who think I was able to write it.'[1] The bishops were much less appreciative. They saw only too clearly the political implication, and indeed Burnet was convinced that it was an unscrupulous device by some opposition politician to embarrass the King's administration. The author, he wrote:

thought the government had so little strength or credit that any claim against it would be well received; he attacked the supremacy of the crown, with relation to ecclesiastical matters, which had been hitherto maintained by all our divines with great zeal. But now the hot men of the clergy did so readily entertain his notions that in them it appeared that those who are the most earnest in defence of certain points, when these seem for them, can very nimbly change their minds upon a change of circumstances.[2]

The noise was so great that early in the New Year Archbishop Tenison decided to read a copy. It gave him an unpleasant shock. Like everyone else, he was unacquainted with the precise historical and legal issues involved, but he was deeply disturbed at the thought

[1] J. Nichols, *Illustrations of Literary History*, iii. 254, Smalridge to Gough, 10 Nov. 1696.
[2] *H.O.T.*, iv. 459-60.

of a general agitation for a Convocation. Now he realized that he had an intricate scholarly debate on his hands, and one with grave consequences for the peace of the Church. He knew only too well that if a Convocation did meet he had every reason to fear a body which would have a majority of clergy in the Lower House who would be hostile to the Government and imbued with a swelling sense of their own grievances. When it was reported to him that William Wake, Canon of Christ Church and Rector of St. James's, Piccadilly, was an expert in the history of the Convocation, he at once summoned him to Lambeth and pressed him to produce a reply without delay. The Archbishop wanted a brief and vigorous tract which would meet the *Letter* on its own terms. But, to his chagrin, Wake insisted on a drawn-out and scholarly preparation and it was not until the very end of 1697 that he produced his book. Tenison read it, grumbled over its length and tedious style, but at last yielded and gave permission for it to be published with a formal dedication to himself and the Archbishop of York.[1]

Wake's book, *The Authority of Christian Princes over their Ecclesiastical Synods*, was a terrible mistake. Even the author's friends and well-wishers started with alarm at what seemed like a completely Erastian line of argument. Almost a quarter of the work was given over to proving that from the age of Constantine Christian rulers had possessed an absolute control over church synods. Indeed this constant stress on a total subordination of Church to State caused immense resentment among the ordinary clergy and tended to vitiate everything else which Wake put forward. Yet the fact was that he made one important scholarly point which laid an axe to the root of Atterbury's whole ingenious argument. He showed that there had been two different types of Convocation. There had indeed once been an assembly which had met in answer to the *Praemunientes*, and it had met in the fourteenth century when the King had tried to tax the clergy in Parliament. But it had not assembled since then and the clause was now a picturesque and meaningless survival. The present two provincial Convocations were of a quite different nature. They were true ecclesiastical synods under the authority

[1] Christ Church, Oxford: MS. Diary of William Wake to 1705. For Wake and his subsequent part in the controversy, see N. Sykes, *William Wake, Archbishop of Canterbury, 1657-1737* (2 vols., Cambridge, 1957).

of their respective Archbishops, but since the clergy had been accustomed to vote taxes in them they had assumed some of the characteristics of a parliamentary occasion. They were not, however, an essential part of Parliament. Wake concluded with an earnest plea that no Convocation should be allowed to sit and debate at the present time since 'nothing at this day preserves us from ruin and desolation but that we have not power of ourselves to do the Church a mischief'.

He staggered before the anger which his book created. By his tactlessness he had succeeded in giving many ordinary priests the impression that the only reply to their pleas for action to preserve the Church was an arrogant declaration of the royal power to silence troublemakers, and that issued with the imprimatur of both Archbishops. Not least his asperities had aroused Atterbury's well-known pugnacity, and the latter determined to devote every minute he could spare to working on the materials of English parliamentary history. He now spent the best part of each week in Lincoln's Inn, working in the lodgings of his friend, Francis Gastrell, who was Reader in chapel there.[1] Each summer he set off on a journey to ransack the archives of cathedrals and to search through diocesan registries. It was only after two full years' study and research that in March 1700 he published anonymously the book known as *The Rights, Powers and Privileges of an English Convocation*. And yet, in spite of the labour, rather than a work of genuine scholarship it was a superb piece of journalism. Wake was spared nothing. He was represented as a literary hack who wrote to the order of the Archbishop, who insulted the intelligence and sense of responsibility of the clergy, and who was undermining the 'good old constitution' in Church and State. Atterbury knew quite well that too much detailed historical evidence was liable to bore and tire his readers, and so it was necessary to write vividly and pungently. As he later explained it, if he had treated Wake 'barbarously, 'twas to inspirit a dull and dry subject'.[2]

The preface sounded a clarion call for the defence of the Church against arbitrary and absolutist notions. Englishmen lived under an ancient constitution which gave them rights and liberties, and

[1] Wake MSS. 17, fo. 130, J. Holt to Wake, 28 Sept. 1700.
[2] Nicolson's diary, iv. 25: 29 Feb. 1708, reporting a conversation with FA.

nowhere were their historic privileges more valuable than in Parliament and Convocation. How came it then that Wake was digging about in the history of late Imperial Rome when churchmen were discussing the terms of the legal establishment of the Church of England? Atterbury perceived, however, that Wake had dealt his position one shrewd blow, and all his powers of resourceful argument were bent to redirect the evidence and obscure its force. The distinction between the two types of Convocation had to be got over, and he now argued disingenuously that this was a distinction without a difference. In the medieval period the English clergy had sometimes met at Westminster as a national body and sometimes they had been allowed to assemble in their provincial bodies. But it was still a parliamentary attendance, and the *Praemunientes* had been kept up to emphasize this. With unfailing energy Atterbury returned to the subject of the Act of Submission, and by a startling conjuring trick of argument produced a truly remarkable new conclusion. The rights of the clergy, he declared, remaineed wholly unaffected, but one person had suffered a catastrophic blow to his authority and powers in Convocation—and that was the Archbishop of Canterbury. The new Royal Supremacy had reduced him to the status of a mere royal officer. He no longer had any discretion in calling Convocation or governing it; his role was limited to 'moderating the debates of the synod, and giving his vote last upon any question proposed there'.

It was a *tour de force*: not the less so for its staggering effrontery. The very style of writing, with its brilliant paradoxes, telling witticisms, and smooth plausibility, made it clear who the author was. As Bishop Burnet put it: the book had 'great acrimony of style and a strain of insolence that was peculiar to one Atterbury'.[1] But, in spite of all criticism, the work sold in great numbers, and soon the publisher was calling for a new edition. It was the main topic of conversation wherever the clergy met, and Wake obviously had much to endure in London clerical society. 'I need not tell you', he wrote on his return from a residence at Christ Church, 'the world here is as full of Mr. Atterbury's book as I left it at Oxford . . .

---

[1] *H.O.T.*, iv. 459; Bodl. MS. Ballard 7, fo. 82, Kennett to Charlett, 14 Mar. 1700.

Some men, I am told, wonder at my impudence that I have not yet hanged myself.'[1] The experience made the iron enter into his soul, and he determined on a reply of monumental proportions. Of his adversary's arguments verily not one stone should be left upon another. In vain the Archbishop pleaded for something lively, readable and above all quickly produced. Wake ignored all advice and retired grimly to his study.[2] When in 1703 his vast folio *The State of the Church and Clergy of England* appeared it was an irrefutable answer to Atterbury's case. The trouble was that only experts could bring themselves to read it, and that by then the immediate political importance of the dispute was over. In the meantime the field was left to his opponent who luxuriated in the acclaim of a popular hero. It served no purpose for Atterbury to make any further pretence about his authorship, and now he resolved that a new and enlarged edition of his book should be issued; and that this time it should not only bear his own name but be dedicated, albeit without permission, to the Archbishop of Canterbury.

All this was reported to Tenison, who became thoroughly agitated. He summoned to his aid two noted medievalists, Edmund Gibson and White Kennett, and charged them to work on small books which might do something to counteract Atterbury's arguments. Anxious meetings were held at Lambeth at which the Archbishop sought some clarification of his real constitutional position. In order to stifle the whole contretemps before it became quite out of hand, it was decided to convene a meeting of the judges and ask them for a public declaration that Atterbury's theories were inconsistent with the Royal Supremacy. The prospect of such a solemn appeal to the twelve men in scarlet did give the author of the work an unpleasant turn. He wrote at once and in alarm to Bishop Trelawny, who had now assumed the role of his chief patron and adviser, and the little group of Tory bishops held urgent consultations with Lord Rochester. But there was no real need to worry. As is the wont of lawyers when asked to pronounce upon the legal complexities of the Church of England, the judges

---

[1] Bodl. MS. Ballard 3, fo. 32, Wake to Charlett, 28 Mar. 1700.
[2] See G. V. Bennett, *White Kennett, Bishop of Peterborough, 1660–1728* (1957), p. 36 et seq.

advised caution and delay, and dispersed to leave the Archbishop to face the coming storm without their assistance.[1]

It was at this point that the Tory lay politicians began to see that Atterbury could be a useful political ally. In November 1700 he was still unknown to Rochester personally and had had to seek an introduction from Trelawny 'so that I might wait upon him, and let him know the measures that are taking'. But by the following January he was in regular conference with the High Tory leader, and even transmitting his opinions and instructions to the bishops of the party. Rochester, of course, understood clearly that ecclesiastical issues were the most powerful weapon of attack in the Tory armoury, and he could see that the clerical agitation had played no small part in the disintegration of the Junto administration. Indeed by the end of 1700 King William's parliamentary arrangements were in such disorder that he had no alternative to putting himself into the hands of Rochester and his allies. When the Earl discussed with the King the terms on which he would serve, one of his prime conditions was that there should be a sitting and acting Convocation.[2]

Elections for a new Parliament and Convocation were fixed for the third week in January, and at once Atterbury found himself in a fevered round of activity. On the first day of the new year the second edition of his book was published with his name on the title-page and a new preface in which the moderate bishops were savagely attacked. Lord Rochester complimented the author and told him he 'was very much pleased with the book, and particularly with the way of handling the Bishop of Sarum'. Large numbers were printed and distributed down to the dioceses where willing helpers carried them from parsonage to parsonage so that the clergy might have them to hand before the elections. The anger among the bishops' party at all this was explosive, but among the ordinary priests it was quite otherwise. Maurice Wheeler, Wake's former tutor at Christ Church, wrote to describe the mood of the clergy who had gathered at Gloucester for the parliamentary and

[1] *E.C.*, i. 53–57, FA to Trelawny, 12 Nov. 1700; H.M.C. *First Report* (1870), pp. 52-3, Blackburne to Trelawny, 16 Nov.

[2] *E.C.*, i. 57–58, 76, FA to Trelawny, 2 Jan., 22 Feb. 1701; ibid., i. 63, Sprat to Trelawny, 14 Jan. See also the series of letters from Sprat and Compton to Trelawny in Coll. Trelawn., p. 263 et seq.

proctorial elections, and even to the author's principal adversary he could not disguise how much he himself agreed with the Atterburian thesis. 'The great subject of the conversation at that time', he reported on 18 January, 'was this book; and you may be sure in a question where the popular side of the argument is against you, you could not have many advocates . . . As to the conclusion which Mr. Atterbury supports, I own myself somewhat staggered by the evidence he alleges for himself. But perhaps some old, fixed prejudices of my own in behalf of the Church's essential and unalterable rights may incline me to favour that side.'[1] Atterbury himself spent the whole of the month writing letters in all directions to ensure that the proctors were formally returned on the writ *Praemunientes*, and he did manage to persuade several Tory bishops to co-operate. But in most dioceses it was the ordinary clergy who demanded that the archdeacons as returning officers should execute the clause.[2] The story of Thomas Naish, a Salisbury incumbent, bears witness to one humble parson's conviction that Atterbury was right. On 24 January he publicly renounced Burnet's patronage and joined his brethren in petitioning for the writ to be formally mentioned in the archdeacon's return.[3]

Amid all the excitement Atterbury considered putting himself up for election in the London diocese, but an unexpected vacancy in one of the archdeaconries of the diocese of Exeter gave Trelawny his chance. Quietly Atterbury travelled down to the South-West and was duly instituted and installed as Archdeacon of Totnes. When he arrived back in town he was amused to discover that his new rank, and the *ex-officio* seat in the Lower House which went with it, was still unknown to the Archbishop and his allies. He speculated pleasantly that they had a surprise in store.[4]

3

It was with the meeting of Convocation that the contest between

---

[1] Wake MSS. 23, fo. 136, Wheeler to Wake, 18 Jan. 1701.

[2] Hardwicke Court, Gloucester, Sharp MSS. 4, A.4, FA to Fell, 14 Jan. 1701; ibid. 4, A.3, FA to Sharp, 4 Feb.

[3] *The Diary of Thomas Naish*, ed. Doreen Slatter, Wilts. Archæological and Nat. Hist. Soc. (1965), p. 43. Naish was later deprived of his benefice by Burnet.

[4] *E.C.*, i. 71, FA to Trelawny, 29 Jan. 1701.

High and Low Church really began. At the opening service in St. Paul's on 6 February it was plain that both sides were tense and apprehensive. Tenison went through his part with grave dignity but his nervous agitation could not be wholly disguised. No one knew what the ensuing sessions would bring.[1] But Atterbury, at least, was clear what his goal was: not just to harass the Archbishop but to make of Convocation an instrument by which urgently needed measures could be taken to restore the authority and status of the Church. And this meant, first of all, that they had to assert that the Lower House was the spiritual counter-part of the House of Commons. They had to establish their constitutional autonomy or else the Archbishop would use his position as President of the Convocation to stifle all discussion. That the battle would be bitterly fought Atterbury did not doubt, but a rapid survey of the membership of the Lower House showed him that there would be at least two to one in favour of the High Church campaign. It was indeed the size of this majority against him which worried Tenison, and at a bishops' meeting at Lambeth he and his brethren determined to stand and fight: to allow no business and to silence all discussion by sending down a schedule of prorogation as soon as any debate got under way in the Lower House.[2] It was a short-sighted tactic and one which made frustration, anger and rebellion virtually inevitable.

Just before the session began, Atterbury was confident that his campaign would receive the warm support of the new Ministry, and he waited on Lord Rochester, ready to tender advice and discuss tactics. To his great surprise and considerable dismay he was coldly received and quickly dismissed. Having achieved office with the aid of the High Church agitation the Minister had no intention of letting things get out of hand or putting himself in the power of this young and impetuous clergyman. Rochester's own clerical friends were elderly Tory bishops who had survived from the pre-Revolutionary era and senior divines such as Henry Aldrich of Christ Church or George Hooper, Dean of Canterbury. Atterbury

[1] Ibid., 8 Feb. 1701.
[2] Lambeth Palace MSS. 934, fo. 41, Moore to Tenison, 8 Jan. 1701; Wake MSS. 17, fo. 139, Patrick to Wake, 17 Jan.; *E.C.*, i. 73, FA to Trelawny, 15 Feb.

had expected that Dr. Jane would again be elected as Prolocutor and he hoped to work through him, but Lord Rochester thought otherwise. At a meeting at his house, to which Atterbury was not invited, it was decided to put up Hooper for the chair.[1] He was, from the activists' point of view, by no means an ideal choice. Pompous, slow-moving and fussy, he was more likely to wait on Rochester for every move than lead the vigorous and all-out attack which the High Church majority so clearly desired.

Business began briskly, however. On the first day, 25 February, the Lower House sat in Henry the Seventh's Chapel in Westminster Abbey and proceeded to act on the basis of Atterbury's theory of the independent status of the house.[2] When, in the midst of their discussion, the Archbishop's prorogation was brought down, they ignored it. Hooper continued in the chair, in spite of some protests, and business went on until they decided 'to adjourn'. On subsequent days Atterbury was delighted when committees were appointed. Dr. Jane was made chairman of the most important of these, charged with the work of examining books for heretical opinions, and they set to work to draw up a detailed indictment of Toland's *Christianity Not Mysterious*. Atterbury, who was also on the committee, was eager to prepare the way for an investigation of Bishop Burnet's well-known commentary on the Thirty-Nine Articles and he insisted that this was also a work of heresy which the committee should consider. Various motions were formulated censuring the previous Whig administration's policy towards the Church.[3] The only drawback to all this party assertion was the obvious alarm and increasing hesitation of the Prolocutor. It was apparent that Hooper had been charged by his master not to let matters get out of hand and to demonstrate to the King that the clergy could be kept under control when Tory ministers were at the helm. He was thus deeply unhappy to find himself in the role of a rebel leader. Indeed when Atterbury rose to propose a fiercely worded Loyal Address to the King from the lower clergy Hooper raised points of difficulty and procrastinated until the Bishops had had time to

---

[1] *E.C.*, i. 76, FA to Trelawny, 22 Feb. 1701.

[2] For an almost verbatim account, see White Kennett, *The History of the Convocation, summoned to meet . . . on February 6, 1700* (1702).

[3] *E.C.*, i. 86, FA to Trelawny, 11 Mar. 1701.

compose a draft of their own and send it down to the Lower House.
Soon the Prolocutor allowed himself to be drawn into an intricate
argument with the Archbishop over the rarer constitutional points,
and it began to seem as if the whole High Church campaign was at
the point of foundering for lack of leadership.

At the end of March the Tory members of the Lower House
were in an ugly mood. There was general disgust at the 'leisurely
and overwary steps' of the Prolocutor and even some outspoken
complaints of lack of support from 'some of our Lay Friends'. They
wanted vigorous action to counter the obstructionism of Tenison
and his colleagues. Now was Atterbury's chance to supplant Hooper
as *de facto* leader of the House, and on 18 April he rose to demand a
direct confrontation with the Bishops. Hooper was still unwilling
for open rebellion and, when he was outvoted, stayed behind while
Atterbury at the head of a throng of clergy marched through the
abbey to present the Archbishop with a formal request that there
should be no further delay in condemning Toland as a notorious
heretic. Tenison had been warned of their coming, and he received
them with grave anger. Where was their Prolocutor? What right
had they to approach him in this irregular manner? He ignored the
paper which they proffered and sent a summons for the Prolocutor.
When Hooper appeared, the Archbishop delivered himself of a
fierce and emphatic speech. In the Church of England there was a
due subordination of presbyters to bishops and he would not tolerate rebellion; he and his brethren had no intention of proceeding
to a formal censure of Toland for the simple reason that they had
no licence from the King to consider heresy. He ordered them to
return to their meeting-place and be ready to receive his schedule of
prorogation.

Back in Henry the Seventh's Chapel the rage of the High Churchmen exploded and Hooper was thrust aside. After much angry talk
Dr. Jane stood to propose a motion which marked a declaration of
war: 'that, since the Upper House refused this correspondence with
them, it was now time for this House to return thanks to Mr.
Atterbury for his learned pains in asserting and vindicating the
rights of Convocation.' It was voted by an overwhelming majority
that a letter should be sent to Oxford asking that the degree of
Doctor of Divinity by Diploma should be conferred on him as 'some

public notice of so great a piece of service to the Church'.[1] Such a doctorate 'by Diploma' was an honour reserved for the most distinguished persons and yet on 5 May the university duly obliged. It was the end of peace in Convocation. In the following weeks the Lower House met, debated and adjourned itself without reference to the Bishops. The Primate was insulted and his authority defied. Articles were drawn up against Burnet, and the Easter recess found the House in a full-scale attack on the former Whig administration. When at last the Convocation was prorogued by the King in June the Bishops and their presbyters were quite unreconciled and all communication between the two Houses was broken off.

During the summer the party conflict raged on with unceasing bitterness, and Tenison and his colleagues were appalled at the vehement abuse poured out against them from clergy and laity.[2] Now they clung to Somers and the Whig leaders as their only friends and supporters. All pretence at keeping the Church neutral was abandoned as the rancour of party attachment drew all men into two opposing camps. It was perhaps with some reluctance that the Archbishop found himself committed to political Whiggery but on 11 September when Lord Sunderland wrote for the King a paper of advice on the political situation, he could speak of it as an accomplished fact that 'the whole moderate Church party, who are not Jacobites, are joined with the Whigs'.[3] It was now clear to William that Rochester had been a disaster. Indeed he later described the year 1701 as 'one of the uneasiest of his whole life'. He had been personally insulted and attacked, his foreign policy had been rejected, and his former ministers impeached. It was true that the Act of Settlement had safeguarded the Protestant Succession but its provisions included much of the Tory 'Country' programme and were an impediment to strong executive government. It was high time to make new ministerial arrangements and to rid himself of faction and irresponsibility.

No one was more disillusioned with Rochester and the old Tory politicians than the new Doctor Atterbury. If his plans for Convoca-

---

[1] *E.C.*, i. 91, for the evidence from the Journal of the House.
[2] See H.M.C. *Bath MSS.* i. 52, for an anonymous letter from Robert Harley to Tenison, 11 Aug. 1701.
[3] *Hardwicke State Papers*, ed. P. Yorke (1778), ii. 445–46: 11 Sept. 1701.

tion were to succeed he needed the support of a Minister of the Crown who could establish himself firmly in office. But by now it was apparent that Rochester lacked not only real statesmanship but a genuine sympathy for the grievances and aspirations of the ordinary clergy. Disgust with such 'tarnished old courtiers' led Atterbury to cultivate new allies and in the early summer he found himself increasingly in the company of Simon Harcourt and William Bromley, the latter of whom he energetically supported in the parliamentary election for Oxford University. When in May he preached before the House of Commons it was his two new friends who were deputed to convey to him the thanks of the House for his sermon.[1] By the autumn it was clear to shrewd observers that there were two sets of High Church divines: an elderly party which did Lord Rochester's bidding and a more radical faction, led by Atterbury and attached to younger Tory politicians.

By the end of 1701 Atterbury had emerged as the man who could exercise the most powerful sway over the minds of the parish clergy. When in November William finally dismissed his Administration and dissolved Parliament and Convocation, it was he who bore the whole burden of the High Church cause. As the pamphlet warfare grew even fiercer, he worked late into the night to confute the efforts of Gibson and Kennett. At times he staggered under the weight of his self-imposed task. 'What can be done', he wrote on 15 October, 'by one poor hand and head, by the blessing of God, I will do, towards stemming matters. But, in the meantime, it is a little uncomfortable to be left to work alone without any assistance or anybody to bear a part in the same cause.'[2] In fact, he scarcely needed to worry himself. In the elections the ordinary clergy again followed his lead and the majority in the new Convocation was now nearly three to one. 'The poor country parsons', reported Maurice Wheeler on his return from the Gloucester election, 'that know nothing of the matter, were instructed to vote for such as would assert their rights against the usurpations of the bishops. This in a trice passed from ear to ear as if conveyed by the magical communication of our famous Whispering Place, and so Will. Thornton was

---

[1] See the extracts from the newspapers, collected in *E.C.*, i. 91 et seq.
[2] *E.C.*, i. 100, FA to Trelawny, 15 Oct. 1701.

presently dubbed Defender of the Inferior Clergy.'[1]

It was apparent, as the last months of King William's reign worked themselves out, that a great new issue had entered the political arena. The Anglican priesthood was now thoroughly aroused. They looked eagerly to the Tory politicians to vindicate their cause, relieve their sufferings, and lead them back to that fair country where they had dwelt before 1685. A new figure, too, had come upon the scene: Francis Atterbury, the man whom the country clergy were beginning to think of 'as the prop and asserter of the Church of England and *the Great Champion of her Cause* in these late difficult times'.[2] It was a dizzy eminence to have attained.

[1] Wake MSS. 23, fo. 135, Wheeler to Wake, 15 Dec. 1701.
[2] B.M. Add. MSS. 27440, fo. 25, Charles Allestree, Vicar of Daventry, writing in early 1702.

CHAPTER FOUR

The Church in Danger, 1702–1705

I

IN March 1702 King William died and there came to the throne the woman upon whom the whole Church party had set their hopes. Queen Anne was old beyond her thirty-seven years, she was almost continually ill, and she had endured great personal sorrow. But she was no nonentity. Her opinions were firmly formed, and in particular she was determined not to be governed by the strong men of either of the two political parties. Tory or Whig, she saw them as tyrants who would monopolize her Government and destroy her discretion in choosing men and policies. Above all, she feared and hated the five lords of the Junto. 'I know the principles of the Church of England', she affirmed, 'and I know those of the Whigs, and it is that and no other reason which makes me think as I do of the last.' And yet, though country Tories might rejoice in manor-house and parsonage, she had no intention of delivering herself into the hands of her uncle, Lord Rochester, or any other of the old Tory party chieftains. Rather her confidence was to be given to the two men who were her trusted personal friends, Sidney, Lord Godolphin, and John Churchill, Earl of Marlborough; and it was they who formed the linch-pin of the new administration. Marlborough became the heir to King William's policies and campaigns, and each year in Flanders he set in motion a vast military machine, voracious in its demands for men, money and munitions. Godolphin as Lord Treasurer became absorbed in the heavy labour of procuring finance and ensuring the smooth working of the administrative machinery; and he dreaded beyond all things an outbreak of party strife at home which would interfere with the voting of supplies. With Anne's ready consent the Treasurer and the General became the apostles of 'moderate' or non-party government. They were determined to work only with men who would be responsible and who were prepared to prosecute the war with the utmost vigour. For this it was essential to keep at bay the high-priests of Whiggism and Toryism, the 'violent' party leaders who manipulated ideologies which worked so powerfully with the backbenchers on either side.

It was obvious from the first days of the new reign that the issue of the Church was to be critical in domestic politics. Anne herself played no small part in giving the impression that the Tory millennium had come, and at the dismissal of the old Parliament she warmed all High Church hearts by declaring that her 'own principles must always keep her entirely firm to the interests of the Church of England and would incline her to countenance those who had the truest zeal to support it'. It was only to be expected that at the General Election in the summer months the Tory rank and file would go to the polls confidently. Banners inscribed with the device 'No Moderation' were carried high to the hustings, and when the first calculations were made it was seen that there was to be a substantial Tory majority in the new House of Commons. Dissenters might well feel apprehensive. 'The fanatics', wrote William Bromley to one of his constituents at Oxford, 'could not be more dejected in Bucks than they seem everywhere else. Most of them are very quiet and silent, though some talk of persecution; they fear its approaches; and their liberty of conscience they expect will be taken from them. The abuse of it I hope will, and a stop put to that abominable hypocrisy, that inexcusable immorality of occasional conformity.'[1] Lord Treasurer Godolphin was well aware in this situation that he would have to face an intense agitation about the Church when the new Parliament opened, and the prospect filled him with utter dismay. For all his financial skill he knew his own limitations. He was a deeply reserved and sensitive man, incapable of dealing subtly with assertive High Church divines. 'A discreet clergyman is almost as rare as a black swan', he opined, and his letters were punctuated with complaints of the 'insolences of the clergy'.[2] It was clear that Godolphin had to find an astute and experienced political manager who could handle ecclesiastical affairs on his behalf.

Fortunately for him such a man was at hand in the glib and

[1] Bodl. MS. Ballard 38, fo. 137, Bromley to Charlett, 22 Oct. 1702.
[2] H.M.C. *Bath MSS.* i. 63, 76, 152.

ingratiating figure of Robert Harley, Speaker of the House of Commons. This son of a Herefordshire squire of Puritan and Whig background had been educated in a Dissenting academy, and retained all his life a facility for speaking and writing readily on religious matters. At his first entry into the Commons Harley had supported the most extreme measures of 'Country' Whiggism, and was even accounted by some 'an enemy of the Church', but by 1702 a remarkable sea-change had been effected in his politics. Indeed he was now accounted a leader of 'Country' Toryism and even a supporter of the Anglican cause. Already his extraordinarily wide and varied political and religious contacts had been established, even if at the same time he had attracted to himself the reputation of being one of the most subtle and slippery of contemporary politicians. In the autumn of 1702 Godolphin took the decision to entrust the Ministry's ecclesiastical management to this brilliant but complex man.

It was inevitable that Harley and Atterbury would soon be brought together. All during the recess the High Church champion had been planning a renewed attack on the 'Moderate' bishops, and he was looking eagerly for some sign that the new Queen and Ministry would lend their support to the cause. It was all the more necessary because in the short session of Convocation in the last months of the old reign the Archbishop of Canterbury appeared to have been completely victorious.[1] On the Tory side Hooper and the other clergy of Lord Rochester's camp had totally refused to work under the direction of a young upstart like Atterbury, and they absented themselves from the Lower House on so many occasions that the Tory majority was actually in continual jeopardy. On the other side Tenison determined to attack and carry the battle into the camp of his enemies. Advised by White Kennett, a precisely learned historian and a formidable debater, he decided that the time had come to intimidate and subdue his presbyters. Just for a moment the Archbishop lost his nerve when he learned that Atterbury had managed to reactivate the committee on heretical books and that the members were drawing up a detailed indictment of Burnet's commentary on the Thirty-Nine Articles. But fate intervened and

[1] See *E.C.*, i. 103–25 for FA's letters to Trelawny. G. V. Bennett, *White Kennett*, gives a detailed account of this session.

the sudden death of the Prolocutor, Dr. Woodward, gave him his opportunity. By refusing to allow a new election the Primate virtually suspended the Convocation, and neither pleas for justice nor argument from precedent could make him relent. In private Atterbury was deeply depressed. It was 'an end of the constitution, unless the Queen or the new Ministry intervened. Meanwhile the only recourse was to carry the clergy's cause to the general public, and in a series of numbered papers, each describing itself as *A Faithful Account*, he trumpeted forth the grievances of the Lower House and the tyrannous conduct of the Archbishop.

It was the virulence of Atterbury's attack on Tenison which first attracted the attention of Robert Harley. In mid-October, just before the new Convocation opened, there appeared a pamphlet somewhat innocently titled *The Parliamentary Original and Rights of the Lower House of Convocation*. It might almost have been designed to provoke the Archbishop into overhasty action. Tenison was outraged to find himself portrayed as a servile party hack who bullied his fellow-ministers of the Gospel on the orders of a faction of Whigs whose real aim was to undermine and destroy the national Church. But what seems really to have unnerved His Grace was Atterbury's announcement that the 'orthodox' clergy of the Lower House now had no other recourse but to invoke the Royal Supremacy and ask the Queen to determine the points at issue. As the Archbishop pondered the matter he began to conceive of the unpleasant possibility that the new Administration might try to buy off the Tory churchmen by sacrificing him, and he hastened to pay a visit to the Lord Treasurer, bearing a copy of the offending work. 'So he desired me', reported Godolphin, 'to take that book, which he said was written by Mr. Atterbury, and to judge if it were possible to be tame and quiet under such provocations'. The Chief Minister at once passed the whole distasteful problem over to Harley, 'not being willing indeed to meddle with it one way or the other, but just as I may have the favour of being instructed and guided by you'.[1]

It was a superb opportunity for the Speaker to recommend himself to the Queen and Minister as the man who could bring about that peace in the Church which they both desired so earnestly. He read the pamphlet and realized that the author of it was a formidable

---

[1] H.M.C. *Portland MSS.* iv. 49, Godolphin to Harley, 19 Oct. 1702.

troublemaker who would have to be bought off. Careful enquiries were made and on the evening of 21 October, the very day on which Harley was formally re-elected to the chair of the House of Commons, he and Atterbury met in the strictest secrecy. It was fortunate that Francis Gastrell was Speaker's Chaplain and could offer his own lodgings for a clandestine discussion. Harley approached the matter with all his habitual dissimulation. He hinted that the Queen in her heart sympathized with the Atterburian case and was ready to support the Tory clergy in their struggle. As if on her behalf he asked what terms the Lower House majority would find acceptable and what advice they had to offer. Words could not express Atterbury's delight. This was the kind of contact for which he had always hoped, and they talked until far into the night. The next morning, still brimming over with the excitement of the occasion, Atterbury wrote to Harley to put his suggestions on paper.[1] He asked that in her reply to the Loyal Address from Convocation the Queen should make it clear to all that she espoused the High Church cause. Tenison should then be informed by the Government that concessions were expected of him in the interests of peace. On this basis a joint-committee could be set up to work out a settlement of the immediate dispute and they could all get on with essential measures for the revival of the Church. It would be necessary to bring Hooper into all this and even for him to think that he was the one principally consulted, but meanwhile Atterbury and the Speaker should continue their secret meetings and correspondence with the aid of the useful Dr. Gastrell.

At once Harley informed Godolphin that he had a plan by which ecclesiastical peace might be secured, and on the evening of 25 October he was ushered in to his first long private audience with the Queen. She received him with special kindness and was delighted when he explained his scheme to her. Its terms were identical with those which Atterbury had so recently proposed.[2] Now, with Anne's enthusiastic consent, Harley was indefatigable in activity. He called on Archbishop Sharp of York, the Queen's confidant and

[1] Ibid., iv. 288, FA to Harley [22 Oct. 1702]. This letter is misdated in the H.M.C. report.
[2] Longleat, Portland papers Misc[ellaneous] vol., fo. 110, Godolphin to Harley, 22 Oct. 1702; Blenheim MSS. E-45, Harley to Godolphin, 25 Oct. 1702.

confessor, and effected a union of their interests. He went to extraordinary lengths to meet and ingratiate himself with George
Hooper. The Dean, whose political reactions were not particularly
fast, was astonished to find himself invited to dinner, engaged in
theological discussions, and even on one slightly absurd occasion
have the Speaker of the House of Commons insist on accompanying
him across the river to Lambeth. In mid-stream the waterman was
ordered to row to and fro so that the two might have an entirely
secret conversation.[1] When Convocation met and elected Henry
Aldrich to the chair Harley organized a series of meetings at which
he, Lord Nottingham, Hooper and the new Prolocutor prepared the
text of the Queen's speech and settled tactics.[2]

Clearly it was well to have secured Convocation, for within a few
days the storm burst in the House of Commons. William Bromley
and Arthur Annesley, members for the two universities and the
acknowledged representatives of the Anglican clergy in the House,
introduced the first Occasional Conformity Bill. It was proposed
that anyone who qualified for office by receiving the Anglican sacrament and then went subsequently to a meeting-house should be
fined £100 on conviction and forfeit £5 for every day on which he
continued in office after committing the offence. It was a draconic
measure, designed to drive a considerable body of Whig voters out
of public life. What could the Ministers do? If they openly opposed
it they would gravely compromise themselves with the Tory backbenchers upon whom they relied for their majority; if they voted
for it and it passed into law then their attempt at moderate or non-
party government was in ruins. They could only resort to an elaborate deceit, and so when the bill was carried in the Commons and
came up to the Lords, Marlborough and Godolphin made a show of
voting for it while at the same time, behind the scenes, they were
moving everything in their power to have it killed. By an alarmingly narrow majority the Lords voted amendments which eviscer-
ated the bill, and the day was saved by a deadlock between the
houses.[3] The anger of the Tory chieftains was terrible when it began

[1] 'MS. account of Hooper by his daughter', quoted in A. Trevor, *Life and
Times of William III* (1836), ii. 478.

[2] H.M.C. *Portland MSS.* iv. 50-51.

[3] William Pittis, *The Proceedings of both Houses of Parliament, in the Years 1702,
1703, 1704, upon the Bill to prevent Occasional Conformity* (1710).

to dawn on them that they had been outwitted and out-manoeuvred by dexterous management.

Similar dismay prevailed among the clergy in Convocation. At first Atterbury trusted implicitly in his secret agreement with Harley, and when the Queen's reply to the Loyal Address arrived it augured well. She expressed her determination to preserve the Church 'in its doctrine and discipline, and to take care of all your just rights and privileges'. In the next few days the Tory divines were delighted to learn that Burnet had been turned out of his grace-and-favour lodgings in St. James's Palace and that the Bishop of Worcester had been dismissed as Lord Almoner for his overzealous Whig electioneering activities. Obviously Tenison had been upset by his conversations with Godolphin, and he made some gestures at a compromise: he offered to allow committees to meet outside the time of the formal sessions and to give proper time for debate in the Lower House before the schedule of prorogation was sent down.[1] But all this Atterbury urged his supporters to reject as insufficient: there had to be a decision on the points of principle, and on 11 December he moved that there should be a formal petition to the Privy Council. It was a complete misreading of the political situation. Above all, Harley was determined that the Queen and the Ministry should not be drawn into the political conflict, and he moved into action at once. Urgent meetings with Aldrich and Hooper were arranged, and it was agreed that Anne should return no answer at all to the petition. The Prolocutor promised to suppress all further mention of it on the floor of the House.

As the days went by Atterbury became more and more puzzled and uneasy. What had gone wrong? What of the Speaker's assurances of Her Majesty's heartfelt support? By the beginning of February he was forced to admit that there was 'no answer, or hope of an answer, that I can hear of, from the Queen; and those of our house, who before were the most sanguine, begin now to despair.' Gradually it was brought home to him that he had been tricked, that 'the Great Ones were not in earnest when the Occasional Conformity bill was carried', and that the two Deans had done a separate deal with the Ministry behind his back. Without doubt he was genuinely and

---

[1] B.M. Add. MSS. 29584, fo. 101, Tenison to Nottingham, 21 Jan. 1703; see also *E.C.*, i. 136-55.

deeply outraged. In his anger he even paid a special visit to Sir
Edward Seymour, that most doughty of old Tory stalwarts, to
'represent our Convocation affairs to him in their true light' and to
'let him see how little we have been beholden to our managers who,
instead of serving their body, have really been playing their own
game'.[1]

2

Atterbury looked forward to the winter session of 1703 with a grim
determination. At least he would not be duped again. Relations
with Harley were abruptly broken off, and his planning and discussions were now with genuine opposition Tories who could be
relied upon to attack without mercy. With barely disguised chagrin
he observed the rise of George Hooper to the position of the
Ministry's principal lieutenant in ecclesiastical affairs; and in May
Harley procured the see of St. Asaph for his pliant ally. Even the
best endowed of the Welsh bishoprics was a poor thing, but
Atterbury writhed at the bitter injustice of it: 'for had not that
book I wrote procured a Convocation, and given him by that means
an opportunity of forming a strong body of the clergy, and placing
himself at the head of them, he could not have made it necessary for
the Crown to take notice of him in order to bring things to a temper.' It may well be that his own fate was to be 'neglected and
sacrificed' but he knew that he had a power over the hearts and
minds of his brethren that Hooper had never had and could never
possess.[2]

Few informed observers really imagined that an Occasional
Conformity Bill would pass into law in the winter of 1703, and
Atterbury himself noted grimly that 'many members who were
zealous for it last session, are cooled in it'. Seymour, Bromley, and
their energetic young supporter, Henry St. John, were fully aware
that the Lords were an impenetrable barrier, and they determined
to lay the foundation of a new party unity by making the debates in
the Commons a ringing appeal to Tory sentiment about the national
Church. Harley made insistent endeavours to dissuade Bromley

---

[1] *E.C.*, i. 155-80, FA to Trelawny, 4 Feb.–4 Mar. 1703.
[2] *E.C.*, i. 209, FA to Trelawny, 1 June 1703.

from actually re-introducing the bill, but received a severe rebuff.[1] Atterbury similarly was clear that his task now was to support his friends in the Commons with a parallel agitation in Convocation, and that their efforts must be closely concerted. It was not an easy task. At first only a handful of members put in an appearance in the Lower House and Aldrich scarcely bothered to disguise the fact that he had no intention of doing any business. All seemed as Harley had arranged it. But the Speaker was uneasy; he nursed at the back of his mind the suspicion that though he might have fixed the elderly Aldrich and Hooper, the incendiary young Dr. Atterbury was not only unpropitiated but now positively hostile. It was decided to invite him to a meeting, and Atterbury was intrigued to receive a summons from no less a person than the Lord Treasurer himself to a meeting with the Archbishop of York and the Bishop of St. Asaph. The encounter with Hooper was acutely embarrassing and the two bishops could obtain no assurances at all. Atterbury came away even more sourly determined 'to see if I can put a little life into our affairs'.[2] And words could scarcely express his disgust when on 13 December he learned that Hooper, so recently consecrated to St. Asaph, had been translated to the splendid and wealthy bishopric of Bath and Wells.

For a while the scene in the Lower House continued to be dispiriting, but suddenly all was transformed by the mounting excitement in Parliament. Atterbury had been following closely the 'very warm' debates in the Commons and he applauded the oratorical efforts of Bromley, St. John and the aged, acidulated Seymour. The postbags of Tory leaders were crammed with letters of exhortation from country squires and parsons, and on 13 December two hundred M.P.s marched together to carry the bill up to the House of Lords. In this fortnight of sleepless excitement even Queen Anne conceived a hankering after the bill and a surprisingly large body of peers actually voted for it, including (to Godolphin's great vexation) the Archbishop of York and the new Bishop of Bath and Wells. At the final vote it was discovered that the measure had failed by the

---

[1] See B.M. Loan 29/191/93, Bromley to Harley, 25 Sept. 1703, where the issue is made clearer than in the extract published in H.M.C. *Portland MSS.*

[2] *Sharp*, p. 349, Godolphin to Sharp, 14 Nov. 1703; *E.C.*, i. 266, FA to Trelawny, 23 Nov. 1703.

narrow margin of twelve. This was clearly the moment for
Atterbury to seize once again the initiative in the Lower House of
Convocation. Tenison had prorogued the assembly to the distant
date of 4 February, but as the members came rushing back to town
it was apparent that their mood would brook no delay. Aldrich was
unceremoniously swept aside, and Atterbury led the majority party
in holding intermediate sessions.[1] It was decided to draw up two
manifestos or declarations of the grievances of the clergy of the
Church of England, and during January these took shape. The first,
a solemn *Representation*, laid all the blame squarely on the bishops.
Canons were being disobeyed, discipline unenforced, and everywhere episcopal administration was inefficient and corrupt. Men of
'plenty and leisure' were filling the dignities and consuming the
substance of the Church, but the ordinary parson was neglected,
impoverished, and disheartened. The second document, *The Protestation of Right*, was a pungent statement of the Atterburian thesis
with regard to Convocation, drawn up in the form of an itemized
account of all Tenison's unconstitutional behaviour over the
previous four years.[2]

At the beginning of February Atterbury was in a mood of
exhilaration. 'I thank God', he wrote excitedly to Trelawny, 'I will
be able to break through all their devices, and show the world (by a
demonstration of what we can do when we please) who betrayed
the Lower House when they sat in it.'[3] When eventually on 12
February the Bishops re-assembled the sight was seen of the whole
body of the lower clergy marching in procession through Westminster Abbey towards Jerusalem Chamber to present the *Representation* to the Upper House. It was generally noted that the
Archbishop was not present to receive in person so offensive a
document. On the 24th the solemn march was repeated to deliver
the *Protestation* but this time Atterbury was vastly amused to find
that their lordships had been 'too nimble for us'. They had packed
up early and just gone home.[4] Naturally the lay-politicians did not

[1] *E.C.*, i. 278, FA to Trelawny, 23 Dec. 1703.
[2] See the broadsheet, *A Representation made by the Lower House . . . Anno
1703* (1704); and N.L.W. Ottley MS. 218, for a draft of the *Protestation*, sent by
FA to Adam Ottley.
[3] Coll. Trelawn., p. 286, FA to Trelawny, 1 Feb. 1704.
[4] N.L.W. Ottley MS. 232, FA to Ottley, 26 Feb. 1704.

miss the parallel between the House of Commons obstructed by the Lords and the Lower House of Convocation thwarted by the Bishops. At the end of March Atterbury received an intimation from 'our friends in the House of Commons' that they would welcome a formal address from the spiritual assembly to its lay counterpart, and this was duly provided in the form of a message of gratitude to all those who had voted for the Occasional Conformity Bill. On 8 March Atterbury again preached by invitation before the Commons, and at the end of the session he could describe himself as a happy man 'because I had prevailed with them to do more than had been done in Convocation for forty years before'.[1]

The lesson was not lost on Robert Harley. If there was now to be any hope for 'moderate' government urgent measures had to be taken to reconstruct the Ministry's basis of support in Parliament, and something had to be done to exorcize this destructive ecclesiastical issue. Increasingly over the two previous years Marlborough and Godolphin had come to rely on the ingenuity and subtle skill of Mr. Speaker, but now it was decided in May 1704 that he would have to come out into the open and take up the Secretaryship of State which Nottingham had resigned in disgust at the failure of the Occasional Conformity Bill.[2] It was a difficult and delicate moment, and in the days before his appointment was announced Harley engaged in an elaborate series of conversations designed to create a new body of support and fend off the great Tory onslaught which would certainly follow Nottingham's resignation. Strangely enough his wiles were not directed towards separating moderate Tories from the extremists. Rather he aimed to deprive the extremists of their most effective leaders. And thus, among the politicians, he secured the co-operation not only of Tories like Thomas Mansel and Simon Harcourt but even of Henry St. John, until this time one of the hottest advocates of the bill. All were younger men without any close ties with Rochester or Nottingham and each was a man of a definite Tory ideology. Harley put forward to each something more than the lure of office or place; he offered them the prospect of abandoning factious opposition, gaining an ascendancy in the

---

[1] *E.C.*, i. 300, FA to Trelawny, 4 Mar. 1704.
[2] See Angus McInnes, 'The Appointment of Harley in 1704', *The Historical Journal*, xi (1968), 255–71.

Ministry and the Queen's councils, and then as a Government creating a new Tory deal in Church and State.[1] In the summer months of 1704 Harley performed a truly remarkable feat in breaking the unity of the Tory leadership and confusing the party rank and file.

The Church was, however, an essential part of the new Secretary's scheme and from this time on he, the Queen and Archbishop Sharp formed themselves into a working partnership to deal with all matters of ecclesiastical preferment. The precise nature of Harley's understanding with Sharp must remain obscure, but the Archbishop's diary and his future course of action would indicate that he too thought that Harley was pledged to a policy of Anglican reconstruction when this was no longer linked to the factious politics of Rochester and Nottingham. It was clear, of course, that the Secretary had to find some ecclesiastical adjutant to persuade and temper the High Church party among the lower clergy. Without hesitation he fixed on Francis Atterbury. Hooper was now useless: his humiliating failure in Convocation and his disobedience in the House of Lords put him in the deepest disgrace. Only in one way was the Bishop of Bath and Wells of service. His constant complaints that the whole disaster of the previous winter was due to Atterbury's intrigues and incendiary activity led both Harley and Godolphin to realize that this above all was the divine whom they needed to recruit.[2]

The Secretary moved quickly. A few days after taking up the Seals he was in his office amid a crowd of suitors when he saw that Atterbury had come into the ante-room. At once Harley made his way through the throng and whispered that 'he must speak with me, and would send me word when he had an hour or two's time'.[3] In the following days the two had earnest secret discussions. Naturally, after their previous dealings there was a considerable barrier of suspicion, but Harley was not entirely at a loss. An urgent message was sent to Godolphin asking that the first available piece

[1] For the kind of persuasion brought to bear on St. John, see his letter to Sir William Trumbull, 16 May 1704 [endorsed], Berkshire R.O., Trumbull Add. MSS. 133.

[2] *E.C.*, i. 279, FA to Trelawny, 30 Dec. 1703.

[3] *E.C.*, i. 313, FA to Trelawny, 6 June 1704; H.M.C. *Bath MSS.* i. 57, Godolphin to Harley, 9 June 1704.

of senior preferment should be conferred on Dr. Atterbury as a token of the Ministry's fair and honest intentions towards him. It was only unfortunate that the sole vacancy which the Treasurer could discover was the deanery of Carlisle. Remotely situated and meagrely endowed, it was by no means an ideal promotion for a busy London clergyman, but Harley promised repeatedly that it was only to be considered as a first instalment of the Queen's favour.[1] Great care was taken to see that Atterbury's acceptance received wide publicity. 'I need not explain to you the meaning of it', wrote the Secretary to his chaplain, Dr. William Stratford at Christ Church. Indeed this open alliance with the Ministry of so vehemently extreme a divine did much to unsettle the minds of country Tories. One of them revealed his complete bewilderment by announcing that 'Mr. Speaker Harley, Mr. St. John and Mr. Mansell (our new Dean's patrons) have deserted the Church, and are looked on as Whigs in the House of Commons.'[2]

3

It soon became clear to the new Dean of Carlisle that his position was embarrassing and exposed. Now he found himself surrounded with animosity on all sides: from Whigs who continued to regard him as a dangerous High-flyer and from Tories who thought he had sold himself to the Ministry. Small insults and the shunning of his company by old friends, particularly those at Oxford, indicated the penalty he had paid for his adhesion to Harley's band of Court Tories. There were compensations. It was satisfying to be admitted to Mr. Secretary Harley's intimacy and quiet political confidences. Harley saw clearly where this restless divine's ambitions and aspirations lay, and he regaled him with plans to distribute ecclesiastical preferment according to a system and exclusively to those churchmen who would serve the Queen and not a faction. By mid-September Atterbury was writing to the Secretary as his 'patron and protector' and offering advice which 'will be of advantage to her

---

[1] Sharp MSS. 4, L. 121, Godolphin to Sharp, 4 July 1704; Nicolson's diary, ii. 197: 10 July.
[2] H.M.C. *Portland MSS.* iv. 98, Harley to Stratford, 8 July 1704; Nicolson's diary, ii. 203: 14 Aug.

Majesty in her right of patronage, and will forward those noble ends which she is pursuing'.[1] But, in return, Harley expected assistance from his ally, and particularly peace in Convocation when the new parliamentary session began. This was an altogether more difficult matter. Indeed at one of their evening meetings Atterbury found himself forced to a promise that he would raise no dispute so long as Tenison on his part offered no provocation. After sleeping on it the Dean became quite agitated lest he should have yielded too much, and he wrote the next morning to seek another meeting.[2] He could see that when Convocation met his position was likely to be uneasy indeed.

Not the least of his embarrassments, however, was the extraordinary conduct of his new diocesan, the Bishop of Carlisle. William Nicolson was an able scholar and an acute observer of the political scene, but he was excitable and impulsive by temperament. When the news of Atterbury's appointment was conveyed to him he was overcome by sheer disbelief that the Ministry could have imposed such a man upon him. And as he thought of the past his heart hardened, for Nicolson had suffered much from the attentions of Atterbury's followers. Indeed because of some criticisms which he had published of the *Rights, Powers and Privileges of an English Convocation* the Bishop had been subjected to an unprecedented humiliation. When in 1702 he had been nominated to the see of Carlisle the Tories of Oxford, by packing the Convocation house, had contrived to refuse him the doctorate of Divinity which the university invariably conferred on those of her sons who had been raised to the episcopate. For the first time a bishop had to be consecrated as a mere Master of Arts, and with that humble degree he remained until Dr. Bentley took pity and procured for him the solace of an Honorary D.D. at Cambridge. It had all rankled badly, and at the end of August 1704 Nicolson took the unwise decision to return humiliation for humiliation by refusing Atterbury institution to the deanery of Carlisle until such time as he had formally retracted three propositions in the *Rights, Powers and Privileges* which, in Nicolson's view, tended to deny the Royal Supremacy. Archbishop Sharp was instant in pleas

[1] B.M. Loan 29/191, FA to Harley, 16 Sept. 1704.
[2] Ibid., FA to Harley, n.d. but clearly early July 1704. It is marked 'Thursd. morn.', which would indicate 3 July.

and counter-arguments, but the Bishop was wholly unmoved and proceeded to summon Atterbury to appear before him in Carlisle.[1] There was nothing for it but to set out for the North, bearing his Letters Patent and taking with him a severe letter from the Archbishop of York warning his headstrong suffragan of the perilous consequences of seeming to deny the Queen's right of patronage. It was a wretched journey. As they went over Stainmoor Atterbury's coach broke down, and he arrived in Carlisle on 15 September in a hired chaise, weary, dishevelled and distinctly out of temper. There was no sign of the civic reception usually accorded to a new Dean and no welcome by the clergy of the cathedral. With surprising self-control he went on to Rose Castle where the Bishop with his lawyers was waiting. But if Nicolson expected to overawe a man of Atterbury's strength of character and natural pugnacity he was wholly mistaken. The Dean was icily formal and legally precise. In spite of much huffing and puffing from the Bishop he carried the attack deliberately into the opposite camp. He would sign no retractions; the demand for these was an improper attempt to impose tests unknown to the law. He requested the Bishop's notaries to witness his solemn written protest against the way in which Royal Letters Patent were being denied and belittled.[2]

It was clear that Nicolson had made a fool of himself, and in London ministerial anger was unbridled. 'The Bishop of Carlisle's perverseness is very unaccountable', complained the Lord Treasurer; and at his weekly audience Harley laid the whole case before the Queen.[3] Disrespect to her prerogative always nettled Anne and she became extremely incensed. Instructions were given to Secretary Hedges, Harley's colleague, to write at once to the Bishop, and on 27 September this letter was received at Rose Castle. Its contents filled Nicolson with horror. Not even he was prepared to disobey a direct royal command, and he hastened to obey; the next morning

---

[1] *Sharp*, pp. 236–41, Sharp to Nicolson, 28 Aug. 1704; H.M.C. *Portland MSS.* iv. 127, FA to Harley, 9 Sept.

[2] Nicolson's diary, ii. 207, 15 Sept. 1704; H.M.C. *Portland MSS.* iv. 129–31, FA to Harley, 16 Sept.; Sharp MSS. 4, V.11, FA to Sharp, 16 Sept.; B.M. Loan 29/313 for Harley's private notes.

[3] H.M.C. *Bath MSS.* i. 63, Godolphin to Harley, 15 Sept. 1704; Sharp MSS. 4, V.17–18, Harley to Sharp, 14 and 21 Sept.; B.M. Loan 29/191, FA to Harley, 18 Sept.

Atterbury received his institution without question or conditions. 'What sits most heavily on me', wailed the Bishop to Archbishop Sharp, 'is my being wholly ignorant wherein I have so far offended the Queen as to deserve so severe a correction.'[1] His plea was disingenuous, though the rebuff he had received was to play no small part in his future attachment to the Junto. By separate routes the Dean and his diocesan travelled the long road back to London where they regaled their respective circles with a tale of insult and wrong endured. Not all Archbishop Sharp's eirenic endeavours could prevent them from publishing to an amused world the graceless story of their clerical storm in a tea-cup.

No one could doubt the deep uneasiness of Harley's friends as the winter session of 1704 drew on. Rochester, Nottingham, Seymour and Bromley were preparing an all-out attack on the Ministry, and informed political observers waited to see what the Court Tories would do. Some open split in the ranks of the Church party now appeared inevitable, and Harley was anxious to explain his position to any country member whom he could get to listen. He and his allies, he argued, were committed to resisting the factious and sterile politics of the present Opposition. What mattered was the goodwill of the Queen and the reputation of being responsible and efficient in office; these qualities alone could give the Tories power and a real opportunity to put into effect their programme of reconstruction in Church and State. It was in this cause that they had to oppose the assault on the Ministry in Parliament and attempt to procure peace on the vexed issue of the Church. As Henry St. John put it: 'the bill of Occasional Conformity is the only handle that can be taken to divide and consequently weaken one side and consequently strengthen the other.'[2]

Peace among the clergy in Convocation was essential to the Secretary's scheme to thwart the Tory attack, and yet this was crucially embarrassing to Atterbury. He was aware how many High Churchmen would be looking to him to renew the great agitation against the Bishops. It was unpleasantly obvious that he would soon 'lie under the imputation of being disaffected, which

---

[1] Sharp MSS. 4, V.4, Nicolson to Sharp, 2 Oct. 1704.
[2] Berkshire R.O., Trumbull Add. MSS 133, St. John to Trumbull, 16 May 1704.

our good friends will be sure to bestow on us'.[1] And in the event the actual sessions in the Lower House proved as personally grievous as he had expected. When he rose to announce himself reluctant to insert any Tory ideological sentiments into the Loyal Address there was a general stir and Lord Rochester's allies began to goad him unmercifully. With some heavy remarks on the wonderful effect which the northern air of Carlisle had had on the clerical champion of the previous year, Henry Aldrich stepped back into the picture as Prolocutor. But the work of agitating the House required a certain flair and Lord Rochester's friends did not possess it. It gave Atterbury no comfort at all to stand by while Tenison triumphed at every turn. Indeed on 10 February things had arrived at such a pass that he began to suspect that he might never again be able to revive the dispute. As he confided to a friend, he was terrified that the situation might 'grow irretrievable, and we ourselves shall sink into the last degree of contempt, if some spirit be not put into matters at the beginning of the next Convocation. Unless that be done, we drop into nothing of course.'[2]

The future of Godolphin's Administration now depended on events in the House of Commons, and at first it seemed impossible that the Government could resist the pent-up feelings of a majority of its backbenchers. Obviously the House of Lords was the rock on which the Tory assault would break, and in mid-November Bromley and his associates fixed upon a tactic by which the peers could be prevented from cumbering the bill with amendments. It was decided to 'tack' the Occasional Conformity clauses to the Land Tax Bill for the ensuing year.[3] And yet this, ingenious as it was, turned out to be a grievous error. Many country gentlemen, who were convinced of the iniquities of occasional conformity, were uncertain that they wished to vote for a measure of doubtful constitutional propriety which might have the additional effect of denying Marlborough the money to put an army in the field in 1705. And Harley, of course, was much happier in fighting the Tack than opposing the bill itself. But with a kind of wild disregard for political

---

[1] *E.C.*, i. 361, FA to Trelawny, 7 Nov. 1704.
[2] N.L.W. Ottley MS. 222, FA to Ottley, 10 Feb. 1705.
[3] Henry Snyder, 'The defeat of the Occasional Conformity bill and the Tack', *Bulletin of the Institute of Historical Research*, xli (1968), 172.

realities the Tackers pressed on until on the evening of 28 November they were defeated in the Commons by 251 votes to 134. It was a most grievous shock to them. Bishop Nicolson described how 'when the coaches began to move, I sent my servant to enquire how matters went; and he presently returned with a lamentable story that *The Church has lost it*. This, he said, he had from several clergymen, as well as others.'[1]

In a sense the triumph of Harley's management was complete; and yet the Government's victory was a sour one for him and his friends. The Treasurer had been severely wounded and utterly alienated by the conduct of the Tory zealots and in the New Year he embarked on a wholesale proscription of office-holders who had voted for the Tack. Harley and Archbishop Sharp protested in vain against the ruthless treatment meted out even to minor Tories, and they were deeply chagrined when in March 1705 the important bishopric of Lincoln fell vacant. Without ceremony Godolphin swept aside their recommendations and appointed a firm Junto supporter, William Wake, Dean of Exeter. In spite of Atterbury's considerable services to the Government and the urgent canvassing of his political friends it was impossible for Harley to procure for his ally this desirable appointment in the South-West.[2] It was an unenviable situation for the Dean of Carlisle and his circle. Neglected by their new masters and vilified by the main body of the Tories, it would require some master-stroke of Harleian ingenuity to restore them to their place in the sun.

---

[1] Tullie House, Carlisle, Bishop William Nicolson's MS. Diary, 28 Nov. 1704.

[2] H.M.C. *Portland MSS*. iv. 156, Harcourt to Harley, 6 Jan. 1705; Wake MSS. 17, fo. 84, Blackburne to Wake, 7 Apr.; Norman Sykes, 'The cathedral chapter of Exeter and the general election of 1705', *E.H.R.* xlv (1930), 260.

CHAPTER FIVE

Mr. Harley's Friend, 1705–1708

I

THE General Election of 1705 ushered in a period during which the High Church cause was at its lowest ebb. Up and down the land Tory squires found themselves rejected in the face of Whig propaganda and electoral efficiency. The survivors who travelled up to Westminster in the autumn were angry men, grimly determined to revenge themselves on their enemies and to spurn those false friends who had frustrated their hopes in the last Parliament. They still looked to Rochester, Nottingham, Seymour, and Bromley to lead them in a new agitation in defence of the Church. But the Lord Treasurer was now unmoved and unafraid. He made his calculations and discovered that the new House of Commons would have approximately equal numbers of Whig and Tory members. Now by throwing the Court or placemen votes to one side or the other he could hold the balance and choose which of the parties to take into partnership. There was no doubt in his mind that henceforth he would rely on the Whigs. It was not only that the old Tory leaders had proved utterly factious in the last session and endangered supplies for the war but also that they seemed to be wedded to an ecclesiastical controversy which Godolphin found repellent and personally distressing. During the elections he had been upset by the continual assertion of 'The Church in Danger', but this was as nothing compared with the grievous wound inflicted on him by the pamphlet known as *The Memorial of the Church of England*. At the very mention of it Archbishop Sharp found him 'in great concern and very near weeping'.[1]

Thus Harley and his friends, lay and clerical, found themselves tied to an Administration which relied in the main on Whig support, and their situation was comfortless and exposed. In letter after

[1] H.M.C. *Bath MSS.* i. 76, Godolphin to Harley, 18 Sept. 1705; *Sharp*, pp. 365–66.

letter the Secretary urged upon Godolphin the necessity of concili-
ating at least some members of the Church party: there were, he
repeated, still reasonable men among the Tories, and they could
be the foundation of a return of their party to the Queen and to
office. Whenever he could find a Tory to listen, layman or divine,
Harley poured out his accusation against the old-guard leaders: by
pursuing party politics to a 'violent' height they had forfeited high
office when they had had it and now they had driven the Queen
into the arms of the Whigs. A future for the Tories existed only if
they could regain a reputation for responsible conduct in government and loyalty to the Crown. Only then would they be in a
position to effect that reconstruction in Church and State to which
they so earnestly aspired.[1]

When the new session of Parliament began, Harley's opinion of
the competence of the Tory leadership received ample confirmation,
for Lord Rochester at once fell into a trap devised for him by the
Junto lords. On 6 December he allowed himself to become excited
at a Whig motion which called for a public inquiry into whether
the Church was in that danger which the Tory propagandists
alleged so strenuously. His opponents had carefully concerted their
speeches, not least with their allies on the Bench of Bishops, but the
High Tory leader was manifestly ill-prepared and made a disastrously inept contribution to the debate. In his usual overheated,
choleric style he launched himself into a wide-ranging attack on
Presbyterianism in Scotland, the Dissenters in England, and a
Ministry which encouraged both by its vilely underhand action
taken to frustrate the Occasional Conformity Bill. He concluded
with a demand that the Electress Sophia of Hanover should be
invited to England to be at hand in case Anne should die suddenly
from one of her many ailments. It was a wretched performance, not
the least foolish in that the Queen herself was present incognita in
the chamber. On a division a majority of two to one proceeded to
vote not only that the Church was in 'a flourishing condition' but
that 'whosoever goes about to suggest or insinuate that the Church
is in danger under your Majesty's administration is an enemy to
the Queen, the Church and the kingdom'.[2] It was a crushing retort

---

[1] B.M. Loan 29/171/2, Harley to Stratford, 10 Oct. 1705.
[2] Wake's diary, fo. 8: 5–6 Dec. 1705; *Sharp*, p. 363.

to Rochester and a blow from which his reputation never really recovered.

Such was the emotionally charged atmosphere in which Atterbury, as Harley's acknowledged lieutenant in ecclesiastical affairs, took up the difficult task of trying to wean the lower clergy from their dependence on the old Tory leaders. On all sides he found himself regarded with the deepest hostility. It might have been thought by this time that he had a claim to the prolocutorship of the new Lower House of Convocation but Rochester's friends were determined to prevent his election, and Dean Aldrich sent round a circular-letter to members of the Church party announcing that 'many of our true friends' had held a meeting and agreed to put up Dr. William Binckes, Dean of Lichfield, as 'one in whose hands the prolocutorship may be safely trusted'.[1] On 25 October Binckes was duly elected to the chair. None of the clergy, however, seems to have realized how carefully the Junto had been preparing for their discomfiture and how anxious the Bishops were to lead their presbyters into some rebellious action which would ruin their remaining credit with the Queen and the Treasurer.[2] A draft address was prepared in the Upper House which declared provocatively that to insinuate that the Church was in danger could, among clergymen, proceed 'from nothing but prejudice, interest and ambition'. When on 19 November the Lower House offered an alternative form, omitting all reference to the vexed topic, Tenison not only refused to accept it but actually ordered the Prolocutor to inform the clergy that they must either pass the Bishop's form forthwith or state in writing why they would not join in condemning those who so falsely asserted that the Church was in danger under Her Majesty's happy administration. As a piece of calculated incitement to rebellion the Archbishop's tactic succeeded well. Atterbury, who had at first spoken on the side of moderation and compromise, was himself swept along in the general sense of outrage. At one session, held to draw up a formal protest, he so far forgot his usually poised manner as to shout down a member of the

[1] N.L.W. Ottley MS. 257, Aldrich to Ottley, 6 Oct. 1705; H.M.C. *Cowper MSS.* iii. 65, Stratford to Coke, 30 Sept.

[2] FA's account of the session was published in 1708 as *Some Proceedings in the Convocation, A.D. 1705, faithfully represented*. It was answered by Charles Trimnell in *Partiality Detected* (1708).

opposition. He attended diligently on all committees and wrote round to his friends beseeching them to travel up to town as quickly as possible. 'Unless this attempt be vigorously resisted, exposed and baffled', he told them, 'we must be content to give up the cause for the future, and so suffer the other side to do what they please with Convocation, and, by that means, with the Constitution itself. But if we can obtain a full appearance of our friends, I doubt not but that the artillery may be turned upon them, and the attempt begun by them prove of service rather than any ways disadvantageous to us.'[1]

It was exactly what the Whigs wanted. Godolphin listened angrily to reports of the clergy's factious behaviour, and early in the new year he decided to admit the Junto to a full share in the direction of ecclesiastical policy. At a meeting with the Whig leaders he and Marlborough came to a formal agreement with them: that 'in the disposition of Church preferment the Queen had made this rule, to give them to such as had shown a due zeal for her Supremacy and respect for their ecclesiastical superiors, and had made it their business to remove that reproach from her that the Church was in danger.'[2] It was small wonder that when Bishop Nicolson visited the Archbishop of York at the end of the month, he found him 'very much over-run with the spleen' and chafing at the state of Church affairs.[3] Armed with their new authority, the Junto began to hold regular conferences with their clerical allies to discuss policy and to make recommendations for preferment. At one such gathering on 7 February they decided to advise the Treasurer that the time had come for Convocation to be silenced.[4] Accordingly on 1 March, the next day of official session, the lower clergy were summoned to attend on the Bishops in Jerusalem Chamber. They suspected nothing amiss until the text of a severe Royal Letter was read out to them. The Queen now declared that she must take firm action 'to maintain our Supremacy and the due subordination of

[1] N.L.W. Ottley MS. 250, FA to Ottley, 3 Jan. 1706.
[2] New York Public Library, Hardwicke MSS. 33, fos. 125–26: memorandum by Somers, written in 1709 but referring to the period Dec. 1705 to Feb. 1706, quoted by E. L. Ellis, 'The Whig Junto' (Oxford University unpublished D. Phil. thesis, 1962), pp. 555–56.
[3] Tullie House Library, Carlisle, Nicolson's MS. diary: 29 Jan. 1706.
[4] Wake's diary, fo. 11: 7 Feb. 1706.

presbyters to bishops'. Atterbury, standing beside the Prolocutor, was horrified; in a moment's confusion he clutched Binckes by the sleeve of his gown to force him to withdraw, and he called out to the rest of the clergy to make their way back to the Lower House. But the Dean of Lichfield had sufficient presence of mind not to lay himself open to a charge of disrespect to a royal letter and, shaking himself free, he returned to the table to hear the writ which formally prorogued the Convocation. It was a black moment for Atterbury. When Harley protested to the Treasurer on his behalf at this harsh treatment of the clergy, he received a cool reply. 'As for the clergy', concluded Godolphin, 'they always say themselves it is easy for the Queen to get them into her interests. I think so too, if they be once thoroughly satisfied which is the right way to preferment.'[1] It was a curiously insensitive view of clerical motivation, but at least the Chief Minister had made it clear that so far as he was concerned the days were over when the Queen, the Archbishop of York and Robert Harley had guided the affairs of the Church of England.

By the autumn of 1706, however, the Secretary's plan of resistance was beginning to emerge.[2] He knew that in theory Godolphin was an earnest advocate of non-party government; and yet in practice his disgust with the old-guard leaders was so alienating him from the Tories that he would soon become wholly in the power of the Whigs. In correspondence and personal interview Harley urged the necessity that at least some Tories should be conciliated and that, above all, the Ministry should not appear to espouse the Whig cause in the Church. This would distress the Queen and make inevitable that very ecclesiastical agitation which Godolphin himself so deeply deplored. He assured the Treasurer that, after the disasters of the previous session, there were many among the younger politicians and clergy who were ready to be co-operative and who would certainly support a Ministry which favoured moderate Tory policies and men. This, he explained, 'hath been proposed to the leading men of the Church party and, if my intelligence is right, the Dean of Christ Church will not come

---

[1] H.M.C. *Portland MSS.* iv. 291, Godolphin to Harley, 22 Mar. 1706. For FA's confusion, see Wake's diary, fo. 12: 1 Mar.

[2] For a fully documented account of the events of 1706–7, see G. V. Bennett, 'Robert Harley, the Godolphin Ministry, and the bishoprics crisis of 1707', *E.H.R.* lxxxii (1967), 726.

into it, nor meddle with anything more of business, but others, namely Dr. Atterbury and Dr. Smalridge, etc. approve of it and promote it very earnestly.'[1]

Atterbury was indeed indefatigable in his master's service, and went constantly among the clergy propagating Harley's ideas. His work was not too difficult, for reflection on the events of the previous spring had proved a chastening experience for many High Churchmen. By the time of the new session of Convocation he was able to assure his patron that the Lower House would be on its best behaviour and would even be willing to insert into their Address a phrase or two which might mollify Godolphin by complimenting him on the wise administration of the public revenue.[2] Such a re-emergence of Atterbury as leader of the Lower House, together with the new spirit of co-operation which he had instilled into his brethren, came as a most unwelcome surprise to the Bishops. They had already sent down an Address couched in terms almost identical to those which had caused so much trouble the previous year, and now they waited confidently for its rejection. They were dumbfounded when it was meekly accepted. 'They agreed to it without any amendment', noted Bishop Wake in amazement, 'What is the meaning of this procedure?'[3] On the following day he was even more puzzled, when the Convocation waited on the Queen to present the Address, to see Atterbury and Aldrich standing side by side at the head of the lower clergy. 'God forgive', he besought heaven through the medium of his diary, 'either their past perverseness or their present hypocrisy.'

It was not so easy, however, to convince the Treasurer that it was possible to work with Tory churchmen. His Whig mentors possessed his mind with a suggestion that the Lower House was about to seize the bill for the Union with Scotland as an excuse for a new 'Church in Danger' agitation, and he readily believed them. He announced himself as determined to 'prevent the designs of the

---

[1] Huntington Library, San Marino, California, Stowe MSS. 57, i. 46–47, James Brydges to Godolphin, n.d. but between 19 and 22 Nov. 1706, for this report of Harley's conversation. Cf. H.M.C. *Bath MSS.* i. 109.

[2] B.M. Loan 29/192/385, FA to Harley, 4 Dec. 1706. This letter is misdated and misquoted in H.M.C. *Portland MSS.* iv. 274.

[3] Wake's diary, fo. 31: 6 Dec. 1706.

firebrands in Convocation', and nothing could be said or done to convince him that his fears were unfounded. On 12 February a royal writ was sent to Tenison requiring him to prorogue and silence the assembly while the bill was passing through Parliament.[1] It was an insult so gratuitous and undeserved that when eventually on 5 March the Lower House was once again permitted to meet, it was all that Atterbury could do to hold back those who advocated some extreme expression of protest. Clearly silence was pain and grief to him, but he sought compromise by composing a very modestly worded 'application', setting out the historical precedents. Yet even so restrained an exercise in historical research was grist to Tenison's mill, and on 2 April he summoned the clergy before him with every degree of awful solemnity. The 'application', he announced, was a reflection on the Queen in the exercise of her Royal Supremacy, and he intended to lay it before her so that she could take appropriate action. In sudden and real alarm Atterbury wrote off to Harley to invoke his protection and to prophesy that with the support of the Treasurer the Archbishop was about to attack the Tory clergy without mercy.[2]

His prediction was entirely justified. Easter was near and most members of the Lower House had departed from Westminster for the pastoral duties of Holy Week. It was generally thought that the meeting fixed for 10 April would be the occasion for a formal adjournment. Atterbury himself was talking with friends in one of the houses in the abbey precincts when, to the general astonishment, Tenison summoned the Lower House to attend him. On being informed that the Prolocutor had left town to keep Easter in the cathedral at Lichfield, His Grace proceeded to pronounce him contumacious of the primatial authority. A Royal Letter, couched in the most crushing terms, was then read. The Queen declared her grave resentment at a recent paper which called in question her rightful prerogative, and she asserted that she was ready to take punitive measures against the author or anyone else who denied or

[1] Longleat, Portland papers, Misc. vol., fo. 119, Godolphin to Harley, [8 Feb. 1707]; *H.O.T.*, v. 297; B.M. Lansdowne MSS. 1013, Kennett to Blackwell, 13 Feb.

[2] N.L.W. Ottley MS. 247, FA to Ottley, 20 Mar. 1707; H.M.C. *Portland MSS.* iv. 399–400, FA to Harley, [2 Apr.].

disobeyed the royal authority.[1] Indisputably this was Tenison's greatest moment in Convocation, and not the least of his satisfactions was the abject terror which the royal missive produced in the Prolocutor. Abandoning the duties of his cathedral, Binckes hurried up to town, and at Lambeth he agreed to sign a formal submission. Nothing that Atterbury or Smalridge could say would dissuade him. It was small satisfaction to note that one of Rochester's nominees for the prolocutorship had once again proved a broken reed. Now not all the requirements of expediency could keep Atterbury's pen from paper and in a small, anonymous pamphlet *An Account and Defence of the Protestation* he published to the world the unhappy story of an archbishop's offensive against his presbyters.

2

The summer and autumn of 1707 saw the Ministry in the grip of a grave ecclesiastical crisis, the roots of which lay in Queen Anne's growing anger at the policies of her Lord Treasurer.[2] Whatever her distaste for irresponsible Tory politicians and factious divines, the Queen retained a deep-seated animosity towards the lords of the Whig Junto. And yet in the winter of 1706, despite her pleas and energetic attempts at delay, she had been forced by Godolphin to accept Charles, Earl of Sunderland, as Harley's colleague in the office of Secretary of State. It was a deeply unhappy time for her. She had recently quarrelled vehemently with her erstwhile bosom friend, the Duchess of Marlborough, and now she found herself surrounded by Ministers with whom she was increasingly out of sympathy. More and more she came to lean upon those who showed her kindness and did not bully her with unwelcome political advice, and in particular she took refuge in the gentle attentions of her dresser-companion, Abigail Hill. In private interviews the Archbishop of York pressed upon her his own discontent with ecclesiastical policy; and Harley, with his gift for facile persuasion, urged her to assert her personal authority, to stand above the parties, and to defend the Church from control by 'violent men': in other words, to be a Queen indeed.

[1] Bodl. MS. Ballard 7, fo. 10, Smalridge to Charlett, 10 Apr. 1707; Wake MSS. 17, fo. 163, Kennett to Wake, 10 Apr.
[2] See G. V. Bennett, art. cit., for a detailed account.

Thus in the spring of 1707, fortified by her friends, Anne absolutely refused to accept the names of two Whig divines whom Godolphin had proposed for the vacant sees of Exeter and Chester. Only recently the Treasurer had angered the Junto by offering the bishopric of Winchester, with its heavy rent-rolls and magnificent episcopal palaces, to Bishop Trelawny. Now he found it virtually impossible to convince the Whig lords that the rejection of their nominees was not a breach of the agreement so recently made with them and part of some deeply laid plan to return to the Tories. And in May it became known that Anne, entirely on her own initiative, had promised Exeter and Chester to two Tory divines, Offspring Blackall and Sir William Dawes. Both were protégés of Archbishop Sharp, and to most observers it seemed clear that Harley and the northern Primate moved in the dark behind the scenes. Yet no bullying, no prediction of political chaos, could bring the Queen to change her mind. She was emotionally, stubbornly committed. As the battle raged about him Harley kept up earnest protestations that he was innocent of all attempts to influence the Queen, and his clerical associates waited on the side-lines in the devout hope that out of the conflict there might emerge some new deal for the Church and freedom from ecclesiastical bondage to the Junto.[1] But at the end of June the Whigs delivered their ultimatum: either their own candidates were appointed or they would break with the Ministry and go into opposition. By the beginning of September they had widened their demands to include the dismissal of Harley.

It was a moment of great uncertainty, but one in which Atterbury perceived that he might be able to play a role. Attention must therefore be turned to his strange devisings in the North, which were themselves to become a national issue. During his uncomfortable residence in Carlisle in 1704 the Dean had occupied himself in characteristic fashion: by undertaking some detailed research into the chapter archives. What he discovered intrigued him greatly. He became convinced that the Foundation Charter of the cathedral, given to it by Henry VIII in 1541, alone had legal validity and that the statutes of 1545, by which the collegiate body was usually

---

[1] B.M. Loan 29/194/82, Smalridge to Harley, 23 May 1707.

governed, had no legal status at all.[1] No small point lay at issue. If Atterbury could establish that the charters of the Henrician 'new foundations' alone held up, then appointment to all canonries and prebends in them, and indeed the very right to act as their Visitor, would belong to the Crown and not to the individual diocesan bishops. In the balance lay a vast amount of patronage which might enable a Tory administration to consolidate a strong body of clerical support. The Dean himself had no intention of spending much time in the bleak North, even for the opportunity of exploiting so promising a cause, but he found in Dr. Hugh Todd, one of the prebendaries, a man after his own heart who was to prove a useful and energetic agent. Todd had already clashed with Bishop Nicolson and now he welcomed the opportunity not only to ingratiate himself with Mr. Secretary Harley but also to torment his diocesan.

During the next two years relations between the Dean and the remaining members of the Chapter deteriorated steadily, and his residence in the summer of 1705 produced such grievous disputes over the decanal rights that it was thought wise to obtain a royal licence excusing him from further attendance. Henceforth from London Atterbury endeavoured to work up support through letters to local Tory political families, while in Carlisle Canon Todd and the Bishop became locked in mortal combat.[2] On 28 June 1706 Todd went so far as to present the Bishop's sister in the consistory court on a charge of adultery. At last, his patience gone, Nicolson addressed a formal letter to the Dean and Chapter, calling on them to cease their disputes. They should not, he concluded sharply, desert their statutes and strike out in new ways, especially when this course was pressed upon them from afar by men who did not reside to perform the duties of their office. From London the Dean replied in his most urbane manner to thank his lordship for his fatherly concern for peace, which was so well known among them, and to assure him that nothing stood in the way of complete

---

[1] See J. E. Prescott, *The Statutes of the Cathedral Church of Carlisle* (1879) for a careful examination of the legal case.

[2] York Minster Library, Hailstone collection QQ.2, 7, for Todd's papers, 1706–08, showing how closely he followed the Dean's instructions; see especially FA to Todd, 5 Mar. 1706. See also Levens Hall, Westmorland, Bagot MSS., FA to Colonel James Graham, 18 June, 23 and 25 July 1706.

harmony but the underhand activities of knaves who were urging the Chapter on to oppose the just and legal rights of the Dean under the Foundation Charter.

This was more than Nicolson's fragile temper could endure, and he announced that he would include the cathedral in his triennial visitation in the summer of 1707. No one, certainly not the Bishop, seems to have realized how carefully the Dean had been preparing for just such a legal contest and an eventual appeal to the Crown.[1] In the months before the visitation everyone wavered but Atterbury. And the moment Nicolson issued his formal monition, he went into action. The Bishop, he protested, had no such authority under the 'pretended local statutes'; only the Queen herself was Visitor of 'this royal foundation'; and he was 'determined not to suffer anything to be done injurious to the prerogative and supremacy of the Crown'.[2] With a minute attention to detail he drew up his legal case and a formal petition, and the two documents were sent off to Harley with a solemn assurance that he would be 'answerable in every particular' for them. Her Majesty could now acquire a principal part of the patronage of half the bishops of England. He begged the Secretary 'that you will please to let this matter be laid before the Queen, so early as that I may have her answer to my petition before you leave town.'[3]

It was a critical moment for Harley. The bishoprics crisis was still unresolved, and the Junto were pressing hard for his dismissal. Godolphin was badgering the Queen almost daily, and it was by no means sure that she would be able to maintain her resistance to the Whig appointments for much longer. During these tormented autumn days the Secretary was trying secretly to lay the foundation of a new 'moderate scheme': a Ministry in which both Whigs and Tories would participate but which would rescue Anne from the 'violence' of the Junto. By mid-September he had many promises, notably from Whigs who were themselves angered by the manner in which the Queen was being bullied. But it was still essential to attract a substantial body of Tory support, and for this

---

[1] Bodl. MS. Add. C. 217, fo. 40, Nicolson to FA, 14 June 1707.
[2] Prescott, op. cit., p. 15.
[3] H.M.C. *Portland MSS.* iv. 437–38, FA to Harley, 29 Aug. 1707. The documents are B.M. Loan 29/313/35 and 29/194/208-9.

there had to be some public sign that Anne was really willing to favour Tory policies. Under Godolphin's baneful eye this was a matter of some difficulty, and it can only have been in an attempt publicly to indicate a new deal for the Church that Harley took the grave risk on 7 September of presenting Atterbury's controversial petition to the Queen. This was the first clear evidence which his fellow-ministers had that he was interfering in ecclesiastical affairs, and they took decisive action. Two days later Lord Chancellor Cowper came to inform him that his colleagues considered him to be a disturber of public business. Such a formal warning could only be a prelude to dismissal, and the Secretary was badly shaken. To Godolphin he sent off an earnest protestation of his entire loyalty and to Cowper a detailed rebuttal of the immediate charge. 'I should be fallen very low', he concluded, 'if the Dean or anyone else could influence in these cases, or be thought capable of it.'[1]

Visiting Harley on the evening of 10 September, Atterbury found him utterly despondent, and ready to throw over their whole plan. The Dean was horrified to learn of the difficulties within the Administration which the petition had caused. 'I beg your pardon for this', he wrote next morning, 'and all the other troubles I have given you, since I had the honour and happiness to know you.' Not unnaturally he did not much relish the prospect of falling under Godolphin's grave displeasure but if 'the honour I have hitherto had of being known to depend entirely on you cannot prevent it, 'tis to no purpose to complain . . . However, if you please to look back at what passed at the beginning of last winter, you will permit me to say I have not deserved such usage. My Lord Treasurer himself knows I have not.'[2] Atterbury, in fact, was still ready for a fight, and within a few days he had hit upon another device which could serve as a manifesto to reluctant Tories. In mid-September he had to hand the proofs of a collected edition of his sermons. What better idea than that it should come out with a dedication to Bishop Trelawny and a preface which could indicate that the Queen was ready to change her policies and embrace the cause of Anglican

[1] Hertfordshire R.O., Panshanger (Cowper) MSS., Box 49, Letters H–O, Harley to Cowper, 12 Sept. 1707; H.M.C. *Bath MSS.* i. 180–81, Harley to Godolphin, 10 Sept.

[2] B.M. Loan 29/194/24, FA to Harley, 11 Sept. 1707.

reconstruction? The text, when it was submitted to Harley at the end of the month, sounded indeed like a High Church programme. The discipline of the Church courts was to be revived, the rights and revenues of the clergy secured, and blasphemers and heterodox writers suppressed. As Atterbury explained to his patron, it was

designed to give such a turn to the thoughts of those who read it, as you desire should be given. And if there should be a little more warmth than ordinary in it, perhaps the occasion will justify it, and coming from me, it may not be amiss; and, I am sure, is the more likely on that account to arouse the clergy, with whom it is necessary to establish a confidence, in order to the promoting any public service.[1]

3

When Parliament met on 25 October the Ministry was in the deepest disarray. No plea could induce the Queen to yield on the ecclesiastical issue, and Marlborough and Godolphin seemed powerless before the storm brewing in the two Houses. Their apprehension proved wholly justified. The Junto spokesmen combined with the High Tories to attack the administration of the Admiralty under the Queen's husband, Prince George of Denmark, and the Ministers found themselves savaged by both sides. A reconstruction of the Government's basis of support was imperative, and on 5 December in the face of the Queen's continuing obstinacy Marlborough and the Treasurer agreed to allow Harley to have his way: to bring in 'reasonable' Tories as well as moderate Whigs and thus establish a ministry which would not have to yield to the extremists of either party. It was a critical moment. In the following days the Secretary busied himself in organizing support, and in the Queen's name a message was sent to the Tories promising that the Junto should no longer monopolize office and preferment. As the opposition in Parliament temporarily died away, it was announced that the bishoprics of Exeter and Chester were indeed to go to the Tory candidates, Blackall and Dawes. In the same week Atterbury's volume of sermons was published and the preface attracted all the attention which its author could have wished. Within a few weeks

[1] B.M. Loan 29/194/267, FA to Harley, [20 Sept. 1707]. The critical passage in the preface is *E.C.*, i. 415.

it was sold out and a new printing called for. That it was understood as an inspired hint to Tory churchmen was shown by the deep anger which the book inspired in the breast of the Bishop of Winchester who, confirmed political trimmer that he was, objected to being associated with so transparent a political device.[1]

These were contented days for the Dean of Carlisle. He now saw the possibility of a new administration in which his patron would have the Queen's grateful favour and a predominant share in management. And, even more satisfactorily, he saw the coming humiliation of his prime adversary, the Bishop of Carlisle. On 25 September Nicolson had formally visited his cathedral, where he found his way barred by the excited figure of Dr. Todd who protested in the most strident terms that the Queen alone was their Visitor. Two days later, after another unedifying altercation, this time in the very choir of the church, the Bishop took the very serious step of formally excommunicating his antagonist. 'I know not', he confided nervously to Bishop Wake, 'what hand it is which moves behind the curtain, but certainly no presbyter would bid that defiance to his ordinary, which Dr. T. (countenanced by Dr. A.) has done me, without a supporter of power and authority equal to his insolence.' Nicolson was right, for at that very moment 'the Pilot of Chelsea' (as he described his Dean) was reporting to Harley and requesting a personal word of encouragement for the embattled Todd.[2] When the Bishop arrived in London and consulted his lawyers he was alarmed to discover just how uncertain his legal case really was. Indeed he began to see looming on the horizon the distinct possibility that Atterbury's carefully defined position would be upheld in the courts.

Harley's 'moderate scheme', however, still hung in the balance. Godolphin had agreed that it should be given a trial with the greatest reluctance and under pressure from Marlborough. Negotiations with the Tories went painfully slowly and it was the third week in January before the Secretary was able to gather even a modest body of support from among their men of influence.

---

[1] See Coll. Trelawn., p. 291, for a letter from Trelawny's son to his father, 13 Mar. 1708, seeking to excuse FA.
[2] Wake MSS. 17, fo. 182, Nicolson to Wake, 29 Nov. 1707; H.M.C. *Portland MSS.* iv. 463–64, FA to Harley, 2 Dec. 1707.

Rochester and Nottingham held out to the last, and the Junto lords were not inactive: they were reported to be 'tearing' Marlborough and Godolphin 'to pieces' in an endeavour to make them jettison Harley. Any way of killing the 'moderate scheme' appealed to them; and Somers, Sunderland, and Halifax approached Bishop Nicolson with an offer to bring forward a bill which would give legislative force to customary statutes. At one blow Atterbury would be ruled out of court and the 'moderate scheme' would be outvoted in Parliament.[1] The Archbishop of Canterbury played his part, and on 2 February he issued out a circular letter to all his suffragans recommending the bill as 'of great concern to this Church, which will never be quiet so long as that evil generation of men, who make it their business to search out little flaws in ancient charters and statutes, meet with any success.'[2] This was war, and Atterbury prepared himself for battle. Just before the second reading of the bill in the Lords he claimed to have the votes of all the Tory bishops; he was sure that when this 'bill of attainder' went down to the Commons it would meet with a warm reception.[3]

Events, however, were moving fast, and at the end of January Godolphin made a sudden decision to break with Harley.[4] The Secretary's position had been dangerously weakened by the unlucky discovery that one of his confidential clerks, William Greg, had been engaged in a treasonable correspondence with France; and he was now vulnerable to a public inquiry. But, more than this, Godolphin had now begun to suspect, with good reason, that his wily colleague was actually projecting his own dismissal; reports had come to him of secret conversations with the Queen and of messages sent to individual Tories in her name promising changes and policies beyond anything that had been agreed. Anne did her frantic best. A message was sent to Marlborough to induce him to abandon Godolphin, but the General decided to stick by his friend. After a dramatic scene in the Cabinet Council on 8 February Harley knew that he had lost. Already a committee had been set up in the Lords to examine Greg, and it appeared that the first steps were

[1] Nicolson's diary, iv. 19: 29 Jan. 1708.
[2] H.M.C. *Portland MSS.* iv. 467.
[3] *E.C.*, i. 422–23, FA to Trelawny, 6 Feb. 1708.
[4] See Geoffrey Holmes and W. A. Speck, 'The Fall of Harley in 1708 reconsidered', *E.H.R.*, lxxx (1965), 673.

being taken towards impeaching the Secretary for complicity in his clerk's treason. On the 11th Harley resigned, accompanied by his political associates, Henry St. John, Simon Harcourt, and Thomas Mansel.

For a while Atterbury seems to have lost his nerve. When early on the morning of 10 February Edward Harley came to call on his brother, he found the Dean of Carlisle already there and in a great state of agitation. As they passed on the stairs Atterbury took him to one side and whispered urgently that 'your brother's head is upon the block, and yet he seems to have no concern about it; you should therefore persuade him to do something which may prevent the impending danger.'[1] Later that same day Todd appeared at Nicolson's house and offered to make a submission which the Bishop, sensing victory, firmly refused. The next day his lordship was amused to receive an embarrassed visit from his Dean who 'stayed some hours in a peaceful temper', and never actually managed to get to the point. But on the following afternoon Nicolson had the satisfaction of having Atterbury wait on him in the lobby of the House of Lords and plead with him to restore Todd without imposing an undue humiliation.

It seemed that disaster had overtaken Harley and his friends. Godolphin remained in office and now had no choice but to rely on Whig men and measures. The Queen was bitterly hurt and resentful at the manner in which she had been coerced, but there was for the present no way by which she could shake off her bondage. And in the weeks following the great crisis the dismalness of the Tory situation was emphasized by the passage into law of Bishop Nicolson's Cathedrals Bill. There was only one glimmer of hope, for the signs were that the Tories were beginning to unite in adversity and sink their differences. In the debate in the Lords Archbishop Sharp berated Nicolson and sounded a clarion call to party unity, in which he was joined 'by all the lords, spiritual and temporal, of that party.'[2] A fierce fight lay ahead in the Commons, and both Nicolson and Atterbury printed off broadsheets, appealing frankly to party sentiment. Dining with Dr. Onley, one of the Canons of

---

[1] H.M.C. *Portland MSS.* iv. 648: Edward Harley's memoir.
[2] *Court and Society from Elizabeth to Anne,* ed. the Duke of Manchester (1864), ii. 284, Addison to Manchester, 20 Feb. 1708.

Westminster, the Bishop of Carlisle was disconcerted to discover that the ladies of the family were firmly 'on Dr. Atterbury's side', and had no intention of disguising their partisan opinions, even in the presence of their guest. Tory enthusiasm was consolidating, and party divisions were once again standing out clearly. One correspondent of Harley, in sending him a copy of one of Atterbury's sheets, congratulated the ex-Secretary on his new freedom in opposition, and that 'the Church party so generally and so heartily take you by the hand.'[1] On 28 February the Cathedrals Bill passed in the Commons after a furious debate in which Harley, St. John, Bromley, and Sir Thomas Hanmer all argued vehemently for Atterbury. Such support was consoling, and when on 29 March the Dean of Carlisle paid a formal visit to Nicolson the Bishop was surprised and not a little uneasy to find him quite composed under his defeat. Clearly the Dean was contemplating the new political scene which was opening out before them.

[1] H.M.C. *Portland MSS.* iv. 478, Lawton to Harley, 27 Feb. 1708.

CHAPTER SIX

The Dilemma of Dr. Sacheverell, 1708–1710

I

THE year 1708 saw a series of veritable disasters for the Tories. In March, just as the country constituencies were preparing for the General Election due in the summer, the Pretender made a feint at invasion. Meagrely equipped, his small fleet set out from France and appeared in the Firth of Forth, but there was virtually no response. Within a few weeks 'King James III' was back in exile at St. Germain-en-Laye, shocked by the fewness of his adherents and the grievous naivety of his advisers. The main effect of the venture was on the British election campaign, for there was nothing to which the Tories were more vulnerable than a charge of Jacobitism. Country gentlemen might sympathize with conservative views but they would have no truck with Popery or the exiled Stuarts. In the weeks before the poll a wave of anger swept through the voters. One small, anonymous pamphlet *Advice to the Electors of Great Britain*, by ingeniously linking the Tory cause with the invasion, was worth more to the Whigs than a whole army of election agents. And when the results came in, it was clear that the Tories had suffered a crushing reverse. In the new House of Commons the Whigs would be a formidable majority and their opponents a remnant.

It was a scene which presented a superb opportunity to a man of Atterbury's undoubted controversial talents. In the face of overwhelming Whig strength the Tory spokesmen could hope for little effective action in Parliament; they had to look for some agitation out of doors: in Convocation, in the press, or in the country. But there was much with which they could work, for country gentlemen and clergy were becoming increasingly fearful that Whig government would mean a comprehensive attack on the influence of the Church of England. It was a uniquely opportune moment for a man who possessed the resource, verve and political sense to lead the

counter-attack. And, of course, Atterbury's new role was less com-
plicated than it had been in the past: he no longer had to subordinate
his activities to Harley's secret machinations within Godolphin's
Ministry. Yet the Dean remained deeply under the influence of his
patron's political notions and the promise of effective power which
they offered.[1] He was well aware of the care with which a new
'Church in Danger' campaign would have to be managed, and of the
danger that it might rebound disastrously on their own heads. This
time it must appeal to the minds of conservative men and be
securely rooted in a defence of the faith and rights of the Church; it
must speak to that religious view of authority and society in which
so many implicitly believed. Only such a campaign could bring together the disparate forces of Toryism and lay the foundation for a
Ministry able to undertake an effective programme of party measures. But the election débâcle of 1708 had shown what was at all
costs to be avoided. Jacobitism was the creed only of a small, insistent minority. If the campaign were not to confuse and divide the
Tory ranks it must not be associated with an attack on the Queen's
title, nor must it seem to endanger those civil liberties which the
Revolution had secured.

Atterbury was the obvious High Church choice as Prolocutor in
the new Convocation, but his candidature had to surmount some
determined opposition. Rumours were circulated in Oxford that he
had made a secret agreement with Tenison to betray the interests
of the lower clergy; and, to prevent the embarrassment of an alternative candidate, Smalridge had to write down to the university in
forthright terms to assert that his friend had 'such an indisputable
title to that post, and is in all regards so well qualified for it' that he
was astonished to hear that anyone else was even being thought of.
By the end of September the dissentient voices had been silenced
and at a meeting in London the High Church divines agreed that
they would be unanimous in voting for the Dean of Carlisle.[2]

But meanwhile it began to seem possible that the Archbishop's

[1] See Blenheim MSS. E.27, Maynwaring to Duchess of Marlborough,
[13 May 1708]. During the summer FA was at work on a justification of
Harley's political conduct.
[2] Bodl. MS. Ballard 7, fos. 22 and 27, Smalridge to Charlett, 3 July and
28 Aug. 1708; N.L.W. Ottley MS. 254, Smalridge to Pool, 25 Sept.; H.M.C.
Portland MSS. iv. 509, Stratford to Harley, 15 Oct.

party might even obtain a majority in the Lower House. The Whig bishops had carefully filled all vacant archdeaconries with their own supporters, and early in May Tenison set up a committee to organize the election of proctors. At the beginning of September, with the crucial London elections still in the balance, something was needed to stem the Low Church tide; and, after some feverish work, Atterbury put out his pamphlet *Some Proceedings in Convocation, A.D. 1705*. With studied irony, a mounting anger, and some judicious selection of the facts, he recounted the story of the Archbishop's humbling of the Lower House three years previously. The Church party, he claimed, could be patient no longer in the face of daily insults: from the press and from Whig divines who used the pulpit to deny and traduce the fundamental doctrines of the Church of England. For the sake of peace churchmen had remained quiet while their case had gone by default, but now 'if the press may be employed to defame the clergy, it may also, and must be, made use of to vindicate them.' During the autumn large parcels of the work were sent down to the dioceses. Tory colporteurs 'very industriously spread' the copies among the country parsons while Trimnell's reply *Partiality Detected* went entirely unnoticed by most.[1]

When he read the pamphlet Tenison's heart sank, and vexation turned to alarm when he heard the news that the Tory divines had united behind Atterbury. Wavering moderates among the newly elected proctors were bullied mercilessly and until ten days before the opening of the Convocation the Archbishop still hoped for a majority, but at the last his advisers could give him no assurance of one. The thought that Atterbury would be Prolocutor was more than he could bear, and on 9 November he capitulated. At a meeting of the Junto at Sunderland's house the situation was discussed at length, and 'at last [Wake] moved that the Convocation might by virtue of the Queen's letter be prorogued, and no Prolocutor chosen at all. It was agreed to.'[2] On 19 November Atterbury arrived at St. Paul's, confident that he would be elected to the chair by a majority of about six, but to his and the rest of the clergy's chagrin they

---

[1] Wake MSS. 23, fo. 187, Wheeler to Wake, 22 Dec. 1708.
[2] Wake's diary, fo. 68, 9 Nov. 1708; Berkshire R.O., Trumbull MSS. LIII, Bridges to Trumbull, 22 Nov.

were not allowed to utter a word: no prayers were said, even the usual sermon was omitted, and they were prorogued to 25 March 1709. Jonathan Swift reported graphically the impotent fury of the Tory divines, and as late as the following January he could describe Atterbury as 'raging at his disappointment'. So vehement indeed was the general reaction that the Archbishop thought it the better part of valour to pretend that the prorogation had been without his knowledge or consent.[1]

Confident in their great party majority, the Junto lords moved on towards single-party government. Godolphin gave ground slowly and grudgingly but he had no real alternative to yielding high office and the direction of policy to the Whigs. When Parliament met in the winter the majority was wielded ruthlessly and with manifest injustice to turn out Tory M.P.s against whom a petition had been lodged. It was clear, as Bishop Burnet noted, that a state of war existed between the parties. But in one sphere at least the Whigs patently overreached themselves, and their moves to reduce the Church of England to subservience were ill-conceived and badly timed. It is significant that during this winter of 1708-9 Jonathan Swift himself became disillusioned with his Whig friends and convinced of their ill-will towards Anglican churchmen. The author of *The Sentiments of a Church-of-England Man* could display an essentially moderate attitude towards all the critical ecclesiastical issues of the day, but even he drew the line at the kind of crude vilification of the clergy which poured forth from the Whig gutter-press.[2] Not that the Junto stopped short at abuse. When Wharton went to Ireland as Lord Lieutenant it was with the firm intention of repealing the Anglican sacramental test for public office there. His unskilled moves to sound out Irish opinion were at once reported back to England and occasioned a kind of sensation of horror. Tory correspondence of the period after Christmas 1708 is filled with apprehension that a repeal of the Test Act in England was about to be sprung upon them and forced through Parliament. So persistent were the rumours that Swift took it upon himself to tell the Whig

---

[1] *Swift Corr.* i. 115, Swift to King, 30 Nov. 1708; ibid., i. 121, Swift to Hunter, 12 Jan. 1709.
[2] Swift, *Bickerstaff Papers*, ed. H. Davis (1957), pp. 8–9.

leaders 'with great frankness, my opinion, that they would never be able to repeal it'.[1]

In fact, the Whig scheme for England was not to repeal the Test Act but so to amend it that the qualifying sacrament could be received either in church or in any registered Dissenting chapel. During January a bill was introduced into the Commons to permit the wholesale naturalization of Protestant refugees from Europe, and in the debate the point was made that Prussia had derived great commercial benefits by offering a complete toleration to skilled foreign craftsmen; the bill specifically provided that the refugees should be naturalized on receiving the sacrament in a Nonconformist congregation.[2] Atterbury was among those who joined in the general excitement. On a visit to Bishop Nicolson he 'bewailed the Church's hazard on a second invasion', and at home he set to work to compose a new pamphlet. His *Reflections on a late Scandalous Report about the Repeal of the Test Act* was not published in his own day, but it remained among his papers as what might have been one of his most powerful pieces: a mocking, ironical attack on the Whigs, professing to defend them from the accusation that they would put forward a measure so directly contrary to the Act of Union so recently passed. In March the Church party was again thrown into alarm by reports of a bill to relieve Fellows of colleges from the obligation to enter into Holy Orders. Even a Junto supporter like Dean Kennett of Peterborough expressed anxiety and his complete opposition to the scheme.[3] And after May 1709, when the Naturalization Bill became law, thousands of refugees from the Palatinate came pouring into the country. Within the first few weeks two thousand had entered and were filling the streets of London. By the end of July their number had increased to eight thousand, and a social and employment problem of serious dimensions was building up. For many churchmen the last straw was a royal proclamation enjoining a collection in all churches in aid of 'the poor Palatines'. That their money should be required to feed aliens who lived off the poor rates, competed with Englishmen for jobs, and boosted the number of

---

[1] *Swift Corr.* i. 118, Swift to King, 6 Jan. 1709.

[2] *Parl. Hist.*, x. 780–84. The bill was bitterly attacked by Bishop Dawes of Chester.

[3] Bodl. MS. Ballard 7, fo. 124, Kennett to Charlett, 26 Feb. 1709; H.M.C. *Downshire MSS.* 1.2, 871, Bridges to Trumbull, 3 Mar.

Dissenters, was more than Tory flesh and blood could stand. It was clear that the wrath of clergy and gentry against their Whig masters was rising fast.

2

The scene was now set for one of the bitterest disputes in English Church history, and for a personal duel between Atterbury and Benjamin Hoadly, the Whig clerical champion. The critical question was how far the old doctrines of Divine Right and Passive Obedience were to remain essential parts of the ordinary teaching of the Church of England. For most conservative churchmen the point at issue was not one of politics alone; they were contending for something much more fundamental and against a new generation of men who would divest human society of his religious character and sanctions.

The traditional belief concerning the duty of a subject towards his ruler was that expressed succinctly and unequivocally in that most widely read popular manual of devotion of the later seventeenth century, *The Whole Duty of Man*. Generations of children had learned and repeated the phrases:

An obedience we must pay either Active or Passive: the active in the case of all lawful commands . . . But when he enjoins anything contrary to what God hath commanded, we are not to give him this active obedience; we may, nay, we must refuse thus to act; . . . We are in that case to obey God rather than Man. But even this is a season for the Passive Obedience; we must patiently suffer what the ruler inflicts on us for such a refusal, and not to secure ourselves, rise up against him. *For who can stretch forth his hand against the Lord's Anointed and be guiltless?*

Such teaching had a venerable medieval lineage; it had been expounded and developed by the apologists of the Elizabethan Church until harangues upon the heinous sin of rebellion had become a regular feature of the ministrations of the English reformed establishment. Naturally in the early seventeenth century such teaching was regarded with suspicion by those who sought to defend subjects' rights against royal encroachment, but after the Restoration and the experience of the Civil Wars men felt again a need to strengthen their institutions and consolidate the social order. In an age when political theory still moved naturally within the categories of Scripture, the doctrine of Passive Obedience was warmly, even passionately, embraced. A parallel theory, that of the Divine hereditary Right of kings, though as fervently preached up by most Restoration divines, presented greater difficulty. While the scriptural texts on submission to rulers were regarded as clear and unequivocal, it clearly required some ingenuity in biblical exegesis to derive from Holy Writ an indisputable hereditary right for the Stuarts to rule over Englishmen. It is sometimes asserted that the Revolution of 1688 shattered the old doctrines for ever, but this is quite erroneous. New ideas, that all governments had to consist with the natural rights of the governed and that the authority of rulers rested upon a contract between them and the people, gained powerful exponents, and were supported by the great name of John Locke himself. But for most Englishmen such notions were founded in irreligion and tended to social and political anarchy.

Continued belief, however, in a divinely constituted order required some judicious handling in the years after 1688.[1] The great, seemingly insuperable, difficulty lay in the resistance offered to James II in 1688; and conforming divines did an extraordinary work in so reinterpreting the old doctrines that they could be accommodated to the Revolution. They did so by calling to their aid the convenient notion of Divine Providence. While many preachers and writers dealt with the same theme, the classic short apologia for the Revolution was and remained Atterbury's sermon delivered before the House of Commons on 29 May 1701 and entitled 'The Wisdom of Providence manifested in the Revolutions of Government'. His argument was direct and simple. Resistance by men to a ruler was sin, but God himself was always free by an act of supreme power to overrule and throw down a regime or government. 'No people', he went on, 'can be reduced to such a wretched and forlorn condition, but that the good Providence of God may and will, if it sees fit, come to their rescue and deliver them; even without hope and against hope.'[2] Such had been the case at the Revolution; subjects did not offer resistance to their ruler; rather they had acted as the

---

[1] See Gerald Straka, 'The Final Phase of Divine Right Theory in England, 1688–1702', *E.H.R.*, lxxvii (1962), 638.

[2] Atterbury, *Sermons and Discourses* (1723), Vol. I, p. 258.

instruments of God, 'for He did it in such a manner as to shew that He was the Sole Author of it, and that it sprang not from Human Wit or Contrivance'. God had removed an unjust and disobedient king so that the succession might continue in a faithful line. It was thus by a dexterous modification of traditional loyalist theory that the chasm of the Revolution was bridged. And similarly, while preachers were careful not to withhold from the Queen the usual titles of sovereignty, it became more and more customary to indicate that the supreme power, resistance to which was sinful, was the legislature of Queen-in-Parliament rather than the monarch in her personal capacity. In a sermon preached before Anne on 8 March 1704 Atterbury came as near as was thought permissible to advancing this point of view. 'The Law', he declared, 'is as much a Rule to her, as to the least of those who obey her; the first Measure, not only of her governing Power, but even of her will to govern; and she makes no other use of that power, with which the Laws have invested her, than to give life and force to them.'

There were not wanting in Anne's reign some trenchant critics of this delicate theoretical construction. On the one hand Nonjuring propagandists, like the formidably precise Charles Leslie, never tired of pointing out that all this was not what Passive Obedience had meant in the Restoration era, while on the other side a host of Whig writers attacked the High Church position as a feeble attempt to make out a case for magic and unreasonable submission in the new age of reason. Of the Whigs Benjamin Hoadly, Rector of St. Peter-le-Poer, was easily pre-eminent. For a generation he teased and sneered at his opponents, and without a shadow of a doubt he was the most detested Anglican clergyman of his day. In no way could Hoadly be described as an attractive figure. He was diminutive in stature with a bulbous, unequally shaped face. An illness during his Cambridge days had left him so crippled that he could walk only with the aid of crutches and had to preach kneeling on a cushion. His mind was logical, his view of religion bare and prosaical, and he had made the whole apparatus of Locke's theory of government his own. That this courted deep unpopularity he was fully aware, and he observed without dismay that his style of preaching had emptied the pews of his London church. His sermons were practically never upon any topic of Christian faith and devotion: heavy, unadorned, remorseless, their one concern was to savage and demolish the Tory view of Church and State.[1]

Atterbury first attracted the animosity of the Whig champion in the winter of 1705-6. In the previous September at the election of the Lord Mayor, Hoadly had preached an aggressive sermon on the text, 'Let every soul be subject to the higher powers'. St. Paul, he declared, had no intention of tying future ages to the absurd proposition that subjects had to give an unlimited submission to evil rulers who sought to deprive them of liberty, property, and religion. 'Therefore', concluded Hoadly, 'to oppose them, in such case, cannot be to oppose the authority of God. Nay, a *Passive-Non-Resistance* would appear, upon examination, to be much greater opposition to the will of God, than the contrary.'[2] For Christian preachers to maintain publicly that a ruler had the right to make his subjects miserable was, pronounced the Whig spokesman, 'against the Laws of Nature and Reason'. Such an exegesis of one of the cherished proof-texts of loyalism deeply scandalized High Churchmen, and on 19 February 1706, at Atterbury's instigation, the Lower House of Convocation proceeded to vote that Hoadly's discourse was not only 'a scandal' but a 'grave dishonour' to the Church of which he was an ordained minister.

The public affront at the hands of his brethren rankled and the crippled little Rector hankered after a personal revenge. And so, one morning early in the new year of 1707, Atterbury was disconcerted to hear his name cried in the streets and to discover on all the bookstalls a new pamphlet which bore the intriguing title *A Letter to the Reverend Dr. Francis Atterbury concerning Virtue and Vice*. It was a truly swingeing attack on a sermon preached the previous August at the funeral of the publisher, Thomas Bennet. As Atterbury freely admitted, the oration had been hastily prepared and was not perhaps very carefully phrased. His theme had been the artless one that without belief in an after-life men were less happy than the brute beasts. In this life the best men were often those who had to endure most: they accepted self-denial and

---

[1] See N. Sykes, 'Benjamin Hoadly' in *The Social and Political Ideas of Some English Thinkers of the Augustan Age*, ed. F. J. C. Hearnshaw (1928).

[2] B. Hoadly, *The Measures of Submission to the Civil Magistrate Considered* (1706), pp. 5–8.

spiritual discipline; they suffered persecution and martydom; and they followed a morality of 'an exalted nature, contrary to flesh and blood, far above our ordinary capacities'. All this would be folly apart from their faith in the Resurrection of Christ and their hope for eternal life. But thus to make morality depend on Christian dogma was deeply alien to the Latitudinarian way of thinking; and so, writing as if in sorrow at an erring brother, Hoadly accused Atterbury of saying that vice was a more pleasant state than virtue and 'that Virtue shall be rewarded in another Life, because it is not in its own nature so great a happiness to man, in this state, as the prosecution of *Bestial* Pleasures.' Such preaching was a standing invitation to men of little faith to continue in their vicious mode of life; he himself would rather recommend virtue as bringing rewards in this life, and conducing to prosperity, contentment and a good reputation. It was clear that in Hoadly's scheme of things morality required no support from Christian faith. A casual visitor to Atterbury's home at Chelsea discovered him fuming under the injustice of this assault, even if not entirely displeased at appearing the victim of Latitudinarian malice. 'He continues', reported Ralph Bridges, 'his resolution of revenging himself upon the pamphleteer that attacked his late sermon, and he tells me, he don't question but that he shall make it appear that he has said nothing but what the best men and greatest divines before him have done. For his sake I wish he may do this; but whether Religion will gain anything by his coming off conqueror, may fairly be disputed.'[1]

By the autumn of 1708 Atterbury had decided that Hoadly needed to be dealt with severely and publicly, and the opportunity for this arrived on 29 September when he was invited to preach in St. Paul's at the election of the new Lord Mayor. It was the same occasion as that on which Hoadly had preached his notorious sermon on Passive Obedience. Mounting the pulpit, Atterbury announced the same text, 'Let every soul be subject to the higher powers'; and before the assembled City fathers he proceeded to deliver a fierce attack on Hoadly and an almost classical exposition of the new modified Tory doctrine. St. Paul, he claimed, had not been concerned to provide the first Christians with a charter for rebellion, but had urged them to be quiet and obedient citizens of

[1] Trumbull Add. MSS. 136, Bridges to Trumbull, 19 May 1707.

the Roman state. The princes to whom he enjoined submission were corrupt and tyrannous men, no less than Nero and Caligula: 'for if we owe entire obedience to good princes only, there's consequently none due to bad. Horrid Doctrine! directly opposite to Primitive Truth and Apostolic Institution; but exactly fitted to their inclinations, who would destroy all Government, and reduce everything to its first Chaos and Confusion.' Warming to his theme, he claimed that Hoadly and his abettors aimed to destroy that sense of obedience which flowed 'not only from a dread of any human punishment, but a sense of the Divine Obligation laid upon us'. Upon reverence for monarchy as a sacred institution depended the whole fabric of the social order. Rising to the emotional high point of his sermon, Atterbury declared that damnation was pronounced against all who misused Sacred Scripture to preach rebellion, and that 'whosoever they are that favour such interpretations, in prejudice of a thing of such moment, as is obedience to princes, are direct enemies to both: and who whilst they are striving to debauch subjects' minds with their pernicious opinions, impiously pollute the pure fountains of Divine and Eternal Truth!' At the conclusion he took some care to protect himself. It was not the function of the clergy to spend their time explaining those exceptional cases where resistance might be in some measure justified: even if such sermons 'bore some resemblances to truth, yet would they be offensive to pious ears, too great flatterers of men's impure and vicious inclinations . . . to be communicated to the unthinking multitude.'

But whatever concessions he was prepared to make, the Whig members of the City corporation were infuriated. At the Court of Aldermen an angry complaint was made that he had preached up an unlimited obedience to tyrants, and it was formally voted that he should neither be thanked for his sermon nor asked to print it. The Dean was undismayed. With some effrontery on 17 May 1709 he preached it again in Latin before an invited audience of London clergy, and went through a show of acceding to their unanimous request that it should be printed. It was, as he explained disingenuously, only right that an English translation should come out at the same time.[1]

[1] H.M.C. *Downshire MSS.* 1.2, 861, Bridges to Trumbull, 1 Oct. 1708; H.M.C. *Portland MSS.* iv. 507, Lewis to Harley, 7 Oct.

In the early summer of 1709 the Passive Obedience debate was gaining momentum. When Bishop Blackall of Exeter had the temerity to preach before the Queen on the vexed topic Hoadly attacked him with sarcasm and a point-by-point refutation. Soon the personal clash and a political issue of such delicacy had sparked off an eager public interest. Dons and country parsons, Dissenters and the heterodox contributed their tithe to the pamphlets and sermons which came off the presses. And when an uncompromising Nonjuror like Charles Leslie added his voice, all subtle qualifications sank out of sight, and the defence of Passive Obedience became synonymous with a denunciation of the Revolution of 1688. It was this association of their cause with overt Jacobitism that the main body of churchmen would not endure at any price. 'Whig and Tory, High and Low Church, are names', wrote one country vicar, 'Hanover and St. Germains are Things!'[1] With an opponent like Hoadly lying in wait, it would be easy for the whole High Church campaign to take a disastrous turn. An unguarded friend was even more dangerous than an open enemy.

3

During the summer Atterbury worked carefully to dissuade the more extreme churchmen from joining publicly in the controversy. Flattery, persuasion, even threats were employed.[2] But there was one divine in particular about whom the Atterbury circle felt deep apprehension. In the spring of 1709 Sir William Trumbull was anxious to find a London pulpit for Dr. Henry Sacheverell, Fellow of Magdalen College, Oxford. Although, after a number of fruitless attempts, he managed to secure a chaplaincy or readership at St. Saviour's, Southwark, he was puzzled and irritated to find that his efforts had been impeded not only by Tenison and the Whigs but the whole weight of the Christ Church interest. When Trumbull then sought an invitation for his protégé to preach before the Lord Mayor he was vexed to find that he was supplanted by Atterbury himself.[3] It was clear that the Tories were reluctant to have

---

[1] Wake MSS. 17, fo. 243, Wootton to Wake, 21 Mar. 1710.
[2] See Bodl. MS. Eng. Th. c. 24, fo. 321, FA to Thomas Brett, 2 July 1709.
[3] H.M.C. *Downshire MSS.* 1.2, 872–78.

Sacheverell come to their aid. The Doctor was only thirty-six, and yet already the epitome of a High-flying preacher. The man was not unattractive: he had boyish good looks, a vigorous charm, and a pleasing light voice. Women found him irresistible, and his passionate sincerity could melt even hard-bitten, elderly Tory politicians. And yet he had a mind of almost total unoriginality. His sermon-matter was derived from some easily discernible source and distinguished only by the fact that it was delivered in an emphatic, exaggerated manner. His early efforts, *The Character of a Low-Church-Man* and *The Political Union*, were sustained rants bordering on a kind of hysteria.

The autumn of 1709 found the political world in a strange state of suspense. Discontent was in the air: money was scarce, prices high, and the war seemed to drag on inconclusively. Behind the scenes the Treasurer was engaged in a last stand to retain some authority in his own Ministry, while Harley was quietly intriguing to oust Godolphin for ever. The Queen herself remained utterly opaque, and not even the attentive Mrs. Masham could discover her real opinions or intentions. Obviously much depended on the state of popular feeling, and during August Harley had busied himself in drafting and redrafting the text of a vehement pamphlet calling on the Queen and the Church to rid themselves of the incubus of the Whigs.[1] No one appears to have thought of Dr. Sacheverell as the man to fire the powder-keg.

The Doctor's great moment came on 5 November when at last he achieved his ambition to preach before the City corporation in St. Paul's cathedral. Influential friends and a High Tory Lord Mayor had at last overcome the obvious objections. The contents of the most famous, or notorious, sermon of the eighteenth century are well-known; but what is perhaps not so apparent about *In Perils among False Brethren* is that it was a mish-mash of other men's sermons and the preacher's own past performances. The furious, overloaded style, the rant against Dissenters and the advocates of Toleration: these were the preacher's own. But when he came to deal with Passive Obedience and to launch himself against Hoadly (whom he cruelly described as a 'Monster'), it is clear that his discourse was a carelessly phrased rehash of Atterbury's arguments.

[1] See B.M. Loan 29/10/1, for Harley's drafts, dated 24 Aug. 1709.

Even Sacheverell was aware that the topic needed some caution. He trumpeted forth that 'the grand security of our Government, and the Pillar upon which it stands, is founded upon the steady belief of the subject's obligation to an Absolute and Unconditional Obedience to the Supreme Power', but he was quick to add the saving phrase 'in all things lawful'. The whole discourse, if examined, is a *mélange* of furious assertions and covert qualifications. As such it is doubtful whether the sermon would ever have been the subject of a solemn prosecution had it not been for the assault on Godolphin, whom Sacheverell classed with atheists, Dissenters, Whigs and Hoadly in his catalogue of enemies to the Church. The picture of the Treasurer was unmistakable; and a reference to 'the crafty insidiousness of such wily *Volpones*', by making use of Godolphin's common nickname, put the matter beyond reasonable doubt. What really seems to have caused the offence, however, was the description of the Chief Minister's relationship with the Junto: 'Such a wise game do our Projectors play, they barter and betray their Friends, only to sell themselves Slaves into the hands of their Enemies, who shall treat them with more Insolence, Disdain and Tyranny, than honest Men do with Scorn and Contempt, if they don't go the whole Lengths of their Party.' Not content with preaching this harangue, against all the advice of his friends Sacheverell insisted on putting it into print.[1]

Irritating and offensive as the sermon was, it was a piece of folly on the Ministry's part to go to the length of actually impeaching Sacheverell. The Queen advised against it, Marlborough was lukewarm, and Somers later claimed that he had earnestly and in vain tried to dissuade Godolphin from it. Once, however, prosecution had been decided upon, it became clear that both sides were committed to a grand parliamentary inquest on the Revolution of 1688. The Tory case would be submitted to a minute forensic examination and, with their great majorities in both Houses, it might be possible for the Whigs to procure a judicial condemnation of the doctrine of Passive Obedience. A defence of 'Revolution Principles' was a cause around which all good Whigs could unite; and on 13 December, when the matter was first raised in the House of Commons, it was agreed to vote the sermon in St. Paul's a

---

[1] H.M.C. *Downshire MSS*. I.2, 884, Bridges to Trumbull, 29 Nov. 1709.

'malicious, scandalous and seditious Libel'. On the following day, when Sacheverell appeared at the bar of the House, the real character of the approaching conflict began to show itself. The Doctor drove to Westminster in the coach of the Vice-Chancellor of Oxford University and arrived to find no less than one hundred gowned clergymen waiting to greet and encourage him.[1]

The Whigs were undeterred, and it was resolved that the Doctor should be impeached for 'High Crimes and Misdemeanours' and that he should be held in custody without bail. Tory protests that a solemn state trial before the House of Lords was out of all proportion to the offence were set aside. And for the High Churchman that day insult was added to injury. The previous week Hoadly had published his *The Original and Institution of Civil Government with a Large Answer to Dr. Atterbury's Charge of Rebellion.* After a lengthy defence of the principles of resistance to evil rulers the Whig apologist proceeded to attack Atterbury with a vehemence and anger which even Sacheverell would have been hard put to to emulate; he concluded with a threat that for the future 'I will endeavour to find time and leisure . . . to pursue you through every winding of what you shall offer; to examine thoroughly every specious word; to search after every false colour, and every inconsistency; and to set them in as clear a light as possible.' Even one of Atterbury's friends had to admit that 'Hoadly has made most sad stuff of his late Latin (sermon), and what is most sad he has maul'd the Dean with his words'.[2] It needs little imagination to plumb Atterbury's feelings when, on the strength of this performance, the House of Commons voted, in a quite unprecedented manner 'that the Reverend Mr. Benjamin Hoadley . . . for having often strenuously justified the principles on which Her Majesty and the Nation proceeded in the late happy Revolution, hath justly merited the favour and recommendation of this House.' In spite of Harley's protest that this was a favouring of 'loose and republican principles', it was agreed that the Queen should be asked to bestow some dignity on Hoadly 'for his eminent services to Church and State'.

It was now war to the knife, as both sides fell under the spell of party passion and began to close their ranks. Harley, who had

[1] Trumbull MSS. LIII, Bridges to Trumbull, 20 Dec. 1709.
[2] Trumbull MSS. LIV, Bridges to Trumbull, 23 Jan. 1710.

neither planned nor foreseen such a crisis, was as genuinely surprised as only an inveterate schemer could be at a state of affairs which he had done absolutely nothing to contrive. He saw clearly, however, that it would 'serve to unite the university and the clergy'.[1] Many Tories agreed with Dr. Stratford of Christ Church that the High Church Doctor's performance was a 'scribble', but they still flocked to visit him in prison and bear messages of support. And it was at this point that Simon Harcourt and Atterbury stepped forward to take over the management of the new Tory champion. In other hands his case might be so badly conducted that the Church interest, and even Harley's own schemes, might suffer a grave blow. Casual observers were thus puzzled to find that the Harleyites 'whom he has used brutally, forget their past resentments on this occasion and visit him'. Indeed as soon as the Doctor had procured bail a series of meetings took place in Harcourt's chambers in the Temple, attended not only by the defendant but also by Atterbury and Smalridge. Clearly the Doctor's defence required the cunning of both lawyers and divines.[2] During the Christmas recess of Parliament a stream of pamphlets, broadsheets and verses came off the presses. No less than forty thousand copies of the famous sermon were printed and distributed up and down the country. Cartoons depicted the Doctor in various guises: in some he is the emissary of France, accompanied by the Pope and the Devil; in others he kneels patiently in prayer while the hovering spirit of Charles I proffers a martyr's crown. One divine, a humble reader in the Chapel Royal, was so transported by the prevailing mood that he prayed publicly for 'Henry Sacheverell under persecution', and promptly earned dismissal at the hands of the Bishop of London.

At last, after many delays, the great trial came on.[3] Sir Christopher Wren had been commissioned to fit up Westminster Hall with

---

[1] B.M. Loan 29/171, Harley to Stratford, 19 Dec. 1709
[2] H.M.C. *Portland MSS.* iv. 530, Stratford to Harley, 21 Dec. 1709; *Memoirs of the Four Last Years of the reign of Queen Anne* (1742), p. 70. In mockery at FA's constant attendance on Sacheverell, *The Tatler*, no. 113 [29 Dec. 1709], gave notice of a forthcoming work: 'A Letter from a Gentleman at the Hague to Dr. F. Atterbury, containing reflections upon the idolatry of the Jesuits in China.'
[3] For a full account of the trial and the riots which accompanied it, see Geoffrey Holmes, *The Trial of Doctor Sacheverell* (1973).

seats sufficient to hold not only the members of both Houses but four hundred spectators as well. A box was constructed so that the Queen might be present incognita. Competition for tickets was brisk and at times acrimonious. Women were especially anxious to have a seat of vantage where they could see and be seen, and the front rows were reserved for peeresses and their daughters. As *The Tatler* remarked, it was no use calling on any lady of quality while the trial was on: they had all risen early to go, bearing their packed lunches, to Westminster Hall.[1] On the first day, 27 February, the streets round Westminster were filled with an ugly and vociferous mob. As the Queen arrived they 'gathered about her Majesty's sedan, crying *God bless your Majesty and the Church. We hope your Majesty is for Dr. Sacheverell.*' When the hero of the hour made his appearance it was to immense cheering, and he went to take his place at the bar of the House, accompanied by Atterbury and surrounded by a distinguished body of divines in the gowns of Doctors of Divinity.

It was not until the second day that the Commons' managers began to make out the case for the prosecution, and they did so against a background of rising alarm. The mood of the crowds outside had become distinctly menacing; M.P.s making their way to the trial had been forced to pull off their hats and stand bareheaded as Sacheverell's coach passed by. But the managers for the House of Commons were not deterred, and all day they hammered away at their case: that the prisoner had intended not only to malign the Revolution but to impugn the Queen's title, insult the Dissenters who enjoyed a legal Toleration, and prepare the way for faction and disorder. At the heart of their argument was the assertion that Sacheverell's covert modifications of his doctrine were specious attempts to disguise the real message that he intended to preach. A powerful speech was delivered by Robert Walpole but the most scathing one came from General James Stanhope. It was reported that the Doctor visibly paled beneath it. Having raked the accused with his fire Stanhope turned his attention to Sacheverell's companion at the bar and began a cutting examination of Atterbury's own sermon in St. Paul's. Here again was that same dishonest

---

[1] *The Tatler*, no. 142 (4–7 Mar. 1710); White Kennett, *The Wisdom of Looking Backward* (1715), p. 11 et seq.; *Pol. Annals*, viii. 265.

inconsistency between a doctrine openly and unequivocally set forth and a few concluding sentences put in to cover the preacher from the logic of his own teaching. The Whig assault was telling, and as news of it spread the mob became entirely out of hand. On that evening and the next Whig peers, M.P.s, and clergy were insulted and terrorized; Dissenting chapels were pulled down, and Hoadly's name howled through the streets by men after his blood.

It was on 3 March, after order had been in some measure restored, that Harcourt opened the case for the defence. In contrast with the Whig managers and their angry denunciations of the prisoner, his speech was calmly, even felicitously delivered, and made a profound impression. 'His reputation for a speaker is fixed for ever', enthused Smalridge, while Abigail Harley reported Harley's own view that everything had been handled 'so well that had there been no watches none had thought the third part of the time spent—no heat or indecent language.'[1] Harcourt's plea was simple. His client was a grievously misused man, whose words had been twisted out of all recognition, but 'a subject of England is not to be made criminal by a laboured construction of doubtful words.' All that Sacheverell had done was to follow the example of countless English preachers before and after the Revolution in assenting to the *general* proposition that resistance to the supreme power was a moral evil. Did his accusers insist that every time a priest spoke to declare the Church's usual teaching 'the particular exceptions, which may be made out of that rule, are always to be expressed?' Harcourt agreed that 'an unlimited Passive Obedience and Non-Resistance is a slavish notion. My Lords, Dr. Sacheverell does not contend for it, nor is there anything mentioned in his sermon of such an Obedience or Non-Resistance.' His client believed that the supreme power in England was the legislature, and it was to preserve its supremacy that the Revolution had taken place. Were the clergy to be prosecuted for setting forth this ancient teaching of the Church of England at a time when any profligate writer was free to deny and insult it? On 6 March defence counsel began to read extracts from recent writers who had attacked and vilified the Church and clergy. And as the day passed the great assembly in Westminster Hall listened

[1] Bodl. MS. Ballard 7, fo. 35, Smalridge to Charlett, *circa* 4 Mar. 1710; H.M.C. *Portland MSS.* iv. 533, Abigail Harley to Edward Harley, 2 Mar.

to a truly chilling catalogue of malice, heresy and irreligion, garnered from the pens of Blount, Toland and Tutchin, and from the pages of the *Review* and the *Observator*. This was surely the Tories' most effective day's work.

On 7 March Sacheverell himself rose to address the House in his own defence. There could have been no greater contrast between the sermon in St. Paul's and this calm, modest, and beautifully phrased address. Contemporaries to a man disbelieved that the Doctor could ever have written a speech so out of accord with his usual style, and were virtually unanimous in ascribing it to Atterbury. Indeed a study of its phraseology, paradoxical manner and quiet emotion would confirm that at least his was the chief hand in its composition. Speaking in his clear voice and with great earnestness Sacheverell claimed that he was only an insignificant, ordinary priest, but 'the avowed design of my impeachment is, by the means of it, to procure an Eternal and Indelible Brand of Infamy to be fixed in a parliamentary way on all those who maintain the doctrine of Non-Resistance, and to have the clergy directed what doctrines they are to preach, and what not.' He had stood silently by while the great men of politics had poured abuse at him; 'no favourable allowances have been made to a minister of the gospel, discharging the duty of his function, and rebutting vice and irreligion with an honest and well-meant zeal.' He denied solemnly and before heaven that he had desired to impugn the Revolution; for her Majesty he had nothing but love and veneration; and he earnestly besought God that the succession might be 'established in the most illustrious House of Hanover, which I look upon as, next to his Providence, the best guard we have against Popery and Arbitrary Power.' But undoubtedly the true burden of Sacheverell's speech lay in an appeal to his brother clergy. The cause for which he was that day called in question was one of 'Eternal Truth'; the age was one in which 'never were the ministers of Christ so abused and vilified, never was the Divine Authority of the Holy Scriptures so arraigned and ridiculed, never was infidelity and atheism itself so impudent.' A man must be 'dead in his love for his country and religion' who could listen to the blasphemies which they had all heard without 'Horror and Astonishment'. He had been imprisoned and separated from his flock; he had been made 'a gazing-stock, both by reproaches and afflictions'; but he had not abandoned the good old doctrine of the Church of England, and he would not do so. As he spoke the ladies sobbed audibly into their handkerchiefs, and Tory lords were seen to be struggling to fight back their tears. It was much to be debated (as one observer pertinently remarked) 'whether ever the Doctor did such a feat in his pulpit'.[1]

By this time the Whigs were demoralized. No one more bitterly regretted the whole affair than the Treasurer. 'This uneasy trial of Sacheverell', he lamented to Marlborough, 'does not only take up all my time, but very much impairs my health.'[2] He began to see his great majority in the Lords visibly crumbling: the bishops were terribly uneasy at this attack on a clergyman, and a number of the great magnates had recently become remarkably devious and uncertain in their attitude to his administration. On 20 March the House of Lords voted Sacheverell guilty by the narrow majority of seventeen; but, to Godolphin's alarm, they showed no disposition to inflict any serious punishment on him. After the vote the Treasurer and Somers met a group of the bishops of their party and, against Wake's earnest opposition, agreed to fix the penalty at suspension from preaching and incapacity to hold any benefice for seven years, imprisonment in the Tower for three months, and the burning of his sermons by the common hangman.[3] Yet on the floor of the House even this could not be forced through, and at the end of an uneasy debate the sentence was reduced to three years' suspension from preaching and the burning of his sermons. 'So all this bustle and fatigue ends in no more', was Godolphin's weary comment.[4]

Yet the case of Dr. Sacheverell was far from ended. The news of his light sentence, after so solemn a trial, was received almost everywhere as equivalent to an acquittal. In London bonfires were built in the streets and houses were illuminated as for a victory. When the Doctor began to read prayers again at St. Saviour's, Southwark, the great church was crammed to the doors. Even more significant was the manner in which the smaller towns in the country were aroused. At Sherborne the news was greeted with ringing of bells,

[1] H.M.C. *Portland MSS.* iv. 535, Abigail Harley to Edward Harley, 7 Mar. 1710.

[2] Coxe, M., iii. 163, Godolphin to Marlborough, 5 Mar. 1710.

[3] Wake's diary, fo. 93.

[4] Coxe, M., iii. 164, Godolphin to Marlborough, 21 Mar. 1710.

and a toast drunk not only in the Town Hall but afterwards at the top of the church tower. Again and again reports tell of the ceremonial burning of the works of Hoadly. One of the many prints circulated at this time shows a group of divines approaching Queen Anne who is seated on her throne. They are led by the Bishop of London and by Sacheverell and his companion, 'Dr. A.' A clergyman on two crutches limps up to demand 'When shall I be preferred?', but the loyal churchmen chant their song:

> The brave Sons of the English Church
>   Come foremost like the Wind;
> And Moderation, out of hope,
>   Comes out limping on behind.
>
> As we Obedience others teach
>   Our practice shall be as we preach;
> We're all agreed, all of a Mind
>   But limping Ben: we left behind.[1]

By careful management and the unaccountable whims of popular enthusiasm Harley's friends had turned what could have been a disaster into a triumph for the High Church cause. It now remained to be seen what use could be made of the great Tory passion.

[1] F. G. Stephens, *Catalogue of Prints and Drawings in the British Museum: Political and Personal Satires*, Vol. II (1873), no. 1549.

CHAPTER SEVEN

High Church Zenith, 1710–1711

I

IN the summer of 1710, as Godolphin's Ministry crumbled and fell, Atterbury seemed to stand before the Promised Land, ready to go over to possess it. He was known to be the friend and ecclesiastical lieutenant of Robert Harley, the politician who now had the Queen's trust. Before such a divine lay the prospect not only of personal advancement but of considerable influence with the Ministers in power. In many ways the year 1710 marked the high-point of Atterbury's personal contentment. To a lonely Irishman like Jonathan Swift, arriving in London poor and insecure, he seemed on all accounts to be envied. In the pleasant riverside village of Chelsea, near the Old Church, he owned a handsome, compact house. There was a quiet garden and a sunny well-furnished study with the books finely bound and neatly shelved. Mrs. Atterbury, retiring and equable beside her volatile husband, was a gracious hostess and mistress enough of her household to invite in a rather forlorn Irish clergyman lodging nearby. Swift noted appreciatively that the food was good and the wine carefully selected. While his wife and three growing children lived mostly out of town, the Dean kept up his official lodgings at the Bridewell near the Temple, and these provided a convenient *pied-à-terre* and a useful place for conducting business. Between Chelsea and London he travelled in a smart light carriage driven by one of his servants. He, at least, did not have to walk home on rainy nights through dangerous and muddy streets, as Swift so often found himself forced to do. His daily life was crowded with a variety of business, and by no means all (or even the greater part of it) was spent on politics. Long hours were passed at his desk preparing sermons, and even Bishop Nicolson on a visit to the Chapel Royal could not withhold his admiration for a careful and scholarly discourse 'in defence of Moses and the Prophets'. Atterbury's range of reading was wide, and in the evenings at home he made copious notes on works of poetry, history and law.[1] But he seemed to regard this knowledge as primarily for use and display rather than as part of a scholar's pleasure in study and research. Thomas Hearne, who was far more charitably disposed towards Atterbury than to most of his contemporaries, was not unjust when he wrote that

> tho' Dr. Atterbury be a man of a very sharp pen and of very quick parts, yet I do not look upon him to be a man of extraordinary depth. He has not a true genius to the study of antiquity; nor has he taken much pains to make himself a master of our English history. He may be cried up for a master of style, and 'twill not be denied; yet this however must be granted withall that affectation of wit and satire does not become a grave subject.

Atterbury would have cheerfully agreed with him. When the same question was once raised in his company by a candid friend, he smiled and declared disarmingly that 'I sometimes know where learning is, and how to make use of it when I want it'.[2] It was rather in the intimate circle of his literary friends, mostly Old Westminsters or Christ Church men like himself, that he felt at ease and could relax, when his quick wits and natural friendliness could flourish, and when for a while he could be free from schemes and obsessions. There were hilarious evenings at Chelsea or in the Abbey precincts or out on visits into the country with Matthew Prior, Henry St. John, Lord Orrery or the brothers Freind: occasions when epigrams were created and impromptu verses composed on the men and events of the day. It gave Swift much pleasure to be welcomed into this charmed company and even to think of himself as 'admitted a Christ-Church man'. But outside the group of his likeminded companions, contemporaries found something unnerving about so restless and able a clergyman. With his usual deft strokes Swift captured something of the spirit of the man as he first knew him early in the new year 1711:

> A little black man of pretty near fifty? Aye, the same. A good pleasant man? Aye, the same. Cunning enough? Yes. One that understands his own interests? As well as anybody. How comes MD and I

---

[1] *E.C.*, v. 191–212, for examples of his careful notes.

[2] *Hearne's Collections*, iii. 108, 16 Jan. 1711; J. Nichols, *Literary Anecdotes*, iv. 456.

don't meet there sometimes? A very good face, and abundance of wit; do you know his lady? O Lord! whom do you mean? I mean Dr. Atterbury, Dean of Carlisle and Prolocutor.[1]

It is not difficult to mark out Atterbury's hopes for the Tory era which he now saw about to begin. Now that his friends, Harley, St. John, and Harcourt, stood on the threshold of office, he looked for a virtual re-establishment of the Church of England and an end to the decline of its influence. With a friendly Ministry and a co-operative House of Commons it should be possible to put through a scheme of measures which would do something to restore the Church to its old position. He was never in any doubt as to its vulnerability, not only to the mental climate of the age of reason, but to the grim possibility that a hostile political regime could, by a ruthless use of patronage, reduce the clergy to subservience and frustrate even the mildest measures of reform. To forestall such a going down into bondage, he hoped for an alliance between Queen, Ministers, and a 'Church of England' Parliament. In all this Atterbury belonged to a high strain of Toryism. As Harley's agent from 1704 to 1708 he had joined in measures to manage and restrain the High Church clergy, but it had been a costly sacrifice thus to leave those who agitated for the rights of the Church. He had done so only because Harley's subtle and ingenious persuasion had convinced him that this was the surest road to gain the Queen's confidence and, eventually, effective power. St. John, too, had quitted the mainstream of Toryism in 1704 with difficulty and regret; and after his resignation from office in 1708 it was not long before he was urging Harley to put himself at the head of a reunited 'Church of England' party. As Atterbury had the vision of a faithful nation united to the ordered ways of the English Church, so St. John looked to a stable and paternalistic society based on the influence of the 'landed interest'.

But the manner of Harley's coming into office consorted ill with the 'Church party's' hopes. The most skilled political artist of the day had given his friends many fair words, but in the end it was not so much the great Sacheverell passion which toppled Godolphin as a carefully contrived palace revolution. During the spring of 1710 Harley had gone to work in his own distinctive way, using the methods at which he was most adept. The influence of Mrs. Masham

[1] *Stella*, pp. 156, 514.

at the Queen's side; visits into the royal presence by way of the privy stairs; and the defection of magnates such as Shrewsbury, Newcastle, and Somerset: all these finally contributed to break the spirit of the Junto. But, having accomplished his aim with the Queen's abrupt dismissal of Godolphin on 8 August, Harley had neither the wish nor the power to inaugurate a High Tory regime. Indeed Anne herself would have been an immovable obstacle to this. For her the new Ministry meant a liberation from being dictated to by party zealots; she had listened to Harley because he had persuaded her to be 'a Queen indeed' and because he had promised her that a 'moderating scheme' was all that he intended.[1] Whatever the crowds may have imagined, she had despised Sacheverell and the extremism he represented: it had been a 'bad sermon', and she had hoped all along that he would be punished. At the height of the uproar she had spoken bitterly to her physician of the need for devotional preaching and 'practical religion'. When the Lieutenancy of London presented her with an extravagant address declaring to the world that her 'Right was Divine', she was visibly offended.[2] The fact was that in the summer and autumn of 1710 her new Minister had no option but to attempt a 'moderate scheme' and a balancing administration. Godolphin had left the finances in a parlous condition, and Harley as Chancellor of the Exchequer had to struggle hard to procure loans from unwilling City financiers. It was understandable in such delicate circumstances that he caballed with Halifax and moderate Whigs like Cowper to persuade them to continue in the new Administration, and he delayed from week to week what the churchmen most desired: the dissolution of the Whiggish Parliament of 1708.

The Church party waited uneasily during the summer months as Harley's obscure manoeuvres went their way. St. John became increasingly possessed of the notion that the new Minister meant to exclude him from the Cabinet; and Rochester and Bromley complained bitterly that, while Harley seemed to be continually at meetings with the Whigs, they themselves were kept entirely in the

---

[1] For Swift's interpretation, see *Political Tracts, 1713–1719*, ed. H. Davis and I. Ehrenpreis (Oxford, 1964), pp. 146–47.

[2] Hertfordshire R.O., Panshanger (Cowper) MSS, Box 48, Sir David Hamilton's diary, 27 Feb. 1709, 6 Mar. 1710, 15 Dec. 1711.

dark.[1] Quite early on it was made clear to Atterbury that he was to be let into no secrets, and that it was not 'safe for me (whose name has been so much tossed about of late) to communicate by letter even that little that I happen to know.'[2] Of course, he did what he could to keep up the Tory temperature. In the spring Anthony Collins had published an insulting and curiously inaccurate history of the Anglican clergy under the title of *Priestcraft in Perfection*, and he devoted long hours to composing a reply. During August Sacheverell journeyed on a kind of triumphal progress through the shires and county towns, and a flood of loyal addresses came pouring in, condemning the enemies of 'our pure and undefiled Mother, the Church of England' and asserting the old doctrine of Passive Obedience. Atterbury and Smalridge were active in promoting these, and assisting their compilers to draw them up in language of appropriate hyperbole. In August they dexterously stage-managed an address from the London clergy. Indeed Queen Anne must have become quite accustomed to seeing Atterbury appear before her: on 23 August he was among the Doctors of Divinity who accompanied the Vice-Chancellor of Oxford with the university's address, and on 11 September he was introduced by Harley to present a high-flown address of his own composition as from the clergy of the diocese of Exeter.[3]

At the height of the ministerial crisis in early August the 'Old Westminster' literary circle, under St. John's direction, decided to establish the Tory political periodical which had been so often mooted. Swift later described the genesis of the *Examiner*; it 'was begun about the time of Lord Godolphin's removal . . . About a dozen of these papers, written with much spirit and sharpness, some by Mr. Secretary St. John . . . ; others by Dr. Atterbury . . . ; and others again by Mr. Prior, Dr. Freind, &c., were published with great applause.'[4] Atterbury's own contribution to these first numbers are relatively easy to distinguish, and they provide a useful clue

---

[1] See Geoffrey Holmes, *British Politics in the Age of Anne* (1967), p. 269; *Wentworth Papers, 1705–1739*, ed. J. J. Cartwright (1882), pp. 128, 135.

[2] Bodl. MS. Eng. Th. c. 24, fo. 361, FA to Brett, 8 Apr. 1710.

[3] *Pol. State*, i. 12; B.M. Lansdowne MSS. 1024, fo. 219; *Pol. Annals*, viii. 238–40.

[4] Swift, *Political Tracts, 1713–1719*, pp. 123–24.

to the two basic themes of his party faith. Number 10 was a vehement appeal to the county freeholders to consider how closely the Church and the 'landed interest' were bound together, and to vote only for candidates who would pledge their support for both; while number 13 consisted of a furious polemic against Hoadly as the arch-patron of the propagators of rebellion and irreligion.

By the second week in September there was still no sign of a dissolution nor of any distribution of places to the members of the Church party. St. John and Harcourt became progressively exasperated at Harley's involved talk and obscure promises, and were at the point of breaking with him and retiring into the country.[1] They discussed the matter at length with Atterbury, and at last with typical impetuosity the Dean agreed to do what they hesitated to do: to risk his credit by going straight to Harley and demanding a clear statement of his intentions. In some respects Atterbury was an unfortunate messenger. There was no man to whom Harley had given fuller assurances, and there was no one whose hopes he was more surely to disappoint. It was surely this which must account for the quite uncharacteristic outburst of irritation with which he greeted the Dean's mission. Edward Harley described vividly the encounter, which seems to have taken place on or about 14 September:

Being alone at dinner one day with Mr. Harley, Dr. Atterbury . . . came in to us; after some compliments, he told Mr. Harley that he came from some of his particular friends to acquaint him how very uneasy they were at his conduct, that the Parliament was not yet dissolved, nor so many of the Whigs turned out as was expected, and that they were wholly in the dark as to the measures he was taking, which had created a very great uneasiness, and that out of his friendship, he had acquainted him with it. This was the only time I ever saw Mr. Harley express any passion in public affairs. He told the Doctor he knew very well the persons from whom he delivered the message, and was so sensible of the difficulties he had to struggle with, that nothing but his duty and promise to the Queen could make him be concerned any further; and therefore desired he would let those persons know that if they expected he should communicate all the measures he thought were absolutely necessary for conducting the

---

[1] J. Macpherson, *Original Papers containing the Secret History of Great Britain* (2 vols., 1775), ii. 531.

Queen's affairs over the difficulties, he would let Her Majesty know that it was impossible for him to be of any further service.[1]

From this moment onwards relations between Atterbury and Harley were to be clouded by mutual distrust. Party men of the Dean's determined cast of mind, and certainly those possessed of high schemes of ecclesiastical revival, were a threat to Harley's whole plan of government. It was especially so when in mid-September it became clear that the Whigs would not co-operate and that the Queen, after all, would have to work with the Tories. Harley did his best to retain moderate elements in the Administration. Between 17 and 20 September, Harcourt became Attorney-General, St. John Secretary of State, Rochester Lord President, and Buckingham Lord Steward but the cautious Lord Dartmouth was retained in the senior secretaryship (which he had held since the previous June) and changes among the minor officeholders were strictly limited. When Parliament was dissolved on the 21st men were not unaware that Harley had set his face against a full party regime, and Tory resentment could not be quietened. During the previous weeks Atterbury had written regularly to William Bromley to keep him informed of political events; and when the great High Church squire replied to send his congratulations to St. John and Harcourt through Atterbury his letter breathed discontent. He wrote bitterly of the discouragement which the delays had given to the Tory faithful and of the Whigs still remaining in lesser offices, in the Commissions of the Peace, and in the Lieutenancies.[2] When the General Election produced an immense Tory landslide, the prospect of an overwhelming majority of untried and mostly young squires in the new House of Commons boded ill for Harley's management.

2

Among the clergy the Convocation which would meet with the new Parliament was a matter of eager expectation on the one side and of a fearful apprehension on the other. This was the moment for which Atterbury had worked and waited, when his programme for renewal could be begun; but he was not, of course, so sanguine as to imagine that Convocation by itself could effect this by canon or resolution.

[1] H.M.C. *Portland MSS.* v. 650.
[2] *E.C.*, i. 444–45, Bromley to FA, 23 Sept. 1710.

Only legislation had the binding power and coercive force required; and so, on the basis of his theories, he looked to establish a working partnership between a High Church Lower House of Convocation and a Tory House of Commons. With himself as Prolocutor and William Bromley as Speaker, business could be carefully concerted. The method was not in doubt. The Crown would license Convocation to discuss and draw up proposals for reform; these would be embodied in a detailed petition to the Queen, and by her referred to the Commons who would then initiate the necessary legislation. The matter would need much careful management behind the scenes; it would require co-operation from the Ministry and a measure of goodwill from the Bishops. But there was yet a real possibility that from it would emerge an Anglican counter-revolution: measures to silence heretics and infidels, to reform the church courts and give them new powers, to define the Toleration, to build new churches and create new parishes, and to give greater protection to the revenues of the parochial clergy.

In the weeks before the opening of the Convocation, set for 25 November, Atterbury went to work confidently. He was encouraged by enthusiastic reports of High Church successes in the proctorial elections, and on the evening before the first meeting in St. Paul's he held a gathering of his supporters at his lodgings in the Bridewell. He was delighted to discover not only that they were unanimous that he should be Prolocutor but that he would have under his command no less than sixty members against the Archbishop's forty.[1] If what they had to do could be carried through peacefully he would be content. 'There may be', he confided to a friend, 'some hopes of healing the breach, and compromising matters so far as to proceed jointly upon business of public importance. A little time will show whether there be any grounds for these hopes.' He was anxious 'not to be construed anyway to infringe the peace of the body—whatever measures of peace may be set on foot.'[2] But here he was certainly being too sanguine. The Archbishop's party was not against all reform; they would even have welcomed some

[1] N.L.W. Ottley MSS. 1534 and 1535, FA to Ottley, 2 and 24 Nov. 1710. For an account of this session, see G. V. Bennett, 'The Convocation of 1710: an Anglican Attempt at Counter-Revolution' in *Studies in Church History*, vii, eds. G. J. Cuming and Derek Baker (Cambridge, 1971).

[2] Bodl. MS. Eng. Th. c. 24, fo. 634, FA to Brett, 7 Nov. 1710.

Plate 1

Henry Aldrich

Plate 2

The Schismatical attack or y^e CHURCH Besieg'd by y^e Ephesian Beast

Lead on your Beast, for the attack prepare,
Ye growling Wolv's who Shepherds cloathing wear;
That Pious Men with weeping Eyes may See
St. Pauls, at last, with Salter's Hall agree:
But Stand to ye Churchmen, guard the Sacred Door,
Beat back the Monster, and Exert your Pow'r;
For, if the Beast prevails, too late you'll find
A Common Wealth come Sneaking in behind.

Atterbury and Bishop Blackall defend the Church against Hoadly and Republicanism, 1709

Plate 3

Henry Sacheverell

Plate 4

Robert Harley as Earl of Oxford and Lord Treasurer

administrative improvements, but they were deeply afraid of Atterbury himself. Many of them detested him personally, and they had convinced themselves that he intended not only to revenge himself on the 'moderate' bishops but to achieve some kind of synodical endorsement of Tory political theory. As the day approached, Archbishop Tenison, old and almost continually in pain, became more and more agitated. His closest advisers were summoned in to him 'at this critical juncture' and urgent consultations took place with the Junto lords on the policy to be adopted in the face of the coming High Church attack. 'God grant', groaned Wake, 'that things may go better than we fear.'[1] On 11 November a meeting of bishops and others took place at Lambeth and they decided for a policy of total resistance: 'to set up a Prolocutor; to get an Address ready that shall meddle in no state affairs.' On the 25th they went to St. Paul's in a great state of trepidation, and their worst fears were realized. Atterbury was elected to the chair by an overwhelming majority, and the triumphant Tory divines even went to the length of voting to suppress all mention of the fact that there had been another candidate, Richard Willis, Dean of Lincoln. The Archbishop's friends were deeply depressed. That evening Wake and other bishops drew up a formal Latin petition to Tenison, praying him to quash the election of a man who was 'not only a disturber of the peace of the Church but indeed the principal enemy of our order and authority'.

Harley was well aware that, in the prevailing climate of opinion, it would be inopportune to set himself directly against the High Church campaign; he determined to go along with it, but to play the game cautiously. Even in this he had to deal very carefully with Queen Anne who was deeply uneasy at the prospect of renewed quarrelling and bitterness among the clergy. To get her to allow the Convocation to proceed to business at all, Harley had to agree that 'it must be such as shall be first agreed upon; and they are to know that they are on their good behaviour; should they be extravagant, they can hurt none but themselves, and are easily sent going.'[2]

---

[1] Wake MSS. 17, Tenison to Wake, 10 Oct. 1710; Surrey R.O., Kingston-upon-Thames, Somers MSS. E/32, Sunderland to Somers, 6 Nov.; Wake's diary, fo. 100, 8 Nov.

[2] *Hardwicke State Papers*, ed. Philip Yorke (1778), ii. 485: 30 Oct. 1710.

Even so, she would not be at ease until Archbishop Sharp had been called in to manage the whole affair in the interests of peace and quiet. Although the Convocation of the Province of Canterbury was properly no concern of his, the Archbishop was asked to preside at a meeting of Harley, Rochester, and Bishops Sprat and Hooper. It can have given Atterbury no satisfaction to be summoned into this gathering and informed that they had already settled the business of the Convocation. The managers proposed that the topics of discussion should be limited to three: blasphemous and heretical books, the use of excommunication in the church courts, and relations with the Lutheran Church in Prussia. While the first two of these were promising enough, the third was irrelevant, and the whole inadequate. It is clear that Atterbury objected strongly and that many hours were spent in fierce argument with Sharp before an agreement could be reached. When eventually the Queen gave her consent to the Royal Licence and Letters of Business, these were in terms far more extensive than had been originally intended and they bore the unmistakable stamp of Atterbury's views.[1] Unfortunately in the process of arguing his case he had deeply offended and alienated the Archbishop of York, and this was soon to be shown in a particularly hurtful manner. In mid-December Henry Aldrich died, and there fell vacant the preferment upon which Atterbury had long set his heart, the magnificent deanery of Christ Church. It had been promised to him by Harley as long ago as 1704, and he could reasonably now claim it as a reward for assiduous service.[2] But, to his utter dismay, Sharp began an energetic campaign on behalf of George Smalridge, and it was apparent even to casual observers that a considerable contest at Court was in progress. Although Harley at last got the Queen to see that it was not expedient that Atterbury should be disappointed, she acted in a way which was entirely characteristic of her when she felt that she was being pressed to do something uncongenial: she delayed and put off a decision from week to week.[3]

Faced on all sides with such hostility, the new Prolocutor knew

[1] *Sharp*, pp. 531–33.
[2] *E.C.*, i. 446, FA to Trelawny, circa Dec. 1710.
[3] *Stella*, pp. 152–53; Bishop Nicolson's MS. diary for 1709–10, 18 Dec. 1710. I am grateful to P. N. S. Mansergh for allowing me to use this section of the diary.

that he must begin by disarming his opponents. While he could count on Government support to spur the Convocation on to business it was important not to give Tenison any legitimate reason for breaking off relations. And so on 6 December, when he was formally presented to the Primate for confirmation, he and Smalridge each made an impassioned plea for peace and for getting down to business. In the decent obscurity of formal Latin rhetoric Smalridge commended his friend's qualities in moving terms: he was expert in the history and privileges of the lower clergy, but he was also a man of peace and a lover of concord. The quarrels of the past between the two Houses had wounded the Church gravely; the ungodly had scoffed, and the whole tribe of infidels had grown to despise the censures of a Convocation. Now they must go on to the necessary work of renewing the life of the Church, setting aside fault-finding and personal pride. There had never been a more favourable moment: the Prolocutor of the Lower House and the Speaker of the House of Commons were not only personal friends but men of the same beliefs and principles, devoted to the Church of England. Atterbury followed in a speech of equal fervour. His brethren had chosen him as a man jealous of their rights and interests, but this did not mean that he intended the least disrespect for the episcopal order. In a truly happy Church bishops and presbyters united in love for their common task and ministry. There was much to do to restore the marred visage of their holy mother, the great and glorious Church of England. Let all uncharity and meanness be put away, and let them now go to work.[1] The old Archbishop, seated in the midst of his suffragans, listened impassively to this flood of oratory. In a terse and somewhat ungracious speech to the clergy he confirmed Atterbury's election, making no mention of the petition which he had received from Wake and his colleagues. As the assembly dispersed from the cathedral, however, the Whig divines were vociferous in their outrage that anyone should have described Atterbury as a man of peace and concord. Wake sourly professed himself as uncertain whether Smalridge had 'really intended to praise or abuse him'.[2]

---

[1] *E.C.*, iv. 291–303. FA's copy of his speech is Westminster Abbey MSS. 65028.
[2] Wake's diary, fo. 101: 6 Dec. 1710.

The first day of business on 13 December showed just how determined the Whig resistance was to be.[1] A letter was read from the Queen in which she added her own exhortation to peace. She was, she declared,

ready to give them all fitting encouragement to proceed in the dispatch of such business as properly belongs to them, and to grant them such powers as shall be thought requisite for carrying on so good and so desirable a work. In confidence that our Royal Intentions in that behalf will not be frustrated, nor the ends of such assemblies defeated by any unseasonable disputes between the two houses of Convocation, about unnecessary forms and methods of proceeding, we earnestly recommend that such disputes may cease.

Clearly the letter was of Atterbury's composition, and Tenison was furious that he had been given no prior notice of it.[2] In reply the Bishops sent down a tepid form of an address, and at once heated controversy broke out as the Tory majority attempted to enlarge it. The Prolocutor found himself engaged in an acrimonious verbal duel with White Kennett, Dean of Peterborough and the leader of the Archbishop's supporters. Grimly and with heavy persistence Kennett now began a campaign which was to last the whole of the life of the Convocation. Both he and Richard Willis could fairly be accounted Atterbury's personal enemies, and they set to work to harass his every action in the chair: protesting, demanding explanations, delaying business, and reporting every move back to their master at Lambeth. It was an undoubted right of the lower clergy to propose amendments to the Address, but on 15 December the Archbishop totally refused to receive or consider their alterations. It began to look seriously as if at its very first meetings the Convocation was to run into deadlock.

This was a miserable beginning, and during the Christmas recess Atterbury brooded over the necessity of overcoming these difficulties and getting on with the measures on which he had set his heart. He was far from pleased when Jonathan Swift, who was now writing the *Examiner* with immense verve and skill, launched himself into an

---

[1] The sessions of 1710–11 are described in W. Pittis, *The History of the Present Parliament and Convocation* (1711) [hereafter referred to as 'Pittis'].

[2] Kennett's diary, fo. 238; Bodl. MS. Eng. Th. c. 24, fo. 632, FA to Brett, 28 Nov. 1710.

eloquent defence of the Prolocutor and a vehement attack on the Archbishop. He was, he wrote, 'unwilling to employ the Press until we see what turn things will take.'[1] Everything turned on the Royal Licence and the Letters of Business; and here he knew he had an ace up his sleeve. On 24 January the Licence was read in the Upper House in the presence of the assembled clergy, and the Archbishop's party staggered under the shock. The whole document was conceived within the terms of Atterbury's convocational theories. Tenison was not named as President of the Convocation but merely appointed first of a quorum of bishops, one of whom had to be present if the assembly were to proceed to business. The clear implication was that the Primate was President by royal appointment and not by right of his metropolitical office. All the other bishops of the quorum were known Tories; and, in view of the Archbishop's fragile state of health, it began to look as if one of the High Church supporters would preside regularly over the whole Convocation.

On the last day in January the Prolocutor moved yet a stage nearer his goal. The Letters of Business communicated to the Convocation appeared innocuous enough but, in fact, they provided topics out of which an effective reforming programme could be constructed.[2] The Queen formally proposed: 'the drawing up of a Representation of the present state of Religion among us, with regard to the late excessive growth of infidelity, heresy and profaneness'; regulation of the practice of excommunication in the ecclesiastical courts; preparation of new 'occasional offices'; extension of the jurisdiction of rural deans; the provision of 'more exact terriers and accounts of glebes, tithes and other possessions and profits belonging to benefices'; and a regulation of the issue of marriage licences. Before the lower clergy withdrew from the Upper House, Atterbury paused to address an urgent plea to the Archbishop that he would allow them to execute the business which the Queen had committed to them and that joint-committees of the two Houses should be set up to consider separately each head of the

[1] Bodl. MS. Eng. Th. c. 24, fo. 664, FA to Brett, 4 Jan. 1711; the *Examiner*, no. 21, 28 Dec. 1710.
[2] Only George Every, *The High Church Party, 1688–1718* (1956), chs. 7 and 8, has indicated the seriousness of the attempt at reform in 1711.

royal proposals. 'Not that I have any reason to doubt', he concluded ominously, '(from the harmony that now seems to be settled between both Houses, after a long misunderstanding) of your ready concurrence with such measures.' In the face of the implied threat, His Grace could only agree to do as he was asked.[1]

The succeeding months, from February round to April, proved a time of the most wearisome labour. The committees met two or three times a week and moved at a veritable snail's pace. Atterbury found himself sitting for hours in endless discussion, and writing and rewriting the texts of reports. He savoured to the full his clerical brethren's propensity for verbose time-wasting, for scrupulosity over minor details, and for chasing false hares over the horizon. From time to time deadlocked committees met at his house in the Bridewell, and he tried to get them again to constructive work.[2] His task was made none the easier by the continual harassment of Kennett and his cronies, ready at every doubtful step to question his conduct and bring procedure to a halt on some point of order. On the whole it must be said that Atterbury kept his temper well. Occasionally the Dean of Peterborough received the sharp edge of his tongue, but mostly he was just swept aside. And some encouraging progress was made. By the latter part of March the joint-committees had reached the point of composing draft parliamentary bills.[3] With regard to the church courts, detailed regulations were drawn up as to their fees and procedures; and it was proposed to increase their effectiveness by making it easier for the ecclesiastical judge to call on the assistance of the civil power. The old draconic writ *de excommunicato capiendo*, which could only be used against truly serious offenders who had first been formally excommunicated, was to be replaced by a more generally useful writ *de contumaci capiendo*, by which even minor recalcitrants might be committed to prison until they promised obedience. To protect the interests of the clergy from the depredations of patrons or the refusal of tithepayers, attested certificates of the rights and revenues of each benefice were to be drawn up, and these were to be admissible as evidence in a court of law. The issue of marriage (and by implication all other)

---

[1] Pittis, pp. 127-29.

[2] Kennett's diary, fos. 260-312, *passim*.

[3] Lambeth Palace MSS. 929, fos. 105-19, for drafts of bills.

licences was to be less in the hands of local officials and more directly under episcopal control. Reports were ready containing recommendations about charity schools, new forms of services, and the extent to which rural deans could become disciplinary officers alongside the archdeacons. It was a not unimpressive achievement, and Atterbury planned to have his drafts and reports ready to be laid before the Queen soon after the Easter recess.[1]

The method by which this preparatory work was to be turned into legislation was revealed on 28 February, when Atterbury proposed to the Lower House that he, as Prolocutor, should pay a formal visit to Bromley, as Speaker of the House of Commons. In the previous week, by Bromley's devising, a Commons committee had been set up to consider the shortage of church accommodation in the rapidly expanding areas of London and its suburbs. Accordingly on 1 March, accompanied by a body of leading Tory divines, Atterbury waited on the Speaker to convey the thanks of 'the whole clergy of this province' for the gesture, and to offer any information or assistance which might be required. On being informed of the visit, the Commons proceeded formally to resolve that they would 'have a particular regard to such applications as shall at any time be made to them from the clergy in Convocation assembled, according to antient usage, together with the Parliament'. On 10 March Bromley announced to the House that Atterbury had been with him the previous evening and had 'delivered to him a scheme of the number of churches and chapels and meeting-houses, within twenty-seven of those parishes in and near the cities of London and Westminster, and the suburbs thereof, where the additional churches were judged to be most wanted.'[2] On the 26th Convocation petitioned the Queen to favour the project, and she graciously commended it to Parliament. Such was the origin of the Fifty New Churches Act of 1711, which was to inaugurate the greatest era of Anglican church-building since the Reformation. Later, in September, Atterbury was to be one of the distinguished body of commissioners, Tories almost to a man, who were to convert the proceeds of a parliamentary tax

---

[1] B.M. Lansdowne MSS. 1013, fo. 150, Kennett to Blackwell, 17 Mar. 1711.

[2] On 20 Mar. FA received a reprimand from Lord Dartmouth to the effect that he had acted without consulting the Queen. See *E.C.*, iv. 306.

on coal into the fabric and endowments of new churches. During the next twenty years the commissioners and their successors were to build only twelve churches; yet even these, cool, classical and ample structures by Archer, Vanbrugh and Hawksmoor, may stand as memorials to a brief moment when Church reform seemed possible. If co-operation with a Tory House of Commons could continue in this manner then the way ahead seemed clear.

3

But after Easter matters suddenly began to look distinctly less favourable. It was in large measure due to the fact that the chief Minister had regained a firmer control over the political situation. All during the previous February and March Harley had had to withstand an immense pressure from the gentlemen in the House of Commons. It was indeed not only in Convocation that a party revolution was being planned. At the Bell Tavern in Westminster a great gathering of squires met regularly to drink 'October Ale', and to pledge themselves to common action to force an all-out Tory programme on the Administration.[1] The 'October Club' consisted for the most part of raw, inexperienced new members, but they were none the less effective for that. From the seventy or eighty who met at the beginning of February, by April their numbers had grown to well over one hundred and fifty; and their fiery crusading zeal had become the talk of the town and a nightmare to the Ministry's managers in the Commons. As part of their anti-Whig vendetta and to force through their programme, the October men did not hesitate to obstruct Ways and Means, and supply. A bill to repeal the Naturalization Act had to be stopped in the Lords; and another to impose a landed-property qualification on M.P.s had to be allowed to pass into law. Soon the squires moved on to attacking the City financiers of the Bank and the East India companies, and a motion was made for resuming King William's grants of land. Clearly moderate Tories were becoming alarmed at this hectic course, yet Atterbury, with Drs. Sacheverell, Stanhope and Moss, appeared at their dinners and joined in their festivities. These were invitations

[1] For the October Club, see Geoffrey Holmes, *British Politics in the Age of Anne* (1967), pp. 116–17, 342–44, and H. T. Dickinson, 'The October Club', *Huntington Library Quarterly*, xxxiii, no 2, Feb. 1970.

which Swift thought it wiser to refuse.[1] But on 8 March Harley suffered an alarming misfortune which turned out in the long run to be an amazing piece of good luck. On that day the Lords of the Committee were interrogating a French spy, the Marquis de Guiscard, when the suspect impetuously leaned forward across the table and stabbed the Chancellor of the Exchequer twice in the chest. Without his heavily embroidered waistcoat, donned especially for the Queen's Accession Day, Harley would certainly have been gravely wounded. But for the moment everyone believed that his injury was far more serious than it was, and an immense wave of sympathy and emotion swept the country at this news of the Queen's Minister almost done to death by a French and Popish spy. When he emerged from his convalescence at the end of May it was to universal congratulations, and to receive from the Queen not only the title of Earl of Oxford and Mortimer but the White Staff of the Lord High Treasurer of England. Harley was not the man to lose so favourable an opportunity. By his usual methods he weakened and divided his opponents: some were given promises, others bought off, and a few menaced. By the beginning of June those who had aided the October men or caballed with St. John in his many intrigues, were under a dark cloud. Even Swift, for falling in with a suggestion that Guiscard's blow had really been aimed at the Secretary and not at Harley, lost some of his former favour.

When Convocation reassembled after the Easter recess, the life and heart had gone out of the High Church party. Perhaps Atterbury had driven his troops too hard, perhaps political events had unnerved them, but soon numbers had diminished and there were not enough for the petitions to the Queen.[2] Now, to those wearied by the intricacies of reform, a more intriguing issue appeared in the person of William Whiston, Lucasian Professor of Mathematics at Cambridge. Whatever his mathematical abilities, Whiston was a heterodox theologian of distinctly strange opinions who had recently been deposed from his chair by the university authorities. In 1711 he added to his reputation for colourful eccentricity by

[1] *Stella*, p. 242. See also *A collection of Hymns and Poems for the use of the October Club. By Dr. S[acheverel]l, Dr. A[tterbur]y, Dr. S[tanhop]e, Dr. M[o]ss, and little T[rap]p of Oxford, Chaplains to the said Club* (1711).

[2] B.M. Lansdowne MSS. 1013, fo. 146, Kennett to Blackwell, 22 May 1711; H.M.C. *Portland MSS.* vii. 30.

publishing *An Historical Preface to Primitive Christianity Revived*, wherein he declared that the Christology of the ante-Nicene Fathers was far more akin to that of Arius than to that of Athanasius. Much of his case was based on an appeal to the so-called *Apostolic Constitutions*, which he ranked in authority above the canon of Scripture. In ordinary circumstances Whiston's efforts could have been safely forgotten. What could not be forgiven was his sheer impudence in dedicating his heresies 'to the clergy of the province of Canterbury in Convocation assembled'. On 16 March the book was formally delated in the Lower House, and soon bishops and presbyters were caught up in the heady experience of a heresy hunt. Atterbury was as fierce as anyone in his irritation with Whiston's wretched work, but at the same time he looked on with dismay at the time and energy being consumed. All other business fell away as the two Houses pored over copies of the book, and became entangled in the immensely complex question of how far a provincial convocation could conduct a trial for heresy. It was not until the second week in June, when everybody was exhausted and out of temper, that the Houses agreed that a petition should be sent to the Queen: not against the man (for it seemed that this could not be safely done) but against his 'pernicious doctrines'.[1]

At the end of May, as the town became hot and unpleasant, the sessions became enormously tedious. White Kennett, still at his post to dog the Prolocutor's every move, described himself as 'a prisoner, I may say a slave in the Convocation House'.[2] But before the assembly was prorogued Atterbury determined that there should be one last effort of party assertion. He knew that the October men in the Commons had drawn up a lengthy 'Representation of the State of the Nation', to be presented to the Queen at the end of the session: it was to be a bold and outspoken assertion of the high Tory case, against Oxford's 'unwarrantable schemes of *Balancing Parties*' and for a thoroughgoing party regime. Obviously it would be a considerable *coup* if this could be accompanied by a parallel 'Representation of the State of Religion' from the clergy in

[1] For Whiston's case and the difficulties involved in it, see Kennett's diary, fos. 290–319, *passim*; *H.O.T.*, vi. 48–52; and N. Sykes, *William Wake*, i. 132–35.

[2] B.M. Lansdowne MSS. 1013, fo. 154, Kennett to Blackwell, 2 June 1711.

Convocation, and if this could be a comprehensive account of High Church views and aims. The Queen's Letters of Business had authorized such a statement, though doubtless she had not intended the clergy to produce a *cahier* of grievances. All sides agreed that Atterbury took the composition of the document into his own hands, and it remains a classic expression of Tory ecclesiastical doctrine, written in an emphatic and denunciatory style and clearly intended for 'country' consumption. In it the origin of all the ills of the Church was traced back to the Civil War, 'that long and unnatural Rebellion which loosened all the bonds of discipline and order, and overturned the goodly frame of our ecclesiastical and civil constitution'. It expatiated on blasphemous and scurrilous writings, on the immoralities of the stage, and the insults daily heaped on the 'ministers of Christ and their holy function'. There were a few signs of hope: charity schools were being founded; parochial libraries were providing wholesome and helpful literature; and there was the 'inexpressible satisfaction' of the fifty new churches which they hoped soon to see rising. But enemies abounded and were growing in strength and impudence: libertines, heretics, the 'importers of foreign vices', and Dissenters who insisted on exceeding the legal Toleration granted to them. The remedies were clear. 'The law, which makes those who abstain from all sorts of religious assemblies still obnoxious to punishment' must be 'exerted in its utmost force'. The press must be put under control, and 'the present excessive and scandalous liberty of printing wicked books at home and importing them from abroad' must be ended. Convocation must be stirred up so that 'some way might be found to restore the discipline of the Church, now so much relaxed and decayed, to its pristine life and vigour; and to strengthen the ordinary jurisdiction of the ecclesiastical courts'. Although Atterbury managed to steer his draft through the joint-committee, and had it enthusiastically accepted by the majority party in the Lower House, it was clear that the Bishops would not co-operate. Encouraged by the new political climate, they resolved to stand and fight. A version of their own, markedly different in emphasis, was sent down to the lower clergy on 16 May: all politically exceptional references were expunged; the tone was modified; and the proposed remedies altered. The Bishops' form of the Representation

was a platitude. Between the two versions there could be no compromise, and the Convocation was eventually prorogued amid a
display of bitter temper and an exchange of hard words between
Kennett and the Prolocutor.[1] The *Representation of the State of
Religion*, although immediately printed and distributed up and down
the country, was never formally presented to Queen Anne.

The ending of the Convocation found Atterbury a bitterly disappointed man. All the tedious labour and all the hope he had put into
the sessions had come to virtually nothing. During the whole summer he continued in a state of depression and nervous tension; and
as a result of his exhaustion he had his first prolonged attack of the
recurrent illness which was henceforth to colour his character and
cloud his judgement. During much of August and early September
he lay at home tortured by gout and unable to walk more than a
few steps. Added to his sense of failure was the humiliation that
nothing had yet been done about the deanery of Christ Church.
Swift reported him as being 'heartily angry' at it. Rumours circulated
the town that the delay was due to the Court's desire to give him
some even greater preferment, the bishopric of Bath and Wells, or
that of London. It was even whispered that he was to be the next
Archbishop, if Tenison should die.[2] But Atterbury, who was close
to St. John and Harcourt and was well aware of the position of his
friends, knew better. On many evenings Jonathan Swift came to
sit with him; and the two divines, between whom there had already
been established a strong bond of mutual sympathy, discussed the
split in the Ministry exhaustively. Both realized how dangerous
these divisions were to the Tory cause, but in their solution they
plainly differed. Swift urged his friend 'to use his interest to prevent
any misunderstanding between our ministers', but the Dean declined to intervene.[3] Harley's abandonment of the cause of Anglican
reconstruction had affected his mind and spirit deeply. In the future
there might be a show of cordiality, but never a real reconciliation.

[1] Trumbull MSS. LIV, Bridges to Trumbull, 8 June 1711; Kennett's
diary, fos. 322–27, 1–8 June; B.M. Lansdowne MSS. 1037, fos. 39–44.

[2] *Stella*, p. 298; B.M. Lansdowne MSS. 1013, fo. 142; H.M.C. *Portland
MSS.* vii. 26.

[3] *Stella*, p. 346: 28 Aug. 1711.

CHAPTER EIGHT

A Strife of Divines, 1711–1713

I

I N the summer of 1711 the Tory party was curiously adrift. Old
connections were breaking up and long-established leaders passing
from the scene. Lord Rochester, for so many years the representative of the old Cavalier tradition, died in May; and soon in December Lord Nottingham, unforgiving and embittered by neglect, was
to astound the political world and shatter his own following by
joining forces with the Junto. The great majority of country backbenchers in the House of Commons looked eagerly for some clear and
definite leadership, but found only divided counsel and confusion of
voices. More and more the party dilemma came to consist in the
rivalry of Lord Treasurer Oxford and his erstwhile friend and disciple,
Henry St. John: two men who represented radically different policies
and who appealed powerfully to divergent elements in the Tory
ranks. Clearly the one who had the power to become undisputed
leader of the whole host was Oxford, and churchmen continued to
look to him. His policy of perpetual moderation was a source of both
strength and weakness. To the professional politicians, the 'men of
business' of all parties, he represented an assurance that politics
would not get out of hand; by his superb manipulative skill he
protected them from the backbench violence which so many of them
feared. It was well understood, too, that behind his policies stood
those of the Queen, and that he retained his position by her goodwill. Influential Tory politicians could never bring themselves to
ruin him, lest in the process they lost the Queen as well. Yet the
Treasurer was an exasperating leader. Intrigue and double-talk had
become so much a part of him that he seemed incapable of dispens-
ing with trickery. His instinctive reaction to any crisis was to
negotiate with the opposition at the expense of his friends. With
him procrastination had become an art of government.

The radical alternative to Harleian management was represented by Henry St. John. It was never doubted by any informed political observer that his policy was the one after which the clergy and 'gentlemen of England' hankered. In a sense the Secretary was not a 'politician's politician', but rather a man who sympathized deeply with the popular cause. For him only single-party government would serve: an immediate proscription of all Whigs from every place, office and preferment; and the whole weight of ministerial influence turned to crush the Whigs into a permanent minority. Increasingly he came to see this as the only security which the party and the cause had in the face of what could not be long delayed: the Hanoverian Succession. Many Tory politicians agreed with him in theory, Swift, Bromley, Anglesey; but they hesitated before the danger which it seemed to involve. If one went along with the wild squires and high-flying clergy into a regime of single-party power, where would it all lead? Would full-blooded Toryism mean bitterness, proscriptions, civil war? Could it end in an attempted Jacobite restoration? The personalities of St. John and his closest associates did not re-assure. The Secretary himself was that 'Man of Mercury' of whom everyone spoke: youthful, effervescent, brilliant, able to cast his spell over those he took into his friendship. And yet he gave an impression of waywardness, precocity and instability. His scandalous private life and his scarcely veiled Deist opinions did little to attract the more cautious churchmen and were known to repel the Queen. And Lord Keeper Harcourt, vain, pushing and greedy, was not an associate immediately to secure sympathy. Indeed St. John's friends as a whole were a strange assortment of 'wild cards'.

The Church reflected the Tory dilemma, and here the divisions were especially crippling. The last four years of Anne's reign were in many ways the heyday of the Anglican clergy, and it would be difficult to overstate their immense value to the party as theorists, writers and election agents. The number of Whig divines remained always very small. They might flourish in the episcopate and among the senior clergy but they were very thinly spread over the parishes of England. In the Rutland county election of 1710 no less than forty-three beneficed clergymen went to the poll: thirty supported the two Tory candidates, nine the two Whigs, and the remaining four split their votes.[1] There is plenty of evidence to show that the

[1] Leicestershire R.O., unpublished Finch papers: Rut. 2 (ii).

voting pattern of the smallest county was repeated across the rest of the country. The clergy provided a great political interest of men deeply conservative, concerned for their personal status, and desperately anxious for the implementation of a full Tory regime. The irony of the Harley administration is that in spite of all the hopes of its supporters, it was determined on ecclesiastical moderation. The Queen, the Treasurer, and the old Archbishop of York acted as a formidable combination to curb the high-flyers and prevent their ever arriving in strength on the Bench of Bishops. The record of episcopal appointments from 1710 to 1714 is, with one significant exception, wholly of moderate Tories, taken out of the troop of Harley's and Sharp's clerical dependants. The first promotions set the theme. In October 1710 the bishopric of Bristol was filled, not by one of the Tory divines who had borne the heat and burden of the day but by Dr. John Robinson, a professional diplomat rather than a priest, an ecclesiastical trimmer who had been close to Harley since 1704. St. Davids went to Philip Bisse, the Treasurer's urbane and socially-minded cousin, whose talents as a genial matchmaker for the aristocratic young were unsurpassed. When even Tory bishops were thus dedicated to moderation, the clerical sheep went politically unshepherded and their zeal was liable to break out in unexpected and embarrassing ways.

In June and July 1711 everything came to be overshadowed by the great issue of the peace. Rumours spread through the coffee-houses that secret negotiations had begun. Peace was what the war-weary squires longed for—but what kind of peace would it be? Even Jonathan Swift had his fears that an 'ill peace' was in the offing; and when so ardent an admirer of both Oxford and St. John had his doubts, it could be taken as certain that the Junto, Marlborough and the Allies would be consumed with distrust. To withstand the coming political storm it was essential that there should be some strengthening of the Ministry's support; and all during July, when the Court was at Windsor, St. John and Harcourt pressed for radical changes: an ousting of every remaining Whig office-holder and the wholesale promotion of Tory stalwarts. Certain minor changes were conceded, and then Anne and the Treasurer again became opaque and non-committal. It was a dangerous situation, and Swift noted the rising tension and anger which surrounded the Queen.

Not the least of the grievances was the question of the deanery of
Christ Church, which was rapidly assuming the status of a symbol
of the obvious and pointed refusal to promote any of the committed
High Churchmen. During June Atterbury had spent much time in
consultation with Harcourt and it was clearly he who suggested the
names of the Tory divines whom the Lord Keeper now regularly
pressed upon the Treasurer. When these were put aside with many
excuses and much confused talk, Harcourt warned Oxford in blunt
terms of the terrible uneasiness which his policies were causing 'and
especially to our Church friends'.[1] As early as April St. John had let
it be publicly known that Atterbury was his candidate for the
deanery, and during July Harcourt tried to urge the matter on: by
inspired leakages that the patent was already approved and by sending down to Christ Church warrants for money which could not be
discharged until a Dean had actually been installed.[2] It was a matter
of everyday comment that at Windsor an earnest struggle was
in progress to overcome the resistance of the Queen and the
Archbishop of York, both of whom insisted still on George
Smalridge.

At last on 12 August, as the peace negotiations entered a critical
stage, St. John delivered his ultimatum. He refused any longer to sit
in Cabinet with Whigs like the Duke of Somerset, that 'man who
had so often betrayed them', and the meeting broke up without
business being transacted. Now the Queen and Oxford were forced
to a choice. As the troubles of the peace came fast upon them, they
could not afford to be without St. John's political support and diplomatic skill. And so, with ill-concealed resentment, Anne agreed
that Somerset should stay away from the Cabinet and that some
gesture of conciliation should be made to the Church party.[3] What
followed was highly gratifying—at least to Atterbury. On 20 August, at a very unusual time of year, the Queen issued an open letter
to the Archbishop of Canterbury, to be communicated to all his
suffragans. White Kennett made no bones about it that in his
opinion the royal missive was a public endorsement of Atterbury's

[1] H.M.C. *Portland MSS.* iv. 695, Harcourt to Oxford, 20 May 1711; ibid.,
v. 12, 17 June; ibid., v. 58, Sharp to Oxford, 21 July.
[2] Ibid., vii. 29.
[3] Panshanger (Cowper) MSS., Box 33, Somerset to Cowper, 28 Aug. 1711.

views and intended as a crushing rebuke to the Bishops for having rejected the Lower House form of the Representation.[1] Anne complained again about the prevalence of heresy and profanity, and called on the bishops 'as you will answer it to Him by whom both we and you are to be judged' to put into execution 'all such ecclesiastical Laws and Canons as have been hitherto provided for the well-governing of the Church'. Somewhat gratuitously she commanded them to visit their dioceses regularly to discover at first hand the needs of the body ecclesiastical. And her final word had unmistakable reference to those reform projects of Atterbury's which still languished, and she ordered 'that before the next sitting of Convocation you would carefully consider what defects there are in the present discipline of the Church, and what further provision may be requisite towards removing them, that when Convocation assembles, such orders and constitutions as are wanting, may upon deliberation be prepared and laid before us for our consent.' Tenison accepted this loaded communication with such good grace as he could muster, and to the outside world it began to seem that the High Church cause was indeed prospering in the royal favour.[2] At the same time Atterbury was informed by a delighted Harcourt that 'the main point has been gained at last': that on 30 August, albeit with great reluctance, Anne had signed his warrant for the deanery of Christ Church.[3] To complete this packet of concessions to the churchmen, the Treasurer offered the Privy Seal to Bishop Robinson of Bristol. Not since the mid-seventeenth century had a bishop held such high office in the State, and that the Whigs at once raised an outcry against priestly power made it all even more welcome to the Tory clergy.

It was now essential that the Tories should put up some show of unity. Whatever their differences, they all desired an end to the war, and St. John's word to his friends was that everything now depended upon the peace. Once that was achieved there need be no limit to their ambitions: they would have the prestige to execute the full counter-revolution which the backbenchers demanded. And on 9

[1] B.M. Lansdowne MSS. 1013, fo. 162, Kennett to Blackwell, 15 Sept. 1711.
[2] William Salt Library, Stafford, Dartmouth Supplementary MSS. 271, Tenison to Dartmouth, 22 Aug. 1711.
[3] Longleat, Thynne MSS. 12, fo. 297, FA to Weymouth, 30 Aug. 1711.

September all the contestants of the previous month joined in a celebration dinner at Windsor, the unity of which was more obvious than convincing: 'Dr. Adams, Canon of that church, made a noble supper for the Lord Treasurer, the Lord Keeper, the Lord Privy Seal, Mr. Secretary St. John, Dr. Atterbury and Dr. Smalridge—the main health was *Peace and Glory!*'[1]

2

Pretences of this sort did not go deeply. Atterbury's allegiance now lay unmistakably with St. John and Harcourt, and as Dean of Christ Church he prepared to do his best to further their interest in Oxford. The Treasurer had had good reason to hesitate before putting Atterbury into the most important headship in the university and the key position in Oxford politics. It was well known that for some years Harley had been trying to build up a personal connection there, and the choice of his title as Earl of Oxford was not fortuitous. He knew that this greatest of clerical seminaries had an influence which spread far beyond the confines of the city and its colleges. A powerful interest of country parsons and Tory aristocrats took their lead in religion and politics from this place of their education, and to be elected to Parliament as one of the two Burgesses of the university had a prestige surpassed only by that of a Knight of the Shire for one of the largest counties. By 1711 Harleian influence was already well established and, in particular, Francis Gastrell and William Stratford as Canons of Christ Church might each be accounted the great man's agents. A year previously the new Dean might have laboured mightily in the same cause, but in September 1711 Atterbury went to the college determined to build up a rival Tory connection for Harcourt and St. John. Success in such an ambition was by no means impossible. Harcourt was the great parvenu of Oxfordshire society, but his estates at Nuneham Courtenay and Cokethorpe betokened a powerful local interest, and his clerical patronage as Lord Keeper could smooth a way into the university's good graces.

It was not only politics, however, which made Christ Church

---

[1] B.M. Lansdowne MSS. 1013, fo. 162, Kennett to Blackwell, 15 Sept. 1711.

view with such apprehension the advent of so formidable a figure as Atterbury. What had occurred at Carlisle was not unknown to them, and the new Dean's temper and masterful ways were already legendary. But by one man in particular the appointment was bitterly resented. Canon William Stratford had served Harley loyally: he had been his chaplain as Speaker of the House of Commons; he had been his son's tutor; and time and time again he had been the recipient of quiet political confidences. A solitary and self-concerned bachelor, the doctor had long cherished the hope that the deanery might be offered to him. His whole life had been spent in Christ Church and the post would have been the height of his personal ambition. Like the politicians they were, the Treasurer and Harcourt had mildly encouraged his expectations. Thus the news of Atterbury's nomination came like a searing blow and he began at once to nourish an intense animosity towards the man whom he conceived of as having supplanted him. To Stratford's malicious pen we owe a detailed and almost day-to-day account of Atterbury's career at Christ Church. It is wonderfully vivid, superbly ill-natured, and to be used with extreme caution.[1]

Before his installation Atterbury concerted his plans with Harcourt at Windsor, and it was decided that the occasion should be of the utmost magnificence, due notice to all that a new and potent interest had arrived. In spite of an excruciating return of his gout, Atterbury wrote letters in all directions: to members of the nobility inviting their presence as his guests and to friends begging a provision of venison for the great feast. The Lord Keeper agreed to come in state bearing the Great Seal and to see that the local gentry were not lacking in respect. Speaker Bromley's son was to be sent down to Oxford to bear his father's felicitations. All this mighty preparation the Canons looked upon with a jaundiced eye. Disquieting rumours had reached them of things which their new Dean had said at Windsor: that the college was in a poor state of discipline and learning, and that radical and rapid changes were required. Eventually resentment was joined to apprehension until they were even ready to attempt a little mild sabotage, and Atterbury was kept in

---

[1] Stratford's letters are in H.M.C. *Portland MSS*. vii, and are addressed to Edward, Lord Harley. The originals in B.M. Loan 29 do not add significant new material.

calculated ignorance of the exact number of speeches to be delivered during the formal reception. Yet, even by eighteenth century standards, it proved a ceremonial triumph. On 25 September Atterbury arrived in his coach at the foot of Shotover Hill, to be greeted by almost the entire body of junior members of the House, who had ridden out to meet him. To his obvious delight he was escorted into Oxford by a great cavalcade of gentry and academics, with applause and an exchange of compliments. One young student described the arrival: 'He was saluted with repeated huzzahs; as he entered the great gate he was welcomed again with huzzahs and all possible demonstrations of joy, so that I verily believe he and all of us were mightily well pleased.'[1]

On the 27th the college was again *en fête*. During the morning Atterbury, dressed in the scarlet of a Doctor of Divinity, received the heads of colleges, the nobility, and the visiting dignitaries. At eleven o'clock he was conducted into the cathedral. After the first lesson at Mattins he presented his Letters Patent and, before the whole glittering company, was duly installed. His first act as Dean was to install George Smalridge into a vacant canony. As the guests moved towards the Hall the formal speeches were made, and Atterbury replied in his customary, elegant style. He paid a moving tribute to Dean Aldrich, and the great company sat down to a lavish banquet. Thomas Hearne, absolutely delighted to find himself virtually the only mere M.A. invited from another college, had his breath taken away; he could think only of the hundreds of pounds that such a feast must have cost. At table Atterbury was in an exceptionally affable mood, and as his guests came up to greet him he was free in promising them his influence with the Lord Treasurer and with Harcourt. It was half past three before the gathering rose, but at four the Dean heralded his new regime of discipline by insisting that all the members of the Chapter should accompany him to evening service. Afterwards the three Harleian Canons walked back to their lodgings in gloomy mood. And, of all the day's events, one in particular had stuck in their minds: the uncanny appropriateness of the psalms for the day chanted by the choir as the Dean had stood waiting to be installed. There had been Psalm 120: 'My soul hath long dwelt among them that are enemies

---

[1] H.M.C. *Portland MSS.* v. 93, Urrey to Harley, 28 Sept. 1711.

unto peace.' And to that had succeeded the supplication of Psalm
122: 'O pray for the peace of Jerusalem.'

The college soon began to feel itself under a masterful hand. The
Dean appeared at every service in the cathedral, morning and evening, and he came each day to dine in Hall. Attendance at church
and at public lectures was carefully scrutinized. It quickly became
obvious that these stern measures were directed not so much at the
undergraduates as their elders, the Canons and tutors. Indeed with
the young, Atterbury put up an energetic show of geniality: the
deanery was open house; they were invited in to talk with their
new head; and he and his wife gave pleasant tea-parties to small
groups. To all and sundry he announced his ambition: to make the
college once again a centre of that humane literary study which it
had been in Aldrich's early days, and for this he was prepared not
only to expend his own efforts but to provide prizes out of his own
pocket.[1] It was clear that the Dean had declared war on the body
of mediocre and easygoing tutors which he had inherited from his
predecessor. But, of course, this academic zeal did not stand first
among his aims. He had come to Oxford primarily to build up a new
political connection and for this he needed, first, to establish his
power as head of the largest and most influential college, and to
bring all Christ Church's great resources of patronage under his
own control. And, secondly, he had to build up among the Heads of
Houses a strong party which would dance to the Atterbury-Harcourt
tune.

He set to work without delay. Stratford noted uneasily that the
Dean was spending an extraordinary amount of time among the
Chapter archives, but in fact all these careful researches proved un-
rewarding. Atterbury found that at Christ Church the decanal
powers were strictly limited and there could be no appeal to the
strict letter of the law, for the House was governed not by statutes
but by ancient custom. But he determined to see what could be
gained. No sooner were Stratford, Gastrell and Smalridge away from
the House for a while than he opened a sudden attack on the elderly
Canons still in residence. To their alarm and confusion he announced
in Chapter that henceforth he would exercise the sole right to present to the college livings. The brethren present raised some feeble

[1] *Hearne's Collections*, iii. 264.

protests, and were imperiously swept aside. But when the three Canons returned they treated their lord and master to a taste of his own medicine. At the Chapter meeting on 7 November 'a train was laid, which he could not avoid, to bring in the business of the curacies'. They were ready with their evidence: charters and books were laid on the table; instance after instance was produced of presentations to benefices being executed under the common seal and not by the Dean alone. In the face of this unanimous opposition and a case which had collapsed into ruin, there was nothing Atterbury could do. He beat a strategic retreat, and endeavoured to put on as good a face as possible. 'As he and I came home together', reported Stratford, 'he took me by the hand and desired me to learn from him to *yield*. I told him that when he and I were students to- gether, I was always for submitting to lawful authority; but that I knew he had been an old mutineer. I believe his courage is cooled a little, and that he will not advance any more new pretensions as hastily as he did these.'[1] In fact the good doctor was being too sanguine, Atterbury had no intention that his feud with the three Canons should rest there, and his natural pugnacity was now truly aroused. Peace descended for a while on the inhabitants of Tom Quad when Atterbury went up for the opening of the new sessions of Parliament and Convocation, but on his return everything was in a sad state of tension. At the Audit on 20 December it proved impossible to find anyone willing to take on college office for the ensuing year, and Dr. Potter had to be dragooned into the post of Sub-Dean. It began to be whispered that at this rate things would soon be as bad as at Trinity College, Cambridge, where the terrible Dr. Bentley was locked in mortal combat with his Fellows.

In eighteenth century Oxford, university politics depended largely on the Heads of colleges: they ran the whole of the day-to- day administration in the Hebdomadal Council, and they could usually count on the votes of the members of their own societies in Convocation, the academic legislative body.[2] In 1711 the most influential man among them was Dr. William Lancaster, the pliant

---

[1] H.M.C. *Portland MSS.* vii. 69–70.
[2] In writing this paragraph I am indebted to the useful account in W. R. Ward, *Georgian Oxford* (1958), ch. 3.

and resourceful Provost of Queen's. He had just laid down the Vice-Chancellorship but a formidable group of his colleagues still took their lead from him and he had become accustomed to fix university elections and to manage the business of Council. Lancaster was the very epitome of a trimmer, usually subservient to the Government of the day and currently obsequious to the Harley interest. It was this Lancaster party which Atterbury now set out to break. His tactics were simple. He schemed to create a new grouping by uniting the forces of the two largest colleges, Christ Church and Magdalen. If these two ancient rivals could be brought together, and if the adhesion of one or two other lesser colleges could be secured, then the reign of Provost Lancaster was over. Thus, immediately after his arrival Atterbury entered into deep consultations with Sacheverell, now after his triumphant travels in residence again on his fellowship at Magdalen. The two plotters put out feelers for support among the Heads, and managed to entice an unsavoury trio into their party. William Delaune, President of St. John's, was a dubious character who, while a Delegate of the University Press, had retained in his own hands the great profits of Clarendon's History. In 1711 he teetered on the edge of bankruptcy and was desperate for preferment. Robert Shippen, Principal of Brasenose, was well-known as an overbearing tyrant within the walls of his college; while Jonathan Edwards, Principal of Jesus, was too senile to know rightly what he was doing at all. They were not impressive allies but Atterbury had an important card to play. At the end of November he let it be known that a scheme was being prepared to annex some of the choicer canonries in the Crown's gift to certain college headships. 'The Lord Keeper', explained Stratford, 'is to ask the Queen's leave, and our Dean is to have the choosing of the colleges. The end of this is too plain to be mentioned. It must draw all applications to him, to be sure before the places are determined, and is to make his Lordship absolute here, where our Governor is to be his Viceroy.'[1]

3

During this Oxford interlude the larger political world was in violent motion. The Whigs were in excellent heart as they gathered

[1] H.M.C. *Portland MSS.* vii. 72–78.

their forces for a great parliamentary assault on the Peace preliminaries for, whatever advantages peace had for Britain, the terms
negotiated included one provision which rocked diplomacy and
politics to their foundations: that Spain should remain under the
rule of King Philip V, the Bourbon claimant. Thus to yield the
point of a French succession seemed to many to jettison the whole
cause for which so long and bloody a war had been fought. It was to
go against solemn obligations made to the Allies and a series of
resolutions passed in previous Parliaments. Marlborough deplored
such a Peace, and the Elector of Hanover protested against it in the
most vehement terms as a betrayal of the whole alliance. He let it
be known that those who negotiated such a settlement were no
friends to him or his family. The Peace was a deeply divisive issue,
and many Tories were themselves uncertain and confused over it.
Unnerving rumours were heard that the Queen was dissatisfied and
planning a new Ministry with the secret encouragement and advice
of the Whig Duke and Duchess of Somerset. But the hardest blow
to Tory morale was the public defection from supporting the
Government of the Earl of Nottingham. Conceiving himself
neglected beyond endurance, he now threw in his lot with the
Whigs and concluded with them a kind of bargain with the Devil:
that he would join them to savage the Peace, if they would at long
last allow through the Occasional Conformity Bill. On 7 December
Nottingham and his new allies carried in the Lords a motion which
struck the Ministry at its most vulnerable point and came near to
bringing Oxford down in ruin: 'that no Peace could be safe or
honourable to Great Britain or Europe, if Spain and the West Indies
were allotted to any branch of the House of Bourbon.' Rumour
spread like wildfire that a dissolution of Parliament was imminent,
and indeed it was only by the closest of shaves that Anne could be
brought to see the seriousness of the situation and take the urgent
measures required. But Oxford's touch was still sure. Marlborough
was dismissed for his outspoken opposition and twelve new Tory
peers were created to oversway the majority in the Lords. But for
the moment it had seemed as if the whole Tory experiment was in
the balance.

Among the churchmen, too, everything was disintegrating. All
the delays to a revival of the authority of the Church had tried the

patience of the parochial clergy to the uttermost, and there were many who now began to express in trenchant terms their disillusion with the whole idea that there was anything to be expected from politicians or Parliaments. For some the conviction was growing that the whole connection with the State was a snare, an incubus on the spiritual life and work of the Body of Christ. Indeed in the autumn of 1711 a powerful propagandist movement on the right wing began to argue for the independent priestly authority of the Church; and its right and duty, if need be, to act in separation from the civil order. For many years Nonjurors like Henry Dodwell, Charles Leslie and Robert Nelson had argued in this strain, and their writings held an uncanny fascination for the Anglican priesthood. They were deep in patristic learning and they knew well how to write with emotion and sympathy. Now they were joined by two Anglican high-flyers who did not perhaps possess their spiritual qualities but who much exceeded them in urgency of message. Roger Lawrence and Thomas Brett were both of them still members of the Church of England, and early in 1712 they became the centre of a doctrinal storm.[1]

Lawrence was perhaps the more influential. Originally a Dissenter, on joining the Anglican communion he had insisted that he should be conditionally baptized, and in a series of tracts sought to defend his action against Nonconformist and Low Church critics. In his *Lay Baptism Invalid*, a widely read small book, first published in 1708 and many times reprinted, he examined the attitude of the Early Church to heretics and schismatics, and came to the firm conclusion that all who had not been baptized by an episcopally ordained minister lacked true Christian initiation. With the baptism of Roman Catholics he had no quarrel, but foreign Protestants and English Dissenters could 'fairly be assumed to be as much in the Church as the *catechumeni*, or candidates for Christian baptism, were used to be in the primitive Church'.[2] It did not take much perspicacity to see where this argument led. The exiled Stuarts and the Nonjurors were safely within the true Church, but the Elector of Hanover and his Lutheran co-religionists lacked valid Christian

---

[1] For the earlier history of this controversy, see the valuable account in George Every, *The High Church Party, 1688–1718* (1956), ch. 7.

[2] R. Lawrence, *Works*, ed. W. Scott (1841), pp. 84–86.

initiation and could at best be regarded as catechumens. The learned reply of Joseph Bingham in his *Scholastical History of Lay Baptism* seems to later ages irrefutable, but to the clergy of Queen Anne's day Lawrence's arguments were irresistibly attractive: they gave to men deeply unsure of their temporal position the assurance of an authoritative status laid up in heaven. Thomas Brett provided a variation on the same theme. In the autumn of 1711 he preached no less than three times, and subsequently published, his celebrated *Sermon on Remission of Sins*. He dealt with the necessity of confession and absolution before a priest before a man or woman could be admitted to Holy Communion, and he was not speaking of this as a practice of private devotion and personal piety. He was arguing for the right and duty of parish priests to refuse Holy Communion to those whom they considered to be impenitent sinners. By the Prayer Book rubric 'open and notorious evil livers' could be repelled from the Lord's Table, if the clergyman was prepared to risk an action for defamation of character, but Brett was pleading for a thoroughgoing discipline at the discretion of the parish priest, and he made no bones about the fact that Occasional Conformists and those who took the sacrament merely to qualify for office ought to be so excluded. By Christmas the controversy in sermon, tract and pamphlet over the new doctrines was in full flood. One work, *The Mitre and the Crown, or a real Distinction between them*, even attempted to claim Atterbury himself as an advocate for a total separation of Church and State. Nothing could be further from the truth. He was theologian enough to know the fragility of the new writers' scholarly case, and certainly his own essential method and aim was to achieve reconstruction in the Church in partnership with the State and the politicians.[1] In the conditions of the early eighteenth century Lawrence and Brett represented a clerical dream-world. High claims to sacerdotal power would never be accepted by the Anglican laity in whom the Erastian spirit was deeply fixed. And, whatever the parish priests might think, the new doctrines were too thin a cover for Jacobitism to be embraced by more than a tiny minority of the higher clergy. To throw them into the realm of

---

[1] The two parts of the work are ascribed to FA in *Somers Tracts* (2nd edn, xii), and Beeching has followed this. The theme of the tract and its continual reference to Nonjuring writers makes this improbable.

public discussion was to risk an open and dangerous division in the High Church ranks

All during the winter the Whig writers worked themselves into a passion against the threat of priestly power. The Low Church bishops led the attack in their visitation charges, and Fleetwood of St. Asaph was prominent in demanding that all covert Jacobites, subtle insinuators of Popery, should be rooted out of the National Church.[1] Disquieting rumours came to Atterbury's ears that Tenison was planning to raise the whole affair in Convocation and press for a solemn censure of Lawrence and Brett. By the end of January he was aware that the Tories were going to be severely on the defensive and that a hard fight lay ahead. Lord Oxford was reluctant that the assembly should sit at all, and only earnest persuasion brought him to see that the clergy would not submit to a silencing of Convocation by a Tory Administration without immense ill-feeling.[2] To preserve the delicate web of High Church unity Atterbury had to go on, playing off the Tory extremists on the one hand and on the other working to prevent the Bishops from raising issues which could shatter his whole cause. He knew, of course, that the Whiston censure would have to be abandoned, for if one heretic were synodically condemned then the way was open for a process against Lawrence and Brett. There was nothing for it but some energetic stonewalling when Convocation met, and when the Lower House did assemble for business on 20 February Atterbury brought into play a most ingenious device: he announced from the chair that all their proceedings would have to be begun anew after the recess and that all committees would have to be reconstituted. As a piece of constitutional doctrine it was highly doubtful, but as a political manoeuvre it served admirably. When the Whig divines moved that the committee on heretical books should consider and report on the dangerous and subversive doctrines of one Thomas Brett, the Prolocutor at once ruled them out of order and refused to allow any more discussion of the topic.[3]

[1] William Fleetwood, *The Judgement of the Church of England in the Case of Lay-baptism* (1712); White Kennett, *The Wisdom of Looking Backward* (1715), pp. 172–94; *H.O.T.*, vi. 114–17.

[2] N.L.W. Ottley MS. 252 and 255, FA to Ottley, 26 Jan., 2 Feb. 1712.

[3] R. Cannon, *A Letter about a Motion in Convocation* (1712); *Pol. State*, iii. 158–76; Kennett's diary, fo. 364.

Tenison was not, however, prepared to lose his opportunity that easily. Long consultations were held at Lord Sunderland's house with other members of the Junto, and a plan was conceived.[1] Matters might be at a stand in the Lower House where the formidable Prolocutor barred the way, but the Tory bishops were an altogether weaker proposition. Custom had it that on Easter Tuesday all the bishops, of both provinces, dined at Lambeth with the Archbishop of Canterbury and joined in a general discussion on the state of the Church. This year, without prior notice, Tenison introduced the topic of Lay Baptism, and the Tory bishops under Archbishop Sharp were asked to declare themselves plainly. A recent sermon by one Brett at an episcopal visitation in the diocese of Exeter had been printed by order of the Bishop: would his Lordship like now to defend the doctrine of that discourse and explain why he thought it worthy of publication? Lawrence had been rebaptized in a London church: would Bishop Compton like to tell them whether this had been done with his consent and approval? This frontal attack threw the Tories into confusion. Compton hurriedly denied giving any such permission. 'Upon which his Grace of Canterbury observed that it was too late to stifle such a noise, that had been already spread so far, and had filled the heads of so many people with doubts and scruples about their baptism; that it was high time something should be done to convince them that such a call to be rebaptized was never the practice or the sense of the Church of England.'[2] Put in this awkward position, Sharp and the rest could only agree that baptism, if administered with water and in the name of the Trinity, was unquestionably valid and ought not to be repeated. They agreed to join in a unanimous declaration to this effect in Convocation.

When Sharp told him what had passed, Atterbury was horrified. A declaration of this kind in the Upper House, backed up by the moral authority of all the Bishops of the province of York, would be disastrously divisive when it came down to the Lower House. Did the Tory bishops wish to shatter the Church party there and ruin its leader? Much troubled, Sharp agreed to think again, and when Tenison wrote to him to propose the terms of their joint resolution

---

[1] Wake's diary, fo. 120: 15 Mar. 1712.
[2] Wake MSS. 17, Kennett to Wake, 26 Apr. 1712; *Sharp*, pp. 369–71.

in the Upper House, the Archbishop of York replied uneasily to the effect that after consulting some of his colleagues he had changed his mind. 'I can by no means', he wrote, 'come into that proposal Your Grace has now made in your letter, in that we should all *declare* under our hands the validity of Lay Baptism. For I am afraid this would be too great an encouragement to the Dissenters to go on in their way of irregular, uncanonical baptisms.' This was an immense relief to Atterbury, and he at once wrote off to Brett, one of the chief culprits in the whole wretched business, to try to bring home to him the danger which they had all so narrowly missed.[1]

In the ensuing session the Prolocutor was often put to desperate measures to stifle discussion on the disputed issues. Lawrence and Brett, of course, were quite incorrigible and only too aware of the support which they were attracting from the rank and file of the parish priests. They were actually anxious for a full-scale debate in the Lower House, and seemed not to care that the Whigs were ready and eager to pounce. Indeed Tenison and his allies agitated constantly for a debate. On 20 April the majority in the Upper House sent down a formal resolution, inviting the clergy to agree that the validity of Lay Baptism was 'in conformity with the judgement and practice of the Catholick Church of Christ'. In the face of this challenge Sharp, Atterbury and Bishop Bisse of St. Davids held anxious meetings and could think of nothing better than that the Treasurer should have the Queen formally forbid any further discussion of the explosive issues.[2] On 14 May matters came to a crisis when there was an exceptionally bitter debate in the Lower House and when the Tory extremists could scarcely be kept in check. All Sharp's and Atterbury's private endeavours with Brett had failed, and the Prolocutor had to risk a public discussion of the Bishops' motion. It was a tribute to his skill and continuing authority that at last he managed to persuade the minority neither to accept nor reject the resolution but merely to put it off 'during the sitting of this synod'.[3] Even White Kennett had to admit that it had been 'craftily done'.

The Bishops had been kept at bay, but the victory had been

[1] *Sharp*, pp. 271–74; Bodl. MS. Eng. Th. c. 24, fo. 442, FA to Brett, 29 Apr. 1712.
[2] H.M.C. *Portland MSS.* v. 257, FA to Oxford, [9 May 1712]; *E.C.*, i. 453–54, FA to Trelawny, 9 May.
[3] Kennett's diary, fo. 380; *Pol. State*, iii. 388–89.

achieved at some cost. All Atterbury's reform projects were now in limbo and he had strained his credit with the Tory high-flyers to the limit: with men like Brett he had been forced to be positively deceitful.[1] For a while during the summer he stayed on in London. The fate of Europe was in the diplomatic balance, and he worked hard sponsoring addresses in favour of the Peace negotiations. It was a sadly tense time. Relations between Oxford and St. John remained difficult; and when the Secretary was created Viscount Bolingbroke, instead of being given the earldom for which he had asked, matters threatened an open breach. Once again the hot weather brought on Atterbury's gout, and it was a sick and exhausted man who at the end of June escaped away to his Oxford deanery.

4

Only some personal disorder can account for the extraordinary scenes at Christ Church over the next six months. For what occurred we rely heavily on the vindictive pen of Dr. Stratford, for whom Atterbury quickly became a kind of devil incarnate; but the fact remains that the Dean now not only wrecked the peace and usefulness of the college but, in the process, shattered a lifetime's friendship with Francis Gastrell and George Smalridge. It was all done to further Harcourt's ambitions and, in particular, to set up young Simon Harcourt as the next university member. To achieve this the Dean required absolute mastery in his own college and all its votes at his command. He intended to reduce the recalcitrant members of the Chapter to subservience by a campaign of calculated terror. The unwisdom of it all was to embark on such a policy when he himself was ill and overwrought.

One thought did disturb him: how the Treasurer would view this attack on his friends and protégés. And so on 24 July he sent off to Lord Oxford a letter plainly designed to obscure what was to follow under the guise of a zeal for reform:

I find [he wrote] the college, at the head of which by your favour I am placed, not altogether what I wish it in point of learning or industry, but I am taking the best methods I can to make it such, and hope in some little time to give you a good account of my endeavours.

[1] Bodl. MS. Eng. Th. c. 24, fo. 460, FA to Brett, 24 May 1712.

Nothing on my side shall be wanting towards raising a spirit of diligence and emulation here, and I doubt not but I shall have your countenance and all proper encouragement towards effecting so good a work. I have nothing at heart but your service, and the public good; and hope, by promoting the one, I may not be altogether useless in respect of the other.[1]

For someone as determined as Atterbury, it was not difficult to find cause of complaint, and before a month was out the Treasurer found himself in receipt of a very different document from the Dean: a formal accusation that the Chapter had been embezzling the trust funds. The Canons, who were away for the Long Vacation, were not entirely unaware of what was preparing, and they had cause to be apprehensive. Letters from the college informed them that Charles Aldrich, the late Dean's nephew, had accused Stratford of stealing money and books from his dead uncle's study, and that Atterbury had charged the Chapter with misappropriating the income from Christ Church meadow. The news spread rapidly and soon even Speaker Bromley was writing from Warwickshire to enquire about the grave scandals which he was hearing reported.[2]

The beginning of the new term was a time of acute embarrassment. The three Canons arranged that they should all arrive back in Oxford on the same day, so that no one of them should alone be exposed to the Dean's attentions. Smalridge, who had been up at Carlisle fulfilling his period of residence as Dean, came back full of stories of his predecessor's conflicts in the North; and these, suitably embroidered, were soon the property of the whole House. That Atterbury was sensitive on this point can be well understood, and he was beginning to find Smalridge's presence near him at Christ Church particularly irksome. It was hard to keep out of one's mind reports that the college had actually expressed their preference for his rival; and it was humiliating when the Chapter now united behind him to resist the Dean's new claims. By the third week of term even their wives were not on speaking terms. But if Atterbury had ever imagined that his colleagues would sue for peace, he was much mistaken. On 22 October the Canons prepared

[1] H.M.C. *Portland MSS.* v. 206, FA to Oxford, 24 July 1712.
[2] B.M. Loan 29/313; H.M.C. *Portland MSS.* vii. 93, Bromley to Stratford, 29 Sept. 1712.

to submit Charles Aldrich to a rigorous cross-examination, and the foolish young man had to be protected by a great diversionary outburst from the chair:

> The Canons took pen and paper into their hands, upon which the Dean said 'Nay, if you write down what is said here, I will go out of the Chapter'. He rose out of his seat and cried 'Goodbye to you' and went out. Dr. Hammond, Dr. Burton, Dr. Smalridge and I followed him to his lodgings, in order to desire him to return to Chapter. He came out of his study, he would not let us speak; he bid us not offer to come into his study, he did not desire to see us in any room of his house . . . As we went out he cried, 'I despise you'.[1]

By the end of November utter confusion reigned. Atterbury and the rest were reduced to shouting at each other in Chapter. Even the peaceable Smalridge felt himself bound to write to the prime Minister's son in defence of Stratford:

> I never yet in my life saw any man bear so ill, inhumane and un-christian treatment with so much temper and patience. I don't look upon myself to be a very fiery man; but I could not promise that I could be so easy under so grievous provocations. My temper has been pretty much tried, but not in such a manner as my poor brother's.[2]

When all his accusations seemed to be falling to the ground, Atterbury decided that he must try to force a Royal Visitation on the college. He knew quite well, of course, that the Queen would not visit in person and that the usual procedure would be for 'the Queen in Chancery' to conduct the judicial enquiry. If the Lord Keeper thus came to probe into the life and disputes of the college, many would run to make their peace and the Harcourt faction would be supreme. The visitation would need to coincide with the next General Election, but it was essential to get the Canons to appeal first. To this end Atterbury determined that they should be starved into taking action against him. He refused to allow the sealing of any document, whether lease, grace, testimonial or pre-sentation to a benefice. Money from rents and fines began to accumulate in the treasury, and the Canons remained unpaid. All this was crucially embarrassing to Lord Oxford, and he groaned under it. Letters poured into him from all sides, and his protégés at

[1] H.M.C. *Portland MSS.* vii. 96.
[2] Ibid., vii. 103, Smalridge to Lord Harley, 31 Oct. 1712.

Christ Church besought him to allow them to appeal but to ensure that the Visitor should *not* be Harcourt. But the Treasurer had no mind for any kind of public conflict; he positively forbade them to appeal, and spoke to Harcourt asking him to use all his private endeavours to bring the whole contretemps to an end. The Lord Keeper, who was clearly looking forward to conducting the visitation, replied evasively: to lament the 'unaccountable differences at Christ Church' but to protest that he was 'not proper to act the part you commanded me in'.[1] The Lord Treasurer's friends would just have to settle themselves down for a long siege.

As Christmas approached Atterbury worked himself into an agitated state. His gout came on with violence and he could only move about on crutches, hopping from room to room in the deanery. In mid-December he made shift to get across to the Students' Common Room to ask their votes for his candidate for the Public Oratorship of the university but to his chagrin at least half the company declined to go along with him. Christ Church was now split irrevocably into two warring factions. Indeed few would have dissented from Stratford's verdict that it was 'the most melancholy' Christmas that he had ever known. A thousand pounds lay undistributed in the treasury, and tempers were fraying. At the Audit the Dean was clearly ill and in great pain:

He fell on a sudden into a violent passion; he hopped up to Dr. Gastrell from whom he had not had the least provocation; he pushed him with great violence several times, and cried 'Get out of my house, you pitiful fellow'. We all expected he would have struck him, it was plain he had much ado to forbear it. I never yet saw any man so much under the power of rage; his face looked black and every joint about him trembled. I was in the bow window at the further end of the room. Dr. Burton and Dr. Potter, who were nearest, ran in between the Dean and Dr. Gastrell, and Dr. Potter begged the Dean to sit down. As he was sitting down, he held up his cane, and shook it at Dr. Gastrell, and cried, 'Dare to give me any indecent language in my own house'.[2]

When Atterbury left for London at the beginning of January he left behind a society the business of which had come to a complete stop.

[1] B.M. Loan 29/138, Harcourt to Oxford, 3 Dec. 1712.
[2] H.M.C. *Portland MSS.* vii. 137: 29 Dec. 1712.

Back in town it was soon borne home to him that his Christ Church campaign had been a dreadful mistake. The Harleian Canons had 'blasted him over all England' and the gossipmongers were revelling in the stories of his uncontrolled rages. In November he had been talked of for the vacant see of Hereford, and the Treasurer may well have considered ending the college's misery by promoting Atterbury and putting Smalridge in to succeed him. But as things went from bad to worse at Christ Church, it was obviously impossible to think of him further. Eventually Hereford went by translation to the serviceable Bishop Bisse and the see of St. Davids to Adam Ottley, a loyal Harleian dependant. The worst aspect of the quarrels was that they had ruined utterly any hope for the Tory cause in Convocation. What, indeed, could the Prolocutor do when he had just parted on such acrimonious terms with his chief lieutenant, George Smalridge? Tenison's adviser, Edmund Gibson, was quite right when he gave it as his opinion that nothing could be done in either House: 'I am told the Prolocutor begins to talk in the same strain, fearing I suppose that if business be entered upon, he may not be so well supported since the irreconcilable breach at Christ Church, which will appear more or less in Henry the Seventh's Chapel.'[1] Indeed for this reason, and because the Bishops still brandished the Lay Baptism issue, Atterbury had not the slightest intention of allowing any business to be commenced. To all enquiries he returned the same excuse for his inaction: new bishops were needed in the Upper House. When the Tory prelates were mostly ancient men like Sprat, Compton and Hooper, who did not even attend, it was hopeless to attempt anything. It was in the next Convocation, after the General Election, that the great Tory leap-forward would take place.[2] But all this was whistling for a wind. The High Church divines were deeply divided among themselves, and by an act of folly their leader in the Lower House had contributed not a little to their confusion. They were wholly unprepared for the critical days which were now close at hand.

[1] Bodl. MS. Add. A. 269, fo. 21, Gibson to Nicolson, 23 Jan. 1713.
[2] *E.C.*, i. 460–67, FA to Trelawny, 10 and 24 Feb. 1713; Bodl. MS. Eng. Th. c. 24, fo. 560.

CHAPTER NINE

Mitre and Crown, 1713–1714

I

I N April 1713, after many delays and obscure manoeuvres, the
Great Peace was signed at Utrecht. It was a moment for which the
Tories had waited with ill-concealed impatience. 'Things which we
pressed', recalled Bolingbroke, 'were put off upon every occasion,
till the Peace: the Peace was to be the date of a new Administration,
and the period at which the millenary year of Toryism should
begin.'[1] And yet, as men waited for the opening of the new parliamentary session, the whole political scene was clouded over with
suspicion and uncertainty; and the Tories themselves were confused
by questions which seemed to have no answer. What had been the
real nature of those protracted negotiations with France? Had there
been secret agreements which only the Ministers knew? Could the
Lord Treasurer be trusted; or would he now abandon his Tory
allies, go back on all the assurances he had given them, and seek
refuge with the Whigs? But the great question, the one on which
all turned during the next troubled year, was the Succession. Those
nearest the Queen knew just how precarious was her hold on life.
At times she appeared in good colour and voice; she made speeches,
received visitors, and moved between Windsor, Kensington, and St.
James's. But she had to be carried from room to room in a chair, and
every step she took required that her immense bulk should be
supported by strong arms. She was often in pain, and life was a
misery to her. Her mind became less and less clear: she was lethar-
gic, irresolute, and disinclined to any troublesome change. News
of her health was relayed by her doctors to chosen political intimates,
and foreign ambassadors distributed a small fortune in bribes to
obtain information from courtiers and servants. In the last year of
Anne's life the politicians became increasingly concerned with the
future—not least with their own futures. What would happen

[1] 'A Letter to Sir William Wyndham' in *Works*, ed. D. Mallet (1754), i. 22.

to the parties, to public order, to the Church, on the day when the Queen's weary frame at last gave up the unequal struggle?

The Junto Whigs waited with ill-concealed impatience and pleasurable anticipation. Their supporters remained a minority in the Commons but their confidence had little to do with numbers: it rested on a conviction that the Hanoverian future belonged to them. No opportunity was lost to represent themselves to the Elector's envoys as the one set of politicians who could be relied upon to support the Protestant Succession. They knew how bitter the resentment had been at Hanover at the manner in which the peace negotiations had been conducted, and they were eager to improve any suspicion that the Ministers were actually engaged on a Jacobite design. In public and in private the Whig lords let it be known that when their day came they would exact vengeance on the authors of the Peace, even to the extent of calling upon them to answer with their lives. Their menaces against Bolingbroke were unremitting and did much to impart an anxious haste to all that he did.

In the face of this grim Whig unity the Tory leadership was perplexed and disunited. While Lord Oxford retained the Queen's confidence and could still exert his old political magic it was virtually impossible for any rival to offer an effective challenge to his supremacy. And, as confusion multiplied in the months which followed, it became increasingly hard to rally the backbenchers to the agitation of some definite party issue There was one topic upon which all the great Tory chieftains agreed: that something had to be done while there was still time to re-establish the authority and status of the Church. But on virtually every other issue they were deeply uncertain and even mutually hostile. If the Tories were now to exert their undoubted parliamentary power to push through a body of discriminatory legislation and if they were to proscribe their opponents from public office, high and low, what would this mean? Was it possible that, when Lord Oxford's moderation was thrust aside, some set of Ministers might seek to secure their regime by a sudden coup on behalf of the Stuart Pretender? It was this possibility which unnerved many influential Tory politicians and senior divines, and made it so crucially difficult to prepare for the critical days which lay ahead.

As the session drew near the Ministers met to discuss tactics, and with all the urgency at his command Bolingbroke pleaded for the scheme which he had preached in season and out of season: **that** there must be an immediate rallying of the Church party and a relentless onslaught against the Whigs. He was not alone in his opinion. Jonathan Swift added his voice, pleading for an agreement: 'Let us be the attackers.' But with Lord Oxford all such pleas were useless. A storm might be building up, but he remained curiously opaque. He reserved all vital business to himself and he alone was the channel of communication with the Queen. When he spoke to his colleagues, even to a friend like Swift, his language was jumbled to the point of unintelligibility. In fact, the strain of office was telling on him badly, but on all sides suspicion was growing that he intended to spring some sudden coup. When at the end of March he spent some hours in the company of four of the Junto lords even Swift began to suspect that he was preparing a deal with the enemy.

The issue which rankled most with the Tories was still that of the Church, and it was at this point that Oxford was at his most ambiguous. Perhaps his own religious convictions made attacks on the Dissenters distasteful to him; perhaps it was the Queen's dislike of high-flying divines which prevented any action: but the paralysis of his administration when it came to ecclesiastical affairs was notorious. Since 1710 only two statutes to further the Anglican cause had been passed: the Occasional Conformity Act of 1711 and the Toleration Act for Scottish Episcopalians in 1712. It was well known that the Treasurer had opposed each of them so far as it lay in his power. For a whole year there had been a stop on ecclesiastical preferments. Deaneries were kept vacant and, as Irish bishoprics fell, no move was made to fill them, though Harcourt plied the Treasurer with the names of prominent High Church divines. Indeed since the autumn he had been pressing that something substantial should be given to Sacheverell when the term of his suspension from preaching expired in March 1713. In February Bromley wrote in exasperation to convey something of the groundswell of anger which was affecting the Tories, politicians and clergy alike.[1]

---

[1] B.M. Loan 29/200, Bromley to Oxford, 18 Feb. 1713: the section omitted from the letter in H.M.C. *Portland MSS.* v. 297.

Among those fast losing patience was a clergyman whose services to the Ministry had been superb. In February 1712 Jonathan Swift had applied humbly, even modestly, to Oxford when the deanery of Wells had fallen vacant. He had received the usual Harleian assurances, and nothing further had happened.[1] Two more deaneries fell in the earlier half of 1712 and he had to endure the misery of denying rumours and observing the amusement of those who enjoyed his discomfiture. At last on 13 April 1713, just after he had spent much labour in helping the Treasurer to draw up the Queen's Speech at the opening of Parliament, he received the shattering news that all three of the deaneries had been given elsewhere. Oxford made some involved excuses but Swift was deeply wounded and disgusted. He announced that he was leaving town at once, abandoning the Ministers to their divisions; and in his distress he received sympathy and encouragement from Bolingbroke, Lady Masham and Atterbury. The Secretary declared that he was 'in the right'; and it now seems to have been by Bolingbroke's intervention with the Duke of Ormonde that at last the Queen's consent was secured to his having the deanery of St. Patrick's, Dublin, a preferment in the Lord Lieutenant's gift. While the matter was still in the balance, Atterbury wrote to send the latest news from Lord Bolingbroke and to convey their joint best wishes for his success. It is clear that both divines were at one in their diagnosis of the situation and in their prescription for a remedy.[2]

The new session of Parliament opened at last on 9 April. The country members had been kept waiting in London by repeated prorogations, and they were in an exasperated frame of mind. Given that there was no direction nor any programme from the Ministry, they were ready to act under whatever leadership offered itself. And there were not lacking dissident Tory politicians prepared to meddle with the squires and lead them in a chase away from the Ministers' control. Since Christmas a 'Hanoverian' group had been acquiring leaders and a definite identity; and its demand for an immediate full Tory regime in Church and State attracted much

[1] For the Queen's and Sharp's determined opposition to Swift, see Panshanger (Cowper) MSS. 48, 15 Feb. 1712 and 25 Apr. 1713; *Stella*, p. 665; Prussian MSS. 39, A, fo. 43, Bonet's dispatch of 8/29 Feb. 1714.

[2] *Swift Corr.*, i. 344, FA to Swift, 21 Apr. 1713.

support while its constant expressions of concern about the security of the Hanoverian Succession in the hands of the present set of Ministers caused confusion and suspicion among the backbenchers. It was difficult for Bolingbroke and his friends to know what to do, and they consulted anxiously. Atterbury was at Christ Church for Easter but immediately afterwards he hurried up to London, where he was in waiting at Court, and discussed matters at length with Harcourt and the Secretary. His own vote was for the Ministry to commit itself without delay to an all-out Tory programme, and he repeated his old argument that there had to be an immediate recruitment of convinced and active Tories to the Bishops' Bench. He joined Swift in lamenting the evil condition into which they had fallen. But it was clear that Bolingbroke and his associates could not do without the Treasurer: their own basis of support among the backbenchers was too narrow and their reputation too much connected with extreme measures. They simply did not dare to ruin the prime Minister. All they could hope to do was to capture him: so to embarrass his Administration that he was forced for his majority's sake to adopt their programme, admit them to the key offices in the Government, and use his influence with the Queen to further their cause. And so, at the end of April, the Bolingbroke group began the delicate operation of secretly consorting with the dissident Tory leaders and encouraging their opposition, in order slowly to break down Oxford's parliamentary position until he was forced to take refuge with them. He, in his turn, was not unaware of what was in progress. As his brother described it:

About this time Lord Bolingbroke, Lord Harcourt, and the now Bishop of Rochester fell into a strict alliance, and endeavoured to raise a great prejudice in the Church party against the Treasurer, upbraiding him for not being a sincere churchman, as they called it; and to make this pass got lists out of every office of the names of such persons as they called Whigs, who were continued in their employments. The Lord Bolingbroke told me, if your brother will not set himself at the head of the Church party, somebody must.[1]

Quietly Bolingbroke was at work among the discontented: Argyll and his scheming brother Islay were approached; Anglesey, Orrery and Hanmer were consorted with; and the kingmaker Shrewsbury

[1] H.M.C. *Portland MSS.* v. 660.

was informed of their plans. According to Oxford, Anglesey later admitted 'that Lord Bolingbroke had told him that [Oxford] was to have terms put upon him and a junto'.[1] It was not long before this dangerous course showed itself in both the Lords and the Commons. While the Secretary and Harcourt went through the motions of doing the Government's business, neither spoke much in the House. In private they adopted the role of sorrowful bystanders, powerless to assist the Administration when its leader refused to listen to advice. Quickly everything got out of hand, as the Whigs joined the Tory attacks, hoping thereby to force Oxford to come into them. The session proceeded with a series of desperately narrow majorities: that 'driving to an inch' which so lacerated the nerves of the new Dean of St. Patrick's.

A vital aspect of Bolingbroke's tactics was to offer to re-create Tory unity around the one issue which could still bring in the leaders and engage the enthusiasm of the backbenchers: the Church. But here, of course, the Secretary was gravely handicapped. His scandalous private life and his heterodox religious opinions made him less than acceptable to traditionally-minded churchmen, and he had to rely heavily on a clerical adjutant. He could deal with the politicians himself but on ecclesiastical issues he needed an agent. It was this role which Atterbury now proceeded to fill.

2

It was not long before he had an ingenious scheme in operation. What Bolingbroke desired above all was to bring into his own plans 'Hanoverian' Tories like Nottingham, his brother Lord Guernsey, Lord Anglesey or Sir Thomas Hanmer. It would be particularly satisfactory to enlist the support of a respected churchman like Bishop Dawes of Chester, who now seemed to be in permanent opposition, setting himself up as a focus for all those who suspected the intentions of the Ministry and thought it necessary to take political action to protect the Protestant Succession. To find an issue on which all could unite, and which in addition would be gravely embarrassing to the Treasurer, was a delicate matter; but early in the session Atterbury drew up a draft parliamentary bill

[1] Ibid. v. 467: Oxford's memorandum of 15 June 1714.

which might serve. Its aim was to revive the power of the church courts by giving them a statutory right to imprison offenders. The method was that which had been proposed in Convocation in 1711: to give the ecclesiastical judges discretion to commit to prison all persons whom they adjudged contumacious of their authority and not merely the small class of serious offenders who had incurred the solemn sentence of excommunication. The title of the bill, 'An act to prevent the too frequent denunciation of Excommunication', concealed its real import. If it passed the courts would have new teeth, not least to enforce a more rigid policy against Dissenters. Hesitating to approach Nottingham directly, Atterbury went instead to Lord Guernsey and was successful in persuading him to introduce the bill into the Lords. Canon Stratford was perspicacious enough to understand what was going on. Atterbury, he wrote,

was then in a ticklish state. He was casting about for new friends, and how to form new parties. He had a design to apply to Lord Nottingham. He had made two or three offers there to no purpose. He knew the aversion both the brothers had to him. He was to recommend himself by giving them an opportunity of doing somewhat that was to be popular amongst the clergy. This was the reason of putting that bill into Lord Guernsey's hands.[1]

On 5 May the bill was duly introduced, when Dawes took it under his wing and managed its progress. At last on 20 June it was sent down to the Commons where it seemed certain to receive a warm welcome at the hands of the majority there.

By the latter part of May Lord Oxford was in as grave difficulties as Bolingbroke and Atterbury could have wished. In both Houses of Parliament his majorities were in ruins. At the beginning of the month the Commons had invited Sacheverell to preach before them on Restoration Day and their gesture of defiance had been the prelude to a hectic session. A Place Bill was introduced and forced through; the Malt Tax was obtained by only one vote; and an attempt to deprive Quakers of their vote in parliamentary elections was barely defeated. And this revival of country Toryism was not all. In the Lords a combination of Whigs, Hanoverian Tories and

[1] H.M.C. *Portland MSS.* vii. 159. For the text of the bill, see H.M.C. *House of Lords MSS., 1712–1714*, pp. 64–65.

Scottish peers attempted to embarrass the Ministry by proposing actually to repeal the Act of Union with Scotland. It was a time of high crisis, not the least so in that all sides were supporting measures contrary to their usual policies in order to produce a political revolution. One of Swift's correspondents professed to find it 'very comical' to observe 'both sides at the same time acting parts which they thought contrary to their interests'.[1] But if Swift's nerves were suffering Oxford himself was scarcely in a better state. Rumours spread as to what his next move would be: now that he would commit himself to the full High Church programme, now that he would go in with the Whigs. Just before the great debate on the Union Halifax offered him an alliance, and he seems to have been sorely tempted. In the course of June a great attack developed on the commercial clauses of the Peace treaty, and one by one Tories fell away to join the opposition.

It was in the midst of this crisis that old Bishop Sprat died quietly in his deanery of Westminster, and vacated a most desirable conjunction of preferments. His bishopric of Rochester had many advantages: it was small in area and involved no great pastoral labour; it was near to town and yet at Bromley it possessed a lovely and peaceful country mansion. Its sole disadvantage was, however, a serious one. The episcopal income was so meagre that it was one of the poorest sees in England. Held alone, it would have involved its Father-in-God in dire penury; but a convenient custom had grown up by which the Bishop of Rochester always held in addition the deanery of Westminster, the ample income of which well made up for any deficiency in the bishopric. At once Atterbury's name was talked of as Sprat's successor, but in view of his recent political manoeuvres a shrewd political observer felt sure that the Ministry 'don't desire him so near the Court'.[2] Obviously for the Bolingbroke group it was a propitious time to test out the strength of their position, and Harcourt at once began an energetic campaign on his friend's behalf. The Queen found herself importuned on all sides, not least by the Secretary's enemy, Lord Dartmouth, who urged Anne to veto the suggestion. She was indeed desperately unwilling to give her consent, and the Treasurer was in a situation which

[1] *Swift Corr.*, i. 361-62, Lewis to Swift, 2 June 1713.
[2] B.M. Lansdowne MSS. 1024, fo. 412, Kennett to Wake, 23 May 1713.

called for all his well-known dexterity. At first he seems to have
decided to divide the preferments, giving the bishopric to Lord
Willoughby de Broke, a High Church divine who had just succeeded
to an ancient barony, and the deanery to the octogenarian Dr.
Robert South, who had been a Prebendary of Westminster when
Atterbury was a schoolboy. At the beginning of June he actually
sent an offer to South, but the venerable old man had the grace and
wisdom to decline.[1] Harcourt and his friends now became insistent:
it must be Atterbury and it must be both preferments. At that
difficult juncture of politics Oxford had to placate the High Tories,
and with the best possible face he agreed to Atterbury's promotion.
Dartmouth reported pungently on the reaction of Anne to her
Minister's insisting that the appointment was a political necessity:

I never knew the Queen do anything with so much reluctancy, as
the signing of his *congé d'élire*. She told me, she knew he would be as
meddling and troublesome as the Bishop of Salisbury, had more
ambition, and was less tractable. I told her, I thought she had a right
notion of the man, therefore wondered she would do it. She said,
Lord Harcourt had answered for his behaviour, and she had lately dis-
obliged him, by refusing the like request for Dr. Sacheverell, and found
if she did not grant this, she must break with him quite; which she
believed, I would not think advisable. I told her, I really thought anything more so, than letting such *boutefeus* into the Church and House
of Lords.[2]

The news of Atterbury's appointment was received in the world at
large with mixed feelings. At Christ Church the first rumour was
greeted with cheers and one of the Censors threw his hat into the
air at the thought of a new Dean. Canon Stratford was, however,
characteristically sour. His mind had been for so long obsessed with
Atterbury's misdoings that the thought of his enemy's going out
of his life was curiously unwelcome to him; and he was deeply
vexed that the Treasurer should have changed his mind about the
disposal of Rochester and Westminster after having let Stratford
know of the first plan. Clearly the good doctor had been confidently

---

[1] Trumbull Add. MSS. 136/1, Bridges to Trumbull, 9 June 1713; H.M.C.
Portland MSS. v. 295, South to Oxford, 8 June.
[2] *H.O.T.*, vi. 165, Dartmouth's note; Bodl. MS. Rawl. Letters 92, fo.
563.

affirming to his colleagues that Atterbury was not being considered, and now he waxed indignant that one who had just been doing his best to embarrass the Ministry should be raised to the episcopate. He would, he concluded acidly, himself 'study the art of being troublesome in order to be preferred'. 'You must allow me to say', he informed Lord Harley, 'that nothing that has been done since your father's Ministry has struck such a damp upon the hearts of all that have honour or honesty, as this promotion.'[1]

But from Atterbury's point of view the whole prospect was pleasing. Not only did this promotion seem the first-fruits of his and his friends' tactics, but his personal status and influence were greatly enhanced. Now he could be released from the wretched deadlock at Christ Church which, he had begun to realize, had done no good either to his health or his reputation. But to be Dean of that great Collegiate Church in the shadow of which he had passed his school-days, where the pageantry of state occasions was enacted, and where wealth and dignity were conjoined: this was indeed after his own heart. On receiving Oxford's letter he accepted at once with great professions of being willing to serve the Treasurer in all he could do, and particularly in the business of restoring peace at Christ Church. Learning that Smalridge was to be his successor, he offered to send him a general proxy to settle the outstanding disputes and to wind up the tangled financial quarrel which had kept them all, Dean and Canons alike, for nine months without money.[2]

Without delay he betook himself to the laborious legal processes of coming into possession of his two new preferments. Westminster presented the fewer difficulties, and he was installed there on 16 June. It was reported that as he got out of his coach at the Abbey door 'a terrible storm' broke overhead. Those moved by such omens were duly impressed, but at first the Chapter was all anxiety to please. It was ordered 'that the Deanery be repaired and made fit for his Lordship's reception and a new room built according to his Lordship's desire'. The college porter was to be fitted out with a new gown 'made agreeable to his Lordship's livery'. Permission was given to him to change the college plate 'into such fashion as his Lordship shall desire'. By the winter session of Parliament he could

---

[1] H.M.C. *Portland MSS.* vii. 140: 12 June 1713.
[2] Ibid., v. 296, FA to Oxford, 13 June 1713.

look forward to being fully settled with his family in a newly fur-
bished lodging.[1] The bishopric presented rather more difficulty.
Stratford speculated pleasantly that the Archbishop might actually
refuse to consecrate a man who had so plagued him, but in fact
Tenison behaved with admirable correctness. Whatever embarrassment either party might have felt was overcome by a visit to
Lambeth, and on 5 July the Primate duly consecrated him as Bishop
of Rochester. Atterbury was the kind of man who took delight in
ceremonies, offices and robes; and the next few days were pleasurable. On 7 July he was introduced into the House of Lords and
afterwards, resplendent in scarlet chimere and new lawn sleeves, he
went with the other bishops to St. Paul's for the great service of
thanksgiving for the Peace. Writing to Bishop Trelawny, in the
excitement of the moment he at first forgot to sign himself with
his new episcopal signature, but later corrected his letter to conclude
with a bold 'Fr. Roffen:'.[2] In all this time of personal triumph
there was only one event which caused a shadow of discontent: the
unexpected death of Bishop Compton of London. To feel that, but
for a few days, he might have gained this splendid preferment
instead of the little bishopric of Rochester was obviously galling.
Dean Swift attempted to mitigate what he knew his friend must be
feeling by suggesting that Tenison could not possibly last long at
Lambeth and that then, at last, Atterbury might succeed Bishop
Robinson of Bristol at London, but it clearly rankled: not least
because of the immense pleasure expressed by the enemies of the
Bolingbroke faction. Indeed while Dr. Stratford rejoiced, the Queen
and Lord Dartmouth congratulated each other that at least it had
not been necessary to promote the Dean of Christ Church that much
above his merits.[3]

At the end of July Bolingbroke and his allies began to feel confident that the game was going their way. The parliamentary session
had ended on a note of complete confusion with the Government's

---

[1] Westminster Abbey Chapter minutes, quoted in *A House of Kings*, ed.
E. Carpenter (1966), p. 197; Bodl. MS. Eng. Th. c. 29, fo. 305, FR to Brett,
14 July 1713.

[2] *E.C.*, ii. 1–3, FR to Trelawny, 6 July 1713. From the time of his consecration Atterbury is referred to by the initials FR.

[3] *E.C.*, ii. 36, Swift to FR, 3 Aug. 1713; H.M.C. *Dartmouth MSS.* i. 315,
Dartmouth to Anne, 8 July.

usual majorities in ruins, and it was clear that on all sides men were waiting to see what the new shape of politics would be. In a situation of such delicacy Atterbury was, of course, quite willing that his Excommunication Bill should be quietly dropped. In a sense it had served its purpose, and he and his friends now wished to propose themselves as able to rescue the Treasurer from his difficulties rather than embarrass him further.[1] The pressure on Oxford was immense, as Bolingbroke urged him to form a genuinely Tory Ministry with himself and his associates in the key-positions. With the coming elections in mind, Atterbury wrote to indicate that he might be able to persuade Bishop Trelawny to use his borough-influence on a new Ministry's behalf.[2] The Treasurer was in a low state of health, but his political wits were unimpaired and he still retained the trust of the Queen. In mid-August he performed his last great act of political wizardry. He did indeed reconstruct his Administration with Tories, but he did it in such a way as to isolate Bolingbroke and push him and his friends into a subordinate position. It was ingeniously done. Quiet negotiations behind the scenes with Bromley and Hanmer procured it that they would serve, the first as Secretary of State, the latter as Speaker of the new House of Commons. The Earl of Mar became third or Scottish Secretary of State and was given the management of the electoral campaign in the northern kingdom. Bolingbroke's rival, Dartmouth, was made Lord Privy Seal, and not only was the Secretary pushed sideways into the senior (but less effective) secretaryship but he had to endure the mortification of seeing the whole of the Government's patronage for the Election put into Bromley's hands. Bishop Robinson was promoted to the see of London as a reward for his diplomatic services at Utrecht and, to the Queen's great pleasure, his bishopric of Bristol was promised to George Smalridge to hold with the deanery of Christ Church. It is clear that both Bolingbroke and Atterbury were deeply shocked. For a while the Secretary seriously considered resignation but in the end realized that he and his allies would have to soldier on, hoping against hope that their plan to capture the Treasurer and the Queen might yet be put into effect.

---

[1] H.M.C. *Portland MSS.* vii. 159.
[2] Ibid., v. 312, FR to Oxford, 27 July 1713; B.M. Loan 29/138, Harcourt to Oxford, 6 Aug.

Oxford's coup was brilliantly devised, but it solved nothing. In the autumn, as Atterbury moved into his new home in Dean's Yard, he saw clearly that the political world was adrift. The General Election proved another triumph for the Tories. The clergy had once again marched to the polls and exhorted their flocks to vote for 'Church' candidates; and once again the electors had returned a large majority of those pledged to bring in the Tory millennium. The number of high-flying backbenchers exceeded even that of 1710. But virtually nothing was heard of the first Minister himself. Oxford was mentally and physically tired. In September he had deeply offended the Queen by asking that his son should be granted the title of Duke of Newcastle; and in November came the shattering news of the death of an adored daughter. All during the winter he was a broken man, unable to summon up the strength to converse with his colleagues or do essential business. When one weekend he travelled down to Windsor in the same coach with Bolingbroke, Atterbury was quick to hope that this meant new life and vigour for the Administration; but when, at Christmas, the Queen was desperately ill her Treasurer unaccountably ignored urgent messages to hasten to her bedside.[1] During this strange, indecisive period both he and Bolingbroke were in touch with the Pretender through the good offices of the Abbé Gaultier, a French agent, and the Marquis d'Iberville, the official envoy in London; and in Paris the Marquis de Torcy read regular reports in which it was learned that the two had pledged themselves heart and soul to the Stuart cause.[2] What this, in fact, meant remains a mystery. In all likelihood it was nothing more than a way by which they kept their options open until the last possible moment.

3

As the first session of the new Parliament drew near it was apparent that the Succession question had grown to the proportions of a national crisis. The Queen's illness had brought home to ordinary people that at any time the country would be faced with its great decision. Steele's Hanoverian pamphlet *The Crisis* sold no less than

---

[1] *E.C.*, ii. 9-10, FR to Trelawny, 19 Dec. 1713.
[2] See the reports in L. G. Wickham Legg, 'Extracts from Jacobite Correspondence, 1712–1714', *E.H.R.*, xxx (1915), 501.

40,000 copies. Nonjuring writers like George Harbin and Charles Leslie put out Jacobite tracts which had an unnerving air of confidence and triumph, and Whig preachers launched themselves into vehement denunciations of Popery and arbitrary power as if a Stuart invasion was actually imminent. At the end of January there was a serious run on the Bank, which could only be quieted by a promise that the Queen would come in person to read her speech from the throne. Lord Oxford was as elusive as ever and it seems to have been left to Bolingbroke to make an effort to unite the Tory leaders. His plea was always the same: let there be now some concerted effort to establish the Tories in undisputed power before Anne died and left them defenceless. As he put it to Anglesey: the Queen had 'but one life, and whenever that drops if the Church interest is broke, without concert, without confidence, without order, we are of all men the most miserable.'[1] Every effort was made to conciliate the 'Hanoverian' Tories who remained fearful for the Protestant Succession. Hanmer was confirmed as Speaker, and Sir William Dawes, Bishop of Chester, was promoted to the vacant archbishopric of York. This appointment was indeed a mighty gesture. Dawes had been one of the Ministry's most consistent critics, and when Archbishop Sharp died on 2 February the Bishop had given no indication that in the coming session he would act differently. The Ministers could easily have promoted one of their more dependable supporters, but instead offered the great preferment to the leading High Church 'Hanoverian'. As Canon Stratford put it gloomily, 'the best you can hope from him will to be whimsical'.[2] When the new Convocation opened on 16 February Atterbury made an attempt to have Thomas Sprat, one of his closest supporters, elected as Prolocutor, but prudently withdrew at the last moment to allow the nomination of George Stanhope, Dean of Canterbury and one of the leading members of the 'Hanoverian' group. As one observer put it, he could not do otherwise 'without hazarding a division of interests', and so he 'put on the face of an unconcerned man'.[3]

But, in spite of all these attempts to keep up a façade of party

[1] *Bolingbroke Corr.*, i. 593-94: 25 Jan. 1714.

[2] H.M.C. *Portland MSS.* vii. 179; Prussian MSS. 39. A, fo. 48, Bonet's dispatch of 19 Feb./2 Mar. 1714.

[3] Bodl. MS. Add. A. 269, fo. 31, Gibson to Nicolson, 13 and 16 Feb. 1714.

unity, the rapidly widening breach in the Ministry itself could not be disguised. It would be quite wrong to attribute this tragic course to Bolingbroke's playing with Jacobitism and Oxford's firm attachment to Hanover.[1] It now seems clear that both Ministers abandoned any real interest in James in mid-March when it became known that he had refused to change his religion. In their separate conversations with Gaultier and d'Iberville they minced no words in declaring that a Stuart succession was an utter impossibility. Bolingbroke even went so far as to say that 'le Grand Turc sera plutost Roy d'Angleterre que le Chevalier tant qu'il sera Catholique Romain'.[2] The issue henceforth was one of tactics: how best to preserve themselves in the face of an inevitable Hanoverian succession. Oxford's overriding concern was to be accepted as guiltless when the new King arrived, and to this end he was prepared to cabal with the Junto and to continue to block any Tory attempts at a radical party policy. Bolingbroke's solution to the problem was, as always, a more direct one: the new dynasty must find on its arrival a Tory party so united and so entrenched that it would be impossible to discard it and rule through the Whigs. The Secretary's assessment of the situation was based on perfectly sound considerations, and historians have been too ready to write of his policy as if it were desperate and unworkable. That there were critical difficulties he and his friends were well aware. The Queen could scarcely bring herself to trust him and he depended too much on Lady Masham's uncertain powers of persuasion. And, as he tried to preserve unity within the party, he found that he had to deal with a vehement and indiscreet faction of Jacobites in the Commons, who threatened to ruin everything. Above all, there remained the ecclesiastical problem: how could a man of notorious morals and doubtful religion appeal to 'the Church interest'?

All during the spring months persistent rumours of a rupture of relations between Bolingbroke and Oxford had a deeply unnerving effect on Tories in Parliament. Soon the 'Hanoverian' group began to recruit to its banner increasing numbers of those who were sus-

[1] See J. H. and M. Shennan, 'The Protestant Succession in English Politics, April 1713 – September 1715', in *William III and Louis XIV*, ed. R. Hatton and J. S. Bromley (Liverpool, 1968).
[2] L. G. Wickham Legg, op. cit., p. 517.

picious that these obscure quarrels in some way touched on the
issue of the Succession. Not least of the Ministry's difficulties was
the gradual consolidation in opposition of the Bench of Bishops. In
April, to Atterbury's great discomfort, two of his former opponents
at Christ Church, George Smalridge and Francis Gastrell, joined
him on the Bench as Bishops of Bristol and Chester respectively.
Smalridge was, in addition, honoured with the post of Lord High
Almoner, which gave him constant access to the Queen. But to the
general surprise even these dedicated Harleians abandoned the
Ministry and joined Bishop Robinson of London in the opposition
lobby. Indeed in a series of divisions the new Archbishop of York led
both his Tory and Whig brethren to vote against measures which
seemed vital to the Administration's continuance. In the critical
vote of 5 April on a motion that the Succession was in no danger
under the Queen's government only three bishops gave their vote
in its favour. On 19 April in sudden alarm Oxford asked Anne
urgently to 'send for such persons of the clergy, besides Lords and
Commons, as she in her great wisdom shall think fit, and let them
know from her own mouth her Majesty's thought about the Succession.'[1] On the 28th she did so send for Dawes and closeted him.
Reports circulated, and were eagerly taken up by the foreign
ambassadors, that he had replied to her politely enough but declared
himself defiantly against the present set of Ministers.[2] By the
middle of May not only the Bishops but Anglesey, Hanmer and a
substantial body of backbench Tories had decided that the conduct
of the Administration was decidedly suspicious.

It was a critical time for Lord Oxford, not least because it was
clear that he was losing the confidence of the Queen. By now indeed
he was often drunk, even in her presence; and his conversation,
never very clear, seems to have consisted of jumbled phrases and
involved personal pleas. Lady Masham was able to convey to
Bolingbroke the message that there was now a chance of greater
personal sympathy in the royal closet, and he and his friends moved
towards some decisive action to force the Treasurer's hand. It was
generally agreed that the initiative came from Atterbury who proposed to Harcourt that they should bring forward a bill in the

[1] B.M. Loan 29/10/9: 19 Apr. 1714.
[2] Prussian MSS. 39. A, fo. 110, Bonet's dispatch of 4/15 May 1714.

manner of his Excommunication Bill of the previous summer, but that this one should deal with the vexed topic of Dissenting education.[1] As Defoe put it later, this was 'the mine to blow up the White Staff'. The bearer of the staff, the Lord Treasurer, had a Dissenting background; since 1710 he had made repeated promises to Whig politicians and to the Nonconformist interest. Now he was in a grievous dilemma. There was no issue on which churchmen felt more deeply. Not to support the bill would be tantamount to forfeiting the loyalty of key-supporters such as William Bromley. That Oxford was horrified at the prospect of this Schism Bill is shown by the disordered character of some notes which he prepared on 14 May, two days after Sir William Wyndham first broached the project in the Commons. Addressing himself to Lady Masham, he pleaded: 'You disable a sure friend to serve you. And thereby you help nobody . . . What is your schism? . . . The first point is to support the Queen . . . Do not terrify her with difficulties of her fast friends.'[2] The alarm was soon up, and on 21 May Wyndham formally introduced Atterbury's bill into the House. It was a draconic measure, intended to enforce the most rigid Tory point of view. As such indeed it went far beyond what had been projected in Convocation in 1711. All teachers, whether in schools or academies, were to be licensed by the diocesan bishop according to the intent of the Act of Uniformity: they had to produce a certificate of having received the Anglican sacrament and they had to pledge themselves in the future to conform to the liturgy of the Church of England. Any teacher so licensed who subsequently went to a Dissenting conventicle was liable to three months imprisonment. That this was a project dear to Atterbury's heart was missed by few, and it is at this point that he began to be spoken of as a kind of *éminence grise*, the intriguer behind Bolingbroke and Harcourt. Peter Wentworth, a Tory supporter himself, reported to Lord Strafford that 'when matters are pretty well between our great folks, there is another Bishop that you have not seen, who renews the breach and widens it worse than at first.'[3]

[1] Ibid., fo. 143, 11/22 June 1714; *The Secret History of the White Staff* (1714). p. 32.

[2] B.M. Loan 29/10/8.

[3] *Wentworth Papers, 1705–1739*, ed. J. J. Cartwright (1883), p. 383: 25 May 1714.

No one doubted that the bill would pass easily in the Commons, and it received a majority of well over a hundred. The real contest lay in the Upper House, where support for such ecclesiastical measures was more precarious and where the attitude of individual Tory peers was so much more uncertain. At the end of May Atterbury was surprised to have a visit from no less a person than Lord Anglesey, who proposed that the scope of the bill should be extended so that it applied to Ireland as well as to England and Wales. At first the Bishop was plainly suspicious. Was this a subtle attempt to defeat the whole thing by embodying a clause which would attract vehement opposition? Or was this a move by Anglesey in his bitter rivalry with the Duke of Shrewsbury, the Irish Lord Lieutenant? On the latter assumption, and because it might conciliate the valuable Irish Tory interest, which Bolingbroke had been wooing for the best part of a year, it was agreed that the new clause should be added to the bill.[1] At last on 4 June the great debate came on, when the Secretary himself introduced the measure. The Junto lords, supported by Nottingham, mounted a furious attack, recalling the fact that both Harley and St. John had received their education in Dissenting academies, and appealing to the grand principles of religious toleration and parental right of choice in their children's upbringing. Though there were some hesitations at first, the Tories warmed to the battle and their party zeal began to create an appearance of unity. It was a terrible time for the Treasurer. In the House he either sat silent with visible embarrassment or went out of the chamber just before the critical divisions. In private, with the Queen or Harcourt, he was at a pitch of excitement. 'Will you have no reserve? Your minister is to have all the insults of the parties', he pleaded with Anne, while Harcourt was told that they were 'running mad'.[2] His appeals were to no avail. In Grand Committee Archbishop Dawes presided over the bill's progress and there was added to it the vital clause extending its operation to Ireland. It is unfortunate that the speeches in the House were reported almost entirely by Whig partisans, and the Tory contributions survive only in an abbreviated or mangled form. Of

---

[1] H.M.C. *Portland MSS.* vii. 186: 3 June 1714.
[2] B.M. Loan 29/10, 9 June 1714; H.M.C. *Portland MSS.* v. 458, Harcourt to Oxford, 13 June; ibid., v. 451, Halifax to Oxford, 29 May.

Atterbury's own speech we possess but an extract, but even this fragment sums up his essential Tory refusal to accept the fact that Dissent had become a permanent feature of English life. He posed to the House a series of questions:

If Schism be about indifferent things, why should children be involved in these differences before they know what they are? If about matters of the last consequence, the Dissenters have gone off from the first and chief pretence upon which a Toleration was granted them. If a Schism was unavoidable, because of the ignorance and distinctions of Forty-One, why should the iniquity of those times be established by a law, or that law be made perpetual and unalterable? If Schism was tolerated on account of its mortality, why should it be allowed the privileges of monarchy, and go by inheritance and succession?[1]

On 15 June, after an embittered debate on the third reading, the bill as amended passed by eight votes. All the Tory prelates united in its passing, while five Whig bishops joined in a formal Lords protest. On 25 June Atterbury was present in the House to hear the Schism Act become law.

4

Now the contest at Court entered its final stage. On 5 July one well-informed observer described the situation as the Tory party waited in increasing doubt and bewilderment to see what would emerge:

Lord Bolingbroke, Lord Chancellor and the Bishop of Rochester are the men chiefly concerned in what they call the New Scheme; and are resolved to out the Treasurer, and Bolingbroke is to have the Staff and be Premier Minister. This the Tories pretty unanimously talk. On the other hand, the Treasurer is endeavouring to retrieve himself with the Whigs; and is, they say, acourting them in order to save himself in that herd. The Lord knows what will be the issue; but sure the Church party do not enough imbibe and consider that maxim, *Divide et Impera*.[2]

Oxford strangely and stubbornly refused to resign, clinging to office in a determined effort to thwart Bolingbroke and his cronies. They themselves were in grave difficulties. There was scarcely any ministerial control over the course of business in Parliament, and

[1] *The History of the Mitre and the Purse* (1714), p. 71.
[2] Trumbull MSS. LV, Bridges to Trumbull, 5 July 1714.

Bolingbroke had just been gravely compromised by an accusation of peculation levelled at Arthur Moore, one of his closest associates. If the Treasurer had lost the Queen's trust, it could scarcely be said that the Secretary had gained it. Though Lady Masham worked away at her royal mistress, for the best part of July the contest was deadlocked. Rumours spread fast as to the composition of a reconstructed Ministry, and the foreign ambassadors agreed that Atterbury was designed to succeed Dartmouth as Lord Privy Seal.[1] Certainly the Bishop was in constant consultations with Bolingbroke and Harcourt. One weekend they drove down to join him at Bromley, and on the day of the famous Lords' address to the Queen, asking her to put a price of £100,000 on the head of the Pretender, he and the Secretary met together no less than three times to discuss tactics. As Dr. Stratford put it: 'if the New Project cannot be prevented, they who are chiefly concerned in it are now so blasted that they must stick at nothing to support themselves.' Everything now depended on the Queen, on a woman who was quite desperately tired and ill. To win her confidence, even a little, Atterbury advised Bolingbroke that he must effect some kind of reconciliation with his shamefully misused wife.[2]

Oxford clung on, intriguing in all directions and writing pathetically to Hanover, but at the end of the month Lady Masham at last managed to get the Queen to the point of taking some action. On Monday, 26 July, before a gathering of councillors Anne announced her intention of taking the White Staff from Oxford and putting the Treasury into commission.[3] The scene which followed was appalling. Oxford launched himself into a tirade against his opponents, accusing them again and again of financial dishonesty. Out in the Long Gallery at Kensington he had a furious quarrel with Harcourt, the sounds of which penetrated back into the Queen's room. All night and all the next day she was in a pitiable state of anxiety about

---

[1] B.M. Add. MSS. 17677 HHH, fos. 268–70, Hermitage's dispatch of 18/29 June 1714; *Swift Corr.*, ii. 51; H.M.C. *Portland MSS.* v. 475.

[2] H.M.C. *Portland MSS.* vii. 190, 193-94.

[3] *Swift Corr.* ii. 86, Lewis to Swift, 27 July 1714. H. L. Snyder, 'The Last Days of Queen Anne: The Account of Sir John Evelyn Examined', *Huntington Library Quarterly*, xxxiv (1971), 261. See Prussian MSS. 39. A, fo. 202, Bonet's dispatch of 30 July/10 Aug.; B.M. Add. MSS. 17677 HHH, fos. 317–18, Hermitage's dispatch of 27 July/7 Aug.

what she had done. And the events of that evening, 27 July, ruined everything for which Bolingbroke and his friends had worked. Between eight and nine Oxford arrived to deliver up his staff and was closeted with the Queen for some two hours. Something of his old magic remained and momentarily he re-asserted his old influence over her; at the end of the interview she was deeply distressed and consumed with suspicion of Bolingbroke.[1] When, late at night, the Cabinet Council met to settle the Treasury Commission all was confusion. Anne refused to accept the names put to her and others, seeing the situation, refused to serve. At past two in the morning the Council broke up, with the intention of reassembling early the next day. But it had been too much. The strain and anxiety had brought the Queen to the point of collapse. Her mind was wandering, and physicians had to be summoned in haste to attend her.

The conduct of Bolingbroke and Atterbury in the last critical hours of the Queen's life shows that neither was party to a plan to bring in the Pretender. It was Lord Harcourt himself who proposed that the dying Anne should be moved to give the White Staff to the Duke of Shrewsbury, and it was under Tory auspices that orders were sent out to put the armed forces into a state of readiness. The well-known story that the arrival of the Dukes of Argyll and Somerset at the Privy Council meeting confused Bolingbroke's plans rests on no tangible evidence. When in the early morning of 1 August Anne's weary frame at last gave up its struggle, the Secretary and his friends were quick to demonstrate their loyalty to the Hanoverian regime. Though it was Sunday morning and Parliament stood prorogued, both Houses assembled with those of their members who were still in town. On that very morning Atterbury, Bolingbroke and Harcourt took the oaths to King George I. Indeed on 5 August the Bishop of Rochester, with his brethren of London and Bristol, was put on a committee to draw up an Address to the new monarch, and this they did in the most fulsome terms. But nothing of this deterred the manufacturers of legends, and within a couple of months Daniel Defoe had set the process on its way.

---

[1] *The Secret History of the White Staff* (1714), pp. 53–61, gives an account of what was said by Oxford to the Queen and his opponents. Defoe seems to have derived this from Oxford himself. See also H.M.C. *Portland MSS.* v. 480-81; and *Swift Corr.* ii. 88-89.

According to *The Secret History of the White Staff* Atterbury is supposed to have fallen into a raging passion on learning of the
appointment of Shrewsbury:

'Give away the Staff' said the Bishop. 'By Lucifer I could not have
believed she durst have done it! What can we do without it, we have
but one way left, France and the Lawful Heir; it must, and shall be
done, By God!'[1]

In later years even Harcourt himself manufactured a story about his
former ally. He 'declared that on the Queen's death, the Bishop
came to him and to Lord Bolingbroke, and said nothing remained
but to proclaim King James. He further offered, if they would give
him a guard, to put on his lawn sleeves and head the procession.'
Even Dr. Stratford, who would let nothing go by that was to
Atterbury's detriment, dismissed the whole tale as a palpable and
malicious fabrication.[2] The death of the last Stuart sovereign was
not an occasion for histrionic and useless gestures but for deep sad-
ness. It was the end of an era, a shattering of old hopes, and the
beginning of a testing-time for the Church of England. As
Bolingbroke wrote to Swift: 'The Earl of Oxford was removed on
Tuesday, the Queen died on Sunday. What a world is this! And how
does fortune banter us.'[3]

[1] *The Secret History of the White Staff* (1714), p. 71; ibid., Part II (1714),
p. 55.
[2] H.M.C. *Portland MSS.* vii. 337. For a variant story, see *Spence's Anecdotes*,
ed. James M. Osborn (Oxford, 1966), i. 284.
[3] *Swift Corr.* ii. 101, Bolingbroke to Swift, 3 Aug. 1714.

PART TWO

THE JACOBITE CAUSE

CHAPTER TEN

'The Tory Party is Gone', 1714–1716

I

T HE death of the Queen was a terrible reverse but it did not necessarily mean that the Tory party was finished. George I was an astute and experienced ruler, and his German advisers had already made a shrewd assessment of the English political situation. They were well aware that if their master were to ruin and proscribe the Tories he would run the risk of putting himself wholly and without reserve into the hands of the Whigs. It soon became apparent even to the Junto lords that their reputation for party assertion was a grave hindrance to their political ambitions and that the King had set his face against single-party government. Indeed Lord Halifax judged the moment expedient to break ranks and offer himself to the Germans as one who could act in the role of a Harley by heading a 'moderate' administration which could preserve the King from being dictated to by any one set of 'violent' party men. Certainly in the autumn of 1714 the appearance of Tory strength was still formidable. It was less than a year since the electorate had returned a House of Commons which was even more fervently Tory in character than that elected in the heady aftermath of the Sacheverell trial. It was only a few weeks since the Lords had passed the Schism Act into law. At the end of September that able political commentator, Frederick Bonet, the Prussian envoy, was convinced that the Whigs would fail to get a majority in the Election and that within a year King George would be forced to work with a Tory administration.[1]

Yet in fact the Tories were at the mercy of events, for not only were their leaders still embroiled in the bitter personal disputes of the last weeks of the Queen's life but those of them who had been concerned in the making of the Peace were in mortal fear. The six weeks which elapsed before the King's arrival in England frayed

[1] Prussian MSS. 39. A, fo. 332, Bonet's dispatch of 28 Sept./9 Oct. 1714.

their nerves badly. Oxford and Bolingbroke were insulted in the
street by mobs and both were utterly disconcerted by what seemed
a complete change in public opinion.[1] A clear majority of Whig
lords on the Council of Regency appeared to indicate the future
direction of royal favour. It was a lacerating time and, as the lay
politicians agonized over their fate, it was left to their clerical
friends to take some thought for the future of the Church party.
Jonathan Swift was well aware of the magnitude of the disaster which
had befallen them and he knew that there was unnerving talk of
impeachments and penalties, but he at once wrote to Bolingbroke.
He begged him

to resume a little courage: to be at the head of the Church-interest is
no mean station; and that, as I take it, is now in your Lordship's
power. In order to which, I could heartily wish for that union you
mention . . . We have certainly more heads and hands than our
adversaries; but, it must be confessed, they have stronger shoulders
and better hearts.[2]

In London Atterbury too tried to salvage something from the wreck-
age. Indeed as his friends wavered he emerged as the one Tory
leader with a clear and courageous policy for the party's survival.
Each day Dean's Yard was thronged with coaches as Ormonde,
Bolingbroke, Harcourt and others went into the deanery to discuss
the situation. To them all the Bishop gave the same insistent advice.
Whatever had happened in the past year, the Tories must now sink
their differences and unite. They must be ready to serve the new
King—but as members of a party with definite policies and acknowledged leaders. George must be brought to see them as a great
political interest, useful in office and formidable in opposition. Only
in this way could they maintain their strength in the country and
continue to defend the cause of the Church and the landed interest.
Above all the leading Tories must not allow themselves to be
frightened into suing for terms as isolated individuals.[3] It was not
easy. In the House of Lords Atterbury sank his pride so far as to go
up to George Smalridge, take him by the hand, and beg him and the

[1] B.M. Add. MSS. 17677 HHH, fo. 329, Hermitage's dispatch of 3/14 Aug.
1714. See also H.M.C. *Portland MSS.* v. 118.
[2] *Swift Corr.* ii. 112: 7 Aug. 1714.
[3] See H.M.C. *Portland MSS.* vii. 199–200, for Stratford's analysis of FR's
position.

other Harleians to forgive and forget their past disputes. They were interrupted by the Duke of Argyll who came across to enquire in a loud voice when he might be permitted to congratulate the Bishop of Rochester on becoming Lord Privy Seal. He received a character-istically fierce reply, but other Tories were not so well equipped to stand up to such taunts and threats, and it was not long before there was something like panic in the ranks.

It was typical of the man that Harcourt should be the first to break and hasten to make his individual submission to Hanover. On 10 August his nerve failed completely and he attempted in some confusion to explain himself to the Bishop:

> My neglect of writing is inexcusable. I doubt it may justly be taken as an affront. I am determined now to do it, late as it is. An ill excuse is worse than none. My station will excuse the presumption. I wish I had your thoughts tomorrow morning in writing. Pray send me two lines, if I must see you no more.[1]

Atterbury knew his Harcourt well, and his reply was only touched with contempt. It should not, he wrote, present a distinguished lawyer with too much of a problem to write to the King and say that he was prepared to serve on any terms, but

> there is one way of addressing him indeed, which would require more skill; that is, if your Lordship thought fit to write not merely as a single person, but in some measure as the head of an interest. This I could wish your Lordship would do; and would take the steps proper to enable you to do it, but I do not find your Lordship so disposed, and therefore am silent on that subject.[2]

Bolingbroke saw the Bishop's point more clearly, and at first showed greater courage. Bonfires blazed before his house in Golden Square to welcome the King's accession and, in spite of a terrible inner apprehension, he went through the motions of a party leader. In the Commons Bromley and Wyndham took the lead in proposing an immense Civil List, and it seemed that the Tories were indeed intent on recommending themselves as the men 'most forward to do the King's business'.[3]

[1] *E.C.*, ii. 12.
[2] *E.C.*, ii. 13: 11 Aug. 1714.
[3] *The Wentworth Papers*, p. 411, 10 Aug. 1714. For a valuable account of Bolingbroke's actions, see H. T. Dickinson, *Bolingbroke* (1970).

But the Whig pressure was relentless, and their talk of impeachments and penalties went on. Bolingbroke knew that it was unlikely that he would remain Secretary of State for long after the King's actual arrival but he was profoundly dismayed to be informed on 31 August that a special courier had come from Hanover bearing an order for his instant dismissal and the seizure of his papers. What appearance of courage he had managed to contrive ebbed away, and he decided immediately to retire into the country and take no further part in party politics. On 3 September he attempted to justify himself to Atterbury, even though he knew that the strong-minded Bishop would regard this as a plain desertion of the Tory cause.

The satisfaction and the advantage of conversing with your Lordship are so great [he wrote] that I shall certainly make use of the opportunity of seeing you which you are so kind as to afford me. About eight tomorrow in the evening I will not fail to be at the Deanery.

I cannot conclude this letter without assuring you that I am not in the least intimidated from any consideration of the Whig malice and power. But the grief of my soul is this, I see plainly that the Tory party is gone. Those who broke from us formerly continue still to act and speak on the same principles and with the same passions. Numbers are still left and those numbers will be increased by such as have not their expectations answered, but where are the men of business that will live and draw together? You, my Lord, know my thoughts as well as you know your own. Nothing shall tempt or fright me from the pursuit of what I know is right for the Church and nation; but the measures of the pursuit must I fear be altered.[1]

With Bolingbroke out of town, the Bishop seemed the only prominent Tory concerned to put the party into a posture of defence. The coaches continued to stand outside his door, but now some of the politicians insisted on coming to him incognito or late at night.[2] It was obvious that the overriding need of the moment was to re-establish a working alliance with the Harleians and the 'Hanoverian' Tories under Archbishop Dawes, but the traumatic events of the previous months were still too fresh in everybody's mind to be easily forgotten. In private among his close friends Atterbury spoke

---

[1] S.P. 35/1/31b, Bolingbroke to FR, [3 Sept. 1714].
[2] S.P. 35/1/48, Duke of Buckingham to FR, *circa* 1 Oct. 1714.

of the 'ten thousand crimes' which had discharged him for ever from any obligation he might have owed to Lord Oxford, but in public he went out of his way to stress the need for all the Tory groups to act together. There was small response. All during the summer the Harleians had been nourishing a bitter resentment which seems in particular to have fastened on the Bishop himself. 'Sure', wrote Erasmus Lewis, 'the earth hath not produced such monsters as Mercury, and his companion, and the Prelate.'[1] Oxford remained strangely confident about his own political future and there was even talk among his cronies of his taking office in the new Ministry and preserving the King from domination by the Junto. Indeed his prime concern was to find some device which would allow him to shift the weight of Hanoverian resentment on to the shoulders of his rivals and to set himself forth as one who had fought and suffered for the Protestant Succession. Just before the Queen's death Daniel Defoe had composed a short vindication of the fallen Treasurer and now the sheets were hastily recalled from the press and revamped to suit the new situation.[2] It was a work which required persuasive skill and literary imagination but Defoe and his master were equal to the attempt, and at the beginning of October they put out a pamphlet which was to cause an immediate sensation under the intriguing title of *The Secret History of the White Staff*. Not even a casual reader could doubt that the author had access to highly confidential information about the struggle around the Queen in the last week of her life. And an ingenious interpretation was put forward. Bolingbroke and Harcourt were represented as dupes rather than traitors; they were weak and personally ambitious, and they had allowed themselves to become the unwitting tools of a secret Jacobite conspiracy. Amid the confusion only Lord Oxford had had the perspicacity to identify the real intriguer who had manipulated his allies and pushed them towards a Stuart restoration. It was none other than the Bishop of Rochester, and his designs had been defeated only when the dying Queen, on Oxford's advice, had handed the White Staff to the Duke of Shrewsbury.

[1] *Swift Corr*. ii. 116, Erasmus Lewis to Swift, 10 Aug. 1714; ibid., ii. 117–18, Bolingbroke to Swift, 11 Aug.
[2] *The Letters of Daniel Defoe*, ed. G. H. Healey (Oxford, 1955), pp. 443–45, Defoe to Oxford, 3 Aug., 26 Aug. 1714.

It is not difficult to imagine Atterbury's reaction to this amazing tissue of lies. The wisest course would have been to ignore the pamphlet and let it pass as a nine days' wonder, for on his arrival in England George I had not shown the slightest inclination to take up with Lord Oxford. The King and his German advisers were even prepared to make conciliatory gestures towards Tories who had not been involved in the peace negotiations; and office was given to Lord Nottingham and offered to Bromley and Hanmer.[1] It was perhaps a time for the Tories to wait upon events and preserve their unity. But old resentments and new insults were hard to swallow down, and Atterbury at last yielded to the temptation to reply in good measure to Defoe's piece of ingenious impertinence. His short tract, *Considerations upon the Secret History of the White Staff, humbly addressed to the E--- of O-----*, was a venting of all the anger and frustration which had been building up within him since the great disappointment of 1711. Oxford was savagely attacked. Did he not recall the large promises made to his supporters among the clergy before 1710? 'But it seems no sooner was the blow struck but your Patriots and worthy Friends, in a moment, became full of Frenzy, hot-headed, factious, and all for the Pretender, only because they exacted from you the performance of the promise you had frequently made them.' The truth was that the Minister had governed by the use of a continual deceit, 'but 'twas your pride, and has since become your boast, to cajole, oppose and disappoint, and to rule the nation by broken sentences and promises.' What, in fact, had Oxford ever done for the Church of England? He had opposed the appointment of genuinely Tory bishops, and he had obstructed every parliamentary measure which sought to restore its discipline and authority; in the great debate on the Schism Bill he had 'sat dumb, and swelling with a discontent that visibly spoke your affections to it'. But now his day was done, and with him went 'a shameful, tricking administration'. Yet, Atterbury concluded, 'there is still some pity for you, and even in him from whom you least deserve it; and I have authority to tell you, the Bishop, when he hears you are next possessed with the spirit of writing secret history, will wait on you,

---

[1] Panshanger (Cowper) MSS., Box 49, Duchess of Marlborough to Cowper, *circa* Nov. 1714; Bodl. MS. A. 269, fo. 36, Gibson to Nicolson, 27 Nov.

exorcize you, and drive out that *Lucifer* with whom you have made him so familiar.' Within a few days three separate printings had come off the presses, and the public appetite was eager for more revelations of intrigue and mutual recrimination in high places. It was useless for either Oxford or Atterbury to deny their involvement. When the ex-Treasurer wrote to Dr. Stratford to disclaim any connection with the *Secret History*, the good Canon was politely incredulous.[1]

At the very height of this pamphlet warfare, on 20 October, Atterbury went through the ceremonial part of a Dean of Westminster at the coronation of George I. He had watched anxiously as workmen erected scaffolding and tiers of seats in the Abbey, and he had coached the choir and his colleagues into performing their duties with dignity and precision. At the climax of the service he bore the Crown from the high altar so that the aged and infirm Archbishop Tenison might place it upon the King's head. It was a moment of muted joy. Standing around among the assembled peers of the realm were all the actors in that sad drama of the Tory party which had been played out in the last days of the Queen's life. And, as soon as the ceremony was over, they fell on each other again with renewed venom. In *The Secret History of the White Staff*, *Part II* Defoe turned on Atterbury without mercy. Now Bolingbroke was completely absolved from complicity in a Jacobite conspiracy; he had been a mere bystander while the real design was carried on by 'a woman, a priest, or a purse-bearer'. But the master-mind had always been the Bishop of Rochester, 'unsufferably haughty, superrogant and enterprising, restless and indefatigable in pursuing his designs, and ambitious beyond measure in their exorbitant extent, vain of directing the greatest heads'. His obligations to Lord Oxford had been immense and yet he had been 'one of the first who fell upon the Staff, plowing with the Heifer, [and] found a cabal in the administration, which opposed all the measures of the Prime Minister'. His whole career had given 'just reason to believe he would be for the Pretender, were it but from a mere inclination to be arbitrary'. When at last it was clear that his designs had come to nothing, 'the

---

[1] H.M.C. *Portland MSS.* v. 501, Oxford to Stratford, 23 Nov. 1714; and ibid., v. 501-2, for the reply. See also *Letters of Thomas Burnet to George Duckett, 1712-1722*, ed. David Nichol Smith (1914), p. 75, 14 Oct.

Ecclesiastic is said to have given loose to his passion, and boiling up
to despair, caused him to go off the stage raving, having neither
grace to repent of what was passed or patience to consider what was
to come'. This was too much, and in mid-November Atterbury
returned to the combat with a vehement piece, *The History of the
Mitre and the Purse*. But it was his last word. Although Defoe teased
him further with a Part III and the Whig writers joined in to improve
the hour with satirical contributions, the Bishop refused to be drawn
further.

The strain had been intense, and he had been deeply disturbed
to be thus publicly branded as a Jacobite. As always when under
some nervous excitement it was not long before he went down with
an agonizing attack from his old enemy, the gout. All over Christmas
he was confined to one room in the deanery, and in the long and
painful hours he had time to assess the political situation.[1] It was
obvious that the coming General Election would find the Tories
and their organization in total disarray. As rumours circulated that
the King had resolved to go on a single-party basis so the morale of
the Tories decayed. Soon they began to fear dismissals, proscriptions and permanent exclusion from the sweets of office. Unnerving
reports came up from the constituencies of men refusing to stand as
candidates, of corporations turning their coats, and of huge expenditure by the Whigs.[2] There were anxious conferences at the deanery
as Bolingbroke, Harcourt, Ormonde and Strafford considered what
could be done.[3] And at last, in a despairing attempt to rouse the
country Tories from a dull acceptance of defeat, it was decided that
Atterbury should publish a powerful pamphlet on which he had
been working in the days of imprisonment in his sick-room. *English
Advice to the Freeholders of England*, put out in the first week in January,
was a bombshell, designed to shock the country supporters and
impel them into realizing what a Whig single-party regime could
mean. It was not, he wrote, 'an affair of small importance. Our *all*,
under God, depends upon the next elections: our religion, our rights,
our liberties, our present laws, and our future security are at stake.

[1] *E.C.*, ii. 14-15, FR to Trelawny, 29 Jan., 13 Feb. 1715.
[2] See J. H. Plumb, *The Growth of Political Stability in England, 1675-1725*,
ch. 6, for a masterly account of the process by which the Tories were excluded.
[3] *Pol. State*, ix. 14-15.

If we make a wrong step at this juncture, all the comfort we can have is that probably it will be our last fault of this kind, because we shall never have it in our power to be guilty of another.' Now the cause of the Church and the 'landed interest' was being attacked by men who had raised themselves on the profits of war. 'Bank bills, lies, threats, promises, entertainments are everywhere employed to corrupt men's affections, and mislead their judgements. Boroughs are rated on the Royal Exchange like stocks and tallies. The price of a vote is as well known as an acre of land; and it is no secret who are the monied men, and consequently the best customers.' Throwing caution to the winds, he went on to deliver a vehement personal attack on George I. Let no one be deceived by this talk of his 'moderation'; it was a mere device to quieten the Tories while the Whigs went about to encompass the ruin of their enemies. In fact, from the beginning the King had shown spite against the vast majority of his new subjects who supported the cause of the Church and the landed interest. His first action had been to dismiss the Duke of Ormonde, and 'by what since hath happened it appears that his being a churchman not to be perverted, is what is not to be forgiven him.' What could really be expected of the King? He was a foreigner, brought up in an alien environment, ignorant of the English language, the English Church, and the English constitution. Even now at St. James's he was attended by 'those two fellows in Turkish habits' who 'seem to have his royal person entirely in their care'. Would he be merciful to those whom he considered to have offended him? Let them enquire after the fate of a certain Count Königsmarck and his lover, the wife of the Elector of Hanover, who even now was immured in a perpetual imprisonment. If the Whigs won the election, Atterbury prophesied, there would be a war in the interests of the King's German territories, a standing army, a repeal of the Triennial Act, and an increasing campaign against the Church of England.

It was well that Atterbury had taken elaborate precautions to preserve his anonymity, for the Government's reaction was immediate and fierce. On 11 January a royal proclamation was issued out against such a 'wicked contrivance', designed to alienate the affections of His Majesty's loving subjects and to encourage the designs of the Pretender. A reward of £1,000 was offered for information leading to the arrest of the author, and on the same day the houses of Lord Strafford and Matthew Prior were searched and their papers seized. At once Erasmus Lewis wrote off to Jonathan Swift warning him to destroy any matter which might incriminate himself or others.[1] As the counties and boroughs went to the poll it was in an atmosphere of wild alarm, with accusations of Jacobitism flying freely and with threats of coming prosecutions in the air. The results, as they came in, showed that the Tories had suffered a major disaster. On a rough count the Whigs had a majority of 152, and it was immediately made clear that they intended to use their new power to the full.

Until this time Bolingbroke had acted the part which the Bishop had counselled. Even a Whig opponent could yield him a grudging admiration and admit that he 'for a coward carries it with the most courage I ever saw'.[2] He attended the House of Lords with an appearance of great calmness and confidence, and on 22 March he attempted to remove from the Loyal Address a clause which contained a severe reflection on those who had negotiated the Peace of Utrecht. To his chagrin and alarm his motion was rejected by 66 votes to 33, and it was revealed just how many peers had decided to trim their sails to the wind.[3] In the next few days his courage drained away, and he decided to flee. On the evening of 26 March he went to the theatre, and the moment the performance was over he slipped down to the coast in disguise and crossed to France. When the news became known, Atterbury was profoundly shocked and dismayed. He had not been consulted and he was never to forgive what he regarded as an act of craven desertion. Although still crippled by the gout, he struggled across to the House of Lords, as if symbolically to fill Bolingbroke's place. And within a few days a broadsheet was being distributed around London which purported to be a letter written by the former Secretary just before his embarkation at Dover. It was a brief, earnest declaration that his flight was due not to any sense of guilt but to a conviction that his enemies were determined to procure his death; and that 'had there been the least reason to hope for a fair and open trial . . . I should not have

---

[1] *Swift Corr.* ii. 156, Lewis to Swift, *circa* 11 Jan. 1715; *Pol. State*, ix. 75.

[2] *Letters of Thomas Burnet to George Duckett*, p. 85: 26 Mar. 1715.

[3] *Pol. State*, ix. 206; J. H. Plumb, *The Growth of Political Stability*, pp. 161-62.

declined the strictest examination.'[1] It concluded with a strong
denial that he had been guilty of any 'criminal correspondence'.
Certainly the letter was timely—but had it really been written by
Bolingbroke? Few seemed to believe so, and one of Swift's correspondents volunteered to 'tell you a secret; it was written by Bishop
Atterbury. It hath done a great deal of good, and we have not lost
a man by his going.'[2] But when news came in August that Bolingbroke had met the Pretender in France and taken service with him
as his Secretary of State, the damage done to the Tory cause was
real and without remedy. A few days later the Bishop chanced to
speak with the Earl of Mar at Court, and in a message which he
knew would reach St. Germains he warned the Jacobites not to
trust their new recruit. King James would find his new Secretary
as unreliable as the English Tories had done in the desperate moment
when they had looked to him for leadership in their party cause.[3]

2

The following twelve months were the most painful of Atterbury's
career. All around he saw the pitiful collapse of the Tory order
which had been at the heart of his hopes and aspirations. Now,
under the regime of Sunderland and Stanhope, the Whigs pressed
on with their party programme. Everything which the 'thorough'
Tories had wanted to do in the spring of 1714 the Whigs now did
in the spring of 1715. Disaster followed disaster, and soon the Tory
leaders were on the rack. In the face of constant threats the Duke of
Ormonde, the last representative of the old Cavalier tradition, lost
his nerve and fled to France. Now was the Junto's opportunity to
brand their enemies as traitors and Jacobites; and all during the
summer the House of Lords sat on to debate Ormonde's and Bolingbroke's bills of attainder and to consider the impeachments of
Oxford and Strafford. In these dreadful days Atterbury stood out as
by far the most effective debater on the Tory side. He intervened
constantly in the House, and his forceful style and biting witticisms

[1] *Pol. State*, ix. 230; H. T. Dickinson, *Bolingbroke*, pp. 135-36.
[2] *Swift Corr.* ii. 168, Barker to Swift, 3 May 1715.
[3] H.M.C. *Stuart MSS.* ii. 47, E. Hamilton to Mar, 8 Apr. 1716; ibid., ii.
386, Mar to FR, 17/28 Aug. 1716.

made him an opponent whom the Whig spokesmen learned to respect. His clashes with the Duke of Argyll became notorious. When on 9 July he rose to argue that Oxford's trial should not be unduly delayed, the Duke turned on him vehemently. The Bishop of Rochester, he declared, 'had of late studied more politics than divinity, and was thoroughly acquainted with the subject matter of the articles that lay before them': perhaps he too had been involved in secret transactions and could enlighten the House on his role in them. On 9 August Atterbury had his revenge. When the Duke proposed that the sacramental test should be abolished and replaced by a simple declaration against the Pretender, the Bishop was at once on his feet to enquire whether his Grace's motion stemmed from loyalty to the King or dislike of religious observance. The noble Duke would forgive them if those acquainted with the frequency of his attendance at church were led to presume that it was the latter. Even the Government supporters on the episcopal Bench joined in the general amusement and, in writing to Lady Cowper, Bishop Wake undertook 'to entertain your Ladyship with the duel fought in the House by Lord Argyll and the Bishop of Rochester'.[1]

The small group of Tory peers fought hard to quash the attainders of Ormonde and Bolingbroke by raising constant procedural objections, but suddenly all their efforts were brought to nothing by news that a Jacobite rebellion had broken out in Scotland. From that moment on the Tories were on the defensive and desperately hard-pressed. As Mar's campaign progressed, the price of Bank stock fell and there was something like panic. Riots were reported in various English provincial towns and the Government eventually decided that it was expedient to demonstrate the loyalty of the City by organizing a series of loyal addresses from all sections of society in and around London. It was, of course, a superb opportunity for the Whigs to compose these addresses with strong expressions of Whig political philosophy, and then to stigmatize the Tories as Jacobites when they refused to sign. Even the advisers of the old Archbishop of Canterbury were not above resorting to such tactics, and on 3 September they produced a document in the name of the Bishops at present in town which could only be interpreted as a

[1] Panshanger (Cowper) MSS., Box 49, Wake to Lady Cowper, 13 Aug. 1715.

scathing denunciation of Tory policy and 'pretended zeal for the Church'[1] Great care was taken to see that the paper was tendered to the Tory bishops, and when the sponsors arrived at the deanery Atterbury knew that he was in a crucially difficult position. But he did not hesitate; he read the document, threw it aside, and 'refused absolutely' to sign what he described as 'a libel'. Bishop Smalridge said that he would sign when the offensive sentiments had been removed, and not before.[2] It was a moment to be relished by their Whig brethren who made haste to improve the shining hour at Court and who were delighted when Smalridge was summarily dismissed from his post as Lord High Almoner.[3] Atterbury's punishment was similarly severe. When at the end of September a new body of commissioners for the Fifty New Churches was set up, his name was omitted from their number and he was thus excluded from any further part in the great project which he had done so much to initiate. After this public mark of disapproval he was sadly prepared for the weight of abuse which now fell on him. Indeed the Whig pamphleteers made him a special object of their attention, and even coined for him a new nickname. In future their readers were entertained with the continuing story of the traitorous doings of 'Frank Scammony'.[4]

The winter months confirmed him in his detestation of the Hanoverian regime. In November the Jacobite army was decisively defeated at Preston, and soon pathetic groups of prisoners were being marched south under heavy guard. Within weeks under Mar's incompetent leadership the Scottish rebellion folded and died. Obviously the real danger to the dynasty was over, but the Ministry was determined to exploit the situation for all it was worth. A great army of Dutch and German mercenaries was retained; the Habeas Corpus Act was suspended; and it was decided that the captured rebels should receive exemplary treatment. It was a dismal winter for the Tories, and during much of it Atterbury was again shut away in his room with an attack of the gout. The weather was bitterly cold and the streets blocked with snow, but after Christmas against

[1] *Pol. State*, x. 451.
[2] Ibid., 457.
[3] Bodl. MS. Add. A. 269, fo. 45, Gibson to Nicolson, 13 Nov. 1715; ibid., fo. 46, 19 Nov.
[4] See John Dunton, *Frank Scammony: or, the Restoring Clergy detected* (1715).

all medical advice he made shift to get across to the House of Lords and hobble into the chamber on his crutches. The effort was made to be present at the solemn and macabre trial of the six peers who had been taken after the battle of Preston and to speak in their defence. But nothing could prevail. They were, for the most part, poor country peers and old-fashioned Roman Catholics who had been romantically attached to the Stuart cause; but on 9 February they were solemnly condemned to death. Even Lord Nottingham was moved to make an emotional plea on their behalf. For his pains he and all his relatives were summarily dismissed from office, and it seemed certain that the extreme penalty was to be exacted. All this needless cruelty preyed on Atterbury's mind, and in his lonely room in the deanery he began to work on yet another trenchant pamphlet. In the middle of March it appeared anonymously and was quickly distributed around by willing helpers.[1] *An Argument to prove the Affections of the People of England to be the best Security of Government* was written in his most deadly style; it was argued with force and passion, and its phrases were carefully chosen. Ostensibly an earnest appeal to the King for mercy on the six lords, in fact it was a vehement attack on him for having allowed himself to become the compliant tool of the Whig faction. Could he not see that this oligarchy was setting him against the wishes of the vast majority of his subjects and forcing him to rely on a standing army to suppress all protest. Already the point had been reached when the only way to throw off the yoke of Whig rule was to rebel against the King. Could his Majesty not escape from this domination and return to all his people? 'Is terror', Atterbury concluded, 'to become the only national principle? If so, I am afraid it will have no other effect than to make men more cautious rebels.'

The Bishop's mind was indeed moving steadily to the adoption of this very role of 'a more cautious rebel', and the parliamentary business after Easter 1716 provided the impulse towards his conversion. Having made a maximum use of the trials, Sunderland and Stanhope attempted to consolidate their position in precisely the manner which Atterbury had predicted, and on 10 April a bill was introduced into the Lords to extend the life of the parliament

---

[1] *Pol. State*, xi. 277. Abel Boyer reprinted the entire text of the tract in his edition for March 1716.

elected in 1715 for four years beyond its allotted three-year span. It was claimed that otherwise there would be danger of a new rebellion at election-time, and that frequent polls 'disturbed the people' and fostered corruption. The arguments for this Septennial Bill were clearly specious, and on 16 April in the Grand Committee the Bishop delivered a speech which was long remembered as a classic of parliamentary oratory. He began, like Shakespeare's Antony, with an echo of his opponents' arguments. For a wild moment his friends imagined that he was actually supporting the bill and praising the Ministry for having introduced it. He spoke in the usual Whig clichés of a 'glorious standing army and a Ministry that knows how effectually to engage the affections of the people', but gradually the note changed and soon the whole merged into a parody of a Whig parliamentary speech. One listener in the gallery reported how he 'complimented, bantered, and lashed the Ministry to a wonderful degree, so that both Whig and Tory wondered at it, and all agreed that it was with a infinite deal of wit. An essential part of it was to admire the happiness of this free nation that now was to be governed by a standing Parliament and a standing Army. It has much increased the hatred of the Court to him.'[1] But pungent witticisms and a powerful protest entered into the journal of the House were not enough. The Tory peers now numbered only twenty-five members, and they were continually outvoted. Indeed the passage of the Septennial Bill marked a definite stage in the evolution of an opposition. While Nottingham and his clan tended still to remain apart, the small body of Tory dissidents in the Lords drew closer in a union of grievance and despair. Bathurst, Arran, Strafford, Gower and Trevor now began to meet regularly at the deanery with the Bishop as their acknowledged parliamentary leader. When he heard of the famous speech on the Septennial Bill Jonathan Swift wrote at once to send his congratulations and to urge his friend to embrace the new position which circumstances had thrust upon him. 'It is a great deal your fault', he concluded, 'if you suffer us all to be undone; for God never gave such talents without expecting they should be used to preserve a nation.'[2]

[1] Timberland, iii. 41; *Pol. State*, xi. 455–56; H.M.C. *Stuart MSS.* ii. 131, Menzies to Inese, 19/30 Apr. 1716.
[2] *Swift Corr.* ii. 197–99, Swift to FR, 18 Apr. 1716.

3

Not all the Bishop's days were spent in the harsh world of political dispute. There were still occasions when cultured friends met at the deanery, when the wine passed quickly, and the talk was of literature or the latest poetry. But for the most part these later years were overshadowed by loneliness. Old friends like Swift, Bolingbroke and Ormonde were in permanent exile, and there were many acquaintances who feared that their political purity might be tainted if they were known to consort with such an inveterate enemy of the regime. Increasingly, too, his life and personality became distorted by punishing attacks of gout. At first they came once or twice in the year, but gradually more frequently. Eventually any minor ailment could bring on a period in which he was confined to bed and unable even to move without excruciating pain. At the height of an attack his hands and legs would swell so that he could neither write nor walk. For weeks afterwards he would be unable to stand and had to be carried from room to room by men-servants. He feared damp winter weather and longed, above all, for a return of the sun and an opportunity to be at ease in the old, rambling mansion of the Bishops of Rochester at Bromley. There, deep in the Kentish countryside, he had the rooms repaired and limped round the gardens planning new lawns and flower-beds. At Bromley he was a kind of squire and he could relax among his neighbours and tenants. He read extensively in English literature and the classics, but above all his time was taken up with an exhaustive study of the synoptic problem of the gospels. Hundreds of pages were filled with careful notes in his elegant handwriting, and he completed the first draft of a substantial scholarly work which sought to demonstrate the relationship of St. Matthew and St. Mark.[1] Perhaps such a theological endeavour was essential to the self-respect of a man who felt conscientious scruples about his own passionate involvement in the secular world and who feared that his reputation as a political priest might lead men to think less of the Church. 'The judicious world', he confided to Alexander Pope, 'is pleased to think that I delight in

[1] FR's notes are now in Westminster Abbey MSS. 65011 and 65014. A lengthy correspondence with Dr. John Potter is *E.C.*, ii. 175-96, 207-18.

work which I am obliged to undergo, and aim at things which I from my heart despise.'[1]

There was little mention of the Bishop's family. Mrs. Atterbury was a quiet woman whose life was bound up entirely with her home and family. Occasionally he spoke of her with affection, but she was never part of his public life nor did she share his literary interests. His son, Osborne Atterbury, born in 1705, was a difficult and wayward boy, intelligent enough to hold his own at Westminister School but excitable and irresponsible. The Bishop treated him with a grave courtesy, and bestowed his real love upon his daughters, Mary and Elizabeth. It gave him great happiness in 1715 to marry Mary to William Morrice, an able young Tory lawyer who subsequently became High Bailiff of Westminster by his father-in-law's influence. In September 1716, however, disaster struck suddenly when Elizabeth died. The child had been Mrs. Atterbury's constant companion, and the shock was more than her homely temperament could bear. Down to her own death in 1722 she was ailing and deeply disturbed in mind. When the Bishop's political activity is weighed in the balance, some consideration must be given not only to his wretched health but to the emptiness of his family life.

He found consolation in the younger men, to whom he gave generous patronage and a warm friendship. Samuel Wesley, elder brother of John and Charles, came to be a master at Westminster School on the Bishop's recommendation, and was subsequently ordained by him. Thomas Moore, his domestic chaplain, was a political sympathizer who could be relied upon not to reveal the identity of secret visitors to the deanery. But the most valued friendship was that with Alexander Pope. Though their correspondence begins only at the end of 1716, it is certain that they were already well acquainted.[2] They had much in common: a similar taste in literary matters, a deep-seated Toryism, and a determined independence of spirit. Atterbury was generally acknowledged a master of style; and his knowledge of literature, both English and European, was extensive. He was delighted to read the younger man's manuscripts and correct his proofs. Pope's polished manner

---

[1] *Pope Corr.* ii. 107, FR to Pope, 16 Mar. 1722.
[2] Ibid., i. 378, FR to Pope, Dec. 1716.

and carefully placed satire were completely to his liking, and he became a fervent admirer of his work.[1] Indeed Pope, who was only twenty-eight in 1716, became something of a son, and from their correspondence between 1717 and 1722 we are able to construct a vivid portrait of the Bishop's daily life. We know of his state of health, his moods, his circle of friends, and his movements between London and the countryside. Here he is to be found writing in a strain of light-hearted banter and familiar nonsense which contrasts pleasantly with the lengthening shadows of his political career.

The pastoral task which faced most eighteenth century bishops was frightening in its size and complexity. Great sees like London, Lincoln and Durham represented a labour quite beyond the reasonable capacity of one man. But beside such whales the diocese of Rochester was a minnow. It had only ninety-nine parishes, grouped in a single archdeaconry. The diocesan boundary came right up to the Thames at London Bridge and included the riverside towns of Deptford, Greenwich and Gravesend. But, for the most part, it consisted of small, unspoilt country towns and villages: Lewisham, Dartford, Bromley, Chislehurst and Tonbridge. At the far end of the diocese lay the cathedral church of Rochester, but from the Bishop's point of view this was of minor interest. The Dean and four of the six Prebendaries were appointed by the Crown and another stall was annexed to the provostship of Oriel College, Oxford. Only the Archdeacon of Rochester was collated by the Bishop of the diocese. In fact, Atterbury seems to have appeared in his cathedral on only one occasion in the whole of his episcopate, when in 1717 he conducted a mild and wholly uncontroversial visitation.[2] The centre of the diocese was his home at Bromley, and his clergy were accustomed to see him there or at the deanery. Indeed so familiar was the association of the Abbey with Rochester diocesan affairs that the Registrar could cheerfully commit the fearful solecism of describing one ordination as having taken place in his Lordship's 'cathedral church of St. Peter at Westminster'.[3]

[1] H.M.C. *Bath MSS.* iii. 451, FR to Matthew Prior, 1 Jan. 1718.
[2] See Beeching, p. 353.
[3] Legal Secretary to the Bishop of Rochester, 1 The Sanctuary, Westminster, S.W.1: 'Diocese of Rochester, Act Book, 1713–1821'. The reference is of date 21 Feb. 1714.

Atterbury proved a meticulous and energetic administrator. Immediately on his consecration he ordered that a new Act Book should be purchased, and thereafter his episcopal acts were recorded in careful detail. Unless prevented by severe illness he ordained in each of the four ember seasons: in the winter at Westminster and in the summer at Bromley, either in the parish church or in his own private chapel. Young Tories from the universities came flocking to him as a bishop who would sympathize with their political views, but there was no relaxing of the strict requirements. Candidates found themselves severely examined by the Bishop himself, and some who prided themselves on their political orthodoxy were disconcerted to discover that they fell short of his standards of theological competence.[1] With so small a diocese it was not necessary to rely on the formal machinery of visitations, and in fact Atterbury held only a primary visitation when in May 1716 he travelled to each of the three rural deaneries to meet his clergy and to entertain them to dinner. His visitation articles were remarkable for only one thing: an insistence on the strict letter of the Schism Act; all persons teaching in grammar schools were solemnly cited to appear and exhibit their episcopal licences in due form.[2] But in his address to the clergy he was entirely uncontroversial; he rejoiced that he was one of the very few bishops who could know each of his fellow-pastors personally, and he offered them advice which was devotional and pastoral in content.[3]

His relationship with the diocese was undoubtedly a happy one, but that with the great collegiate church at Westminster was decidedly more ambivalent. In one sense the Abbey represented the very essence of the Anglican tradition to which he was so genuinely devoted. The great church, the choral foundation, the splendour of state occasions, and the famous school: all these he cherished. He was jealous of the immunities of so privileged a royal peculiar, and insisted that even archbishops should observe the niceties of them.[4] But in many ways the Abbey brought out the worst in him. He disliked the dark rooms in the deanery and hated the foetid slums which

---

[1] Bodl. MS. Ballard 10, fo. 79, North to Charlett, 6 Jan. 1718.
[2] Beeching, pp. 217, 349.
[3] For the text, *E.C.,* iv. 339-52.
[4] Wake MSS. 6, FR to Wake, 10 Apr. 1716.

came up to the very gates of the precincts. And there was the uneasy fact of the existence of his colleagues, the Prebendaries of Westminster. It was unfortunate that among Atterbury's many gifts there was not to be counted the kind of patient courtesy which would allow him to work amicably with a distinguished body of senior clergymen. Even a hint of opposition called forth from him a display of temper and pugnacity, and trouble seems to have begun in earnest in 1715 over the disposal of the furniture and hangings used at the coronation of George I. By 1719 divisions among the members of the Chapter had gone so far that they produced what was perhaps the most virulent of all Atterbury's controversies: that over the siting of the new dormitory of Westminster School.[1] As long previously as 1710 a bequest had been received towards erecting a new building for the use of the King's Scholars but matters were still hanging fire when the new Dean arrived in 1713. Sir Christopher Wren was consulted and he advised that the building should be placed on a site in the college garden. Obviously the scheme now envisaged would be very costly but the Dean was successful in attracting some large donations including, surprisingly, one from the King and the Prince of Wales. But the moment the project became financially viable, trouble appeared in the Chapter. Certain of the Prebendaries seem suddenly to have realized that they would be deprived of a section of their garden, and they persuaded the headmaster, Dr. Robert Freind, to oppose the scheme and take the Dean to law. It was not until May 1721, and then after fighting the case up to an appeal in the House of Lords, that Atterbury won his case and Dr. Freind was dismissed with costs. In fact, the Dean was never to see the new dormitory, erected in 1730 to the Palladian designs of the Earl of Burlington, but by his persistence he had provided the King's Scholars with a home which was to endure until its destruction by incendiary bombs in May 1941. Today, in its reconstructed form, it may stand as a memorial to a truly formidable Dean of Westminster.

[1] Westminster Abbey: Chapter Minutes, 28 Jan. 1724, for a protest of right over the coronation perquisites, made after FR's deprivation. See also *A House of Kings*, ed. E. Carpenter (1966), pp. 200-1, for an account of the dormitory dispute.

CHAPTER ELEVEN

Jacobite Schemes, 1716–1720

I

IN the summer of 1716 the Jacobite cause was at its lowest ebb. After the miserable failure in Scotland the Pretender had been required to quit French territory and his little Court had come to rest amid the decayed palaces of the papal enclave at Avignon. James Francis Edward Stuart was an English prince who knew England only by report, and he had entered into a bitter inheritance. As a boy he had been brought up in a world of suffocating piety in the old house at St. Germain-en-Laye, and as a man he was surrounded by impoverished exiles who made self-pity a way of life. He was recognized as honourable, brave and invariably courteous. In the winter of 1713 he had been advised on all sides to renounce his Roman Catholicism and had resolutely refused to do so. He had the dark good looks of his family and a kind of quiet melancholy as of one who had come early to accept defeat and failure as his inevitable companions. The truth was that, for all his virtues, James was a cold and deeply reserved man and, for one who had to live his life amid intrigue and treachery, he was a fatally poor judge of character. Now, with the Earl of Mar as his Secretary of State, he came to fix all his hopes on exploiting some revolution in the diplomacy of Europe which might enable him to launch a new expedition against England or Scotland. He applied himself to any ruler whose ambitions or grievances might lead him to assist a Stuart 'restoration'. With the benefit of hindsight we may think James's efforts forlorn and hopeless, but it did not seem so to contemporaries. The magic of the Stuart name was still powerful, and the romantic cause of a legitimate heir had a strong attraction for those at home who had watched the crude process by which the Hanoverian oligarchy had established itself.

Surprisingly it was not until 1716 that the Jacobites fixed on the Bishop of Rochester as the man to organize their work in England.

Bolingbroke had suggested his name in May 1715 but no action had been taken and James seems to have been totally unaware of his existence. Now, with the loss of major Tory leaders into exile, the Jacobite agents in London found themselves in a real difficulty: they had no one of rank and political ability to act as the 'King's' representative in England. The Earls of Arran and Orrery were unwilling to assume the responsibility while Lord Oxford, in the Tower on an impeachment for high treason, was ready to dictate copious letters of advice but at the same time protest his complete inability actually to do anything. On all sides James was advised that the Bishop of Rochester was the only man for the task, though some of the correspondents sent warnings of his uncertain temper and independence of spirit. It was, however, easier to decide that Atterbury should be employed than to recruit him. In April Sir Redman Everard, a seedy gentleman who acted as a Jacobite messenger to and from England, was sent to try the Bishop out, but his reception was distinctly cool. Atterbury accepted with due respect the greetings which he brought from James and Mar, but for the rest refused to commit himself in any way. He gave it as his opinion that no Jacobite expedition to England or Scotland had the slightest chance unless it were backed by a full-scale professional army and was led by an experienced commander. He advised Mar to devote his energies to negotiating with the Regent of France or the King of Spain for a joint expedition. If that were procured, he promised 'to do his part in animating the clergy and warning the City of London from the pulpit the Sunday before the invasion is expected'.[1] But until that time he would do nothing, and he declined unequivocally an invitation to write regularly to James in his own hand. He knew only too well the efficiency of the British Secret Service and the assiduity with which the Cross-Channel mails were watched.

Despite all the facile accusations levelled at him, Atterbury had not been a Jacobite before 1716. He had no romantic or theoretical attachment to the cause of Stuart legitimacy, and for the policies and persons of Roman Catholics he continued to have a profound distaste. His loyalty was to the Church of England and to a vision of its place in English life and society. He became involved in

[1] H.M.C. *Stuart MSS.* ii. 67–70, Hamilton to Mar, 7 Apr. 1716; ibid., ii. 73-74, 8 Apr.

Jacobitism only when he despaired that the Tory party would ever be able to rise again in sufficient strength to restore the Church to its ancient status and authority. In 1716 it seemed that both Church and State had fallen into bondage to a Whig oligarchy which rested on a standing army and a ruthless exploitation of political corruption. A Jacobite military intervention now represented the only way to break the Whig hegemony and call back the opportunity lost in the last four years of the Queen. He was, of course, well aware of the perils and uncertainties of plotting to procure an invasion from abroad, and indeed he might have remained wholly uninvolved in intrigue had it not been for an unexpected change in the international situation in the late summer of 1716. Suddenly the Chevalier was presented with what seemed like the opportunity for which he had always prayed, when the Swedes began to discuss with the Jacobites the possibility of a joint expedition. It was, in fact, a moment of desperate crisis for Charles XII. His arch-enemy, George I of England, had been successful in creating a great Northern Alliance of powers pledged to expel the Swedes from Pomerania and the rest of their German possessions. All during the summer an Allied army had been collecting outside Copenhagen, ready to cross the Sound and invade Scania. Charles needed peace badly, but he could not go to the conference table empty-handed and all over Europe his ministers were ordered to search for allies and ready cash. Baron Görtz, the King's agent-at-large, applied himself to the governments of France and Holland, to private bankers, merchants and even to pirates, in an attempt to produce money. It was inevitable that eventually he should be led to the Jacobites, and in mid-August he made contact with General Arthur Dillon, James's agent in the French capital.[1] Dillon was loyal and assiduous, but a professional soldier without any training as a diplomat and quite unequipped to make an accurate assessment of the situation. It is clear that the Swedes made no actual promises but they hinted that in return for immediate financial assistance their King was ready to join the Jacobites in a strategic blow against England and George I. Even the bare suggestion was enough to excite men who existed precariously on a diet of schemes and rumours, and at once they wrote off in all directions to drum up money and support.

[1] Ibid., ii. 380-81, Mar to Dillon, 16/27 Aug. 1716.

Mar now regarded it as essential to recruit the Bishop of
Rochester, and on 17 August he ordered one of his agents, John
Menzies, to carry a personal letter to him in London. He did not
hesitate to describe in detail the advanced state of preparations for a
joint Jacobite-Swedish expedition, and he appealed to the Bishop
now, at this critical moment, to accept a commission as James's
official resident in England with full power to collect the money
which the Swedes demanded before setting out. A similar missive
was sent to Lord Arran, asking him to receive appointment as
commander-in-chief of all James's forces in England.[1] Atterbury was
cautious and very suspicious. He questioned Menzies repeatedly
and he absolutely refused to have in his possession any official
letter or commission; but the bait of a foreign, professional army
was too tempting to refuse, and he agreed to organize a collection
and to liaise with Count Gyllenborg, the Swedish Minister in
London. It was to prove a nerve-racking business, and he warned
Menzies again and again not to use the ordinary Cross-Channel
mails and in no circumstances to mention his own name or that of
any of his associates. As Gyllenborg himself put it: 'they run the
hazard of their lives and fortunes in declaring themselves, so that
they will not speak but upon good security.'[2] At times the whole
operation was only borne up by the ever optimistic reports which
Mar and Menzies regularly supplied.

James's initial request was for £50,000, but this the Bishop
realized was an impossible amount. He would undertake only for
£20,000 and even this, he stressed, would require a united effort
from all the various Jacobite groups in England.[3] An essential first
step was to ensure the co-operation of Lord Oxford, and the political
world was astonished to learn that the Bishop of Rochester had
actually been to call on his old adversary at his lodgings in the
Tower. But, in fact, the interview was not a success. The memory of
those abrasive pamphlets of 1714 still rankled on both sides, and
Oxford treated his visitor to a full measure of his usual devious
conversation. It was clear that nothing much was to be expected

---

[1] Ibid., ii. 386–87, Mar to FR, 17/28 Aug. 1716; ibid., iv. 62, report of
John Ogilvie, Aug. 1716.
[2] *Parl. Hist.* vii. 401, Gyllenborg to Görtz, 2/13 Nov. 1716.
[3] H.M.C. *Stuart MSS.* v. 527–31, Downs to James, 6 Jan. 1717.

from the Harleian faction and in the end the money was raised from three principal sources.[1] Atterbury and his friends subscribed £5,000; a group connected with Charles Caesar, one-time M.P. for Hertford, found another £5,000; while a body of Roman Catholic gentry, organized by the eccentric priest, Father Thomas Southcott, gathered in no less than £8,000. All had to be carried on in the greatest secrecy, and Atterbury would have nothing to do with the Papists or their money, and insisted that they send it directly to France; but even so the quantity of gold coin was vast and its possession put them all in great danger. The strain of all these elaborate precautions and clandestine meetings told severely on Atterbury and he kept up a continual barrage of complaints to Menzies, who reported back to his masters in piteous terms the indignities he endured at the hands of this irascible Bishop.[2] By mid-December all the Jacobites in London were in a sadly jittery state.

Everything depended on the Swedish expedition, but in this Atterbury had been grossly deceived. Baron Görtz had in no sense committed his King to an expedition to England. The Swedes were not dishonest men; they had great sympathy with James's cause; and they knew that Charles XII would never countenance a direct lie.[3] In fact, on 12 November, with commendable frankness Görtz explained the precise position to Gyllenborg: his hope was that the money being collected in England could be regarded as a loan, to be repaid as soon as opportunity allowed. The Swedish envoy in his turn was entirely honest with the English Jacobites, and he took Görtz's letter to 'one of the principals at his own house'. This was Menzies who acted between Gyllenborg and the Bishop. But the revelation that the Swedes had no definite plans shocked the little Scots agent to the very core:

He asked me [reported Gyllenborg] whether I had spoken of it to anyone of his party? And I telling him I had not, he desired me, for the love of God, not to do it. We were made to believe from Avignon, said he, that all went on currently: that Baron Görtz had accepted our

---

[1] Ibid., iii. 111, 219, Ogilvie to Mar, 10/21 Oct., 5/16 Nov. 1716; ibid., iii. 235-38, Menzies to Mar, 8/19 Nov.

[2] Ibid., iii. 285, Menzies to Mar, 22 Nov./3 Dec. 1716.

[3] For a useful account of Swedish diplomacy, see John J. Murray, *George I, the Baltic and the Whig Split of 1717* (1969), ch. xi.

offer, and had given positive assurances on the part of the King of
Sweden, of his assistance.

Menzies was overcome with fear that this news would come to
Atterbury, and he besought Gyllenborg

that you do not make it known to any person what I see our Court of
Avignon conceals with so much care. If you act otherwise, you will
destroy the credit of the Chevalier de St. Georges here . . . and you
will make his adherents your implacable enemies.[1]

On a visit down to the Bishop at Bromley Menzies made no mention
of this latest news, and allowed Atterbury to give him 'further
directions how to spur and promote matters as much as possible.'[2]

Thus far the Swedes had been perfectly straightforward in their
dealings, but at the end of November Görtz in Holland became
desperate. With the news of a famine at home he knew that he had
to have money, and so on his own responsibility he sent off to his
colleague in London a wholly imaginary plan for an expedition to
England, mentioning the readiness of 13,000 Swedish troops, of
whom no less than 4,000 were cavalry. When Gyllenborg showed
this letter to Menzies the agent was overwhelmed with relief, and
he assured the envoy that the £10,000 in gold was ready if only he
could be given an official receipt 'that he might have something to
show those who made this collection, supposing that hereafter they
should ask for it'.[3] Unaccountably Gyllenborg refused to give one,
and Menzies returned to Atterbury at Bromley to report. The
Bishop's patience with this tortuous and dangerous business was
now exhausted, and he took an instant decision. On New Year's day
he travelled up to Westminster and made arrangements for the
immediate disposal of all the cash in hand. Menzies was ordered to
have it packed into small parcels and dispatched at once to Mary of
Modena at St. Germains. As far as Atterbury was concerned that
was an end to the matter, and on 3 January he was back at Bromley
with a great load off his mind. When Gyllenborg thought better of
his refusal and offered a receipt in return for an immediate delivery

---

[1] *Parl. Hist.* vii. 404–5, Görtz to Gyllenborg, 12/23 Nov. 1716; ibid., 405–6,
Gyllenborg to Görtz, 23 Nov./4 Dec.

[2] H.M.C. *Stuart MSS.* iii. 307, Menzies to Mar, 29 Nov./10 Dec. 1716.

[3] *Parl. Hist.* vii. 412-13, Gyllenborg to Görtz, 21 Dec. 1716/1 Jan. 1717.

of the cash, he was adamant. 'He who had the direction of the whole affair' had washed his hands of it.[1]

He would have done so with even greater alacrity had he known how great his danger really was. In fact, the British Government was well aware of a Swedish-Jacobite negotiation, and as early as October the Post Office had begun to intercept the letters between Görtz and Gyllenborg. Soon the Secretaries of State were reading with mounting alarm a sequence of correspondence which seemed to reveal definite and detailed plans for an invasion.[2] Fortunately for Atterbury and his associates no specific names were mentioned and the Ministry could only guess at the identity of the conspirators who had collected so large a sum of money. For months they copied the letters, had them deciphered by their team of experts, and then allowed the originals to continue on their way. But in January 1717 things seemed to have reached a note of sufficient menace for action to be imperative, and on 29th a special meeting of the Cabinet Council was summoned.[3] Orders were given to arrest Gyllenborg, in spite of his diplomatic immunity, and for all his papers to be seized; Charles Caesar and Sir Joseph Banks were taken into custody; and an official request was made to the Dutch Government that they should detain Görtz and his entire staff. Amid such public excitements Atterbury and his friends did what might have been expected of them; they froze into silence and inactivity. Only Menzies had the temerity to write a guarded letter to his masters in Avignon to report that 'our plot is at present at a stand'.[4] It is ironical that it was just at this moment that the Bishop of Rochester received what by Jacobite standards was a mark of signal honour. On 15 January King James had written him a letter in his own hand, thanking him for his diligence and suggesting that the collection should now be raised to £70,000.[5] But there was no reply. The Bishop had gone to ground.

[1] H.M.C. *Stuart MSS.* iii. 429–30, 446; *Parl. Hist.* vii. 414–19.

[2] Coxe, W., ii. 89, Townshend to Stanhope, 23 Sept./4 Oct. 1716; ibid., ii. 114, 12/23 Oct.

[3] *Pol. State*, xiii. 147. Copies of the intercepted correspondence are S.P. 107/1A, 1B. Swedish correspondence in the Uppsala Archives has been printed in *Handlingar rörande Skandinaviens historia* (Stockholm, 1822), vol. x.

[4] H.M.C. *Stuart MSS.* iii. 538–9, Menzies to Inese, 11/22 Feb. 1717.

[5] Ibid., iii. 475, James to FR, 15/26 Jan. 1717.

The Swedish plot was a welcome gift to Sunderland and Stanhope, and they determined to extract every possible political advantage from it. At the State Opening of Parliament on 20 February King George's speech made great play with the complicity of 'desperate and designing men' among his own subjects, and he appealed for supplies sufficient to allow him an army large enough to repel any would-be invader. Atterbury, sitting in his place on the Bishops' Bench, listened grimly; and the day was not to end before he was submitted to an hour of exquisite discomfort. By the King's command the Duke of Roxburghe began to read the texts of the intercepted letters of Görtz and Gyllenborg, and the Bishop could now realize the full extent of the manner in which he had been misled by Mar and Menzies. All that he could not know was that even Görtz's invasion plan had been a figment of the imagination of a hard-pressed diplomat. Atterbury's anger, vented principally on the head of the luckless Menzies, was terrible. He became convinced that the management of business in Avignon and Paris was not to be trusted, and that Mar in particular was a dangerous and deceitful man. For a while Lord Oxford could attribute all this to the Bishop's well-known irascibility and suggest in characteristic fashion that a little well-placed flattery might help the mood to pass, but by the summer of 1717 James had become very alarmed lest he should have lost his most useful supporter in England.

2

After the debâcle Atterbury resolved to have nothing more to do with Jacobite intrigue. He had no illusions about the efficiency of the Government's intelligence service nor about the crassly unreliable character of those who served James. It was apparent, too, that only a severe disturbance of the diplomatic system established at Utrecht would allow any military power to undertake an invasion of the British Isles, and that an increasing concord between England and France made it less and less likely that they would permit so dangerous a breach of the European peace. And yet emotionally and politically it was hard for the Bishop entirely to abandon his involvement in the Stuart cause. The Hanoverians had become inseparably linked in his mind with the destruction of the Tory party and the diminution of the influence of the Church of England; for him, and those other Tories who had watched the establishment of the oligarchy, Jacobitism held out the only hope for a sudden and complete revolution in English political affairs. Atterbury decided on many occasions to sever all connection with the cause, and yet every new political opportunity in England and every fresh rumour of a change in the international situation had him once again listening to the persuasive talk of Jacobite emissaries.

In fact, the Tories were presented with an unexpected opportunity to challenge the Government in the first half of the year 1717. Until this time the strength of the Whig position had been a firm unity among their leading men, and this had resulted in assured majorities in either House. But this concord proved increasingly difficult to maintain in face of the controversial foreign and domestic policies of the two leading Ministers. Sunderland and Stanhope pursued schemes in Northern Europe which were highly congenial to George I but repellent to backbenchers and City merchants who deeply feared involvement in some new continental war with its inevitable high expenditure. And the gradual movement towards aristocratic political supremacy had begun to raise up widespread fears in sections of the community upon whose acquiescence the regime relied. Eventually, at the end of 1716, personal tensions and disagreements in the Ministry resulted in a sudden coup by which Viscount Townshend and Robert Walpole were summarily dismissed from office by the King. By the end of February they had embarked on a course of opposition which jeopardized the Government's normal majorities, and in this they were enthusiastically seconded by the Tories under Shippen and Wyndham. For the first time since 1714 the Administration had to face a really dangerous parliamentary attack. Indeed almost immediately the opposition in the Lords revived sufficiently for Atterbury and his friends to procure the formal acquittal and release from the Tower of Lord Oxford.

But the Bishop's real hope lay in a revival of 'the Church in Danger' theme. Sunderland and Stanhope were generally understood to be deeply anti-clerical and they were determined, as far as possible, to dismantle the structure of Anglican privilege and admit Dissenters to full political rights. In this they clearly went too far

and too fast. Their nominations to the Bench of Bishops were confined to the most compliant of their political clients, and the
appointment of Benjamin Hoadly to the bishopric of Bangor in late
1715 shocked even their own supporters. By 1717 there was a
serious division of opinion in the existing episcopate. Ministerial
supporters like Bishop Trimnell of Norwich and Edmund Gibson,
from 1716 Bishop of Lincoln, stressed the need to build up a strong
body of 'Church-Whigs' who could provide a bridge between Whig
politicians and the Anglican clergy; but even they found the substance of their masters' policy hard to digest. Rumours were heard
of bills to regulate the universities and control charity schools, and
in 1716 a bill to displace the minister of the parish from his traditional control of the charity funds was narrowly defeated. All this
was deeply abhorrent to the man who in late 1715 had been promoted to the archbishopric of Canterbury: not because he was the
Ministry's choice but because he was the friend and confessor of the
Princess of Wales. William Wake had been the principal episcopal
supporter of the Junto in the days of Queen Anne, but he now
became convinced that the Ministry was intent on inflicting
gratuitous harm on the Church. He was grievously distressed when
on 13 March 1717 he learned privately from Lord Chancellor Cowper
that they intended to repeal not only the Occasional Conformity
and Schism Acts but the sacramental Test as well.[1]

It was at this tense moment that Bishop Hoadly intervened with
a sermon preached on 31 March before the King. Apparently intending to prepare the way for the repeal legislation, he launched himself into a characteristic exegesis of the text, 'My kingdom is not of
this world'. In his usual remorseless manner he examined, and rejected, the notion that Christ had committed any power or
authority to the Church. The Saviour had 'left behind him no
visible humane authority, no Vice-gerents, who can be said properly
to supply his place; no Interpreters upon whom his subjects are
absolutely to depend; no Judges over the consciences or religion of
his people'.[2] The only thing of importance in theological matters
was the sincerity with which individuals held their private religious

---

[1] See Norman Sykes, *William Wake* (1957), p. 115; Panshanger (Cowper)
MSS. 49, Wake to Cowper, 14 Mar. 1717.
[2] B. Hoadly, *The Nature of the Kingdom, or Church, of Christ* (1717).

opinions, and therefore there could be no compulsion 'in affairs of conscience and eternal salvation'. The storm of protest was immediate and terrible. By the end of the year nearly one thousand separate publications had testified to the emotions aroused, and the atmosphere recalled the heady days of the Sacheverell Trial. When the Lower House of Convocation proceeded to draw up a 'Solemn Representation', naming Hoadly as an 'enemy to the Doctrine and Authority of the Church of England', the Government took justifiable fright. The repeal legislation was withdrawn and two days later, as the lower clergy prepared to deliver their protest, the Archbishop sent down a schedule of prorogation. He did so with a heavy heart on the direct instructions of the Ministers.[1] His distress would have been even greater had he known that Convocation would not again be allowed to do business for more than a hundred and thirty years.

All this found the Bishop of Rochester in excellent spirits. He was, of course, deeply disgusted at the Government's policy towards the Church and yet he was delighted that they should thus overplay their hand. The immense agitation against Hoadly gave him hope that there would be a strong revival of Tory sentiment and a nation-wide movement of opinion against the Sunderland Administration. It was, too, a new and pleasant experience to cross the Thames to Lambeth and find there a cordial welcome from the Archbishop of Canterbury. Jacobite correspondents in London reported all this back and were amazed at the change in the Bishop's mood; and their accounts were sufficient for James to essay a new approach. It was, in fact, a moment when he badly needed advice and assistance, for in the spring he had been forced to leave Avignon and retire beyond the Alps into Italy. Against all reasonable hope he still believed in the possibility of a Swedish expedition if only £100,000 could be raised from his supporters in England, and he resolved to send across to London the one man who might be able to persuade the Bishop to act. The Honourable James Murray, a younger son of Viscount Stormont, had been one of the rebels of 1715; he was youthful, charming, intelligent and deeply ambitious. In the midst of the acrimonious rivalries of the Jacobite Court he had

---

[1] Wake's diary, fo. 190, 8 May 1717; N.L.W. Ottley MS. 1716, FR to Adam Ottley, 7 May.

already established considerable personal influence with James. Now at the deanery at Westminster he listened patiently to the Bishop's stream of complaints, flattered him, sympathized, and promised fair dealing and complete security in the future. All letters would now be carried to France personally by the Reverend George Kelly, an Irish Nonjuring clergyman with a long experience of undercover work.[1] At last, after long hesitation and with much grumbling, Atterbury agreed once again to co-operate.

He did so because his mind had begun to nourish a new and bold plan, based on the current political situation. Any invasion would be perilous in view of the Government's massive military forces, but it might have a chance of success if it had supporters in high places and even within the Government itself. His assessment of the present state of affairs was that the Ministry could not last out the session. Walpole and Townshend could never be brought to work with Sunderland and Stanhope again, and eventually the Ministers would be forced to approach the Tories. But the Tories must not accept any of their early offers. Atterbury in the Lords and Shippen in the Commons must keep up the attack until the Government was at the point of collapse. Then, at that moment, James must contact Sunderland and secretly offer to take him into his service: 'they are men of vast ambition and no principles; one may therefore think it would be no unreasonable measure for them to serve the King, and thereby at once secure themselves and gratify their ambition.'[2] In Paris General Dillon's response to this advice was wholly in character. Kelly was ordered to return to London at once with a highly optimistic account of current negotiations with the Swedes and with a request for an immediate collection of the £100,000.

As Atterbury dwelt on his scheme to suborn the leading Ministers the more its boldness and directness appealed to him and, on Kelly's return, he took an important decision. Until this time he had judged it an unnecessary risk to write personally to James, but now as a token of his earnest expectation he resolved to do so. Disguising

---

[1] H.M.C. *Stuart MSS.* iv. 453, Murray to Mar, 3/14 July 1717; see also *Memoirs of the Life, Travels and Transactions of the Reverend Mr. George Kelly* (1736).

[2] H.M.C. *Stuart MSS.* v. 557–60, a memorial dictated by FR to Murray, 3/14 July 1717; R. A. Stuart 22/8, FR to Mar, 15/26 Aug. On 17 Sept. Mar wrote to Sunderland offering to open negotiations with him: B.M. Add. MSS. 9129, fos. 41–46.

his distinctive hand and adopting the pseudonym 'Robert Young', he penned a letter which revealed something of the longing which lay behind his support for the Stuart cause:

> I have often reproached myself for my silence, after so many encouragements to write; but I depended upon it that the best construction would be put upon that silence by one who was well acquainted with the manner in which I was employed. My heart is better known to you, Sir, than my hand; and my actions, I hope, have spoken for me better than any letters could do; and to those actions I shall always appeal, which I intend, by God's blessing, shall be uniform and entirely of a piece to the last moment of my life.[1]

Now he looked forward eagerly to the winter session of Parliament when the attack on the Ministry could be resumed. He managed to collect some money, and with elaborate secrecy parcels of coin were dispatched to Dillon in Paris. He made continual enquiries about Sweden and Russia, and strict instructions were given that he was to be informed immediately there was news of an expedition, so that he and his friends could co-ordinate their action in the Lords and Commons. Events were already preparing for a hard-fought battle when it was learned that Bishop Gibson had held a meeting with other episcopal supporters of the Ministry to plan for the repeal of the Occasional Conformity Act. Atterbury was amazed that they should thus play into the Tories' hands. Reporting all this to old Bishop Trelawny, he remarked acidly that 'these are very extraordinary steps; the effects of wisdom, no doubt, but of so deep a wisdom that I, for my part, am not able to fathom it'.[2]

Within days, however, his hopes were rudely dashed. Just after the State Opening of Parliament news came of a dramatic quarrel in the Royal Family and a complete rupture between the King and the Prince of Wales. The scandal and upheaval were immense, but for the Tories it was a disaster. Walpole and Townshend could now press home their parliamentary attack secure in the knowledge that they had the support of the heir to the throne and his personal following of M.P.s; and their interest in co-operation with the Tories, never very intense, withered away. In the Commons Shippen

---

[1] R. A. Stuart 22/7, FR to James, 15/26 Aug. 1717.
[2] *E.C.*, ii. 46–48, FR to Trelawny, 8 Nov. 1717; Wake MSS. 20, Gibson to Wake, 22 Nov.; Bodl. MS. Add. A. 269, fo. 71, Gibson to Nicolson, 28 Nov.

failed dismally when he launched an attack on the size and expense of the standing army. In the Lords things went even worse, for at this critical moment the Bishop of Rochester was removed from leading the opposition peers. As the battle commenced he lay at home in a darkened room, prostrate with the worst attack of the gout he had yet endured. When at last George Kelly was allowed in to sit by his bedside he found him feverish with fears and anxieties, and far too ill to give coherent advice. He could only repeat that the Ministry was to 'be so pressed and distressed as to be forced by the end of the session to take shelter under a scheme'. He asked again and again whether news had come that a powerful invasion force was on its way.[1] But as he emerged from his pain and confusion the Bishop realized that all his plans had gone astray. As he lay in his sickroom he had time to reflect on the poor showing of the Tories in Parliament and he grew more and more embittered. What had Lord Oxford and all that clan contributed? Had Lords Poulett, Foley, Dartmouth, Mansel or Bingley, or Bishop Bisse of Hereford, played a vigorous part in the House? Had they or Auditors Harley and Foley taken any part in the dangerous business of collecting money? It began to look as if Atterbury and his friends, Lords Arran, Strafford, Orrery, North and Bathurst, with Shippen and Wyndham in the Commons, were to do all the work and take all the risks, while Oxford wrote fulsome letters to James and received all the thanks.

The English supporters were divided and discouraged, but were yet capable of being revived by news, real or imaginary, of an impending expedition. What they did not expect was the sudden collapse, in the late spring, of the whole Jacobite chain of communications across Europe. The death of Mary of Modena meant that St. Germains ceased to be a Stuart palace and a staging-post between Italy and England. Soon even the lesser agents who provided the postal service had been expelled or moved on. In April James Murray left London to join his master in Italy, and in July even George Kelly was withdrawn. Before contact was finally broken, Atterbury described for James's benefit the despair and lassitude

---

[1] H.M.C. *Stuart MSS.* v. 286, Kelly to Dillon, 5/16 Dec. 1717; R. A. Stuart 25/71, FR to Mar, 14/25 Dec. [Kelly's handwriting]; H.M.C. *Stuart MSS.* v. 609, a memorial of same date, dictated by FR.

which afflicted those who had been his supporters: 'they sit quiet, without making any step towards the men in power, and live upon hopes of schemes which have no colour of probability in them . . . That one word, the Army, is a charm that lays all of them to sleep.'[1] He was right. So out-of-touch were the English Jacobites that when in November 1718 James was actually presented with his greatest opportunity since 1715, a real Swedish-Spanish-Jacobite expedition, the British Government knew far more of what was going on than did Atterbury and his friends. The Secret Service was well aware that Cardinal Alberoni, as an act of revenge for the destruction of the Spanish Mediterranean fleet by Byng off Cape Passaro, had invited the Duke of Ormonde to Madrid.[2] The Abbé Dubois, the French first Minister, supplied regular and accurate information to the British envoy while Atterbury, who had heard nothing from James, had to confess that he was 'much in the dark and confounded with lies'.[3] When on 10 March King George publicly announced that an invasion fleet was actually on its way, none can have known better than the Bishop of Rochester that the English Jacobites had made no preparations at all to receive it. But on the night of 18 March the armada was shattered by a storm off Finisterre, and the battered and dismasted ships limped slowly back to Spain. If they had attempted a landing in England their annihilation would have been inevitable. The Jacobite reputation for continual ill-fortune held fast.

3

It thus turned out that the opposition was at a grave disadvantage when in the winter session of 1718 the Sunderland Ministry decided that the time had come to force through their repeal of the Occasional Conformity and Schism Acts. The project was kept a close secret until the last moment, and even Archbishop Wake knew nothing of it until the morning of 13 December, the very day on

---

[1] R. A. Stuart 32/145, a memorial of FR, dated 15/26 June 1718. In a letter to James, 14/25 June [ibid. 32/142], a letter from Shippen was enclosed.
[2] H.M.C. *Stuart MSS.* vii. 644; S.P. 78/162/245, Stair to Craggs, 13/24 Oct. 1718; see W. K. Dickson, *The Jacobite Attempt of 1719* (Edinburgh, 1895), for an edition of Ormonde's letters.
[3] Bodl. MS. Ballard 32, fo. 66, Bishop to Charlett, 16 Sept. 1718; B.M. Stowe MSS. 231, fo. 225, Stair to Robethon, 29 Oct./9 Nov.; H.M.C. *Stuart MSS.* vii. 652, Mar to Dillon, 9/20 Dec.

which Stanhope introduced his bill into the Lords. Atterbury had
had enough foresight to organize a private whip to ensure that the
Tory peers came up in good time, but he was out of the House and
it was with difficulty that his friends secured time for a full-length
debate.[1] But on the 18th the chamber was crowded with peers who
knew well that they had come to hear a debate of major constitutional significance. The measure before them, 'for strengthening the
Protestant interest', was designed not only to repeal the two acts
passed in Anne's reign but to abolish the Anglican sacramental
test as well. It was an issue which deeply divided the Bench of
Bishops, and the first day was given over to their speeches.

The Archbishop of Canterbury began with a judicious plea not
to effect this deliberate alteration in the alliance of Church and
State in England; a repeal of these acts would be taken by many as
a formal renunciation of the terms of the establishment; the Church
would be left with all the disadvantages of a connection with the
State without any corresponding advantages.[2] Archbishop Dawes
of York spoke rather more vehemently on the same theme, and
became involved in a personal clash with Bishop Hoadly who declared for complete religious freedom for Dissenters coupled with a
complete subordination of the Church of England to the civil
authority. It was this outrageous proposition which brought the
Bishop of Rochester to his feet in a fiercely attacking speech. The
bill, he declared, was not designed merely to relieve Nonconformists: it was part of a deliberate policy on the part of the present set
of Ministers. Successive measures from them showed that they
wished to damage the Church and ruin its place in English life. He
had always known that this latest attempt would be made and
'he was sorry to have been a prophet, since, in his opinion, this
Bill overturned the foundations of the security of the Church'.
Let none doubt the importance of the change. The Whigs proposed
to abrogate part of the Act of Uniformity, because henceforth
schools would no longer be subject to episcopal authority. He
concluded on a threatening note: that 'we live in a changeable

---

[1] Wake's diary, fo. 211, 13 Dec. 1718; H.M.C. *Sutherland MSS.*, p. 189,
FR to Lord Gower, 10 Oct.

[2] For the best account of the debate, see the notes of Dudley Ryder in
the Harrowby MSS. 432, document 29, part 3.

country, and the hardships which the Dissenters bring now upon the Church may, one day or other, be severely, and with more justice, retaliated upon them.'[1] Bishop of Kennett of Peterborough, in the next speech, drew the attention of the House to a remarkable fact: that whereas all the other speakers had defended the Occasional Conformity Act, the Bishop of Rochester had been 'pleased to offer most in defence of the Schism Bill; from whence your Lordships, with submission, may learn to be wise: for the very wisdom of Solomon, my Lords, was discovered by this test, that he could discern who was the parent of the child.'[2]

Tempers were rising fast, and the next day it was the turn of the lay peers. Among other speeches, Lord Coningsby attempted humour with Atterbury's description of himself as a prophet. He

compared the Bishop of Rochester to Balaam the prophet and designed to be witty on it, in making the Bishop a false prophet, to whom the Bishop rose up and answered pungently, and concluded that Balaam was reproved by his ass, but that he was never reproved by anyone but the Lord Coningsby, upon which the House for some time was in a great laughter, and that noble Lord has got by it a new title: the *Bishop of Rochester's Pad*.[3]

For weeks the town echoed with this devastating piece of repartee, but it was small compensation. Though the Tories managed to delete the clause on the sacramental test, the Occasional Conformity and Schism Acts could not be saved. In the face of the Government's majority, Atterbury and his allies fought the repeal step by step, entering their protests in the journal of the House; but on 23 December, by 55 to 33, the bill was given its third reading. In the immediate aftermath the Bishop meditated sadly on what he could only regard as a public disavowal of the Anglican character of the Constitution, and he thought with bitterness of those of his fellow-bishops who had gone into the voting lobby at the Ministry's behest. He could see in the future only a going down into bondage as the episcopate was recruited with the pliable adherents of a political oligarchy.[4]

---

[1] Timberland, iii. 104.
[2] B.M. Lansdowne MSS. 1039, fo. 197.
[3] Bodl. MS. Ballard 32, fo. 76, Bishop to Charlett, 26 Dec. 1718.
[4] N.L.W. Ottley MS. 1704, FR to Ottley, 3 Jan. 1719.

The defeat in Parliament and the Jacobite catastrophe produced in him a kind of nervous collapse. In May 1719 he was ill so continuously that he became alarmed about his health and left his country retreat at Bromley to go in August to take the waters at Bath. At the spa he found the Archbishop of Canterbury, and those two former opponents sat and complained together about the persecuted and betrayed state of the Church.[1] But the cure was ineffective, and in late September his friends were worried to find him still unable to walk or even write, and with his natural brightness diminished by constant pain.[2] He was forced to ask other bishops to ordain his candidates, and on the rare occasions when he appeared in the House of Lords he was treated as an invalid and not asked to serve on committees. It was a wretched time when personal quarrels and disputes multiplied, and he was too ill to deal with them effectively. It seemed indeed as if all chance for Jacobite plotting had come to an end.

[1] Ibid. 1702, FR to Ottley, 24 May 1719; Wake's diary, fo. 220: 24 Aug.
[2] Bodl. MS. Ballard 32, fo. 103, Bishop to Charlett, 23 Sept. 1719.

Plate 5

The Rt. Honourable
John Ereskin Earl of Marr.

W. Hyffell ad Vivum delin.   L. True excudit.   P. Vanderbank Sculp.

John Erskine, Earl of Mar

Plate 6

Robert Walpole

Plate 7

James Francis Edward Stuart, 'the Old Pretender'

Plate 8

Jacobite medal, dated 1721, showing the white horse of Hanover trampling on the lion and unicorn, and offering James as 'the only salvation'

CHAPTER TWELVE

The Atterbury Plot, 1720–1722

I

THE revival of Jacobite conspiracy was due not to any recovery of spirit by James's English supporters but to the shattering financial crisis which struck the Sunderland-Stanhope Ministry in the autumn of 1720. Until this moment the political regime had seemed invulnerable. In the spring George I was reconciled to his son, and Walpole and Townshend were able to rejoin the Administration. Their co-operation with the chief Ministers was more apparent than real and they could do nothing to challenge Sunderland's position in the King's confidence and regard. Indeed political activity was at such a low level that the directors of the South Sea Company were allowed to engage in a complex financial transaction: to take over the Government's outstanding debts and receive in exchange a fixed rate of interest. Clearly the success of such a project depended on public confidence and an expectation of vast profits; and so, aided and abetted by Ministers, the directors embarked on the promotion of a 'bubble' in the shares. For a while their efforts were wildly successful and the price of stock rose to a staggering height, but in late August the pace began to slacken and in September a ghastly fall gathered momentum. Thousands who had bought shares on credit were ruined. Aristocrats, clergymen, pensioners, colleges, and charities sustained enormous losses while some individuals were seen to have made vast profits. As the full extent of the upheaval became clear the Government found itself caught up in a major political crisis.

No one was more astonished than the English Jacobites.[1] The Bishop of Rochester was still an invalid at his country house, and the

---

[1] A useful general account, making use of the Stuart papers, is G. H. Jones, *The Mainstream of Jacobitism* (Cambridge, Mass., 1954). They have also been used in Paul S. Fritz, 'Jacobitism and the English Government, 1717-1731' (Cambridge unpublished Ph.D. dissertation, 1967), though this differs in detail and argument from the present book.

other leaders had ceased to meet or consult together. Indeed when James on his return from Spain into Italy had written to them one by one in his own hand, the response had been pathetic. Atterbury did not even reply for seven months, while the rest returned urgent pleas that absolutely nothing should be attempted which might bring down upon their heads the full weight of their enemies' spite vengeance.[1] The Bishop alone could hold out a vestige of hope. In May 1720 he wrote to inform James that the financial world was 'to the highest degree uneasy, and will be found to be so in a remarkable manner should anything happen from abroad'. But even he was not prepared for the full magnitude of the disaster when it came, and he could only express to Alexander Pope his amazement at the suddenness and extent of what had happened.[2] At once the English Jacobites wrote express to Paris and to James in Urbino to tell of the wonderful, unexpected opportunity which now presented itself. But what could they do? They had no plans and they had no money. The Chevalier was equally nonplussed. He drew up a dramatically phrased declaration; urgent appeals were sent off to the Courts of France and Spain; and Dillon drew up a scheme for an immediate small-scale invasion which would not require foreign assistance. But in mid-October it was decided that everything must wait upon a reconstruction of their organization in England and that above all they must fix upon a definite leader. It was agreed that the Bishop of Rochester must be their man.[3]

When, however, Kelly travelled across to England he found the situation there far more complex than anyone in Paris had suspected. The Bishop at Bromley was still half-crippled and distinctly short-tempered. He read the Chevalier's declaration and gave it a cursory approval, but he poured scorn on Dillon's plan for a small-scale, unsupported invasion. It was dangerous nonsense: 'the time is lost for any attempt which shall not be of force sufficient to encourage people to come into it.' He was ready to travel up to town and

---

[1] R. A. Stuart 45/57, James to FR, 6/17 Oct. 1719; 46/93, Orrery to James, 1 May 1720; 46/147, Sir William Wyndham to James, 14 May 1720; 46/110, FR [signing himself '1376'] to James, 6 May 1720.

[2] *Pope Corr.* ii. 56, FR to Pope, 28 Sept. 1720.

[3] R. A. Stuart 49/99, Dillon to FR, 14/25 Oct. 1720; 49/98, Dillon to James, 17/28 Oct.

consult with other leading Jacobites, but his own advice was clear: they must wait until the spring of 1722 when Parliament would be dissolved and a General Election was in progress. Against that time James must plan for a really substantial military invasion with a professional army, and the Tory politicians at home must find ways to keep the excitement and discontent at fever-pitch.[1]

The obvious course was to launch an all-out parliamentary attack on the Ministry. Sunderland and his colleagues had been involved in some very shady transactions, and they were undoubtedly in grave danger of impeachment. Robert Walpole's scheme to restore financial confidence and raise the price of South Sea stock was coldly received, and it was soon apparent that the two Houses were bent on revenge. Shippen in the Commons, and Cowper, Wharton, Gower, and Orrery in the Lords joined in an attack the fury of which seemed to compare with past moments of high constitutional crisis. By the end of January select committees of each House were sifting the evidence, and their enquiries moved inexorably towards the Ministers themselves. Soon John Aislabie, Chancellor of the Exchequer, and Charles Stanhope, Secretary of the Treasury, were fighting for their political lives. As one perceptive Tory put it, 'Will the Chief Minister himself stand firm, when underlings are torn off?'[2] Lord Sunderland was well aware of his own peril. He knew that in Walpole and Townshend he had colleagues who would seize any opportunity to strip him of influence and power. But he was a politician of subtle resources, and to secure himself he determined to open negotiations with the Tories through the Bishop of Rochester. That he should do so was not entirely strange. For some time the commentators had been speculating that he might try to form a new 'mixed administration' with the King's consent, and thus reduce his dependence on Walpole and Townshend. Indeed in the spring of 1720 the Prince of Wales had been persuaded to submit himself to his father by just such a report 'that the Ministers were sure of the Tories [and] that Atterbury

---

[1] Ibid. 49/78, FR to Dillon, 22 Oct./2 Nov. 1720 [Kelly's writing].
[2] H.M.C. *Portland MSS.* vii. 287, 24 June 1721. C. B. Realey, *The Early Opposition to Sir Robert Walpole, 1720-1727* (Lawrence, Kansas, 1931) has useful material on the politics of this period but is wholly unreliable on Jacobite affairs.

said he would come up to anything personal against the Prince'.[1] In the days before Parliament met, Lord Coningsby had sent a private letter to Sunderland urging him to break with his Whig colleagues, dissolve, and use the Secret Service money to produce a moderate Tory majority in the new House.[2]

Atterbury himself was by no means averse to such an intrigue. He had always doubted whether any Tory attack in Parliament would do anything more than cement Whig party spirit, and he had always believed that the surest method by which James could be restored was by a secret agreement with the Ministers in power. And he had another, more personal, reason for some *rapprochement* with the Chief Minister. His great legal case over the dormitory at Westminister was due to come before the Lords early in the new session. Without Government support he would certainly lose. And so the Bishop of Rochester, at this moment of high political crisis, remained curiously detached. He spoke in the great South Sea debate in the Lords on 10 January and compared the company and its directors to the pestilence then raging in southern Europe, but significantly he did not blame the Ministry nor did he join in the protests which other Tory peers entered into the journal of the House. Indeed his strange reluctance to press home the attack moved Lord Orrery to complain to James himself of his old tutor's conduct and of 'the ill consequences of some false steps which several of them have lately taken. Their business is certainly to give George and the Ministry all the disturbance, all the uneasiness and all the opposition possible in Parliament.' But the fact was that a significant body of Tories, led by the Bishop, was abstaining from real action, and soon rumour was going about that a reconstruction of the Ministry was in the offing.[3]

Sunderland's first approach to the Bishop was dexterously managed. When on 6 February the dormitory case came on, certain of the Ministers gave Atterbury a tentative support. But the hint was enough, and in the next few weeks he and the Chief Minister had some wary meetings. Though some of the Harley faction professed

[1] *The Diary of Mary, Countess Cowper, 1714–1720*, ed. Spencer Cowper (1865), p. 133.

[2] S.P. 35/23/170, Coningsby to Sunderland, 30 Nov. 1721.

[3] R. A. Stuart 51/52, Orrery to James, 16 Jan. 1721; H.M.C. *Portland MSS.* v. 614, Edward Harley to Oxford, 17 Feb.

to be outraged by this 'snivelling and cringing to Lord Sunderland', the effect was quite remarkable.[1] On 3 March, when the case came on again, the Government spokesmen were all in favour of the Bishop, and the Lord Chancellor from the Woolsack announced that he had reconsidered his verdict in the Court of Chancery below. Dr. Stratford was outraged. 'This', he wrote, 'is a full proof of Ruff's secret correspondence with Sunderland . . . and this is a juncture in which Sunderland will be willing to oblige anyone, especially one that is supposed . . . to be capable of influencing a great many of a whole party.'[2] It was indeed the Minister's moment of greatest danger. His colleague, Lord Stanhope, in the stress of the crisis had just collapsed and died; Aislabie was on the rack before a parliamentary committee; and his own case was due to be debated within a matter of days. He determined to lay some definite proposals before the Tories, and see how far they would take the bait.

After a preliminary meeting with Lord Orrery, which failed because of a mutual distrust, Sunderland approached Atterbury directly and set out his offer. As reported to James on 10 March, he promised that if the Tories would preserve him from impeachment he 'would order all things as they desired'. Parliament would be suddenly dissolved and 'if the Tories do not take the opportunity then it will not be his fault'.[3] On the 15th in the great debate in the Commons Sunderland was acquitted by a handsome majority, and it was noted that a good number of Tories were on his side. On the 29th he returned the compliment in the Lords by warmly espousing Atterbury's case over the dormitory. When the House went on to resolve that so valuable and useful a building should not be obstructed by disagreement in the Chapter at Westminster, the Bishop was almost overcome with joy. The next day he sat down to write to Sunderland a letter 'to return you my heartiest thanks for what your Lordship did yesterday. I will never forget it.'[4] The basis had been laid for the serious discussions which were now to begin.

During the Easter recess the Minister's negotiations with Atterbury and Lord Trevor were an open secret. Dr. Stratford, as well

[1] Ibid. v. 619, Edward Harley junior to Abigail Harley, 19 Mar. 1721.
[2] Ibid. vii. 293: 7 Mar. 1721.
[3] R. A. Stuart 52/105, James Hamilton to James, 10/21 Mar. 1721.
[4] Blenheim MSS. F. 1-31, FR to Sunderland, [30 Mar. 1721].

informed as ever, was scandalized to find that even ordinary Tory backbenchers were now prepared to mark time in the expectation of a new mixed administration. 'Some gentlemen we know', he complained to Lord Harley, 'have been and still are miserable dupes. Those too, I am afraid, who are the very chief of the party. And Ruff has been the instrument used in deluding them.'[1] Of course, the Bishop knew only too well that he was playing a dangerous game. He was elaborately careful not to reveal any Jacobite secrets and his meetings with Sunderland took the form of a wary sparring-match. As he recalled it later: 'he could assure the world that whatever he made of Lord Sunderland was a secret, but that Lord Sunderland made nothing of him.'[2] It is virtually certain that the Minister had no serious Jacobite intent himself and that his manoeuvres were merely to confuse his opponents and win valuable time. Yet the offers made to the Jacobites were unnervingly tempting and presented with every appearance of sincerity. At the end of April Sunderland went so far as to say that the Prince of Wales was his deadly enemy, and that rather than such a creature should come to the throne he was prepared to embrace the cause of the Chevalier. He was ready to procure a dissolution of the present Parliament and form a new administration in which Trevor, Orrery, Strafford and North would each hold office.[3]

They knew that Sunderland was quite likely using them as pawns in his game with Townshend and Walpole. But the prospect was intoxicating to the Jacobite inner circle, and they threw caution to the winds. Until this time every Jacobite leader of any standing had insisted that no expedition to England was possible which did not have the assistance of a strong military force provided by a foreign power. But now, in the excitement of the moment, Atterbury and his associates dispatched a letter to James which invited him to come immediately, even if he could muster only a small contingent of Jacobite supporters. Since there was no other messenger available, Sir Harry Goring was commissioned personally to carry the message to Paris and on into Italy. 'The time is now come', the Bishop

---

[1] H.M.C. *Portland MSS.* vii. 295: 9 Apr. 1721.

[2] C(H) MSS. 1292, Sample to H. Walpole, 19/30 Mar. 1726, reporting FR's conversation.

[3] R. A. Stuart 53/79, Charles Caesar to James, 4 May 1721.

announced in his letter to James, 'when, with a very little assistance from your friends abroad, your way to your friends at home is become safe and easy. The present juncture is so favourable, and will probably continue for so many months to be so, that I cannot think it will pass over without a proper use being made of it.' Even Lord Orrery, usually the very soul of caution, was won over to hope for success 'without foreign assistance.'[1]

As the summer days came, however, there was still no definite agreement with Sunderland. In the Lords Atterbury went so far as to speak on behalf of John Aislabie, and in return the Government peers dutifully supported him on 16 May when the Westminister dormitory came before the House for the last time. The case was hotly debated and the Bishop just managed to scrape home with a majority by 28 votes to 26. But this was small gain, and the Tories became increasingly confused. So far from keeping his discussions with Atterbury a secret, Sunderland seemed almost to parade them. The town buzzed with speculation when the coaches of Cabinet Ministers stood outside the Bishop's door in Dean's Yard. Sunderland himself went in with Lord Trevor, and Lord Carteret was 'often in close conference' with them. Atterbury later described how Sunderland repeatedly 'pressed him several times to act with him' and how they discussed the disposition of portfolios in the new Ministry. But what did the Minister really intend? Sometimes the Bishop was convinced that it was all a trick 'to render him suspected by the Tory party', and in later years he always insisted 'that neither he nor Lord Trevor would engage till we saw the Church and the Army new modelled'.[2] The fact was that Sunderland never really got to the point. When old Bishop Trelawny died on 19 July he came to Atterbury and offered him translation to the rich see of Winchester if only he and his friends would now come into the new scheme.[3] But the difficulty was that 'he could never be prevailed upon to come into necessary measures for securing a good Parliament, though he professed his zeal for one'. Whatever Sunderland

---

[1] Ibid. 53/48, FR to James, 22 Apr. 1721; 53/87, Orrery to James, 6 May.

[2] H.M.C. *Portland MSS.* vii. 299, 23 June 1721; B.M. Add. MSS. 9129, fo. 61, Sample to H. Walpole, 31 Oct. 1726.

[3] B.M. Add. MSS. 32686, fo. 330, J. Macky to R. Walpole, 21 Sept. 1723.

intended, however, none can doubt the serious intent of his manoeuvre. In August he and Carteret entered into a test of strength
with Walpole and Townshend, and their attempts to rally support
extended to Hanoverian Tories such as William Bromley and even
to sturdily independent Jacobites like William Shippen. In June
Walpole had thought it worth his while to call on Atterbury but
whether to warn him or plead with him we cannot know. Now at the
end of August the negotiations with the Tories, conducted with the
King's knowledge and consent, seemed to have reached the point
at which he and Townshend might be dismissed from the Administration. In the face of such a menace he abandoned his summer
pursuits in Norfolk and returned in haste to London.[1] It was a
situation that he would find it hard to forgive or forget.

2

By the end of September, however, Atterbury found himself in a
wretchedly exposed position. Many Tories had been uneasy from
the start at these negotiations with Sunderland and as time went on
and there was no result, they exploded with anger. On a visit south
to London the Scottish Jacobite, George Lockhart, called on William
Shippen and found him seething with resentment against the
Bishop and his collaborators, and worried 'how far some of their
number might be taken off the right scent, in case, as the consequence of such conjunction, they found the sweets of power and
preferment'.[2] To Atterbury's distress and grief many of his personal friends now took measures to dissociate themselves from him.
He was deeply shocked when the amiable Lord Bathurst, whose
house he had visited with Alexander Pope, announced that he was
'sick of some late transactions' and wished to retire to the country
and have nothing more to do with his former partners.[3] The anxiety
and tension of the moment played havoc with the nerves of a man
who was still an invalid. When Pope wrote to enquire kindly after
his health, he received back from Bromley a letter which made a

[1] J. H. Plumb, *Sir Robert Walpole*, i. 363 et seq. See also R.A. Georgian
Add. MSS. 28/74, Princess Caroline of Wales to Mrs. Clayton, 23 Sept. [1721].
[2] *The Lockhart Papers*, ed. [A. Aufrere], (2 vols., 1817), ii. 68–71, G. Lockhart
to James, 5 Dec. 1721.
[3] S.P. 35/28, Bathurst to FR, 19 Aug. 1721.

brave attempt at wit and banter, but it could scarcely disguise the dark mood of depression which enveloped him. 'I have been ill', he wrote, 'almost ever since I saw you; and as soon as I thought myself free from one fit of the gout, persecuted by another.'[1] He struggled up to Westminister for the new session on 19 October, though he was unable to walk without assistance and menservants had to carry him up and down stairs.

What little hope remained that Sunderland would keep his promises was shattered by news that the Government intended another short session of Parliament. It could only mean that the Ministers wanted time to make elaborate preparations for an Election in the spring of 1722, and that the full weight of influence at their command was to be exerted against the Tories. Orrery reported back to James in pungent terms the lame excuses which Sunderland made. It had been, the Minister explained, not his doing but the malign influence of Walpole with the King; he assured them that he himself was 'still a well-wisher to the Tories'.[2] But this time the Bishop and his friends were no longer to be deceived, and there followed a sudden and remarkable closing of the Tory ranks. Atterbury, Orrery, Strafford, Bathurst and North, for the Jacobites, held an emergency meeting with Archbishop Dawes of York and Lords Guilford and Foley for the Hanoverian Tories, and Earl Cowper was invited to their discussion. Under the shadow of the coming Election it was resolved to sink their differences and work under a single leader in the House of Lords. Letters were sent out summoning up all the absent Tory peers, so that the Ministry should now be faced with an opposition at full strength.[3]

Within a week or so the newswriters were commenting on a new style of opposition in the Lords under the able direction of Lord Cowper. 'Cowper's Cabal', as it came to be called, was outnumbered by three to one; and its defeat in the lobbies was certain. But even this could be turned to a kind of advantage. It was the ancient right of any peer, when the vote went against him, to have his reasoned protest entered into the journal of the House. Now it was designed

---

[1] *Pope Corr.* ii. 83-84, FR to Pope, 27 Sept. 1721.
[2] R. A. Stuart 55/67, Orrery to James, 28 Oct. 1721.
[3] See S.P. 35/40/423, for a paper in FR's handwriting, giving a list of the peers to be written to by the various attenders at the meeting.

that Cowper, Atterbury and Trevor, with the aid of the young
Duke of Wharton, should attack the Ministry on a whole series of
controversial topics, and when they were outvoted enter a pungent
statement of protest into the journal. These could then be published
as broadsheets to add fuel to the election campaign which was
even then raging around them. Battle was commenced on 13 November when Cowper forced a debate on the vast debt which the
King had incurred in his use of the Royal Navy. Contemporaries
long remembered Atterbury's vehement speech. Although he had
to struggle into the chamber on crutches, he hammered home the
constitutional point that at no time had George's foreign policy
received parliamentary sanction.[1] When they were defeated the
Tories joined in their first formal protest, and in the following
weeks the campaign continued. Each morning the leading speakers
met together to plan their tactics and write up the previous day's
protests. It is not difficult to detect in them the traces of Atterbury's
characteristic style. As Dr. Stratford put it, 'Ruff is doing everything possible to regain credit with his old friends. He enters
warmly into all opposition that is given. He knows he will be despised by the others, if they see he is not trusted by his old friends.'[2]

In fact, behind the scenes the Jacobites were wrestling with an
agonizing problem. Were they to fulfil the promises which they had
made to James so enthusiastically in the summer, and organize
support for an invasion by the Duke of Ormonde with a small force
of Irish officers? The Chevalier had been transported with joy to
receive their letters, and now he enquired anxiously why he heard
no more from the Bishop and his friends. Why did they not write?
The moment they gave the word, he and Ormonde would put in
hand preparations for their dramatic but desperately perilous expedition.[3] As autumn turned to winter he sent off new pleas to all the
foreign powers who might be sympathetic to his cause, and instructed his agents in Paris to reactivate his English followers and make
them live up to their promises.[4] And it so happened that this criti-

---

[1] *Parl. Hist.* vii. 923; Arch. Aff. Etr. 338, fo. 233: report of the French
ambassador, 16 Dec. 1721.

[2] H.M.C. *Portland MSS.* vii. 307: 24 Nov. 1721.

[3] R. A. Stuart 55/62, James to C. Caesar, 16/27 Oct. 1721.

[4] Ibid. 55/137, James to Strafford, 11/22 Nov. 1721; 55/82, James to
Lansdowne, 22 Oct./2 Nov.; H.M.C. *Moray MSS.* (1895), p. 159.

cal moment coincided with the re-appearance of the Earl of Mar upon the Jacobite scene in the French capital. Although he had been in virtual disgrace since his precipitate resignation from James's service in 1719, Mar was determined to resume his old place in the Chevalier's inner councils. Now, by sheer force of personality, he virtually took over the direction of affairs from Dillon and Lord Lansdowne, who were James's authorized agents in Paris; and in mid-October he drew up a new set of plans for an invasion of England during the General Election.[1] He argued that, though no foreign aid was forthcoming, the matter could be accomplished if an element of surprise were preserved. The Anglican hero, Ormonde, was the man to rouse instant support and he must land unexpectedly at some strategic spot in England. If necessary, diversionary forces could be timed to land just previously in Scotland or the West Country to draw off the Hanoverian army. But everything would depend on the support which the English Jacobites could mobilize. Money had to be provided in really large amounts, and there had to be the kind of local military preparations which would ensure some immediate support for the Duke: he must not be overwhelmed and captured before the revolution was properly under way. At once George Kelly was dispatched to England to carry the scheme to Atterbury and demand an instant reply; and in the meantime the three managers in Paris plunged into an intense activity, even to the extent of drafting new constitutions for England and Scotland when once King James's Restoration had been achieved.

Kelly's arrival with this demand for action put Atterbury at once into a terrible dilemma. He consulted Orrery and the rest and found then utterly divided. Orrery made his own position clear: the scheme was bordering on lunacy and he believed that every penny which could be raised should be put into the Tory election campaign. It was nonsense to send money abroad when there was little enough already for buying votes and entertaining voters. 'There are', he wrote off to James, 'so many little venal boroughs that 'tis to be apprehended a majority will hardly be carried by the inclinations of the people only.'[2] Lords Gower and Bathurst agreed with him, but

---

[1] Ibid. 65/18, the memorial, dated 4/15 Oct. 1721; 53/48, Mar to James, 9/20 Oct.

[2] Ibid. 55/67, Orrery to James, 28 Oct. 1721.

Strafford, Arran and North took the opposite view. The sudden appearance of Ormonde, the great Tory hero, in the midst of the Election could accomplish the King's Restoration far more certainly than any amount of tedious electioneering. Atterbury himself was utterly at a loss what to think. He had always opposed a small-scale, unsupported expedition, but this was to be led by his own friend and hero. There was also the unpalatable fact that if he developed hesitations now he might forfeit for ever any claim he had to be the leader of English Jacobitism. Under insistent pressure, he agreed and suppressed his unease at the rash and ill-considered scheme from Paris. He 'gave into it at first, before he had well considered the particulars of it; the others were transported with seeing him approve what they had proposed themselves, which approbation violence and zeal confirmed him in the reasonableness of their proposition.'[1] An enlarged plan was drawn up. Arran was to be in command until his brother actually landed. Ormonde was to arrive secretly in a small ship which would sail up the Thames bringing sufficient Irish officers and enough arms to provide the nucleus of an irregular army of twenty thousand. Strafford was to organize the North, as Danby had done in 1688, and Lansdowne was to land in Cornwall to raise the West Country. Money would be collected in England to finance the foreign preparations. On 24 November, in the name of five conspirators, himself, Strafford, Arran, North and Sir Harry Goring, Atterbury dictated the details of the plan to George Kelly. He asked for commissions, letters of authority and blank receipts for money to be sent immediately. On the 25th Kelly left London and was quickly on his way to Paris.[2] A train of events had been set in motion which was eventually to involve the Bishop of Rochester and his associates in utter disaster.

3

The arrival of Atterbury's letters in Paris threw the whole Jacobite world into violent motion. An express messenger was sent on to

[1] Ibid. 65/33, Hay to Mar, 3/14 Mar. 1722; 63/33, Hamilton to James, 9/20 Nov. 1722.

[2] The letters to James and Dillon have not survived in the Stuart papers, but their contents are clear from R. A. Stuart 57/1-7, James's replies of 24 Dec. 1721/4 Jan. 1722.

James in Rome; Dillon dispatched a new appeal to the Czar; Sweden was asked instantly to repay the money lent to Charles XII in 1718; and orders were sent to agents in Hamburg to begin purchasing arms and ammunition. Arrangements were made for Irish officers in the French service to hold themselves ready to move to ports in Brittany to embark for England. Ormonde in Spain was given the glad news, and all during January and February he was engaged in feverish activity to fit out a small expedition and have it sail in time for the British General Election. He was fortunate that in the port of Cadiz there was already a Jacobite force of three small ships under the command of Captain William Morgan and that they had on board over two thousand sets of military equipment.[1] On 24 December in Rome James sat down to write letters which overflowed with excitement and gratitude. To Strafford, Arran and North he sent military commissions and warrants of promotion in the Jacobite peerage, but his real enthusiasm was reserved for Atterbury. He was not able, he wrote, to express 'the deep sense I have of the great share you have had in managing and bringing matters to the point they are arrived at. I am truly mortified not to be able to give you a like token of my favour, but I hope the time may come in which you may enjoy a rank superior to all the rest after having been so signally instrumental to my Restoration.'[2]

In London it was necessary for the conspirators to disguise their secret activity, and early in the new year Atterbury accepted with some enthusiasm a proposal from Cowper that they should prepare for the elections by a renewed attack on the Government in the Lords.[3] Debate followed debate, and at the beginning of February the Bishop slipped away, exhausted, for a few days' rest in the country. As he explained to Bishop Ottley: 'the minority there have been struggling all this winter upon points of consequence, wherein they have had, you may be sure, no successes within doors; but have constantly entered their protests with reasons. The fifteenth of that kind, I believe, is entered today.'[4] Indeed in the middle of the month the Government became sufficiently rattled by

[1] See *C.R.*, AA.5, Ormonde to Lansdowne, *circa* 4/15 Apr. 1722.
[2] R. A. Stuart 57/1, James to FR, 24 Dec. 1721/4 Jan. 1722; 57/58, James to Lansdowne, 6/17 Jan.
[3] S.P. 35/40/386, Cowper to FR, 8 Jan. 1722.
[4] N.L.W. Ottley MS. 1705, FR to Ottley, 2 Feb. 1722.

the circulation of printed protests for Sunderland to use his majority to have the texts erased from the journal. When on 10 March the old Parliament was dissolved, the Tory peers could feel a mild satisfaction. As the French ambassador reported: 'the discontented group consoles itself with the thought that what the Court gains in Parliament it loses in the minds of the nation.'[1]

Atterbury and his fellow-conspirators knew that they ran great risks. Both the French and British Governments maintained extremely efficient intelligence services, and the post offices on both sides of the Channel were skilled in the delicate art of opening letters, copying their contents, and resealing them again. In London the Ministry possessed what was virtually a department of cipher-experts; and these men, ably led by the Reverend Edward Willes, had already had immense success in breaking the code of the Görtz-Gyllenborg correspondence of 1716. It was, of course, fairly easy for the members of the House of Lords to preserve strict security: they could meet at their country houses or pretend to be about their parliamentary business. The danger lay in the Cross-Channel correspondence and with the lesser agents whom it was necessary to employ.

It was with the latter that the Bishop showed himself especially nervous. He would allow no visits to the deanery and insisted that any discussions had to take place at Bromley, where his chaplains and servants were sworn to silence. He insisted that his own part in the conspiracy should be kept a close secret from the lesser fry, and all were enjoined to take the most elaborate precautions. He would write nothing in his own hand and forbade the use of the ordinary letter post. All packets to and from Paris were to be carried across personally by a trusted messenger. It was not, of course, easy for Dillon to provide men who matched up to these standards, but at the end of November he sent across to London a reliable and astute man to supervise operations and to act as the financial agent who could transfer money to Paris and Madrid. This was Captain Dennis Kelly, a well-connected soldier who set himself and his family up in fine lodgings in Whitehall and proceeded to play out the role of a gentleman of means and leisure. He was assisted by the Reverend Thomas Carte, a scholarly Nonjuring divine who under pretence of

[1] Arch. Aff. Etr. 340, fos. 191-92, 16 Mar. 1722.

historical research, made two extensive tours into the country liais-
ing with supporters in the provinces. The role of the Reverend
George Kelly was to provide a rapid Cross-Channel messenger
service and to act as special assistant to the Bishop. Atterbury found
him intelligent and determined, and he alone had permission to
arrive unannounced at Bromley.

If, however, the Bishop had known the true state of Jacobite
security he would have been horrified. It was, for example, almost
incredible that Lord Mar should have been allowed to work himself
into virtual control of business in Paris and into possession of the
most confidential information.[1] The fact was that ever since his
resignation in 1719 Mar had made repeated approaches to the
British Government to obtain a pardon and the restoration of his
titles and estates. He was a man of mercurial temperament, and the
miseries of his poverty-stricken exile gnawed at his mind. On his
arrival in Paris in 1720 he pestered the British ambassador constantly,
and eventually the Ministers decided to use him. In February he was
actually given the promise of the income of his Scottish estates on
condition that he supplied genuinely useful intelligence of Jacobite
activity. Strangely enough, the transaction was not entirely unknown to James, who appears to have permitted it on the grounds
that Mar was no longer in his service and could have no secrets to
communicate.[2] Indeed from the summer of 1721 James recognized
Lord Lansdowne as his chief minister in the French capital.[3] It was
thus all the more absurd that Mar should have been allowed in
effect to make plans and assume the direction of the English
conspiracy.

The situation in London was not much better. In spite of all the
Bishop's warnings, Dennis Kelly, Thomas Carte and even George
Kelly, when he was in England, used the ordinary mail. Like Dillon
and his two secretaries they put their trust in an elaborate system
of ciphers and false names. Everything was written in the oblique

---

[1] See M. Bruce, 'The Duke of Mar in exile, 1716–1732', *Transactions of
the Royal Historical Society*, 1937, for an account of Mar with which this study
is in disagreement.

[2] S.P. 78/169/87, Sutton to Craggs, 30 Oct. 1720; ibid., fo. 123, Sutton
to Stanhope, 9 Nov.; R. A. Stuart 50/123-52/54 *passim* for Mar's correspondence
with James, 23 Dec. 1720 to 22 Feb. 1721, N.S.

[3] R. A. Stuart 52/83, James to Orrery, 20 Feb./3 Mar. 1721.

style and veiled language beloved of Jacobites, but which as frequently confused them as much as any casual reader. The ciphers, in particular, were a standing invitation to prying Post Office clerks to investigate further.[1] In spite of all his promises to Atterbury George Kelly was far from cautious, and his acquaintance with a host of desperately poor Irish Jacobites in London was a real danger. In fact he went so far as to employ one of them, the Reverend Philip Neyno, an old friend from Trinity College, Dublin, as a copyist for secret memoranda and correspondence. He showed him Atterbury's dictated letters and allowed him to use the code-books. It was indeed tempting fate to put such matter into the hands of a man poor enough to be on the verge of actual starvation. But even this faded into insignificance compared with the peril represented by the tragi-comic figure of Christopher Layer. Layer was a young barrister, son of a Norfolk gentleman, and he had been raised in an atmosphere of romantic, sentimental Jacobitism; he was gullible, vain and incurably meddlesome.[2] In April 1721, accompanied by James Plunket, a down-at-heel Irish adventurer, he actually set out on a long journey to Rome to pay his respects to the Chevalier. Since he had no credentials, James should have sent him packing but instead he allowed the foolish young man to have scraps of information and messages to friends at home.[3] When Layer returned to England in September it was in a kind of frenzy of loyalty, and at once he began to attempt to force himself into the company of known Jacobite sympathizers. In February 1722, in the face of a series of rebuffs, he began to draw up his own plans for a rebellion. Orrery, North and the Duchess of Ormonde were horrified to be pestered by this slightly mad but very dangerous would-be conspirator.

At the beginning of February the Bishop of Rochester became

---

[1] The keys to the ciphers may be found in the Stuart papers at Windsor, where many of the letters have been deciphered by James's private secretary. The principal code is R. A. Stuart 5/65, and had been in use since 1719. The list of cant-names employed is R. A. Stuart 5/69, and is of date 1720. An important addition to the latter list was sent on 15 Apr. 1722, and is R. A. Stuart 5/91.

[2] For an account of Layer, see R. W. Ketton-Cremer, *A Norfolk Gallery* (1948), pp. 125-48.

[3] R. A. Stuart 65/9, Layer to James, June 1721. See also ibid. 65/10-11 for memorials submitted by Layer when in Rome.

very alarmed. The election was now only two months away. Ormonde was engaged in feverish preparations for his expedition. And yet it was apparent that the English supporters were wholly unprepared to receive him. No plans had been made to divide the country into military districts, the commissions had not been distributed and, worst of all, virtually no money had been collected. The scheme for a vast uprising was still only a dream. This was made clear when, at a clandestine meeting, the Bishop was informed by his partners that they had promises for about £10,000 but that even this could not be collected for some months. Dillon had asked for £100,000 and stipulated that £50,000 was the bare minimum for which an expedition could be mounted. At once Atterbury demanded that Ormonde should be informed by an express messenger of the true state of affairs in England, but to his horror Strafford and the rest were wholly unmoved.[1] Sir Harry Goring even had ready a letter which urged the Duke to set out without delay. At once there was a furious quarrel in which the Bishop lost all control over his temper; in his rage he seized Goring by the collar and shook him. Clearly bitter things were said which gravely wounded the aristocratic self-esteem of men like Strafford and North, and they were never wholly to forgive him. In spite of his vehement protests they resolved to press on with their plans without him: to hire a ship in the Port of London and to send it to Spain to convey Ormonde, with or without his other ships, to England.[2]

What could Atterbury now do? He was convinced that his former partners were leading Ormonde to an inevitable disaster. And when in early March Dillon sent over a detailed plan for a general military rising to take place when an agreed signal was given, it became clear that the managers in Paris were completely misinformed and that they had no idea that virtually no preparations had been made.[3] Somehow an urgent warning had to be got through and yet it was doubtful whether the conspirators would allow such a message or whether any of the couriers would carry it. In the end the Bishop had to adopt a characteristically ingenious

[1] R. A. Stuart 58/74, Mar to James, 5/16 Mar. 1722; 65/33, Hay to Mar, 3/14 Mar.
[2] *Pol. State*, xxv. 429: evidence of P. Caryl, 29 Mar. 1723; R. A. Stuart 59/118, Strafford to James, 18 May 1722.
[3] R. A. Stuart 65/60 for Dillon's memorial of 26 Feb./8 Mar. 1722.

device. He composed a letter and persuaded George Kelly that it was a draft of a letter designed to be intercepted by the British Government: if it were approved by the managers in Paris it could be used to deceive the Ministers at home into thinking that the Jacobites were powerless and inactive. In fact, if Dillon and the rest had any powers of perception, it was intended as an urgent cry of warning. The contents were sombre. The present scheme was described as 'wild and impracticable'; the Tory party was 'without concert and without a head, and few of them are men of any capacity or courage'. The ordinary backbenchers were 'a Rope of Sand; there is no union, no spirit among them; their thoughts both within doors and without are employed about nothing but securing their approaching elections'. So many leading Tories had declined to join in the present scheme that they were to judge 'whether it be worth your while to press us any longer upon that head'.[1] The arrival of this 'mysterious letter' in Paris was a terrible shock. While Dillon could at first make nothing of it, Mar at once saw its importance. As he explained it to James:

it is [the Bishop of Rochester's] real opinion of things, and he took that pretext only of showing it to his partners as if he intended it to be intercepted, but truly to let his real sentiments be known to [Dillon], [Lansdowne], and [Mar] which for his partners he was not otherwise at liberty to do . . . There is certainly a great deal of truth in it; but if it be all so, any undertaking, on that foot, against the Government, were almost madness to be attempted.[2]

In the weeks after the dissolution of Parliament on 10 March the Bishop retired to the quiet of his country house and stayed there. He had delivered his warning as best he could, and he had severed his connection with the conspiracy. Now he was exhausted and utterly dispirited. He was determined, he told Pope, to give up all political 'business':

It has been my fate to be engaged in it much, and often, by the stations in which I was placed: but God that knows my heart, knows

---

[1] *L.R.*, item 6: an anonymous letter, dated 12 Feb. 1722, a copy of which was secretly delivered to the office of the Secretary of State on 31 Mar. 1722.

[2] R. A. Stuart 58/140, Mar to James, 26 Mar./6 Apr. 1722.

I never loved it; and am still less in love with it than ever, as I find it less a temptation to act with any hope of success. If I am good for any-thing, 'tis *in angulo cum libello*: and yet a good part of my time has been spent, and perhaps must still be spent, far otherwise.[1]

There was another, more pressing, cause of his melancholy. As the spring came the doctors could see that Mrs. Atterbury was in the last stages of a consumption. For a while he clung to some hope for her recovery but eventually he had to accept the inevitable. There was nothing to do but watch by her bedside as she became increas-ingly weak and emaciated. For a man of Atterbury's temperament it was a crushing experience, and he was soon in one of his own fits of the gout. As he wrote to his young friend: 'Under all the leisure in the world, I have no leisure, no stomach to write to you. The gradual approaches of death are before my eyes.' The moment it was all over, he would slip away to Twickenham and refresh himself in the pleasant company of Pope and his mother.[2]

[1] *Pope Corr.* ii. 107, FR to Pope, 16 Mar. 1722.
[2] Ibid. ii. 113, FR to Pope, 6 Apr. 1722; N.L.W. Ottley MS. 1705, FR to Adam Ottley, 2 Feb. 1722; R. A. Stuart 59/14, Kelly to Mar, 16/27 Apr.

CHAPTER THIRTEEN

Walpole and the Jacobite Threat, 1722

I

As the Bishop passed these melancholy days at Bromley, disaster moved steadily towards him. In spite of all warnings the Jacobite leaders in Rome, Paris and Madrid were desperately reluctant to cancel the expedition to England. Ormonde, indeed, had gone almost too far to draw back. By the beginning of April he had pledged his personal credit to the limit and his little armada was almost ready to sail, first to Bilbao to pick up the officers and then on to Morlaix in Brittany where a cache of ten thousand sets of weapons was waiting. It would be heartbreaking, as well as financially disastrous, to countermand such elaborate preparations.[1] In Paris Dillon and Lansdowne, in the midst of fitting themselves out for journeys to Scotland and the West Country, were almost distracted with the worry and uncertainty. It was a superb opportunity for Lord Mar to seize the initiative, and with his usual aplomb he proposed that the plan should not be abandoned but merely postponed. Let the invasion be timed for the late summer when Parliament was in recess and George I had left on his annual visit to Hanover. This would give time for money to be collected and a chance for James once again to press the Czar and the French Regent for military assistance. But, above all, it would provide an opportunity to do something about the miserable divisions which prevailed in England. Obviously it was impossible for supporters there to unite under the Bishop's leadership, and it would be necessary to find some new figure who could command a much wider range of Tory loyalty.[2]

James and his advisers in Rome adopted Mar's advice without a moment's hesitation. Without stopping to enquire whether the

[1] *C.R.*, AA.5, Ormonde to Lansdowne, *circa* 4/15 Apr. 1722; AA.4, Ormonde's secretary to D. Kelly, 16/27 Apr.

[2] R. A. Stuart 58/91, Mar to James, 12/23 Mar. 1722; ibid. 58/113, 19/30 Mar.

plan was realistic or whether Mar himself was to be trusted, the Chevalier sat down to write a completely new set of instructions to all his agents. In Paris Dillon and Lansdowne were like clay in the hands of a man of stronger personality and superior intelligence, and imperceptibly he slipped into the position of director of the whole Jacobite enterprise. He wrote to Ormonde with advice and instructions, supervised Dillon's foreign correspondence, and took over from Lansdowne the conduct of relations with the aristocratic supporters in London. Between 2 and 3 April he wrote a series of letters designed to reconstruct the leadership in England, and George Kelly was given detailed instructions for a visit to the Bishop of Rochester. Indeed, in order to re-introduce himself to Atterbury, who had not heard from him for over four years, Mar took over from Kelly a small personal commission: to find a little French-bred dog to amuse Mrs. Atterbury in the last days of her illness. On 8 April Kelly left Paris on what was to prove a disastrous mission.

He arrived in London on the 11th and the next evening travelled quietly down to Bromley. Atterbury received him in his private study and was visibly astonished to be handed a packet of letters from Lord Mar.[1] He asked what Mar could have to do with their affairs. It was a tricky moment, but Kelly took the plunge and explained that all the managers in Paris were anxious that there should now be an expedition to England in the late summer and that this should be under the direction of the Earl of Oxford as the only man who could now unite the whole Tory party. It was the prayer of the King's friends in Rome and in Paris that the Bishop would support him and act as his chief lieutenant. For a moment it looked as if there was going to be an outburst of rage but in the morning Kelly was delighted, and mildly surprised, to find that Atterbury was in a genial mood. He was, he said, willing to join heart and hand with Lord Oxford, to whom he owed many past obligations; it was true that there was 'not much to be expected from the present managers'; and he could think 'it no great vanity to say that the Earl of Oxford and himself were the fittest persons for this purpose'. Rejoicing as a man who had succeeded in an important assignment, Kelly returned to town and soon the good

[1] R. A. Stuart 59/14, Kelly to Mar, 16/27 Apr. 1722. See also 58/131, Mar to FR [Motfield to Illington], 2/13 Apr.; 58/134, 3/14 Apr.

news, disguised in ciphers and false names, was on its way to France—by the ordinary letter post.

The Bishop's reaction to Mar's proposal was not, in fact, as simple as Kelly imagined. He was indeed willing enough that Strafford, Goring and the rest should be dismissed from any future control of Jacobite affairs in England, but he had no illusions about Oxford. That lord had been dangerously ill for much of the previous year and had made no move to come up to Parliament. Only recently Atterbury had received from him a letter which demonstrated his complete withdrawal from the world of active politics.[1] Nothing was to be expected from Oxford and to agree that he should be in charge of the preparations for an invasion was, in effect, to ensure that absolutely nothing would be done. And the Bishop's view of the situation was almost immediately confirmed on 19 April, when Kelly came rushing back to Bromley with the dramatic news that Lord Sunderland had just dropped dead of an apoplexy. While that Minister was in power the Jacobites had little to fear. He and Carteret had remained in contact with them, and it would have been impossibly embarrassing if all these offers and negotiations were to become public knowledge. Certainly Sunderland would never have initiated a prosecution for treasonable activity. But now the Ministry was to be dominated by Walpole and Townshend —and that was a very different matter.[2]

Atterbury was now distinctly alarmed and before Kelly returned to town he dictated to him three letters which were designed to make his own position perfectly clear.[3] Using the pseudonym 'Illington', he wrote to Mar to explain that 'my present sad circumstances . . . will not suffer me to be active soon, or even to set forward the preliminaries entrusted to me'. Writing to Dillon and using the name 'Jones', he attempted to explain the circumstances of the quarrel with his former partners and to warn those in Paris to exercise great care because 'the death of Lord Sunderland makes

[1] S.P. 35/31/41, Oxford to FR, 10 Apr. 1722.

[2] B.M. Add. MSS. 9129, fo. 61, Sample to Walpole, 31 Oct. 1726, reporting FR's conversation. See also *Pope Corr.* ii. 110, Pope to FR, 19 Mar. 1722.

[3] The ciphered letters, all dated 20 April, are to be found in C(H) MSS. 69/4. The Government experts' decoded versions are in *C.R.*, D.10–12, and the versions corrected from the codes in the Stuart papers are in Glover, appendix, pp. 11–15.

such a caution more indispensably necessary; for you may depend upon it, those in power here will now employ all their vigilance as well as power on such occasions.' His third letter was to Lansdowne. Signing himself as '1378' and addressing himself to 'Jackson', he reminded him of the 'mysterious letter' which he had been forced to write, and 'if you guessed at my right mind, I dare say it was agreeable to your own, and that you could not but see through the weakness of all those unsupported pretending people'. Perhaps later, when the time was ripe, he would come into business again but 'in the meantime give me leave to withdraw myself seemingly from any engagement of this kind'.[1]

Kelly put the letters into cipher and dispatched them under a single cover to the Jacobite agent in Boulogne. But, despite all his promises to the contrary, he sent the packet cross-Channel by the ordinary British mail, and even enclosed a note asking that replies should be addressed to him under various false names at Will's Coffee House in Covent Garden.[2] Seemingly oblivious of danger, Jacobite correspondence crossed in both directions, bearing news, instructions, and reports of meetings and conversations. Dennis Kelly sent a bill of exchange for £6,000, and on 30 April George Kelly announced the arrival in London of a French spotted dog. Poor little 'Harlequin' had been a fortnight on the journey and had arrived with a broken leg. Unfortunately he had come too late, for 'Mrs. Illington' had died on the 26th of the month. On 2 May Dillon acknowledged receipt of 'Illington's' packet of letters. Although it must have been clear to the triumvirate in Paris that hope for any immediate action in England was dim, the chatter through the post continued.

2

In fact, since 23 April the whole correspondence had been opened and copied by clerks in the British Post Office, and was being closely studied by Cabinet Ministers. For some time there had been vague

---

[1] Glover and *C.R.* are in error in saying that this letter was for James himself. 'Jackson' is always used for Lansdowne in the cipher R. A. Stuart 5/69. James later affirmed that no letter to or from him had been intercepted.

[2] *C.R.*, E.26, G. Kelly [J. Johnson] to Gordon, 22 Apr./3 May 1722.

reports of Jacobite naval preparations at Cadiz, but on the evening of 21 April Lord Carteret received an express which brought alarming news from Paris. Cardinal Dubois, the French Minister, had communicated an urgent warning to Sir Luke Schaub, the British envoy, that an invasion of England was due to take place on 10 May. His Secret Service had picked up reliable information that Irish officers were travelling to ports in Spain and Brittany, and that money was being sent in large quantities; recently his Government had received a request from the Jacobites to assist them with a force of thirty thousand men.[1] In London there was at once considerable alarm. At a meeting of the Cabinet Council on 23 April it was ordered that all letters between England and France were to be opened at the Post Office; ships of the Royal Navy were to stop and search cross-Channel traffic; and a strong military force was to be encamped in Hyde Park to defend the capital.[2] That very evening the Post Office intercepted Atterbury's three letters under George Kelly's cover to Boulogne, and in subsequent days a rich harvest of other letters was gathered in, copied, resealed and allowed to pass on through the post. The numerical cipher was broken by the code experts within hours and, though the pseudonyms were puzzling to the Ministers, they were able to make some informed guesses. That Atterbury was involved they did not doubt. All the personal circumstances of illness, retirement in the country, and the prospect of personal bereavement pointed to him. And there was a host of intriguing clues to be followed up—not least that of the French spotted dog.

For Robert Walpole it was a golden opportunity. The death of Sunderland had cleared from his path his chief rival for the King's favour, and now only lesser supporters of the dead man, like Carteret, stood in his way. Walpole was well aware of George I's fear of Jacobitism and that he had regarded Sunderland's negotiations with the Tory leaders with extreme unease. Indeed Walpole himself had always made a show of taking 'the other point, of standing or falling with the Whigs, which was not only the King's own entire opinion, but had been much confirmed in time past by my Lord

---

[1] B.M. Stowe MSS. 250, fo. 73, Schaub to Carteret, 19/30 Apr. 1722.
[2] S.P. 35/31/72: 'At the Duke of Newcastle's house, 23 Apr. 1722.'

Sunderland himself.'[1] Here then was a chance to represent his dead rival and his associates as having been involved in an intrigue far more dangerous and extensive than the King had ever imagined or approved, even one itself bordering on treason. It was also an opportunity to put himself forward as an efficient minister and the relentless foe of Jacobite traitors.

On 25 April Walpole and Townshend had a private meeting with Carteret, and the luckless young Secretary realized that his political career now depended on his joining in the energetic pursuit of a plot. A reply was sent to Sir Luke Schaub, telling him of the absolute unanimity of the three Ministers in the face of this grave crisis, and their determination to maintain the French alliance.[2] It was decided to send Colonel Charles Churchill, Marlborough's bastard nephew, to carry a letter to the Cardinal, signed by the three, asking him in the strictest confidence to divulge all he knew. But Churchill's mission was to have an even more secret and delicate purpose. He was to take with him a 'peremptory message' to the Earl of Mar, requiring him 'on account of the favours conferred upon him by King George for some time past' to reveal everything he knew of the plot and the intercepted correspondence.[3] Within hours Churchill was off on his journey to Paris and the Ministers waited expectantly. But there yet remained one source of information which had always intrigued Walpole and which he believed might yield useful matter; and on 28 April he had Sunderland's papers examined. In spite of the excited protests of the Duchess of Marlborough, the dead man's desk was opened and his secret files scrutinized. The contents were disappointing. There was a letter from the Pretender but it contained no clue to any of the English plotters and was immediately burnt.[4] The search had at least given notice to the

[1] H.M.C. *Carlisle MSS.*, p. 38, Sir John Vanbrugh to Carlisle, 5 May 1722. See also G. V. Bennett, 'Jacobitism and the Rise of Walpole' in *Historical Perspectives: Studies in English Thought and Society in Honour of J. H. Plumb*, ed. Neil McKendrick (1974).

[2] B.M. Add. MSS. 22517, fo. 48, Carteret to Schaub, 25 Apr./6 May 1722.

[3] R. A. Stuart 60/88, James to Lansdowne, 17/28 June 1722; 75/136, FR to James, 31 July 1724, quoting from letters found in Mar's papers.

[4] J. H. Plumb, *Sir Robert Walpole*, ii. 40; C.R., E.35, G. Kelly to Glascock [J.H. to Howell], 30 Apr./11 May 1722; H.M.C. *Sutherland MSS.* p. 190; H.M.C. *Onslow MSS.*, p. 510.

world that Sunderland's friends were under suspicion, but so far Walpole was no further in unravelling the conspiracy. There were some interesting clues but nothing like clear evidence.

Churchill got to Paris on the 29th and at once went to Mar. To that lord's alarm he produced the Ministers' letter with copies of the intercepted correspondence, and demanded that he should now do something to justify his pension and his request for a restoration to his title and estates. Clearly Mar was in a dreadful dilemma, and he played for time. But within days Churchill came back with another letter, written by Mar to Kelly on 24 April, with the cipher accurately broken and with the Ministers' suggestions for the cant-names neatly added in the margin.[1] For a while the Earl kept up some show of resistance. He informed James, Dillon and Lansdowne of this visit of an English agent but insisted that he had given nothing away. And they, with touching faith, believed him. But on 11 May he yielded to Churchill's insistent pressure. Although he had no business to communicate, he agreed to write a letter into England which could be intercepted by the Government and used to provide evidence against the Bishop of Rochester. It was addressed to 'Illington' from 'Motfield'; it acknowledged his of 20 April, referred to 'a loss you have had since', exhorted him 'to submit with resignation to what the just and great God thinks fit for us in this vain and transitory world', and added the comment, 'but you know such things better than I'.[2] It was all a transparent device, as Atterbury later insisted it was: '[He] writes a letter to me . . . and sends it by the common post (which he knew at that time to be most carefully watched) and in that letter owns the receipt of mine, and describes me by my function, the late death of my wife, and a fit of the gout, from which I was just recovering: characters that agreed to no other person in the kingdom, but myself.' The Bishop had indeed been betrayed, and in the days following the dispatch of the letter Mar and Churchill were in constant consultation. On the afternoon of 18 May, for example, the Earl wrote submissively to offer to come secretly to the agent's lodgings 'if you want to say

[1] B.M. Sloane MSS. 4204, fo. 66, Carteret to Schaub, 4/15 May 1722; B.M. Add. MSS. 22522, fo. 229, Schaub to Carteret, 9/20 May.

[2] *C.R.*, D.24, Mar to FR [Motfield to Illington], 11/22 May 1722. It was enclosed in *C.R.*, F.23, Dillon to D. Kelly, 16/27 May, which refers to 'the opening of all letters'.

anything to me, or ask me about [anything] before you write tomorrow'.[1] Churchill had been extraordinarily successful; and when Cardinal Dubois expressed his amazement at such contacts with the Jacobites, the Secretary of State was able to reply with diplomatic understatement: it was all 'parcequ'il y a longtemps que Mar a eu des obligations au Roy.'[2]

Now the Ministry could draw the net more tightly, and on 7 May troops were moved into London, where they set up a huge camp in Hyde Park. The price of Bank stock fell heavily and there were wild rumours as to what was about to break. The next day, in a public letter to the Lord Mayor, Townshend announced to an expectant public the discovery of a detestable plot, the existence of which would soon be proved by the King's Ministers. In fact, there was precious little evidence of a really tangible nature. Walpole had secured information from the Regent which seemed to indicate that Sunderland had gone far beyond what the King had authorized in his relations with the Jacobites, but even this was inconclusive. Much careful detective work was required in England, and this was now to be concentrated on the correspondents who answered to the names of 'Hatfield', 'Johnson', 'Vernon', 'Saunders', and 'Baker'. A small army of Government spies watched by relays at Will's Coffee House, to which letters addressed to these names were usually sent. It was soon discovered that the Reverend George Kelly called for them all.

Walpole had suspected the Bishop of Rochester from the first, and now he knew that he was getting near him. On 16 May he actually called on Atterbury and, though it is probable that their business was only with Chapter finance, the tension must have been immense. Then in the small hours of the morning of the 19th the Government pounced. A party of King's Messengers waited near Kelly's lodgings, and on his return from some midnight errand they seized him. But, as they proceeded to search his room, he threw off his captors, caught up a sword, and with a ferocity hardly becoming a Clerk in Holy Orders drove them all out through the door. He was busily burning his papers when a file of musketeers was brought up

---

[1] R. A. Stuart 75/136, FR to James, 31 July 1724, quoting letters from Mar to Churchill, 17/28 May and 18/29 May 1722.
[2] B.M. Add. MSS. 22517, fo. 116, Carteret to Schaub, 7/18 June 1722.

and he was forced to surrender. On 21st he and his landlady, Mrs. Barnes, were brought before a committee of Council and rigorously interrogated. Walpole and Townshend asked him repeatedly what he knew about Mar and Dillon. Who were the conspirators represented by the false names in the correspondence? But again and again the question returned to 'Illington' as 'the person chiefly struck at'. Kelly, of course, protested that he knew nothing, but when he was asked about a certain dog which had been sent across from France, he somehow failed to perceive the full significance of the question; and both he and Mrs. Barnes talked on about poor little Harlequin and his broken leg. Two days later, at a specially summoned meeting of the Cabinet Council, Mrs. Barnes repeated her testimony: that 'the said dog was for the Bishop of Rochester; that the dog was called Harlequin, a very fine spotted dog; that Kelly promised her, the said Barnes, to get the dog from the Bishop of Rochester in case it did not recover its lameness.'[1] This was Walpole's break. There was still much evidence to be sifted, but there was no longer any doubt in his mind. As he reported it to his brother, the little dog 'served to fix the certainty of the names. We are in trace of several things very material, but we fox-hunters know we do not always find every fox we cross upon; but I doubt not but this matter will come out so as to shame all gainsayers.'[2] It was decided, after a discreet interval, to release Kelly on bail; and then to watch him day and night. The hunt was up.

Atterbury was quickly aware of his peril. In the days after his wife's death on 26 April he had stayed in the country until her funeral on 2 May. He buried her in the Abbey in a vault which he had prepared for himself and his family, 'at the West Door of it, as far from Kings and Kaisers, as the space will admit of'.[3] In spite of all the fuss over the encampment, on 17 May he went to Twickenham to stay with Alexander Pope. But when he got back to Westminster two days later he was faced with the shattering news of Kelly's arrest and interrogation. Now began the long ordeal of anxiety. The members of the Council committee who had examined

---

[1] *C.R.*, E.47, G. Kelly to J. O'Brien, 11/22 June 1722; *C.R.*, E.4, 'At a committee of Council, May 23rd, 1722'.

[2] Coxe, W., ii. 220–22, R. Walpole to H. Walpole, 29 May 1722.

[3] *Pope Corr.* ii. 114, FR to Pope, 6 Apr. 1722.

Mrs. Barnes were not discreet, and the whole affair was too exciting not to be whispered about town. Dr. Stratford in Oxford had the story in detail by the beginning of June, and soon it was common gossip that a Jacobite correspondence had been fixed on the Bishop of Rochester by means of a spotted dog.[1]

3

In early June the whole Jacobite scheme for an expedition collapsed. Certainly the British Government was no longer in any fear, for their precautions had been massive. And the strain went out of the situation entirely when British envoys abroad reported on their successful representations at the Courts of France and Spain. The Regent ordered all foreign officers in the French army immediately to return to their regiments, and the Spanish Government agreed to arrest Ormonde's ships and, if necessary, prevent their journey to England by force. It was soon apparent, even to Lansdowne and Dillon, that their whole project was ruined. In the first week in June there was a meeting at St. Germains during which recriminations flew thick and fast, and after it Dillon sat down to write letters countermanding all his previous instructions.[2] Within a few weeks the Jacobite expedition just faded away. And all this was reported back to London by the British embassy in Paris, whose spies excelled themselves in the detail of the information which they procured. In the middle of June the Ministry received definite news from Spain that Ormonde's naval force would not sail. The three small ships of the Duke's armada had arrived in Bilbao to find no sign of their leader and not one of the soldiers they were supposed to embark. Everything had been cancelled, and Ormonde was in Madrid trying to stave off his creditors. The blow to Jacobite prestige and credibility had been crippling. From Rome James made some attempt to keep up the spirits of his followers. He wrote to assure them that the expedition was not cancelled but only put off to a later date

---

[1] H.M.C. *Portland MSS.* vii. 326: 5 June 1722. See also R. A. Stuart 60/26, Freind to Lansdowne, 14/25 June.

[2] H.M.C. *Polwarth MSS.* iii. 138, Stanhope to Carteret, 15/26 June 1722; B.M. Stowe MSS. 250, fo. 81, Schaub to Carteret, 27 May/7 June; B.M. Add. MSS. 22521, fo. 284, Crawford to Carteret, 2/13 June.

when, once again, the element of surprise would be on their side.[1] But this was mere bravado. The next Jacobite expedition was far distant indeed.

In London Walpole knew quite well that any real danger was past. But he was determined that his plot should not fall to the ground. The difficulty was how to exploit it to its full political value when the evidence was so confusing. The Post Office was still intercepting up to five or six letters a week but most of them were useless. Atterbury remained inactive in the country; letters were written to him but he was obviously determined not to reply. The lesser agents were badly frightened men and their correspondence was concerned mainly with their plans to get away out of the country to France. Indeed, if this had been all there was to go on, Walpole might never have taken the decisive step of prosecuting the Bishop. But, fortunately for him and his plans, this was not all the evidence. There were other letters of a much more exciting nature. Addressed to Dillon in Paris and coming from someone calling himself 'Rogers', they were full of the direst menace. 'Rogers' claimed to know all the leading Jacobites and to be admitted to their plans. He discussed schemes for a general rising in England in the autumn and described in detail discussions in which the French and Spanish envoys in London had agreed to co-operate. He seemed confident and definite, and on 4 July he went on to outline a plan for the assassination of George I. It could be said that the reaction of the Ministers was one of both alarm and pleasure. Urgent representations in Paris and Madrid produced energetic denials that their ambassadors were engaged in any such Jacobite conspiracy. Sir Luke Schaub professed himself amazed, on reading copies of 'Rogers's' letters, because they were so out of accord with everything else he knew about the state of Jacobite diplomacy.[2] In fact, of course, Walpole had intercepted the correspondence of James Plunket, written on behalf of Christopher Layer. It was a world of pure fantasy and it had been deeply stupid of Dillon to engage in such an exchange of letters and to encourage the unbalanced young man to put his nonsense on to

[1] R. A. Stuart 60/24, James to Lansdowne, 4/15 June 1722; C.R., D.35, Dillon to FR [Digby to Weston] 14/25 July.

[2] C.R., C.59–62, for Plunket's letters to Dillon. S.P. 78/177/84; B.M. Sloane MSS. 4204, fo. 80; B.M. Add. MSS. 22517, fo. 145, for the comments of Schaub and Carteret.

paper and pass it through the post. Now, as the English Jacobites tried desperately to fade into obscurity, Layer would not be quiet. He and his egregious companion went on inventing schemes and plots and submitting them for approval.

On 28 July Walpole had Dennis Kelly arrested. For some time it had been clear that he was a key-figure in the conspiracy, and that he had transmitted large sums of money abroad. When the correspondence revealed that Kelly and his family were on the point of taking ship to France, the Government took instant action. Every passenger and crew member was seized and the vessel searched from stem to stern. The result was deeply disappointing. Kelly had destroyed virtually all incriminating matter, and neither threat nor intimidation could make him disclose a scrap of useful information.[1] Indeed Walpole might well have despaired but, on the very evening of Kelly's arrest, he found himself on the edge of a new breakthrough. In his post was a letter which offered to sell him secret information about the plot. Surreptitious arrangements were made to meet the writer, and on 1 August, at his home in Chelsea, Walpole received a visit from the Reverend Philip Neyno.[2] Neyno had not actually come to sell his friends. All he hoped for was to obtain some money by feeding Walpole with a few snippets of unimportant fact. But at once he found himself in the hands of an utterly ruthless politician who was considerably cleverer than he was. When Neyno began to talk of a correspondence which the Jacobites had conducted with Dillon and Lansdowne in Paris, Walpole offered to test him and produced a piece of paper which he said was a cipher taken out of Dennis Kelly's papers. If Neyno really knew anything, he would be able to say who 'Illington', 'Digby', and 'Hatfield' were. Anxious to establish his credit, Neyno replied that these names stood for the Bishop of Rochester, Dillon and George Kelly. And thereby he placed himself irretrievably in Walpole's power. There had been no such cipher in Dennis Kelly's papers. Walpole had merely given him a list of names taken from the intercepted correspondence, and Neyno had provided the first independent evidence of their meaning.[3]

[1] B.M. Add. MSS. 32686, fo. 227, Poyntz to Newcastle, 28 July 1722.

[2] Ibid. fo. 232, 3 Aug. 1722. See also B.M. Add. MSS. 34713, fos. 55–56, for Walpole's evidence before the Lords, 13 May 1723.

[3] R. A. Stuart 100/45, J. Hamilton to James, n.d. but after 29 Sept. 1722. Hamilton had a personal account from Neyno.

Neyno was now trapped. In subsequent sessions at Chelsea the pace quickened. Walpole caught him out in a number of lies, and the mood changed from blandishment and the offer of bribes to menace, and from menace to terror. On 4 August the little Irishman was so demoralized that he broke down completely. Soon he was blabbing out everything he knew: plans for Ormonde's expedition; the involvement of Strafford, North and Goring; the way by which Dillon's letters came from France; and George Kelly's work as messenger for the Bishop of Rochester. He repeated over and over again that Atterbury was the real leader of the Jacobite movement in England. He did not scruple to inform on his lesser colleagues, and he gave details of the Reverend Thomas Carte and of John Sample, a servant in the employ of Sir Robert Sutton, formerly ambassador in Paris. His one stipulation was that he should not have to sign a statement nor give any public testimony.

Now indeed the Government could close the net even more tightly, and warrants were issued to take up the smaller fry. Carte managed to evade the messengers and escape into hiding, but Sample was caught and on the evening of 4 August subjected to a terrifying ordeal. The young Irishman was not of the stuff of heroes and yet he found himself ruthlessly interrogated by Walpole, Townshend and Carteret. He was shouted at, struck, and threatened with 'gibbet, racks and fire' and the lowest dungeon in Newgate prison if he did not swear out information against Strafford, Orrery and Cowper.[1] Soon he was weeping, whining and offering to tell anything he knew. But the fact was that he had been let into no secrets and had virtually nothing to give. It was nevertheless particularly vexing for the Ministers when they learned next morning that their bird had flown. During the night Sample had summoned up courage enough to leap from an upper window in the messenger's house, and he had disappeared into the alleys and warrens of Westminster.

All these incidents, and the reports on them in the newspapers, meant that the strain on the leading Jacobites was now intense. Obviously, if Walpole could panic one of the former conspirators

---

[1] S.P. 35/33/313–14 is an account of his examination by Sample, dated 15 Oct. 1722; 35/32/105 is a set of minutes by Walpole and Carteret, dated 4 Aug.

into a false move, many of his problems would be solved, and he carefully stepped up the war of nerves. Rumours were circulated that important discoveries had been made, and that fresh arrests could be expected hourly.[1] Most of those threatened chose to stay in the country, though they waited in an agony of fear and doubt. Atterbury, in particular, was obsessed with the problem of what had gone wrong. As the days passed at Bromley, he set out his evidence: the sequence of correspondence and the timing of the Government's moves. And he became convinced that they had been betrayed by someone at the highest level of the Jacobite leadership. Sometime in the week beginning 22 July Viscount Falkland came across from Paris on the express orders of James himself to assess the situation, and when he was smuggled down to Bromley he found the Bishop in explosive mood. How could the traitor be anyone other than Lord Mar? No man was given a pension of £3,000 a year by the British Government without being expected to perform 'some essential services' for it.[2]

It was in such an anguished mood that on 4 August Atterbury had to travel up to Westminster to supervise the elaborate preparations being made for the state funeral of the Duke of Marlborough. His own condition of anxiety made him regard the whole occasion with irritation and distaste. He complained bitterly to Pope of being forced to attend on 'the last scene of pompous vanity' of a man whom he had never honoured in life.[3] On the actual day, 9 August, wearing one of the venerable purple copes of the Abbey, he received the body at the West Door, and conducted the funeral service. Perhaps he might have been more moved had he known that this was to be the last occasion on which he himself would officiate in the Abbey as Dean. Back at Bromley he had some quiet visits from Bathurst and North and a consultation with the eminent Tory lawyer, Sir Constantine Phipps; but they could only wait.[4] On 15 August Walpole stepped up the pressure by refusing to sign the Chapter accounts in

[1] *C.R.*, E.68, G. Kelly to Dillon, 6/17 Aug. 1722.
[2] *C.R.*, D.40, Falkland to Dillon [Stanley to Drake], 26 July/6 Aug. 1722; R. A. Stuart 61/51, Falkland to James, 18/29 Aug., written on his return to Paris.
[3] *Pope Corr.* ii. 129, FR to Pope, 3 Aug. 1722.
[4] *C.R.*, E.69, Kelly to Dillon, 9/20 Aug. 1722; B.M. Stowe MSS. 750, fo. 409, FR to Orrery, 18 Aug.

his capacity as Chancellor of the Exchequer. Clearly something was about to break, and on 20 August Atterbury came up to town at what he knew was a critical juncture.

I have a little time left, and a great deal to do in it [he wrote to Pope on the 19th]; there are those that intend to employ me this winter in a way I do not like. If they persist in their intentions, I must apply myself to the work they cut out for me, as well as I can. But withall that shall not hinder me from employing myself also in a way they do not like: the givers of trouble one way shall have their share of it another; that at last they may be induced to let me be quiet, and live to myself, and with the few (the very few) friends I like. For that is the point, I now aim at.[1]

There was, in fact, now not long to wait. Early on the morning of 23 August Sir Harry Goring made a break for it. His private yacht slipped away from its moorings and took with it a number of heavily disguised passengers, including John Sample. Goring's escape, which went undetected by the Royal Navy or the Secret Service, was a grievous shock to Walpole, and he knew that he had to act quickly. The next afternoon, 24 August, Atterbury was working in his study at the deanery when a party of messengers, led by an Under-Secretary of State, burst in.[2] The Bishop was in his dressing-gown and unshaven. Despite his furious protests, they went through every drawer and cupboard, turning out every scrap of writing. Even the toilet paper in the lavatory was added to the pile on the floor and sealed up in a large sheet. In the confusion one of the messengers searched the Bishop roughly, going through his pockets and pulling out his wallet. He was given a few moments to put on some clothes, and then hurried to the Cockpit in Whitehall where a specially summoned meeting of the Cabinet Committee was waiting. Among those present was Archbishop Wake, visibly distressed and embarrassed at seeing one of his suffragans in so humiliating a condition.[3]

By this time Atterbury had recovered something of his usual composure. He greeted Walpole ironically and answered questions with some spirit. He demanded to know on what evidence a bishop

---

[1] *Pope Corr.* ii. 131–32, FR to Pope, [19] Aug. 1722.

[2] For FR's arrest and examination, see H.M.C. *Portland MSS.* vii. 332; C.R., D.45; E.C., ii. 223.

[3] B.M. Add. MSS. 32686, fo. 236, Newcastle to an unknown correspondent, 25 Aug. 1722.

of the Church of England had been thus arrested and manhandled. He was sent out and called in again to learn that he had been remanded to the Tower of London on a charge of high treason. His request to be kept under house-arrest at home in the custody of a messenger was refused. It was later whispered around the town that he had used the words of Christ before the Jewish Council: 'If I tell you, ye will not believe me; and if I also ask you, ye will not answer me, nor let me go.' Two servants were allowed to accompany him, and he was sent through the City streets in his own coach to avoid attracting the attention of a crowd. That evening he found himself in the Tower, closely confined in one room, with a sentry at the door. He was forbidden to speak with relatives, other prisoners, or even his lawyers.

CHAPTER FOURTEEN

The Bishop on Trial, 1722–1723

I

IN arresting the Bishop of Rochester, Walpole had staked his
political career on a successful prosecution of the Jacobite plot.
For the next nine months he was to devote himself day and night to
proving to the satisfaction of the King and Parliament that there had
been a grave threat to national security and that Atterbury had been
the principal director of this 'detestable and horrid conspiracy'. Of
course, in the summer of 1722, Walpole had sufficient information to
know that the danger from abroad had been slight and that the
English plotters had been unprepared and divided among themselves.
Jacobitism had a strange fascination for him, but it is impossible to
avoid the conclusion that he intended the plot to serve as a catalyst
in domestic politics. Walpole had virtually secured the pre-emi-
nence among his colleagues, but he still needed something to overcome the residual distrust which George I had for him, and he
wanted an issue with which to face the new House of Commons in
the autumn. No one could doubt the King's real fear of Jacobitism,
and any Minister who could represent himself as having broken a
dangerous Stuart conspiracy was assured of the royal regard. Indeed
in later years Speaker Onslow had no hesitation in pointing to the
trial of Bishop Atterbury as the real beginning of Walpole's premier-
ship. It was, he wrote, the 'most fortunate and the greatest circum-
stance of Mr. Walpole's life. It fixed him with the King, and united
for a time the whole body of Whigs to him, and gave him the universal credit of an able and vigilant Minister.'[1] If it was not going to be
easy to convict the wily Bishop of Rochester, the rewards for doing
so were certainly rich indeed.

The main drawback was that the evidence was still remarkably
meagre, and fell far short of the legal proof required in the Common
Law courts. There were the intercepted letters, but not one of them

[1] H.M.C. *Onslow MSS.*, p. 513.

was in the Bishop's handwriting and all were in code. There were the secret revelations of Neyno, but none of these yet had the status of a sworn testimony. The haul from the Bishop himself was very disappointing. A party of messengers went down to Bromley and tore the fittings apart but as at Westminster they found only a few scraps of correspondence. It was clear that the Ministry urgently required fresh information, if it were to sustain anything of a case. That this was so was quickly shown by the enormous storm which the arrest provoked. Word spread of the grievous indignities which the Bishop had suffered, and some Tories even began to relish the prospect of another Sacheverell Trial. Broadsheets were sold in the streets containing exhortations to the prisoner in the Tower, furious sermons were preached in London churches to congregations which stood in the aisles, and on one Sunday it was reported that Atterbury was prayed for in nearly all the churches in the City and Westminster 'under the pretence of his being afflicted with the gout'. A print was made, showing him looking through the bars of his prison, and it was hawked about the town. There can be no doubt that the Government was worried. An official statement was issued to the effect that the Bishop was under an honourable confinement and well treated; and Dr. Jeremy Pearce, Vicar of St. Martin's-in-the-Fields, was commissioned to write a long and earnest defence of the Ministry's action.

In fact, Atterbury was being closely watched and dealt with with great severity. In these early days in the Tower he first came into contact with Colonel Adam Williamson, an inflexible and heavy-handed professional soldier who had been chosen by Walpole to guard this difficult prisoner. From the pages of his bad-tempered diary Williamson appears to have been one of those military men who regard civilians as basically spineless and potentially unpatriotic.[1] Religion he regarded as mere ceremonial and clergymen as useless parasites. To his mind Atterbury was already guilty and to be treated as any traitor to King George. The Secretary of State's directions for the prisoner's confinement were already severe; Williamson determined to make them even severer. Even a request from the Bishop that he might be allowed to receive the Sacrament

[1] *The Official Diary of Lieutenant-General Adam Williamson, Deputy-Lieutenant of the Tower of London, 1722-1747*, ed. J. C. Fox (1912).

in the Tower chapel was roughly refused, and difficulties were made about the visits of a doctor. By 6 September Atterbury was ill and in distress at the constant searches of his personal possessions and at being deprived even of the company of his children.[1] On 7 September William Morrice, his son-in-law, tried to get him released by suing out a writ of habeas corpus, and to the surprise of competent lawyers it was refused.

Walpole's search for evidence began with an attempt to prise something useful out of the lesser characters of the Jacobite world, and on 18 September Christopher Layer was taken into custody. All during August he and Plunket had continued to live in their fantasy world. They had tried to recruit British non-commissioned officers to the Stuart cause, and had written off their weekly letters to Paris, promising the coming triumph of a spontaneous insurrection. Even the arrest of Atterbury did not give them a moment's pause.[2] At his first examination Layer was calm and relatively confident, but the brutality of his subsequent treatment was more than his courage could sustain. Soldiers were brought in to confront him; and he was reminded that if a quick death by hanging was the penalty for suborning members of the armed forces from their allegiance, that for treason was the horror of being hanged, disembowelled and quartered. Before the end of this session Layer was blabbing out all he knew. The brave romantic plotter was reduced to the status of a mere informer against King James's real friends. Within hours warrants were out for Orrery and North, and by the evening of 29 September both of them had been seized and sent to the Tower to join Atterbury in close confinement. But that same evening Layer's own doom was sealed. To Walpole's delight two large bundles of material, which was plainly treasonable, were discovered at his lodgings. The wretched young man had preserved virtually every item of his imaginary conspiracy, including an elaborate 'scheme' for seizing the City of London.[3] It was mostly nonsense, but sufficient to give the impression to the King and the

[1] S.P. 35/33/28, FR to Townshend, 6 Sept. 1722; fo. 40, Townshend to FR, 7 Sept.; *Pope Corr.* ii. 133, Pope to Gay, 11 Sept.

[2] *C.R.*, C.64, Plunket to Dillon [Rogers to Digby], 16/27 Aug. 1722; C. 65, 23 Aug./3 Sept.

[3] The originals are preserved in C(H) MSS. 69/9, and a selection printed in *C.R.*, B.X.20 and B.Y.21.

members of the Cabinet that they were probing a really widespread and dangerous movement. On 1 October Layer appeared before a full meeting of the Cabinet Council, and at the conclusion he was ordered to be sent to the Tower and loaded with irons on his hands and feet. He had already admitted enough to make him a dead man.

This was satisfactory from Walpole's point of view, but it brought him no nearer the Bishop of Rochester. It was clear that the only real witness against him was the Reverend Philip Neyno, and at their private meetings Walpole pressed continually for some written, legal evidence: a key to the codes, some letter in an identifiable handwriting, or even some scrap of paper which the Jacobites had used in laying their plans. By now Neyno was in a pitiable condition. He made an attempt to escape to France but was captured on the Dover Road, hauled back and subjected to the kind of calculated cruelty which was reserved for the smaller fry.[1] On 18 September, when he had been sufficiently softened up, Walpole dictated to him a list of questions to which written answers were required within one week. Pathetically the little Irish priest wrote to Townshend and Walpole to have mercy upon him and help him 'to rectify the fatal mistakes which have been as prejudicial to the public service as to my own quiet'. On 25 September he produced his answers to Walpole's questions, but still he could not be persuaded to sign anything. To do so would be to incriminate himself in high treason, and so nothing would induce him to convert his oral evidence into a sworn legal document. He was told of the horrors of Newgate, the stench and the fever, and the other prisoners with whom he would share the lowest, filthiest cell. That night he was returned to to the messenger's house with Walpole's threats ringing in his ears and the fear of Newgate heavy upon him.[2] At three o'clock the next morning his despair was so great that he, too, made a bid for freedom. His room was three stories high and overlooking the Thames. By tying his bedclothes together he managed to slide down to the ground, only to find himself trapped in a walled garden which

[1] R. A. Stuart 100/45, for Hamilton's detailed account. S.P. 35/40/37 is a list of the dates on which Neyno was examined.

[2] S.P. 35/33/170, Neyno to Townshend, 24 Sept. 1722; C.R., E.7 is the verbal answer produced by Neyno on 25 Sept. and E.10 is the unsigned statement of 27 Sept.

opened only on to the river. So great was his desperation that he
had the courage to throw himself into the water, though it was
flowing past at full flood. When first light came watermen discovered his drowned body floating against the wall of the Privy
Stairs; in his pocket was found the sodden paper bearing Walpole's
list of questions.[1] Philip Neyno had done great harm to the Jacobites
but he had gone to his Maker without swearing out a formal testimony, and legal evidence for a case against the Bishop of Rochester
had still failed to materialize.

2

In the autumn all the Jacobites were confident that the Bishop
would not be convicted. James himself, writing from Bologna,
affected to take his plight lightly: he was 'persuaded they will find
no proof against him and in that case, bar a little personal incon-
venience to himself, it will, I think, do more good than hurt.'[2] But
the Speech from the Throne at the opening of Parliament on 11
October showed that Walpole was determined to pursue the matter.
King George devoted himself almost exclusively to the enormities
of the plot, and the very first business proposed was a bill to suspend
the provisions of the Habeas Corpus Act. Shippen and his small band
of Tories did all they could to delay the passage of the bill, but on the
17th it was hurried through to the Royal Assent. On 6 October
James Plunket had been arrested, and now the Ministry decided
that George Kelly's freedom could serve their purposes no longer.
All the conspirators were now secured and imprisoned without hope
of legal redress, and the Jacobite correspondence with France was
completely severed. It only remained to be seen how Walpole would
proceed.

He decided to begin with Christopher Layer, against whom
there was at least legal proof. It was a deeply unpleasant business.
On 21 November Layer was taken in irons to the Court of King's
Bench in Westminster Hall to appear before the Lord Chief Justice,
Sir John Pratt, and two other judges. The court was grossly over-
crowded with spectators who pressed against lawyers and witnesses,
and impeded movement to and from the witness-box. Layer himself

---

[1] The water-stained paper is in C(H) MSS. 69/5.
[2] R. A. Stuart 62/66, James to Dillon, 19/30 Sept. 1722.

chose to act the buffoon, breaking in when others were speaking and making grimaces at the jury. But the case against him was easily proved. The 'scheme' for seizing the City, which had been found in his papers and which he had admitted to be his, was damning. That the whole project was a figment of his busy imagination was never really made clear and perhaps would have counted for nothing at law. Sir John Pratt curdled the jury's blood with his passionate description of the heinousness of Layer's intention, and the twelve men took only minutes to return their verdict. On 27 November the prisoner at the bar was sentenced to the most terrible death prescribed in English law. It was, of course, as Walpole had expected, and in the next few months he proceeded to play a cruel game with the condemned man. On the chance that Layer might yet be able to contribute some scrap of evidence against the Bishop of Rochester, it was arranged that there should be a series of last-minute reprieves before execution, and that after each Layer should be pressed for further information. By now he would certainly have done anything to save his life or mitigate the horror of his death, but there was simply nothing at all which he could add.[1]

During December Walpole and his assistants, Charles Delafaye and Stephen Poyntz, spent hours going through the evidence. The committee of Council met continually to examine a host of servants, watchmen and coffee-house keepers who might have some clue to Kelly's or Atterbury's movements. Colonel Williamson at the Tower was given instructions to watch the Bishop like a hawk and secure any paper which might be smuggled to or from him. It was a task which he carried out with pleasure. During November Atterbury's children had been allowed to speak with him at a barred window on the ground floor, and it was even possible for Alexander Pope to have a conversation there with his friend. But all this Williamson was determined to stop, and on 25 December he marked the season of goodwill by issuing out a new and draconic set of regulations. It was more than Atterbury could endure. To be continually sneered at by this loutish soldier, to be deprived of all conversation except with servants, and even to have his pen and ink taken from him,

---

[1] C(H) MSS. 989, Layer to Walpole, 27 Nov. 1722; S.P. 35/34/167, Layer to Townshend, 4 Dec.; fo. 217, 12 Dec.

were all too much for his fragile temper.[1] Relations were at boiling point when on 28 December Williamson decided to submit the prisoner to an interrogation. At once the Bishop flared up on being addressed as 'Sir' rather than 'My Lord'. There was a sharp exchange as to whether the servants were to remain as witnesses of Williamson's actions, and Atterbury put himself between the door and the colonel when the latter went to call for assistance. A scuffle developed in which Williamson fell back on the bed with his boots in the air. Within hours the story was circulating round town that a large and fierce-looking soldier had been downed by an elderly and gouty Bishop. But it was no real victory for the prisoner. Henceforth Atterbury was allowed to speak to his children only by shouting from a top-story window at a distance of a hundred feet. His vehement protests produced from Carteret the curt answer that Williamson's conduct was approved by the King and his new regulations confirmed.[2]

Walpole spent Christmas in Norfolk, working on the trunkload of documents which he had taken down with him. For a while he seems to have cherished the hope that something new might come to light but, when he got back to Westminster with the papers now sorted into neat folders, he had reached a painful decision. It was impossible to proceed at all against Orrery, North or even Dennis Kelly. And if he wanted to go on with the prosecution of Atterbury, George Kelly and James Plunket, it would have to be done by some extraordinary method which set aside the ordinary demand for legal evidence. Even an impeachment, with its intricate processes and with the final penalty left to the House of Lords, would be unsafe. There remained the arbitrary method of a bill of pains and penalties, where all that had to be done was to persuade a majority in each House that it was expedient to pass into law a bill inflicting criminal penalties on an individual. It was a constitutionally dangerous and an unpopular procedure, and as such it would have to be very carefully stage-managed. Thus on 15 January a Select Committee was set up in the Commons, composed of utterly reliable party supporters. That very evening, at 10 at night, they

[1] S.P. 35/34/286, FR to Harcourt, 27 Dec. 1722.
[2] S.P. 35/41/3, FR to Carteret, 2 Jan. 1723; fo. 11, Carteret to FR, 3 Jan.; Wake MSS. 22, fo. 187, FR to Wake, 13 Jan.

began their investigation of the plot. The pace was furious and it was difficult to keep these 'great devourers of paper' supplied, but the fact was that in all essentials their work had already been done for them by Walpole, Delafaye and Poyntz.[1] Though they spent six weeks examining a succession of witnesses, there was nothing new to be discovered.

Nevertheless, when their report appeared it caused an immense sensation. Walpole had created a massive and intricate piece of detective work which managed to construct an intelligible and convincing narrative of the plot from a bewildering variety of evidence, and contemporaries found it fascinating. On 1 March William Pulteney spent no less than six hours reading the text to a House which remained crowded and attentive throughout.[2] Clearly at this point the vast majority of ordinary M.P.s made up their minds, and accepted without further hesitation the committee's unanimous verdict that Atterbury, Kelly and Plunket had been the leading figures in a dangerous and detestable conspiracy. That the report conflated a number of quite separate movements, that it was founded on circumstantial evidence alone, and that there was no living witness to the essential facts, mattered not at all to the politicians. In the course of the following week Walpole held private meetings with leading ministerial supporters, and was able to persuade them that it was necessary to adopt the extraordinary step of proceeding by a bill of pains and penalties.[3] On 6 April the Commons met to consider what punishment should be inserted in Atterbury's bill and, as proposed by Walpole, it was truly draconic. He was to be deprived of all his preferments and banished for ever from the kingdom; if he ever set foot again on British soil he was to suffer the penalty of a convicted felon, and not even the King would have the power to grant him a pardon. No subject of the Crown was to communicate with him by speech or writing except under licence of Privy Seal. In the face of such a proposal the members of the Tory minority were powerless to effect any change. In silence they rose

---

[1] S.P. 35/41/50, Poyntz to Delafaye, 15 Jan. 1723; fo. 93, 27 Jan.; fo. 105, 29 Jan.
[2] *The Parliamentary Diary of Sir Edward Knatchbull, 1722–1730*, ed. A. N. Newman (1963), p. 14.
[3] H.M.C. *Onslow MSS.*, p. 514.

from their places and left the chamber. Disaster for the Bishop of Rochester was now inevitable.

The news of the bill of pains and penalties was a searing blow. At the end of February William Morrice had managed to smuggle into the Tower a brief summary of the contents of the report, which had been 'leaked' to him by someone in the Ministry's confidence. Atterbury was amazed at what they had discovered, but not especially disheartened. Much of it was quite new to him. 'If the narrative', he commented, 'relates chiefly to Neyno's, Sample's and Layer's affairs, so far it cannot affect me: for I never heard of the names of either of these three till after this plot broke out.' His hope was that, for lack of proof, he would be imprisoned until the crisis was past and he could beg for his release.[1] But the voting of the bill destroyed this optimism at a stroke. Now he knew that he had to figure in one of those elaborate State trials which so often marked crises or great changes in English political life. In writing secretly to Pope, he accepted that nothing could avert his banishment. But already his mind was forming plans for a truly epic defence: it was going to be 'such that neither my friends need blush for me, nor will my enemies have great occasion of triumph, though sure of victory'.[2] He intended to go down fighting with a massive personal attack on Walpole himself. He assured Bromley and other friends that he realized that they could do nothing to help him. He alone would contrive this last piece of propaganda for the Tory cause.[3] There was reason in his approach. All over the country a wave of sympathy was manifest, in spite of the Government's immense press campaign. Indeed Hoadly's caustic articles in the *London Journal* under the pseudonym 'Britannicus' caused wide and bitter resentment. Even that old foe, Dr. Stratford, viewing the scene from Christ Church, surprised himself by discovering that he was moved to pity and sympathy for the Tory champion.

---

[1] S.P. 35/41/254–60, FR to Morrice, 25 Feb. 1723. This letter was seized on one of the Bishop's servants.

[2] *Pope Corr.* ii. 165, FR to Pope, 10 Apr. 1723; see also S.P. 35/42/85, FR to Harcourt, 12 Mar.

[3] H.M.C. *Bromley-Davenport MSS.*, p. 78, FR to Bromley, 9 Apr. 1723.

3

On 6 May the Bishop was conveyed from the Tower to his trial. Although Williamson sat with him and a guard of soldiers marched beside the carriage, the journey proved alarming. Rival Whig and Tory mobs in the City streets grew large, and the jeers mingled with cheers and shouts of encouragement. At the door of Westminster Hall Atterbury transferred to a sedan chair and was carried through to the chamber of the House of Lords. Here a massive attendance of peers was waiting, with members of the Commons pressing at the bar to view the scene. With some difficulty the Bishop mounted a scarlet-covered stand which had been set up for him and faced the assembly, presided over by Lord Chancellor Macclesfield on the Woolsack. Near the throne sat the Prince of Wales, an attentive listener who was not to miss a single day's session. The business before the House was not, of course, technically that of a state trial. It was to hear counsel for and against a bill before its third and final reading was moved. In spite of the appearance of a formal judicial occasion, the presence of lawyers and the lengthy examination of witnesses, the ordinary rules of evidence had been set aside and procedure was entirely within the discretion of the House. This Atterbury and his two counsel, Sir Constantine Phipps and Mr. William Wynne, knew very well. The two lawyers were both noted Tory sympathizers and they recognized to the full that the contest on both sides was political and not legal.

In fact, technically the Bishop's cause was lost on the very first day, when the majority voted that the extracts of documents as printed in the report of the Select Committee could be admitted as evidence.[1] At once Atterbury was on his feet with a vehement and eloquent protest. How could there be a proper cross-examination if he were denied the original letters and papers? How was the House to know that this selection had not been put together deliberately to present a false picture? When counsel for the bill proposed to

---

[1] T. B. Howell, *State Trials* (1816), xvi. 490–695, has a confused account of the trial; it is wholly derived from *Pol. State*, vol. xxv. *L. J.*, xxii, gives the formal record. Most valuable is the detailed précis made by Lord Chancellor Macclesfield, and preserved as B.M. Add. MSS. 34713, fos. 34–78 [hereafter cited as 'LCM'].

read the letters intercepted at the Post Office in the versions prepared by the Government's decipherers, the Bishop was on his feet
again. Why could the House not be given the letters in the original
code form, as they had been copied? Why should they be forced to
accept on trust the efforts of these supposed experts? Though his
plea was rejected, he was allowed to cross-examine the chief deci-
pherer. The Reverend Edward Willes was a clergyman skilled not
in theology but in the intricate work of code-breaking, and one day
this expertise was to carry him up the ladder of preferment as far as
the rich bishopric of Bath and Wells. Atterbury was not at all unwilling to pit himself against this brother-priest who did the
Ministry's work, and his trenchant questions revealed that he too
had been studying the finer points of ciphering. How had Willes
been able to work out so complete a key to the codes? Was it not
true that this was an impossible achievement, and that in fact he
had had access to information which had not been revealed to the
House? Had there not been some betrayal of the Jacobite codes? So
remorseless was the pressure that Willes eventually had to be
rescued by a majority vote which declared it 'not in the public
interest' that further questions should be put to the witness.

The defence had rather more success on the second day, when
the prosecution introduced the subject of Neyno's reported state-
ments before the committee of Council. This was a crucial issue,
and it was essential for the Bishop to show that they had been
extorted from a man who had been in an extremity of fear. His
cross-examination of Lord Townshend on this point was something
of a forensic triumph. Under skilful pressure the Secretary of State
had to admit that he himself had had virtually no contact with
Neyno; all had been dealt with by Mr. Walpole in private.
Townshend even agreed with Atterbury that the committee had
failed to ask a number of highly pertinent questions which might
have tested the truth of Neyno's accusations; he admitted that much
else had been said during the course of the committee's examination
of the informer but that this had been omitted from the record.
This was a feeble performance and an excellent opportunity for the
Bishop to launch himself into a bitter attack on Ministers who contrived evidence by underhand means, edited it to suit their purpose,
and then used it to ruin their political opponents. If this procedure

were condoned, who in political life would be safe in the future? A warm debate ensued, in the course of which it was apparent that the Government's supporters were deeply uneasy. When the Bishop was conveyed back to the Tower late that night he could feel a certain grim satisfaction, and the next day was even more encouraging when the prosecution began the task of trying to prove that George Kelly had acted under Atterbury's direction. Amid the complexities of letters and ciphers the question came to turn on the evidence of Mrs. Barnes and the destination of the dog Harlequin. In the august surroundings of the House of Lords and repeatedly pressed by the Bishop, the poor woman became hopelessly confused. She could not remember whether she had said that Harlequin was intended for the Bishop of Rochester or for George Kelly himself, and she was completely lost when asked to recall exact times and places.

On 9 May the prosecution was plainly discouraged. They declined to sum up their evidence or apply its meaning. In spite of Atterbury's protest that it was an unheard of way of proceeding to have to defend oneself against a case which had not been made out, he and his counsel were required to go ahead. Their tactic was at once revealed. It was to assert again and again that Walpole had fabricated or exaggerated the plot in order to ruin his political enemies and to terrify others who might henceforth oppose him. Indeed, observing the Chancellor of the Exchequer standing at the bar with other M.P.s, Atterbury rose to object that 'it was not proper he should hear dispositions which affected him', and Walpole withdrew from the chamber.[1] Three defence witnesses were called to discredit Neyno's testimony. All insisted that he had been almost terrified to death; and one, Edward Bingley, said that Neyno had been offered money by Walpole to swear out accusations against all the leading Tories and even against his own colleagues such as Carteret and Macclesfield.[2] Atterbury's servants were examined at length and could not be shaken under cross-examination in their testimony that no strangers had come to Bromley or Westminster and that it would have been impossible for anyone to have come without their knowledge. Alexander Pope, in a great state of agitation, took the stand to testify that his friend was a man who

[1] *Pol. State*, xxv. 613.
[2] LCM., fos. 43–45.

kept open house to writers and poets. Secret visitors would not have been able to come and go undetected in such a household.

In the afternoon of 11 May Atterbury rose to speak in his own defence.[1] The public galleries were packed and members of the Commons deserted the business of their own House to crowd at the bar to hear what was expected to be one of the great oratorical performances of the decade. They were not disappointed, though the Bishop had a terrible task before him. In spite of all his fervent denials and protestations of innocence he knew himself to be guilty in large measure, and the careful reader will note in the speech the ingenuity of language and expression employed to preserve himself from the lie direct. He began with a dignified protest against his long imprisonment 'in which I have been treated with such severity and so great indignities as I believe no prisoner in the Tower, of my age, infirmities, function, and rank, ever underwent'. Evidence had been brought against him which would have been inadmissible in any court of law, and yet what did it amount to? The intercepted letters were a tissue of circumstances, possibilities and hints; and in a version dubiously deciphered they added up to nothing. Neyno ought to be deeply pitied: he had been ruthlessly used and had been so terrified that he would have been 'prepared to have sworn backwards and forwards, to have affirmed or denied anything'. The real truth was that the whole plot was a fiction. 'After a twelvemonth's search for the contrivers and conductors of this scheme, no consultations appear to have been held, no money to have been raised, and (which is stranger) no arms, officers or soldiers, to have been provided. Not a man of the army is engaged in it. A poor Bishop has done all, and must suffer for it.' The speech ended on a note of passionate appeal. 'For God's sake, my Lords, lay aside these extraordinary proceedings! Set not these new and dangerous precedents! And I, for my part will voluntarily and cheerfully go into perpetual exile, and please myself with the thought that I have, in some measure, preserved the Constitution by quitting my country.' After two hours of such oratory he was conveyed back to the Tower as Whig and Tory mobs fought a pitched battle in the streets.

Monday, 13 May, was the last day of Atterbury's attendance at

[1] Westminster Abbey MSS. 65007 is a corrected version in FR's hand. It is printed in *E.C.*, v. 365-94.

the House, and in some ways the most dramatic. It was clear that the Ministry had to do something to erase the impression which had been created of inventing a plot and manufacturing evidence, and it was the charges against Walpole personally which really rankled. He now decided to go into the witness-box to refute them, even if this meant submitting himself to a cross-examination by the Bishop. This was the great personal confrontation which contemporaries recalled as the highspot of the trial: between the secularist politician on the threshold of power and a priest who represented all those Tory religious and political opinions which Walpole so whole-heartedly detested. Arthur Onslow, standing at the bar with other M.P.s, was awed by the encounter:

A greater trial of skill this way scarce happened between two such combatants, the one fighting for his reputation, the other for his acquittal. The expectation of people in it as they were differently inclined to the politics and the cause, and the solemnity of it from the place and the audience it was in, made it look like a listed field for a combat of another sort, and the joy of victory as great as there.[1]

Atterbury used every device 'to perplex and make Mr. Walpole contradict himself', but the Chancellor was amazingly dexterous. He insisted that he had known nothing of Neyno until the informer had volunteered his services. He had met him secretly at Chelsea and alone because this was the only way to give him confidence enough to make further revelations. No words had ever been put into his mouth. The paper found on his body had not been Walpole's instructions but Neyno's own memorandum of what he wished to impart. It was true that the informer had mentioned various Tory peers, but the suggestion of a plot to destroy the opposition leader-ship was quite untrue: the Government had ignored everything said to this effect. On the other hand, whenever he had spoken to Neyno, in private or elsewhere, the latter had repeated that the Bishop of Rochester was principally concerned in the plot. This, insisted Walpole, he had done without any prompting at all. The cross-examination went on for nearly an hour with barbed question and firm reply, and if anything the honours were with Walpole. By

[1] H.M.C. *Onslow MSS.*, p. 463.

his assured performance he had done much to mitigate the force of the accusations against him.[1]

The Bishop's role in the trial was now over. As the mob surged round his carriage and the guards beat a way through, he could feel a certain satisfaction. He had made the best possible out of a hopeless cause, and for a while he could bask in the admiration of countless Tories who saw him as an ancient hero, smitten but unbowed before his enemies. Alexander Pope voiced the emotion of many when he sat down to write a letter full of the excitement of the moment:

To tell you my heart is full of your defence, is no more than I believe the worst enemy you have must own of his. You have really, without a figure, had all the triumph that antient eloquence boasts of. Their passions and consciences have done you right, though their votes will not. You have met with the fate frequent to great and good men, to gain applause where you are denied justice.[2]

That the vote would go against him was certain. On the 15th the grand debate took place in the Lords on the third reading of the bill, and his friends did their utmost. Earl Cowper's vehement denunciation of the whole proceeding as a disgrace to the good name of British justice was received with manifest unease, and in later years was held to provide the decisive arguments against such bills of pains and penalties. The young Duke of Wharton earned instant fame with his cogent analysis of the manner in which the Government's case had been put together. But it mattered little what was said on the one side or the other. When the peers went into the lobby the bill was passed by 83 voices to 43, and on the 27th King George came in person to the House to give it the Royal Assent. Disaster had come to the Bishop of Rochester. On 1 June he was to be deprived of all his preferments, and if after the 25th he had not gone into perpetual exile he was to suffer the penalty of a convicted felon. The other actors in the drama received their various fates. On 17 May Layer was publicly hanged. It was seen that he was dead before the grisly business of drawing and quartering was carried out. Later the Jacobite antiquary, Dr. Richard Rawlinson, picked up his

---

[1] LCM., fos. 55–56, for the only account of the examination of Walpole.
[2] *Pope Corr.* ii. 168–69, Pope to FR, *circa* 11–15 May 1723.

skull, which had blown down from the South Gate of London Bridge, and kept it as a memento. According to the provisions of their bills, Kelly and Plunket were to remain in the Tower under sentence of perpetual imprisonment. Plunket died there, while Kelly escaped to take part eventually in the Scottish rebellion of 1745. Lords Orrery and North and Dennis Kelly were released on their sureties to be of good behaviour. The Jacobite plot had come full circle.

4

The last days were unbearably sad, as the Bishop began to make urgent preparation for his exile. He was particularly anxious to be released from the Tower so that he might sell his books and furniture, and set his financial affairs in order. For this privilege he was even prepared to humble himself in a letter to Townshend, but the most which could be obtained was that his friends should be allowed free access to him until the time of his final departure. He recognized the reason for this enduring animosity. 'My examination of [Walpole] at the bar of the House of Lords', he wrote, 'can never be forgotten, and will scarce be forgiven by him, and much less he forgive me the injuries he has done me. For he is the author of all I suffer, and has pushed the point to the utmost in every article.'[1] Without sparing his feelings, the Government rushed through the procedure for appointing Samuel Bradford, Bishop of Carlisle, as the new Dean of Westminster and Bishop of Rochester.[2] In the *London Journal* Benjamin Hoadly kept up his savage attack and launched himself into a mordant examination of the defence case, extended into weekly parts. It was little compensation to learn that engraved portraits of the ex-Bishop of Rochester were being sold in the streets and that Tory pamphlets were proclaiming him as the latest martyr for the good old Church of England.

So many friends and admirers wanted to visit him in the Tower that it was hard to find times for them all. There were few whom he could ever hope to see again. Wharton, Trevor, Bathurst and Bishop

[1] *The Orrery Papers*, ed. the Countess of Cork and Orrery (2 vols., 1903), p. 39, FR to the Duchess of Buckingham, 2 June 1723; see also S.P. 35/43/225, for a memorandum in Walpole's hand.
[2] Bodl. MS. Add. A. 269, fo. 102, Gibson to Nicolson, 23 May 1723.

Gastrell, all of whom had spoken at his trial, came to receive his thanks. The Duchess of Buckingham, with whom popular rumour had linked his name for a second marriage, was admitted at a special time. When the senior boys of Westminster School came to recite their verses to him, he gave them his own quotation from Milton:

> Some natural tears he dropt, but wiped them soon.
> The world was all before him, where to choose
> His place of rest; and Providence his Guide.

William Morrice was a tower of strength, and arranged for the sale of his household goods at the deanery and Bromley. The Chapter at Westminster was surprisingly generous, and they met no less than six times between 17 and 31 May to ensure that the Dean had his share of the fines from leases sealed before the actual day of his deprivation.[1] Lord Bathurst undertook a collection, and many country Tories pledged themselves to a regular contribution towards the Bishop's expenses abroad. In the end he could look forward to an income from a capital of about £10,000 together with the rents from his small patrimony in Buckinghamshire. The newspapers circulated stories of his great wealth. The truth was that there was a sober competency.

As the departure drew near, he saw some last friends. Pope came on the final evening and was given a Bible with a farewell inscription. The last letter of all was written to Lord Oxford, whose son had come to convey his father's sympathy and good wishes. It was no time to recall old feuds, and Atterbury sent back an assurance that 'I shall preserve to the death a grateful sense of your Lordship's past favours'.[2] The Admiralty pressed for a date, and eventually he named Tuesday, 18 June. Colonel Williamson was ordered by Walpole to deliver his prisoner into the hands of the captain of H.M.S. *Aldborough*, and remain until the ship had departed. On the day Atterbury appeared at the quayside dressed in ordinary episcopal day clothes, and was calm as his boxes and possessions were loaded into a navy barge. But as they moved down river the months of bitter tension and resentment came to a head, and he began to berate Williamson with the force and skill of a man who knew how

---

[1] *A House of Kings*, ed. E. Carpenter (1966), p. 204.
[2] H.M.C. *Portland MSS*. v. 643, FR to Oxford, 16 June 1723.

to make words tell. 'Among other his bitterness to me', reported the indignant soldier, 'he asked me whether I did not think there would come a time when he would call me to account.'[1] In the Long Reach they came to the *Aldborough*, lying surrounded with small boats, filled with friends who had come to shout a final fare-well. The Duke of Wharton presented him with an inscribed sword, and there was cheering and counter-cheering. Eventually the Bishop, Mr. and Mrs. Morrice, their servants and baggage were aboard; and in the late afternoon sails were set and the ship moved away. Williamson and his men raised three lusty cheers for King George, intended for the 'great mortification of the proud, banished prelate', and it was all over. An era in English politics and in the history of the Church of England had come to an end.

[1] S.P. 35/43/337, Williamson to Walpole, 18 June 1723; B.M. Stowe MSS. 251, fo. 14, Walpole to Townshend, 20 June.

CHAPTER FIFTEEN

King James's Minister, 1723–1728

I

IN the early morning of 21 June the Bishop, with his family and baggage, was unceremoniously deposited on the quayside at Calais. Even after three nights on board a small ship in a Channel gale he had enough spirit left to be grimly amused when he learned that Bolingbroke was, at that very moment, in a hotel in the town, waiting to be conveyed back to England at the end of his own period of exile. 'Then, I am exchanged!' he is reported to have exclaimed. But there was no meeting of the two former friends, for in the summer of 1723 there was nobody whom Bolingbroke wished to meet less. His permission to return home had been obtained by elaborate professions to Walpole and Townshend that he had utterly broken with Jacobitism and that 'there is not a man under the sun, whom I have less reason to trust, or more to complain of, than the late Bishop of Rochester'.[1] For the rest of Atterbury's life Bolingbroke was to take careful precautions to ensure that the two of them never met, and now he feigned illness in his room to avoid a critically embarrassing encounter.

At last on the 27th the Bishop's little party arrived in Brussels, where he collapsed utterly. For a sick man who had spent most of the last ten months in a room in the Tower of London the effort of the journey had been too much, and he was soon seriously ill and confined to bed in some lodgings which had to be hastily engaged. There he was to remain for almost three months, wrestling not only with the pain of his swollen hands and feet but with a fit of depression which overwhelmed him as the full misery of his situation came over him. A few English Jacobites came to see him, but for the most part he was ignored. Even that doughty old exile, the Earl of Ailesbury, intimated that he wished to have nothing to do with a

---

[1] *Pol. State*, xxv. 672; Coxe, W., ii. 327, Bolingbroke to Townshend, *circa* 1 Feb. 1724.

man with whom it was a felony even to hold a conversation.[1] Alone in his room, the Bishop became almost desperate for news and company. He could read French easily and understand it almost perfectly when it was spoken to him, but he found it hard to make himself sufficiently well understood in the language and, for a man who loved fluency and wit, this was intolerable. As he lay in bed he pondered whether there was some chance that Lord Anglesey or some other friend might one day re-open his case. At his darkest moments his thoughts ran on Lord Mar, and in his mind he became convinced that this was the man who had betrayed him and from whom all his troubles stemmed. Not a word was heard from England. After the terrible events of the last year his friends were understandably terrified to put pen to paper. In these wretched weeks he seemed like a man without a future, isolated, neglected and abandoned.

In fact, he was by no means ignored. Robert Walpole, with his vested interest in Jacobitism, was indeed determined to dog every step which the Bishop made; and he was ready to spend the Secret Service money without stint to get his information. At the end of August he decided that the best spy in the Government service must be sent to Brussels and, after a clandestine meeting at Chelsea, he dispatched John Macky, a most experienced secret agent, across the Channel. Macky knew his profession well. He assumed the character of a gentleman art-dealer of Jacobite sympathies, supplied himself with all the latest English newspapers, and lingered in the coffee-houses where Morrice and the Bishop's secretary, Salkeld, were usually to be found. The bait worked. Soon the agent had been invited home to meet the ailing Bishop and was engaging him in vehement conversation on the state of English politics and the future of the Jacobite cause. And week by week detailed reports on Atterbury, his visitors and opinions arrived on Walpole's desk and were circulated to other members of the Cabinet.[2]

Walpole was convinced that James would be eager to recruit the

[1] *Memoirs of the Earl of Ailesbury*, ed. W. E. Buckley (London, 1890), ii. 652. After FR's arrival in Brussels all dates will be given in the New Style, unless otherwise noted.

[2] C(H) MSS. Correspondence 1023, Macky to R. Walpole, 9 Sept. 1723; B.M. Add. MSS. 32686, fo. 321, 18 Sept.; fo. 330, 21 Sept.; Coxe, W., ii. 284, R. Walpole to Townshend, 18/29 Oct.

Bishop into his service, and indeed no sooner was it clear that Atterbury had come to rest in Brussels than a stream of letters came from Rome welcoming him in the most affectionate terms. James was genuinely distressed at the disaster which had befallen one of his most faithful supporters. 'I can never do too much for him', he wrote to Lord Lansdowne, 'and I cannot but hope he will be able to do me more service now than ever.'[1] He pressed the Bishop to join him in Italy and recover his health and spirits in the Mediterranean sunshine. The first response was deeply depressive. Atterbury professed himself useless for any work. After weeks of pain he could not possibly travel, and anyway he could hold out no prospect of any action in England: James's friends there were utterly crushed 'and under a firm persuasion that any motions of that kind (as far as they were able to judge) would be fatal'. He offered the 'King' the benefit of his continual prayers.[2] But James was not going to leave it at that, for the truth was that at that moment he badly needed some independent advice. In the summer of 1723 his affairs had come to a crisis, and he had to appoint a new Secretary of State and devise a new policy. It was a painfully difficult choice because he was being urgently pressed by two rival Jacobite factions. On the one hand there was the Earl of Mar himself, who now seemed to be in complete control in Paris and writing letters which gave an impression of confidence, vigour and impending success. On the other hand there were Mar's enemies, and notably James Murray and the Honourable John Hay, brother of the Earl of Kinnoul, who plied the 'King' with accusations that the management in Paris was both treacherous and deadly dangerous.

The arrival of Atterbury seemed like a godsend, and James determined that he should solve the problem. 'At this time', he wrote enthusiastically, 'there is nobody can give me better light and information on my affairs than you; nobody more capable of suggesting the proper measures to be pursued by me; and nobody whose advice and opinion I lay greater weight upon.'[3] Clearly to gain the Bishop's support was a matter of urgency for Murray and

---

[1] R. A. Stuart 67/136, James to Lansdowne, 5 July 1723.

[2] Ibid. 84/171, FR to James, 1 Aug. [1723]: not posted until 12 Aug., and signed '3607'.

[3] Ibid. 68/124, James to FR, 31 Aug. 1723.

Hay, and they took immediate action. In the middle of winter and with the most elaborate secrecy Hay travelled from Rome to Brussels. He found Atterbury in a despondent state, still unable to walk or write, and convinced that the damp Belgian climate was slowly killing him. But after a single interview all this was changed. Hay told of James's search for a new and realistic policy, and stressed his own suspicions about Mar and the whole conduct of business in Paris; he conveyed an invitation to the Bishop to go there in the King's name and conduct a thorough investigation of the way in which affairs had been managed there. Ill though he was, Atterbury rallied. He voiced his own grievances against Mar and after earnest discussions he and Hay came to an agreement: that Hay himself should be the new Secretary of State and that Atterbury, as soon as he was well enough, should travel to Paris and become King James's Minister there. From that moment Mar's fate was sealed; and now that the possibility of determined action had opened up the Bishop was all impatience to be on the road. He chafed and complained at his forced convalescence until in May he was at last able to get away from his hated lodgings in Brussels and set out for the French capital.[1]

Mar awaited his arrival with something approaching despair. He knew that he could handle his two colleagues, for Dillon was a blunt soldier, utterly without guile, while Lansdowne was equally unperceptive, a littérateur of muddled and romantic ideas and with a swollen sense of self-esteem. For months the triumvirate had been protesting their utter innocence to James, but this news that the Bishop was on his way armed with a special commission of inquiry produced from them a veritable shriek of alarm. It was not just the fiasco of 1722 which terrified them. Mar's whole course of diplomacy in Paris since the summer of 1723 had been highly suspicious, and it did not take an antagonist to characterize it as that of a man in the pay of the British Government. Indeed in May, when the English Jacobites were utterly crushed, he had actually proposed that the time was ripe for an armed invasion of England and Scotland in order that James might 'relieve his subjects who were imprisoned and suffering for him at that time'. Dillon and Lansdowne had

---

[1] Ibid. 73/138, FR to James, 20 Apr. 1724 [A letter written entirely in code; the deciphered version is 73/139].

solemnly assured the Chevalier that money and immediate support would be forthcoming. It was, of course, all nonsense, but on the basis of it in September Mar had sent Dillon to the French Court to present a Memorial requesting their immediate assistance in an invasion. What service such a wild document could do, other than to provide excellent propaganda in England against James, was hard to tell.[1] Mar was now in very deep water. As the time drew near for the Bishop's arrival he launched himself into a campaign of rumour and slander, designed to obscure the main issue and create a party for himself among the minor Jacobites. Atterbury was accused of having insulted Queen Clementina and of being an enemy to the Catholic religion. By mid-May James's supporters were in a state of mingled fear and excitement, while Murray in his eagerness travelled ten leagues out along the road on a bare rumour that the Bishop was coming.[2]

Atterbury travelled via Cambrai, where his appearance caused a flutter of surprise among the delegates at the great diplomatic congress gathered there, and he got to Paris on 20 May. Horace Walpole, the British Ambassador, had made official representations that he should be expelled from France, but the French Government would agree only that he should be accorded no recognition or reception.[3] The Bishop could not fail to sense the tension in the air. There were no French visitors, and as he settled into lodgings and arranged for the hire of furniture and a sedan chair, a spy in the Ambassador's pay watched from a vantage-point across the road.[4] Mar called at once, and the interview was as painful as might have been expected. Without more than a pretence at formal courtesy, Atterbury demanded in the King's name to see his official papers, and with great protestations of innocence the Earl agreed that he should have them. This was a fatal error on his part. For a week the Bishop went through the bundles, reading, noting, comparing dates. Tucked between the folios he found evidence of the meetings with Churchill in the spring of 1722; there were details too of the British

[1] Ibid. 74/143, Hay to FR, 13 June 1724, in which he encloses an abstract of the Memorial, as it had been presented on 29 Sept. 1723.

[2] Ibid. 73/151, Mar to James, 24 Apr. 1724; 74/71, Murray to Hay, 15 May.

[3] B.M. Add. MSS. 32739, fo. 156, H. Walpole to Newcastle, 21 June 1724.

[4] Ibid., fos. 254–70, for the spy's notes, written in French, for the months of June and July.

pension and the 'peremptory demand' that Mar should do something
to justify King George's favour. Mar had put himself in the position
of a double agent, and all the circumstantial evidence went to show
that he had taken full advantage of it. It was all no more than Atterbury had expected; and it confirmed what Murray and Hay had
been saying for months. Now he had enough material evidence to
ruin the man who had betrayed him.[1]

Even James was now convinced. Constantly pressed by Murray
and Hay, and now by Atterbury, he was only too anxious to get rid
of Mar as quickly as possible; but he hesitated to dismiss him openly.
Not only did he want to avoid scandal, but he realized how poorly
he himself came out of the whole affair. He had, after all, agreed to
the British pension; he knew of Churchill's visits; and he had even
consented to the 'wretched scheme' for the invasion of England in
1723. If all this came out, his reputation would be blasted for ever
and no one would feel safe in his service. But he was prepared to be
honest, and on 4 July he dispatched to the Bishop a shamefaced
letter. 'Past mistakes', he admitted, 'give one experience for the
future, and I plainly see that the cause can never prosper without I
act in a firm and masterly way.' Now his mind was made up: Hay
should be Secretary of State with a Jacobite peerage as Earl of
Inverness, and a letter should be dispatched immediately to the
Duke of Bourbon informing him of Atterbury's appointment as the
new Minister in Paris. 'It is on your honour and advice', James
concluded, 'that I do and ever shall chiefly depend for the carrying
on successfully my affairs, and your endeavours towards that will,
I know, never be wanting.'[2] At the end of August Mar was formally
dismissed and the news circulated to all Jacobite agents and correspondents. It was no use the disgraced Minister issuing out reams of
vehement self-justification. The blow had been struck and his day
was past.

2

The Bishop of Rochester (as he continued to be called by everyone)
could now pause for reflection, and it took him virtually no time at

---

[1] R. A. Stuart 75/6, FR to James, 19 June 1724; 74/130, Murray to James,
10 June.
[2] Ibid. 75/60, James to FR, 4 July 1724; 75/62, James to Murray, 4 July.

all to realize how unpropitious his situation was if he hoped to conduct important diplomacy. In spite of James's earnest commendation he received no summons to the Court at Versailles, and eventually even he came to see that attendance there would have been bizarre on the part of a Protestant Bishop who could neither stand without assistance nor express himself fluently in the French language. It was apparent, too, that many Jacobite exiles in Paris had been terrified by the hatchet-work performed on Mar, and they now ostracized his successor. Even Lord Lansdowne declined to visit his one-time friend, though his reticence may well have been in some measure due to the large sums of Jacobite money which he had used to pay his private debts. For a while Atterbury hoped that he might be able to use Dillon as his agent at Court, but even this proved impossible. The soldier's political ignorance and foolish optimism began to irritate the Bishop to such a degree that he found himself unable to keep his temper in his presence. Eventually after one furious altercation Dillon emerged so shattered by the invective heaped upon him that he wrote off to James to demand that one or the other of them should be dismissed: 'since persons bred and born in the same climate, and of the same profession, could not agree with him, can it be well expected that I will meet with better success?'[1] It was indeed clear that Dillon himself had to go, but his departure had one serious consequence: the Bishop was now entirely alone. James appointed a young French-educated Irishman, Daniel O'Brien, to act as secretary and carrier of messages to Versailles, but he was in no sense an adviser or friend. Atterbury became increasingly isolated and dependent on his domestics; he lived in one room and rarely went out, even in his chair. Soon his temper, uncertain at the best of times, began to deteriorate badly and the whole household waited in expectation and fear of sudden outbursts of uncontrolled rage.

Even in this solitary existence he was continually spied upon. Horace Walpole, the British Ambassador, was spending a small fortune on espionage and he had informants high and low among the Jacobite exiles in Paris. From a window across the road from the Bishop's lodgings, a relay of agents watched and noted all who came and went, and what letters were received or delivered. It was a

[1] Ibid. 77/54, Dillon to James, 2 Oct. 1724.

formidable apparatus, and yet the Ambassador soon discovered one especially useful spy. Since his escape from official custody in the summer of 1722 John Sample, Sir Robert Sutton's former manservant, had hung around the streets of Paris without employment. He had talked far too freely to Robert Walpole's committee to be any longer acceptable among the Jacobite community and when Atterbury arrived in the city he was on the verge of actual starvation. Of course, he at once seized his opportunity. He came to offer supposed secrets about Mar's dealings with Sir Robert Sutton in 1721 and, since the Bishop listened eagerly and accepted everything, the tale lost nothing in the telling.[1] Within weeks Sample had become a regular visitor to the household and even in some measure the confidant of a lonely and disappointed man. The ingratiating young Irishman sank into the background as someone of humble status before whom it was safe to talk and discuss business. It is, however, an error to confide valuable secrets to starving men, and Sample's information was a marketable commodity. At the end of July 1724 he went to the British Embassy and offered to spy on Atterbury in return for a regular stipend. His proposal was accepted on the spot, and for the next seven and a half years he submitted a thrice-weekly report. Not a detail was neglected: visitors, table-talk, ailments, and even gestures, were recorded. In these last years more is known of the Bishop's daily life than at any other time. If Sample had been better educated he would have been Francis Atterbury's Boswell.[2]

In all these wretched circumstances the one thing which gave the Bishop courage was a conviction that he could devise a Jacobite strategy which would be both realistic and diplomatically effective. The policy of Mar and Dillon had rested upon the naïve assumption that at any moment France would break away from the Quadruple Alliance and support the cause of James III with a military expedition against England. This, the Bishop believed, was to live in a fool's paradise. Since the Settlement of Utrecht in 1713 the

[1] Ibid. 74/17, Sample to Hay, 30 Apr. 1724; 74/130, Murray to James, 10 June.
[2] C(H) MSS. Corr. 1157, H. Walpole to R. Walpole, 5 Aug. 1724, sending a copy of Sample's first report [Corr. 1153]. Sample's later letters are in the Cholmondeley (Houghton) papers, the Newcastle papers, the State Papers, Foreign and Domestic, and in the Waldegrave MSS. at Chewton House.

major powers of Europe had existed in an uneasy concert which was threatened periodically by sudden alarms and flurries of diplomatic activity. The peace, such as it was, depended basically on the concord of England and France, and that there was no war of any importance depended in the long run on the determined statesmanship of two men: Robert Walpole and André-Hercule de Fleury, one-time Bishop of Fréjus.[1] It is a sign of Atterbury's real diplomatic understanding that he realized at once that both these statesmen were determined to preserve the peace of Europe, and that their co-operation was firm and durable. In fact, Dillon's policy had been wholly misconceived: his negotiations at Versailles had been regularly reported to the British Embassy, and it was certain that the Jacobites had little to expect from the French Court beyond fair words and polite requests for more detailed information about the Chevalier's plans. As Atterbury explained it to James himself: 'The steps here taken are all so manifestly opposite both to your present and future interest, and tend so directly to eat it up by the very roots (being the result of applications made, and the advices given by the English Ministry) that one cannot conceive that there is any sincerity in the professions.'[2]

His own scheme was rather to work for a grand alliance of Spain, Austria and Russia, in the hope that they could be persuaded to combine in a war against England. He was aware that it was virtually impossible to find any one ruler prepared to break the peace of Europe and launch an invasion of the British Isles. The strength of the Royal Navy and the memory of Alberoni's humiliating failure in 1719 were sufficient deterrents. And yet the bitter hostility of each of the three powers towards the Hanoverian dynasty was not to be doubted. Spain, in particular, was deeply aggrieved by the provisions of Utrecht; and Elizabeth Farnese, second wife of Philip V, regarded England as the chief obstacle preventing her creation of a Spanish sub-state in Italy. In central Europe the Emperor Charles VI found himself continually thwarted by the English and the Dutch in his attempts to set up an East India Company at

[1] On the diplomacy of this era, see A. McC. Wilson, *French Foreign Policy during the Administration of Cardinal Fleury, 1726-1743* (Harvard, Cambridge, Mass., 1936). J. H. Plumb, *Sir Robert Walpole*, vol. ii, has much valuable material.

[2] R. A. Stuart 80/61, FR to James, 20 Feb. 1725.

Ostend. In the North the new power of Russia had shifted all the traditional alliances, and the rivalry between Peter the Great and George I had become notorious. The Court at St. Petersburg was thronged with Jacobites, and English Ministers lived in constant fear of some naval or military expedition out of Russia launched against one or the other of the dominions of their master.

It had always been a Jacobite dream that one day the diplomacy of Europe would produce a vast coalition, but suddenly in early 1725 their wishful thinking seemed to be overtaken by reality. In February the Duke of Bourbon sent back to her parents the Infanta Maria Anna Victoria, a mere child who had been affianced to the teenage King Louis XV. Such an insult to a Spanish princess was deeply resented in Madrid and national pride was outraged. At once the world of international diplomacy was in rapid motion and by the end of April the Duke of Ripperdà, on behalf of King Philip, had pulled off a remarkable coup: the first Treaty of Vienna, by which Spain and Austria agreed to sink their past differences and act together. Even if Ripperdà's later assertion that the 'Restoration' of James III was a secret article of the treaty is not believed, there can be no doubt that both the high contracting parties were deeply sympathetic to the Jacobite cause. Soon the Spanish armies and fleet were being put into readiness for immediate action, and Europe was in the grip of a war-scare. Everything depended on whether the new alliance could be worked up into an effective and widespread coalition, and soon the chancelleries of Europe were on tenterhooks as the Spanish and Austrian diplomats attempted to persuade the smaller states to join them. The prospects for King James were suddenly hopeful indeed.

When the crisis broke Atterbury was already hard at work. Hay in Rome was now Secretary of State and Earl of Inverness by his Jacobite title, and the two were in constant touch. They agreed that the Jacobites had a critical role to play in persuading the new Czarina Catherine to join the new alliance and to attack King George's Northern allies. Soon Captain William Hay was sent post-haste to St. Petersburg; Sir John Graham was in Vienna trying to extort definite assurances for James from the Emperor's ministers; while Ormonde was in close cabal in Madrid with representatives of the Spanish King. Paris was obviously the pivot of this strategy

of Jacobite diplomacy, and Atterbury had the difficult task of acting
as link man in the secret correspondence which had to be carried on
between St. Petersburg and Madrid. To his great delight he was
approached by Prince Kurakin, the Russian envoy at the Court of
Versailles, and the two became heavily involved in a discussion of
the ways by which the Czarina might be able to aid the Stuart cause.
In April Kurakin revealed that she was considering an invasion of
Norway and suggested that there was a possibility that a military
and naval force might be detached to land in Scotland to engage the
Hanoverian army there. In June the envoy brought news that
Catherine had rejected Anglo-French offers of an alliance and that
she was preparing a great armament to be used in the Baltic, or
even further afield. On the basis of these conversations Atterbury
could write, with obvious pleasure, to James 'that a war in the
North not only is, but is here thought to be, unavoidable'.[1]

Now the Bishop became the centre of urgent preparations. He
sent to inspect the arms and ammunition which had been in store
since the project of 1722, and he accepted at once an offer by one
fiery Jacobite to provide a frigate, fully equipped and crewed for war
service. On 15 June James granted him full powers to organize the
Jacobite rising in England and Scotland, and 'to give such orders and
directions to all my subjects now residing in France, relating to the
present situation of my affairs . . . and especially in relation to
the present intended expedition into Scotland'.[2] But this was a
commission easier to give than to fulfil. The Bishop made great
efforts to re-establish some correspondence with the English Jacobites but they obstinately refused to reply to his urgent letters and
appeals. Eventually a hired agent had to be sent over and his account
of the shuffling and prevarication he met with was so dismal that
James was forced to agree that there were no men of note who could
do his work there.[3] But in Scotland the situation appeared to be
entirely different, and in May the Bishop held secret meetings with
the most notable men among the Scottish exiles. He was aware that
he had to deal with proud and difficult chieftains who might well

[1] R. A. Stuart 81/28, FR to James, 26 Mar. 1725; 81/133, FR to Hay,
23 Apr.; 83/67, FR to James, 25 June.
[2] Ibid. 83/5-12, 15-18, 20. See also 83/28, Hay to FR, 16 June 1725.
[3] Ibid. 81/71, James to FR, 11 Apr. 1725; 81/133, FR to Hay, 23 Apr.

resent the management and interference of an Anglican cleric, but James supplied him with fulsome letters of recommendation and a credit for 180,000 livres, and so with elaborate courtesy he applied himself to the great men. To his delight they received him well, and the Marquess of Seaforth, the Earl of Clanranald, Sir Hector Maclean and Cameron of Lochiel all agreed to co-operate in an expedition.[1]

Such an undertaking depended, however, on the international situation and the secret diplomacy of the great powers, and here the Jacobites were almost entirely in the dark. But they were determined to exert what influence they could, and at the end of June, at James's request, the Duke of Wharton set out from England on a secret mission. To all outward appearances he was an English aristocrat on a continental tour; in fact he was *en route* for Vienna to plead with the Emperor's ministers that the time was now ripe for an allied expedition against the British Isles. Atterbury put an immense store of hope into this attempt to conduct high-level diplomacy, and he was eager once again to meet the brilliant and wayward young man who had been his champion in 1723. Above all he wanted a chance to give Wharton a cool and realistic account of Jacobite prospects before he came into the hands of the professional diplomatists. He knew how difficult it was going to be for the young Duke to avoid ruining everything by embarking on a course of drinking, gambling and general debauchery, 'that company which misled him sometimes into frolics at home', as the Bishop gently put it.[2] But Wharton had absolutely no intention of calling on Atterbury in Paris. He knew that Horace Walpole's spies were everywhere, and that the full details of such a meeting would be known in London within two days. And so, to the Bishop's distress and alarm, he went on directly to Vienna—to a world of sophisticated diplomacy in which he was sure to be utterly out of his depth.[3]

Jacobite hopes remained high until on 1 July the Bishop sustained a most grievous shock. He was under the firm impression that extensive preparations were being made in Scotland to receive an invasion force, and a meeting was arranged with Lord Seaforth

[1] Ibid. 82/38, FR to Hay, 14 May 1725; *E.C.*, ii. 287, a report by Seaforth and Clanranald, 26 May; *E.C.*, ii. 289, FR to Cameron of Lochiel, 27 May.

[2] R. A. Stuart 84/49, FR to James, 16 July 1725.

[3] Ibid. 84/6, 54; 85/96, FR to Wharton, 11, 17 July, 26 Aug. 1725; Glover, pp. 220-21, Wharton to James, 4, 13 July.

and Sir Hector Maclean to hear the latest news and to issue further orders. The conference took place, but Atterbury could scarcely believe his ears when Seaforth blandly informed him that ten days previously he had cancelled all their plans and ordered his followers to surrender their weapons. The Scotsmen would give no reasons for this extraordinary volte-face and Seaforth loftily refused to countermand his instructions. There could, of course, be no explanation other than that the exiles had done a deal with the British Government. All Atterbury's meetings with them in Paris had been reported and in return for revealing the Jacobite plans Lord Seaforth had been promised a pardon and restoration to his title and estates. His clansmen had been giving up their arms even as their chief was discussing plans for an armed rising.[1] Further information, smuggled in from a few Scottish loyalists, made the situation abundantly clear and the Bishop knew that his whole scheme was in ruins 'and that there could in such a divided state be no hope of success: so I determined, by their joint advice, to stop short in this matter and proceed no further'.[2] It was a terrible disappointment and according to the usual course of his illnesses he at once collapsed and had to be confined to bed. Mr. and Mrs. Morrice came across to Paris to nurse him and were alarmed to find him overwrought and on the verge of physical and mental exhaustion. Meanwhile the egregious Sample chattered away to his employers in the British Embassy of all the Bishop's fears and griefs, of his swollen limbs and his pain-filled nights.[3]

There was even worse to come. At the end of November news was received of a shattering quarrel between James and his wife, Clementina. The 'Queen' herself was unstable and capricious, and her moods and affections varied without warning. She and James were wholly unsuited to each other: he cold, melancholy and meticulously correct; she emotional and unreasonable. In the summer of 1725 she took violent exception to the appointment of James Murray

---

[1] See R. A. Stuart 83/31 for Allan Cameron's very exciting journal of his travels in the Highlands, 17 June 1725–13 Mar. 1726; and 86/11, Cameron to FR, 11 Sept. 1725.

[2] Ibid. 82/74, FR to James, 2 July 1725; *E.C.*, ii. 293, Maclean and Lochiel to James, 2 July.

[3] S.P. 78/182, for the series of letters from Sample to H. Walpole, Aug.–Oct. 1725.

as governor to the young Prince Charles Edward, and with the encouragement of the Roman Catholic faction among the courtiers she demanded that this Protestant heretic should be removed from any influence over her son. Neither arguments nor pleas could move her and when James refused to comply she at once left his house, taking up residence in a convent as a martyr for the Catholic faith.[1] The news of this wretched quarrel and its cause put a damp on the Jacobites everywhere, but it had the worst possible effect on the Bishop of Rochester. Though still grievously ill, he struggled to sit up in bed to dictate a letter to James urging him to be absolutely firm. It was a critical issue: the Pope and the Roman party stood fair to ruin James utterly in the eyes of his English Protestant subjects. Yield on this point and he might as well abandon all hope of becoming King in England.[2] Lying back on his pillows, Atterbury seemed utterly dispirited and he admitted to Sample that his patience with the Jacobite cause was almost at an end: 'he has met with nothing but vexation since he undertook to concern himself with the Chevalier's affairs, but as he has begun with them he meant to go through with them, though he believed himself upon his decline, and that he should soon leave this troublesome world for an ever-lasting enjoyment of heaven.'[3]

The new year 1726 was critical for the Jacobites. If it went by without a decision for war by the great powers and an espousal of James's cause, then the great opportunity had been lost—perhaps for ever. James's correspondents were on tenterhooks and just for a while in the spring it did seem that a conflict was imminent. The aggressive activities of the Royal Navy on the Spanish Main, in the Atlantic and in the Baltic, designed as a show of force by the British Government, were provocation enough to create an international crisis and in Spain a widespread demand for a declaration of war. The British Ambassador in Madrid was repeatedly on the point of demanding his passports and breaking off diplomatic relations. In Paris Atterbury scanned the newspapers and waited day by day for the letter which would tell him that war had broken out and that

[1] R. A. Stuart 87/97, James to FR, 19 Nov. 1725.
[2] Ibid. 89/20, FR to James, 2 Jan. 1726. See also 88/118, FR to Hay, 24 Dec. 1725 [written in O'Brien's hand].
[3] S.P. 78/182/186, 189, 207, Sample to H. Walpole, 14, 15, 19 Dec. 1725.

Spanish support for an attack on England was at last a reality. Surely, he asked, the anti-Hanoverian alliance would not miss this chance: it must be 'that Madrid would be pressed and influenced by the Emperor; on that I built and build.' Something had to be done by the Jacobites to precipitate matters and he urged James to transfer Wharton from Vienna, where he had had no success, to Madrid, where he might yet achieve the diplomatic breakthrough which had so far eluded Ormonde. With a kind of desperation he demanded that the Chevalier should hold himself in readiness to travel to Scotland with the expedition the moment news of war came: 'I am satisfied that things there are thoroughly ripe, if a little assistance can be given.'[1]

But when August came, and still there was no word from Vienna or Madrid, the Bishop recognized that it was all over. The season was too far advanced and there could be no expedition. It was no use disguising the plain truth and he admitted the fact to his household and in the hearing of John Sample. Within hours a report to this effect was with Horace Walpole and within days it was being read by the Ministers in London.[2] In fact Atterbury now had only one card up his sleeve, and he decided to play it in a last desperate gamble. For years he had nurtured the belief that it might be possible to seduce Sir Robert Walpole himself into supporting the Jacobite cause, and so in the late summer of 1726 he composed a long secret letter to the British Prime Minister, had it smuggled across to London and secretly delivered.[3] It was a dramatically phrased plea for Walpole to consider his own position and think of the advantages which could come to him if he entered King James's service. George I was old and ailing, and could not last much longer; the Prince of Wales was Walpole's bitter enemy; vengeance and eventual impeachment were his inevitable lot, whether from Hanoverian or Jacobite. Why not ensure his future by a secret understanding with the Stuart Minister in Paris? Old scores would be forgotten. Now was the moment to avoid the wrath to come. As this letter was dispatched to London so another of Atterbury's carefully

[1] R. A. Stuart 92/8, FR to James, 20 Mar. 1726.

[2] S.P. 78/184/68, Sample to H. Walpole, 7 July 1726; fo. 115, H. Walpole to Delafaye, 9 Aug.; R. A. Stuart 96/72, FR to Hay, 19 Aug.

[3] R. A. Stuart 96/134, FR to R. Walpole, Aug. 1726. See 113/97, FR to James, 19 Jan. 1728, explaining how the letter was sent.

composed epistles was smuggled into the château at Versailles and laid upon Fleury's desk. It was an ingenious re-arrangement of the English letter.[1] Now Walpole was represented as already a secret Jacobite, and it was claimed that the recent aggressive naval policy was designed to provoke Russia, Spain and Austria into an invasion of England which would then allow the Prime Minister to reveal himself in his true colours. The wily old Cardinal was not much impressed by such stuff but he read it with interest and saw that it could be useful. At his next interview with Horace Walpole he produced it with a little flourish and handed it over as a proof of his firm attachment to the alliance with England. The Ambassador was not to worry about such letters, he intimated; the French Post Office was continually intercepting Atterbury's correspondence with Ormonde in Spain. Would Mr. Walpole be interested to have copies? They would be delivered immediately to the embassy.[2] It was clear that the last gamble of King James's Minister in Paris had failed.

3

In the autumn the whole management of Jacobite affairs fell into disorder. Lord Inverness's influence as Secretary of State declined and Queen Clementina's hysterical campaign against the Protestants among her husband's followers seemed to be succeeding. James still wrote letters and he went through the motions of diplomacy and conspiracy, but it was all designed to keep up some kind of reputation with his adherents at home. Now he had settled down to a semi-retired existence in Rome and he feared nothing so much as an international crisis which might force him into taking real decisions or travelling away from Italy. When Inverness finally resigned his office in despair James was left with no policy at all, and soon the vacillation and lethargy at the top communicated itself to all the local agents in the form of a paralysing loss of nerve.

The first manifestation of this came in some terrible news from Madrid. Wharton's embassy there had proved a complete failure. Though at first he had been accorded recognition as an ambassador,

---

[1] Coxe, W., ii. 227–29, for the copy in Walpole's papers.
[2] B.M. Add. MSS. 32747, fo. 374, H. Walpole to Newcastle, 10/21 Sept. 1726. See also ibid. 32748, fo. 130, 14/25 Oct.

he was not invited to Court to meet the King and Queen. Weeks passed and it was only gradually that he came to learn the full measure of his offending. It was that he was a Protestant. The Spanish Court had wholeheartedly espoused the cause of Queen Clementina and amid the suffocating piety which surrounded Philip V it appeared that even James himself was suspect as a man who favoured heretics. At first Wharton strutted around Madrid, wearing the insignia of the Order of the Garter which the Chevalier had given him, but soon he sank ito a state of low debauchery with the riff-raff of the town and was scarcely ever to be seen sober. The British Ambassador revoked his passport and conveyed to him a message from King George requiring him immediately to return home; by ignoring it he put himself out of the protection of the British Government.[1] Finally, in some kind of muddled endeavour to get himself received at Court, he announced his conversion to Roman Catholicism. On the part of a man who had never previously shown the slightest interest in religion it was a singularly unconvincing performance. Even James was deeply mortified by his conduct.

In Paris Atterbury was inconsolable. For days he could think or speak of nothing but the disaster of Wharton's conversion.[2] With Inverness dismissed to placate the Queen, it would be concluded on all sides that only Papists could serve King James and enjoy his favour. Wharton's tragedy made it appear that allies could only be procured if James's repeated guarantees to his Protestant subjects were abandoned. During the autumn the Bishop lamented in his letters to Ormonde the seeming impossibility of serving their master when this accursed confusion of religion and politics remained the achilles-heel of the Stuart cause. Were they truly serving the cause of the Church of England by seeking to set up such a King and his followers? For a while Atterbury remained in James's service because he still retained a belief in his kindness and personal integrity, but even this was rudely shattered when he made the astonishing discovery that for months the Chevalier had been systematically

[1] *Hardwicke State Papers*, ii. 636, Keene to Robinson, Madrid, 5 Apr. 1726; B.M. Add. MSS. 32748, fo. 136, Hamilton [Ormonde's secretary] to FR, 23 Sept. [intercepted letter].

[2] R. A. Stuart 96/145, FR to·Hay, 2 Sept. 1726; 96/80, James to FR, 21 Aug.

deceiving him. At the very time when he had been writing to the Bishop as his Minister in Paris he had been sending private letters and memoranda to Daniel O'Brien, who was supposed to be merely Atterbury's assistant or secretary. O'Brien was receiving secret information and he was actually carrying messages to Versailles about which the Bishop had not been informed. It was crude double-dealing which was certain eventually to be found out.[1] Henceforth Atterbury regarded James as a man who had no real claim on his loyalty; and he treated him like some high-born but dishonest schoolboy.

By the summer he had come to realize that a break could not be far off. 'My interest', he admitted to a friend, 'has been a good while in a declining way, and will go on to decline.'[2] When at the end of May 1727 Britain, France and Austria signed in Paris the preliminaries for a new peace treaty, he accepted that this was the end of the road for Jacobite diplomacy—and was curiously unmoved. As he wrote bluntly to Ormonde: 'If these preliminaries are agreed and if they lead to a Congress, then the cause of the King is utterly ruined.'[3] Soon the Quadruple Alliance would be revived and, with a general peace, it was certain that 'the Prince who now occupies the English throne will continue to occupy it'. Indeed all the Jacobites knew that for them it was the end of an epoch. Sir Harry Goring, in his 'unspeakable grief', urged James to risk everything by sailing to England with a few friends and appealing to the common people.[4] But this was romantic nonsense, and Atterbury would have no part in it. In great weariness he sat down to write his letter of resignation and to release into it all his pent-up feelings of disappointment and frustration:

As things have been managed [he informed James], it will scarce be in my power for the future to do anything considerable for your

[1] B.M. Add. MSS. 32748, fo. 298, FR to Ormonde, 11 Nov. 1726 [letter intercepted by the French intelligence service]. Inverness's letterbook [R. A. Stuart 83/90] shows that the 'private' letters to O'Brien had begun in Sept. 1725.

[2] R. A. Stuart 107/4, FR to Williams, 2 June 1727.

[3] B.M. Add. MSS. 32750, fo. 280, FR to Ormonde, 10 May 1727 [intercepted letter, translated into French at the French Post Office and enclosed in fo. 278, H. Walpole to Newcastle, 21 May].

[4] R. A. Stuart 107/34, Goring to James, 8 June 1727.

service . . . I have been left, in all my disadvantages, to work as well as I could, without any assistance or support. The methods I have taken of serving you have been disapproved of, and many ways traversed.[1]

Even the death of George I on 22 June made no difference. The Jacobites had neither money nor alliances, and their English supporters were utterly broken and demoralized. As Atterbury put it succinctly: 'Nothing, I fear, will at present come of that matter. All at home is perfectly quiet; nor do I see when it will be otherwise: there being no appearance of any encouragement from abroad. If there be any it is a secret to me. The great Tories, who have hitherto stuck out, are going in apace, and as ready as any to make their court.'[2] Within weeks it was clear that Sir Robert Walpole had reconciled himself to the new King and was even more firmly in power than ever. William Morrice's cool and accurate reports on the political situation in England dispelled the last lingering hope.[3] Horace Walpole's influence at Versailles was absolute. Now Atterbury began to speak of himself as old and defeated. Confined to his room, without even the consolation of work to do or plans to make, he became more and more dispirited. He was weary of the Stuart cause with its continual false dawns and its constant disappointments. His only pleasure was in his books or in the eager expectation of visits from the Morrices and their small children. Sometimes in his many sleepless nights he pondered the possibility that somehow he might be able to make his peace at home and return to live as Thomas Ken had done, as an elderly deprived bishop, quiet and harmless in the depths of the English countryside.[4]

[1] Ibid. 107/70, FR to James, 16 June 1727.
[2] Ibid. 108/48, FR to Williams, 7 July 1727.
[3] Ibid. 113/97, FR to James, 19 Jan. 1728; *E.C.*, v. 102, Morrice to FR, 9/20 Jan.
[4] B.M. Add. MSS. 32776, fo. 138, Waldegrave to Newcastle, 6 Mar. 1732.

CHAPTER SIXTEEN

The End of a Cause, 1728–1732

I

To admit that the Stuart cause was hopeless was deeply painful, for it left the old Bishop without any expectation that the Church of England could be rescued from her bondage. Jacobitism to Atterbury was a means not an end in itself. He had never been possessed of a high loyalist ideology of the kind propagated by men like Henry Dodwell or Charles Leslie, and he had not shown the slightest inclination to join the ranks of the Nonjurors. If the Tories had managed to survive after 1714 as a powerful Church party he would certainly never have embraced the Jacobite cause at all. His real loyalty was not to the Stuarts but to an old-fashioned vision of the alliance of Church and State given to him by an education in Restoration Oxford. It was a uniquely English version of the union of a national Church and a regime of absolute monarchy, deriving from Archbishop Laud and developed under Sheldon and Sancroft in the era after 1660. In it the Church of England, with its ordered worship and a conservative theology rooted in patristic learning, received from the civil power continual support and comfort in its role as guardian of the morals and religious duties of the nation. And in return the Church fostered loyalty and obedience with all the ideological resources at its command: in the education of the young, in the elaboration of social and political theory, and by its influence as a major landowner. This vision of the co-operation of a loyalist Church and a pious Anglican ruler could hardly survive King James II and the onset of the 'Age of Reason', and it foundered utterly after 1714. It was Atterbury's tragedy that, in spite of his great religious and pastoral gifts, he was convinced that the well-being of the Church of England was still primarily bound up with the political regime and that her cause was best furthered by political agitation. When all had failed in England he turned to the Stuarts as the one means by which the ecclesiastical past might be restored.

It was a desperate expedient. He had known all along of the Chevalier's weakness of character, his indecision, and the bigotry of his entourage, but these had been overlooked and excused because he alone seemed to be the man who could challenge the Hanoverian regime.

As the bitter years of exile went by, Atterbury's Anglicanism became more and more the linchpin of his daily existence. When he was well, he read the morning and evening offices of the Book of Common Prayer with his household, and he had a weekly celebration of the Holy Communion at which he gave a short pastoral address. He would receive no visitors on Saturday afternoon or evening so that he could be quiet and make his preparation.[1] Many of the Anglicans abroad were, of course, Nonjurors and he did his best to act as a bishop to the whole flock. In a rudimentary way he tried to organize a system of Jacobite chaplaincies, so that there was some pastor in each of the major European capitals. It was not easy. His patience was sorely tried by the perpetual quarrels of the Nonjuring clergy, and he was exasperated by their liturgical innovations which he regarded as a plain betrayal of the heritage of the Prayer Book.

Long residence in France did nothing to diminish his antipathy to Roman Catholicism, and it is clear that from time to time he suffered from the attentions of zealous priests who sought to make a convert of him.[2] They were usually instantly put to silence, but eventually to avoid embarrassment he had to refuse to enter any church in Paris and to receive visitors only on strict condition that they confined the discussion to literature and the arts. Yet there was one French priest whom Atterbury took entirely to his heart: the gentle and devout scholar, Pierre François le Courayer. With him there was no reserve, for this Canon-Regular of Ste. Geneviève was a convinced protagonist of the Church of England. In 1721 Courayer had completed a scholarly examination of Anglican Orders, and had pronounced them to be unquestionably valid.[3] But when Atterbury arrived in Paris in 1724 he found that a vehement

[1] *E.C.*, ii. 298, FR to Williams, n.d., but 'Saturday between 11 and 12'.
[2] C(H) MSS. 1338, Sample to H. Walpole, 7 June 1726.
[3] *Dissertation sur la Validité des Ordinations des Anglais* (Nancy, 1723, though printed as if published in Brussels). English trans. by D. Williams (London, 1725).

campaign was being waged against the author by the Jesuits on the grounds that the book was nothing more than a covert attempt to propagate the teachings of Jansenism. The two friends spent hours together composing the outlines of Courayer's defence, and the Bishop looked on with mounting dismay as an official process for heresy went its way. When eventually a commission of twenty bishops formally condemned Courayer's book and launched themselves into a scathing denunciation of the Anglican position, he was outraged. For a moment he considered himself writing an elaborate justification of Courayer, but saner counsels convinced him that as a stranger in a foreign country he had better keep silence. But his opinion of the Church of Rome and its methods was confirmed: they were enemies both to truth and charity.

In February 1728, however, this zealous espousal of the cause of Courayer brought Atterbury to the edge of personal disaster. All during that winter he had grieved over the continual persecution of his friend and, when the attacks of the Jesuits reached the point of a trial for heresy, he advised Courayer to flee to England. There he could be assured of a warm welcome, for the Archbishop of Canterbury was his earnest admirer. One of Atterbury's friends accompanied the nervous little priest in disguise to Calais and on the morning of 19 January he escaped across the Channel. But if the Bishop imagined that his part in all this had gone undetected he was soon undeceived. The anger of the French Court was immense, and the diplomats of the British Embassy were able to report on it with unvarnished pleasure.[1] Indeed Cardinal Fleury decided that it was now time to administer a severe public rebuke to this meddlesome English clergyman, and on 14 February M. Herault, the Lieutenant de Police of Paris, paid Atterbury a formal visit. He was exquisitely polite and expressed his personal sorrow that he should have to convey a disagreeable message from His Majesty the King and His Eminence the Cardinal. But it appeared that one who enjoyed refuge and hospitality in France had encouraged Courayer in his heretical writings, and had now assisted his clandestine flight from justice. The Lieutenant affected to listen sympathetically to the Bishop's horrified protestations but, the moment he had taken his leave,

[1] *E.C.*, v. 101, Sparrow to FR, 18 Jan. 1728, Calais; S.P. 78/196/5, Robinson to Delafaye, 3/14 Feb.

word was spread around Paris that this English exile was under the displeasure of the Court and a dangerous person to visit. When Atterbury wrote to defend himself, the reply was chilling. Fleury returned the message 'that it was the King's pleasure that the Jansenists should find with you neither succour nor advice, and that in particular you should send away from your house those priests whose teaching is contrary to that of the Roman Church, for His Majesty is determined that this shall be uniformly observed throughout his dominions'.[1]

The clear threat that he might find himself expelled from France was a terrible shock. He became convinced that his enemies among the Jacobites and in the British Embassy were all working to this end. And he came quickly to a decision. He would demonstrate to the world that he had resigned all connection with James's affairs by quitting Paris and retiring out into the neighbouring countryside.[2] As soon as it could be arranged he vacated his lodgings and moved into a small villa in the little hamlet of Suresnes. As the summer days came, he read and rested, and virtually ignored all correspondence. The Chevalier was not at all sure how to take it. In many ways he was glad to be rid of a servant whose letters had become increasingly censorious but he was disturbed to realize that he had now lost one of his most able and clear-sighted advisers. Though O'Brien was officially appointed as the new Minister in Paris, he was instructed to visit Atterbury at Suresnes with every mark of respect and to speak to him as if it were expected that he would at some future date rejoin the service. On 6 June James himself wrote to say that 'if I acquiesced to what you so much insisted upon, you will have seen from my letters how far I was from thinking that the reality or the appearance of your retreat from business could be for my interest'.[3] Atterbury was unmoved; and he even refused any longer to allow himself to be upset by the follies of old friends. Wharton came to visit him, but was befuddled by drink. He 'begged my blessing, swore he was no more a Papist than a Turk, proffered himself to the Ambassador upon any terms, and fain would have

---

[1] *E.C.*, ii. 348–51, FR to Morrice, 3/14 Feb. and 5/16 Feb. 1728; *E.C.*, ii. 358, Herault to FR, 16/27 Feb.

[2] R. A. Stuart 115/21, FR to James, 22 Mar. 1728.

[3] Ibid. 117/7, James to FR, 6 June 1728.

gone over to England. When he was refused and prosecuted, he turned Papist and Jacobite again.' Lord North and Grey, who had now taken up a military career abroad, announced his own conversion to Rome, and Atterbury declined to have anything more to do with him. On a visit out to Suresnes O'Brien could only report that the Bishop was in excellent spirits and that his temper had actually become 'doux et humain'.[1]

At the end of July Atterbury felt able to contemplate an even longer journey: south to Montpellier, right out of the way of all political contact. A new scheme was forming in his mind. It was usual for a new reign to begin with an act of general pardon and, if George II's Ministers advised such an indemnity to all prisoners, it might just be possible that a clause could be inserted permitting him to return home. It was a forlorn hope. Secure in his position as Minister to the new King, Walpole had just refused earnest applications from Mar and Wharton.[2] He was certainly not willing to allow the return of a man whom he regarded as much more dangerous, and whose career he still followed in minute detail through the reports of spies. But the Bishop was determined to see what could be done. As he explained to his daughter, he was going to travel the length of France 'that I may be out of the very appearance of managing anything for a certain person who so manages his own business that it is impossible to do him any service.'[3] Morrice was instructed to inform Lord Harcourt, and by the autumn the message had got through to Sir Robert Walpole. The Minister was cruelly amused, and talked loudly in public of the way in which Atterbury was licking the dust in order to be allowed to return home. There was not much mercy in that quarter.

In early October the Bishop and his household travelled the long way south to Montpellier. The weather was warm and the roads good, and part of the journey was by boat down the river Rhône. He arrived in excellent spirits, refreshed by the trip and the sights he had seen. The old town of Montpellier, with its university and

[1] *E.C.*, ii. 412–15, FR to Morrice, 8/19 Sept. 1728; R. A. Stuart 117/57, O'Brien to James, 14 June.

[2] S.P. 36/4/13, R. Walpole to Newcastle, 6/17 Nov. 1727; Coxe, W., ii. 634, H. Walpole to Newcastle, 25 June/6 July 1728; ibid. ii. 632, R. Walpole to Townshend, 29 June/10 July.

[3] *E.C.*, ii. 373, FR to Mary Morrice, 3/14 Aug. 1728.

beautiful setting, pleased him immensely; and it amused him to recall that the first Earl of Clarendon, another state-exile, had made his home there. It was a quiet life. The local library was well-stocked and there was a complete absence of political news. As he described it in a letter to Sample: 'we are as ignorant of affairs here as if we lived at the Cape of Good Hope.'[1] James and then his secretary wrote to enquire after him, and he left their letters unanswered. His concerns were primarily domestic, and he waited eagerly for the post from England which brought news of his children and grandchildren. He learned with distress of the doings of his graceless son, 'Obby', who had inherited his father's mercurial temperament but without anything of his keen wits or strength of character. The young man's career at Oxford had been an unmitigated disgrace, and to save him from his debauchery Morrice had to ship him off to China as fourth mate in a merchant vessel.[2] An even greater grief was the condition of his daughter Mary, his 'dearest heart', upon whom he poured out his affection. It was now clear that she was a victim of the tuberculosis which had killed her mother, and that the doctors could do nothing for her. At last, after much doubting and hesitation, it was decided that she should come to join her father in Montpellier in the autumn of 1729 to avoid the fogs and cold of London.

Sea voyages in the eighteenth century were always perilous, but this one was a disaster. It was planned that the Morrices should take ship to Bourdeaux, where they would meet the Bishop's servants with a carriage to take them over the excellent road via Toulouse to Montpellier. But all Atterbury's plans for the invalid went hopelessly awry. After twelve days beating down the Channel in the face of westerly gales, the ship managed to put into Plymouth with crew and passengers utterly exhausted. It was over six weeks after setting out before William and Mary Morrice finally reached Bourdeaux, and by this time she was desperately ill. Her weakness was such that her husband realized that she had only a little time left, but the two agreed to go on, hoping that there might be one last meeting with the Bishop. A servant was dispatched to ride like the wind to

[1] C(H) MSS. 1644, FR to Sample, 23 Oct. 1728.
[2] In fact, after his father's death, Osborne Atterbury became a reformed character, was ordained by Bishop Hoadly, and lived to become a respected country parson and the father of a clerical dynasty.

Montpellier to bid him set out at once towards them. It was obviously impossible for her to travel in a carriage, and a barge was hired to take them up the Garonne and through the canals to Toulouse. The journey went at a snail's pace until, in the late evening of 6 November, she seemed so weak as to be actually dying. The boatmen were bribed to continue all night, and at dawn the sad travellers came into Toulouse. Here the Bishop was waiting after a frantic drive from Montpellier, and he was able to spend a few short hours with his daughter before she died in his arms. She was clear-headed and composed to the last, received the sacrament at his hands, and died with professions of love and gratitude to him.[1]

It was the final blow which broke the old man's spirit. Back in Montpellier, although he did his best to comfort William Morrice, the Bishop seemed in a daze. Sleep deserted him, and his mind kept returning to that sad and terrible scene in Toulouse. The emotion of it overwhelmed him, and he was unable to keep his composure.[2] Writing to Alexander Pope, he revealed something of the spiritual desolation of an elderly and infirm exile whose only close relative was now a wastrel son. He asked his friend to use his gifts of poetic imagination to judge 'what I felt, and still feel, on this occasion; and spare me the trouble of describing it. At my age, under my infirmities, among utter strangers, how shall I find out proper reliefs and supports? I can have none, but those which Reason and Religion furnish me; and on those I lay hold, and make use of as well as I can.'[3]

In May 1730, when the first shock of his grief was over, he returned to Paris. He had had enough of the enervating climate of the Mediterranean coast, and was apprehensive that the fierce heat of summer would bring on a return of his illness. He now lived a very quiet life in a hired apartment in the centre of the old city. Though the resentment of the French Court seemed to have passed, his visitors were few and he hesitated to be seen much in public. Naturally the British Embassy was concerned to find out whether the Bishop intended once again to manage the Pretender's affairs,

[1] See *E.C.*, iii. 59 et seq., for Morrice's anguished series of letters.
[2] Ibid. iii. 85, FR to Morrice, 9/20 Dec. 1729.
[3] *Pope Corr*. iii. 78, FR to Pope, 20 Nov. 1729.

and they sent John Sample to visit him. But there was now remarkably little to be gleaned from his table-talk. Much of it turned on the past, but mostly his mind dwelt on the Chevalier, to whom he usually referred as 'the poor wretch'. His cause, Atterbury repeated, was hopeless; the powers of Europe would do nothing for him: 'France gives him a little encouragement now and then to support a little grandeur, in order to keep him fast to them, and that they may have it in their power to frighten or assure the Ministry of England, as they shall require. But they never have nor never will think of doing him real service.' 'I know', reported Sample in August, 'that the Bishop is no longer a Jacobite in his heart and wants to make his peace and go home; and indeed I believe he would be glad to embrace an occasion of that kind, for I am positive he has a mean opinion of the Chevalier and will never think otherwise.'[1]

2

The last eighteen months of Atterbury's life were passed amid gathering shadows. In the autumn of 1730 Morrice came across with the children, and they stayed long enough to revive something of his natural brightness and warmth. But winter brought a severe bout of illness from which he emerged weak and depressed. The post from England contained much sad news: old friends were dropping off with alarming frequency and the Church of England seemed to be in a state of utter bondage to the Whig politicians. Letters from Spain told of the pathetic condition of the Duke of Wharton, whose profligacy had at last carried him down to the lowest ebb of poverty and physical decay. When in May the news came of his wretched and lonely death the Bishop grieved within himself over this tragedy of wasted talent. The Duchess of Buckingham came on a visit to Paris *en route* to Rome, but she refused to risk even a brief meeting with her old friend.[2] In fact, on hearing how ill he had been, she asked James to send an order requiring him to return all her letters lest they should fall into the hands of the British Govern-

[1] C(H) MSS. 1720, Sample to H. Walpole, 17 May 1730; ibid. 1763, Aug. 1730.
[2] Chewton House, Waldegrave MSS., Waldegrave to Newcastle, 20 Apr. 1731.

ment on his death. James did not scruple to write just such a letter, and even saw fit to conclude it with a threat that unless he obeyed forthwith the Bishop could expect to receive no further favours from him. As a gesture of contempt Atterbury threw the bundle of the Duchess's letters on the kitchen fire.[1]

At the end of November 1731 he wrote to Alexander Pope and, though he made an effort to be bright and witty in the old style, his depression and unhappiness could not be disguised. He was now a man convinced that his days were numbered. 'I, who squandered away whole days heretofore', he wrote, 'now husband hours when the glass begins to run low, and care not to misspend them on trifles. At the end of the lottery of life, our last minutes, like tickets in the wheel, rise in their valuation.'[2] There were many intimations of mortality. In August the death of his one-time pupil, Lord Orrery, shocked him; and yet he had to recall that it was well over thirty years since they had battled together against the formidable Dr. Bentley. The news of the passing of his elder brother, Lewis, increased his gloom. And in December he learned that Lord Inverness had publicly renounced his Protestant faith at Avignon and been received into the Roman Catholic Church. Atterbury knew Hay well enough to be sure that this was no genuinely religious conversion. It was rather a desperate bid by a discarded minister to be allowed to serve a master who was feeble before the religious bigotry of his entourage.

As the weather became colder the Bishop's health took an alarming turn for the worse. He spent January in excruciating pain, and at the end of the month had a week in which his household thought him at the point of death. Morrice and another English Jacobite, Francis Bulkeley, watched and waited by his bedside, and gradually he emerged out of the fit, though now shaken and weakened. It was clear that he might die at any time, and that some rapid action had to be taken to protect his papers. While he lived he had been naturally reluctant to destroy this vast record of his political activity since 1723, but he was well aware that if it were to fall into hostile hands after his death the security of hundreds of Jacobites would be

---

[1] R. A. Stuart 143/106, FR to James, 5 Mar. 1731; B.M. Add. MSS. 32776, fo. 140, Waldegrave to Newcastle, 6 Mar. 1732.
[2] *Pope Corr.* iii. 247, FR to Pope, 23 Nov. 1731.

in jeopardy. Family and business affairs compelled Morrice to return to London and on 6 February he sent Bulkeley to Lord Waldegrave, the new British Ambassador, to ask whether he would be willing to secure the papers in the event of the Bishop's death by applying to them the Embassy's diplomatic seal. It is obvious that Waldegrave should have agreed at once, the more so since Bulkeley was in fact a spy in his pay who could supply regular reports on the patient's state of health. But foolishly he and his masters in Whitehall prevaricated, and thereby lost what could have been their great chance. Accordingly Atterbury sent to the French Court and obtained from the Garde des Sceaux, or Minister of Justice, a definite promise that the seal of his office would be applied and the effects secured from intruders.[1]

Morrice left on 9 February, and the Bishop began to recover. A number of friends had written in alarm at the news of his grave illness, and he replied to assure them that he was still alive. He was strangely weak and quite unable to walk. As he lay sleepless at night he was alarmed by a new phenomenon: a sharp pain in the chest which suddenly took his breath away. But otherwise he felt clear-headed enough, and his mind was taken up with the question which really rankled: that of Inverness's conversion to Rome. To force the conversion of this one Protestant adviser was the height of stupidity. As he wrote to the Nonjuring chaplain in James's household in a letter which he knew would reach the Chevalier: 'If the Romans' thoughts of this matter are as you present them, they have no more of the wisdom than they have of the bravery of their ancestors.'[2] In spite of his weakness he spent his days, now that he could write again, composing a long and blistering rebuke to Inverness. Why had he not consulted with the only Anglican bishop available to him before he took this step? Why had he taken no steps to enquire into the theological points at issue, for 'seldom any man, who has a sense of piety and honour, quits a religion in which he has been educated, without carefully considering what may be said for and against it'. The truth was, as everyone said, friends and

---

[1] B.M. Add. MSS. 32776, fo. 122, Waldegrave to Newcastle, 22 Feb. 1732; C(H) MSS. 1869, Bulkeley to FR, 13 Feb.; *E.C.*, v. 182, 18 Feb.

[2] R. A. Stuart 151/165, FR to Williams. 25 Feb. 1732; 152/46, James to FR, 12 Mar.

foes alike, that this was a contemptible act of self-interest, and it was 'odious'.[1] This formidable epistle was finished on the evening of Monday, 3 March, and lay on the desk ready for the post. Before going to bed the Bishop wrote a number of other letters. He was free from pain and seemed to expect a good night's sleep. But at two in the morning he was in obvious distress. As his servants were discussing whether to send for a surgeon to bleed him, he had a sudden seizure and died instantly.[2]

There ensued an unseemly struggle, virtually over the corpse, to gain control of the papers. For a whole day the servants concealed the death while 'Lord' Semphill, one of the few Jacobites whom the Bishop had trusted, took rapid action. That evening the boxes of correspondence were smuggled out of the house and removed to the Scots College, and late at night the Lieutenant de Police arrived to apply the official seal to them. Both Daniel O'Brien and the British Ambassador were caught unawares. When the news got out their chagrin was great, but nothing could be done until William Morrice arrived from England.[3] Meanwhile the mails carried the urgent instructions of all the principals to their agents, stressing the necessity that the papers be secured, at no matter what cost in effort or corruption. But in the end it was the French Government which decided the game. Indeed Cardinal Fleury was determined that the British Embassy should not have even a sight of letters which would show the various dealings which he himself had had with the Jacobites. Accordingly a meeting was arranged at the Scots College under the supervision of the Lieutenant. Many papers were burned, some were handed over to their writers, and Morrice himself took all the family letters and purely personal papers. Neither O'Brien nor Lord Waldegrave obtained anything. The Jacobite agent called on Morrice with a written order from James to hand over everything in his possession, but found himself instantly ordered out of the house as a man who had deceived the Bishop and supplanted him.

---

[1] Ibid. 151/185, FR to Inverness, Paris, 3 Mar. 1732.

[2] Waldegrave MSS., FR to Bulkeley, 'Monday night, 8 o'clock' [3 Mar. 1732]; B.M. Add. MSS. 32776, fo. 138, Waldegrave to Newcastle, 6 Mar., 'most private'.

[3] R. A. Stuart 152/22, O'Brien to James, 10 Mar. 1732; 152/28, Semphill to James, 10 Mar.; C(H) MSS. 1872, Sample to James, *circa* 10 Mar.

John Sample, on Waldegrave's instructions, appeared and endeavoured to ingratiate himself with feigned grief and talk of his 'dear
Bishop'. At once Morrice cut him short. Did he really imagine that
they had been deceived? Atterbury had known for years that he had
been selling information to the Embassy. Whine and protest as he
would, Sample was dismissed with contempt. His future life was to
be bleak indeed. Without his income from spying he was to sink
down into utter degradation and die on the streets of Paris of actual
starvation.[1]

Morrice's journey back to England with the body was closely
watched, and the moment the ship *Moore* arrived in British terri-
torial waters on 30 April the Government acted. Customs men from
Deal came aboard and impounded the coffin, the baggage and all
Morrice's effects on a trumped-up charge that contraband lace was
being concealed in them. A warrant for his arrest was issued, and
he was hurried up to Westminster to be questioned by the two
Secretaries of State. But Morrice was not a professional lawyer for
nothing, and he had obviously expected just this kind of treatment.
Newcastle and Harrington could get absolutely nothing from him,
and all Delafaye's rummaging through the family correspondence
was fruitless. Eventually public anger at the manner in which the
Bishop's coffin had been opened grew so strong that it was thought
expedient to restore the corpse to the family for burial.

Yet the British Government had not entirely abandoned its fear
of Bishop Atterbury. A message was sent to the Dean and Chapter
of Westminster to the effect that the King did not wish there to be
any kind of public funeral. Such a royal message was not to be dis-
regarded, and Bishop Joseph Wilcocks, the Dean, and his brethren
stayed away. A single Minor Canon was present on 22 May to
receive Atterbury's body into the Abbey. It was a quiet funeral,
conducted in an almost empty church and attended only by William
Morrice and two of the Bishop's former chaplains, Thomas Moore
and Richard Savage. He was laid to rest beside his wife and two
daughters in the vault which he had had prepared as long previously
as 1722. In exile he had composed an inscription for his tomb: an

---

[1] B.M. Add. MSS. 32776, fo. 323, Waldegrave to Newcastle, 2 Apr.
1732. See also Waldegrave MSS., R. Walpole to Waldegrave, 10 Nov. 1733,
for the end of Sample's income, and *passim* for his desperate letters.

account of the injustices which he had suffered and an appeal to those who came after to judge between him and his principal adversary.

Robertus iste Walpole
Quem nulla nesciet posteritas

Rather than such a superscription it was better for the stone to remain bare. Until 1877, when Dean Stanley opened the vault and had the name 'Francis Atterbury' carved simply above it, there was nothing to mark where he lay.

3

Atterbury passed quietly from the English scene because in the new age of Walpole and Newcastle the ecclesiastical strife of the reign of Anne was an echo from a distant era. Writers of the Bishop's obituary notices rehearsed his career with something approaching incredulity. The power of his oratory in pulpit and Parliament, his pungent wit, and the elegance of his style: all these they could assess. But his conception of the place of the English Church in the life of the nation had already become incomprehensible, and men found it hard to understand how issues like Passive Obedience or Occasional Conformity had ever set the world of politics into violent motion and toppled Ministries.

It might have been expected that the Jacobites would have preserved in honour the memory of a man who had laboured so mightily in their cause and suffered so much for it. But this was not so. After the Bishop's death James Stuart could reveal his princely resentment at this Anglican ecclesiastic who had chided him so remorselessly, and the last letter to Inverness provided occasion for a harsh verdict. 'I was well acquainted with that Bishop's temper', he complained, and Atterbury was dismissed as a man of 'spleen and malice'.[1] His name was not mentioned again in the Jacobite correspondence. The year 1732 marked indeed the virtual end of James's efforts to secure his Restoration. He continued to correspond with Tory politicians in England but there was a tacit understanding on both sides that nothing be done which involved risk or undue exertion. In July he actually wrote to Sir Robert Walpole, admitting that all his plans had failed and throwing himself on the English

[1] R. A. Stuart 152/106, James to Inverness, 26 Mar. 1732.

Prime Minister as the only person in the world who could now assist
him.[1] Henceforward Jacobitism was the politics of nostalgia, a faith
of Tory backbenchers who had come to accept permanent exclusion
from office and influence. It was a philosophy of perpetual opposition
not a dynamic of rebellion. James lived on in the papal capital,
surrounded by his seedy entourage, increasingly gloomy and pious,
and something of a joke in sophisticated society. He feared nothing
so much as some sudden change in the internal affairs of England or
Scotland or in international diplomacy which would require him to
set out on his travels again. When in 1745 conditions in the Highlands made a rising of the clans under Jacobite auspices a real possibility, it was his eldest son, Prince Charles Edward, who had to be
sent to sustain the royal presence.

By 1732 all Atterbury's aspirations for the Church of England had
been brought down to the dust. So far from achieving its aims the
High Church movement had attracted a terrible reaction. The
churchmen had sown discord and now they reaped a bitter harvest
of pastoral ineffectiveness. Now the Bishop of Rochester was remembered as the symbol of a tribe of arbitrary ecclesiastics who had
threatened the nation with 'Church Power'; and, in an age when
public decency and private principle were at their lowest ebb, there
ensued a vehement and persistent campaign against the Church.
Obviously much of this hostility was derived from the current vogue
for an extreme rationalism in religion, when any appeal to the tradition of the past was equated with mere superstition and the Deist
challenge to orthodox Christianity was regarded as unanswerable.
But antagonism stemmed also from the fear and resentment which
the High Church campaign had instilled into Whig politicians.
Those who had lived through the great Sacheverell crisis could
never forget the raw passions aroused, and they were resolved that
churchmen, lay and clerical, should never again be in a position so
to inflame popular sentiment. Thomas Burnet, himself the son of a
bishop, recorded the dramatic shift in opinion among the political
classes. 'I cannot but remind you with joy', he wrote in 1719, 'how
the world's changed, since the time when, as we know, a word
against the clergy passed for rank atheism, and now to speak toler-

---

[1] Ibid. 163/57, James to R. Walpole, 13 July 1732.

ably of them passes for superstition.'[1] In the 1730s indeed the prevalent cry was of a danger to the State, and even the Church's lay supporters affected the role of 'candid friends' who had to temper the inordinate drive of the clergy towards priestly domination. The reality was of a crushing secular power over the Church, which denied both the clergy and active Christian laymen the right to promote its gospel and extend its pastoral work. Inexorably the Anglican establishment came to depend on the goodwill of Ministers of the Crown who, even when they paid a formal respect to religion, tended to think of it as primarily an engine of civil order and social subordination.

Francis Atterbury may be justly described as a tragic figure: one who by defect of vision and a flawed personality hastened the events which he most feared. He came to exercise his undoubted powers of leadership and persuasion at a time when the clergy of the Church of England were faced with a critical choice, and he urged them to agitate for a return to the past. For one hectic period ecclesiastical issues and the grievances of the clerical order formed the very stuff of political conflict—but it was for the last time. In the political and intellectual conditions of the eighteenth century religious affairs were destined to recede from the centre of the political stage. But before 1714 it was by no means obvious that this had to be the case. Lord Macaulay, in one of his magisterial judgements, dismissed Atterbury as a man of 'great powers' who 'troubled Church and State during forty eventful years'. But the verdict is, at best, superficial. Anglican Toryism with its vision of a stable society, built on religious assumptions and compacted into a moral order, was a faith which certainly the majority of Englishmen embraced in 1688; and it was to take a veritable shaking of the foundations before it appeared as obsolete as it did in 1730. A defence of the Church and 'the landed interest' against minimizing rationalism, political oligarchy, and the power of money, engaged the energies of some of the most talented men of the age.

It is of the nature of doomed causes, however, that their agitation falls to strange champions. Of Francis Atterbury's force of personality, restless intelligence and subtle ingenuity there can be no question. He was superbly equipped for the public persuasion and

[1] *Letters of Thomas Burnet to George Duckett,* p. 161.

private manoeuvre involved in the business of politics, and yet his disadvantages were also many. His character was flawed by excitability and obsession, and his political judgements were in the long term faulty. At a critical time his extraordinary career was that of the most notable English churchman of the age, but his influence was one which the Church of England learned bitterly to regret.

Bibliography

I. MANUSCRIPT SOURCES

THE principal material is listed with a brief note of its location and nature.

BRITISH MUSEUM

Loan 29	Robert Harley, Earl of Oxford
Additional MSS.	
4291	Lewis Atterbury
5143	Nichols's Atterbury collection
6116	William Wake, Bishop of Lincoln and Archbishop of Canterbury (transcripts)
9129	Coxe transcripts
17677 HHH	L'Hermitage to the States-General (transcripts)
22515–24	Official papers of Lord Carteret
22908	Dr. John Colbatch
27440	Charles Allestree
28055	Earl of Godolphin
29579	Viscount Hatton
29588–89	Earl of Nottingham
32096	George Harbin
32686–87, 32738–40, 32747–48, 32750, 32776,	
33199–200	Duke of Newcastle
34713	Earl of Macclesfield
35837	Sir Luke Schaub
35839	Earl of Hardwicke
35854	Earl Cowper
36139	Earl of Hardwicke
36707	James Harrington
Stowe MSS.	
231–32, 242	Hanover State Papers
250	Jacobite intercepted correspondence

251	Viscount Townshend
750	
Lansdowne MSS.	
515	Petyt correspondence
773	Charles Davenant
1013, 1024, 1039	Correspondence and diary of White Kennett
Sloane MSS.	
4204	Sir Luke Schaub
4274	Thoresby collection
Harleian MSS.	
4712	J. Anstis

BODLEIAN LIBRARY, OXFORD

MSS. Additional	
A. 191	Gilbert Burnet
A. 217	William Nicolson
A. 269	Edmund Gibson
MSS. Ballard	
3–7, 10, 17, 29, 31–32, 38	Arthur Charlett
MS. Eng. Th. c.	Thomas Brett
MS. North c.	Lord North and Grey
MS. Rawl. Letters 92	
MSS. Tanner	
30–31, 37, 300	William Sancroft, Archbishop of Canterbury
MS. Top. Oxon.	
MS. Top. Wilts c.	Thomas Naish: autobiography
MS. Willis 45	Browne Willis

PUBLIC RECORD OFFICE

State Papers	
Series 35	Domestic, George I
Series 36	Domestic, George II
Series 78	Foreign (France)
Loans	
Series 30	Lord Bathurst
Transcripts	
Series 3	Baschet transcripts

ROYAL ARCHIVES, WINDSOR CASTLE

Stuart Papers, 5 163   James Stuart, the Old Pretender
Georgian Additional   Caroline, Princess of Wales
  MSS. 28

CAMBRIDGE UNIVERSITY LIBRARY

Cholmondeley (Houghton)
  MSS.   Sir Robert Walpole
Strype MSS.

LAMBETH PALACE LIBRARY

MSS. 929, 934   Thomas Tenison, Archbishop
                       of Canterbury
MS. 1770   William Wake: diary, 1705–1725

HOUSE OF LORDS RECORD OFFICE

Records 1716/1717, item 249

QUAI D'ORSAY, PARIS (Archives du Ministère des Affaires
  Etrangères)
Correspondance Politique, Angleterre, 338–40

WESTMINSTER ABBEY

MSS. 65007–65031   Francis Atterbury

OTHER COLLECTIONS

Bagot MSS.   Mrs. O. R. Bagot, Levens Hall,
                    Westmorland (Colonel James
                    Grahame)

Blenheim MSS.   Duke of Marlborough, Blenheim
                       Palace (1st Duke of Marlborough,
                       3rd Earl of Sunderland, Robert
                       Harley, Arthur Maynwaring)

Dean and Chapter of
  Carlisle,
  Minute Book 10
Chatsworth MSS.
  Finch-Halifax MSS.   Duke of Devonshire, Chatsworth
                              House, Derbyshire (Heneage
                              Finch, Lord Guernsey)

Dartmouth MSS.
  Supplementary MSS. 271   William Salt Library, Stafford
  Cabinet minutes   (1st Earl of Dartmouth)
Finch MSS.   Leicestershire R.O. (Daniel Finch,
    Earl of Nottingham)
Gower MSS.   Staffordshire R.O. (Sir John Leveson
    Gower, Lord Gower)
Hailstone Collection   York Minster Library (Dr. Hugh
    Todd)
Hardwicke MSS. 33   New York Public Library
    (Lord Somers)
Harrowby MSS. 432   Earl of Harrowby, Sandon Hall,
    Stafford (Dudley Ryder)
Lloyd-Baker-Sharp MSS.   Miss Olive Lloyd-Baker,
    Hardwicke Court, Gloucester
    (John Sharp, Archbishop of York)

Longleat MSS.
  Portland Miscellaneous   Marquess of Bath, Longleat House,
  Thynne MSS.   Wiltshire (Robert Harley, Earl of
    Godolphin, Viscount Weymouth)
Nicolson MS. Diary
  1702–8, 1710–14   Tullie House, Carlisle
  1709–10   P. N. S. Mansergh
Orrery MSS.   Harvard College Library, Cambridge,
    Massachusetts (Charles Boyle, Earl
    of Orrery)
Ottley MSS.   National Library of Wales (Adam
    Ottley, Bishop of St. Davids)
Panshanger (Cowper)   Hertfordshire R.O. (William Cowper,
  MSS.   Earl Cowper, Sir David Hamilton)
Prussian MSS. 39A   Deutches Zentralarchiv, Merseburg
    East Germany (Dispatches of
    Frederick Bonet)

Diocese of Rochester,
  Act Book, 1713–1821   Rochester Diocesan Registry,
    1, The Sanctuary, Westminster, S.W.1.
Somers MSS.   Surrey R.O., Kingston-upon-Thames
    (Lord Somers)
Stowe MSS.   Henry E. Huntington Library,
    San Marino, California (James
    Brydges)

Trelawny MSS.

    Collectanea Trelawniana   Mr. Francis Williams (Sir Jonathan
                             Trelawny, Bishop of Exeter and
                             Winchester), transcripts.

Trumbull MSS.

    MSS. LIII–LV   Marquess of Downshire, Berkshire
    Additional MSS. 133, 136 R.O. (Sir William Trumbull, Henry
                             St. John)

Wake MSS.

    Arch. Epist. W.,   Christ Church, Oxford (William
    Lincoln, Canterbury,   Wake, Bishop of Lincoln and
    Miscellaneous   Archbishop of Canterbury)
    Autobiography to 1705

Waldegrave MSS.   Earl Waldegrave, Chewton House,
                             Chewton Magna, Somerset (1st Earl
                             Waldegrave)

II. WORKS PUBLISHED BY ATTERBURY

Pamphlets attributed to Atterbury but which cannot definitely be
ascribed to him have been placed in square brackets.

Absalom et Achitophel: *poema Latino carmine donatum* [with F. Hickman]
    (1682).
Anthologia Seu Selecta Quaedam Poemata Italorum Qui Latine Scripserunt
    (1684).
*An Answer to Some Considerations on the Spirit of Martin Luther and the
    Original of the Reformation* (Oxford, 1687.)
The Duty of Praise and Thanksgiving: A sermon preached before the
    Queen at Whitehall, 24 May 1692 (1692).
The Power of Charity to Cover Sin: A sermon preached before the
    President and Governors of the Hospitals of Bridewell and
    Bethlehem in Bridewell-Chapel, 16 August 1694 (1694).
The Christian Religion Increased by Miracle: A sermon preached before
    the Queen, 21 October 1694 (1694).
A Scorner Incapable of True Wisdom: A sermon preached before the
    Queen at Whitehall, 28 October 1694 (1694).
*A Letter to a Convocation-Man concerning the Rights, Powers and Privi-
    ledges of that Body* (1697).

[*Dr. Bentley's Dissertations on the Epistles of Phalaris, and the Fables of Aesop, Examined.* By the Honourable Charles Boyle (In fact, composed by Atterbury, Smalridge, and Freind). 1698].

A Discourse occasioned by the Death of the Right Honourable the Lady Cutts (1698).

The Rights, Powers, and Priviledges of an English Convocation, Stated and Vindicated in Answer to a Late Book of Dr. Wake's, Entituled, The Authority of Christian Princes over their Ecclesiastical Synods Asserted (1700).

A Short Review of the Controversy between Mr. Boyle and Dr. Bentley. With suitable Reflections upon it (1701).

The Rights, Powers, and Priviledges . . . The Second Edition, much enlarged (1701).

Additions to the first edition of the Rights, Powers, and Priviledges (1701).

The Wisdom of Providence Manifested in the Revolutions of Government: A sermon preached before the Honourable House of Commons at St. Margaret's, Westminster, 29 May 1701 (1701).

The Power of the Lower House of Convocation to Adjourn itself, vindicated from the Misrepresentations of a late Paper (1701).

A Letter to a Clergyman in the Country, concerning the Choice of Members, and the Execution of the Parliament-Writ for the Ensuing Convocation (1701).

A Second Letter to a Clergyman in the Country (1701).

A Third Letter to a Clergyman in the Country, in defence of what was said in the two former (1702).

A Faithful Account of some Transactions in the Three last Sessions of the Present Convocation. In a Letter to a Friend. Numb. 1 (1702).

A Faithful Account of what past in Convocation, Febr. the 19th. 1702. In a Second Letter to a Friend. Numb. 2 (1702).

A Continuation of the Faithful Account in a Third Letter to a Friend (1702).

The Case of the Schedule Stated (1702).

The Parliamentary Original and Rights of the Lower House of Convocation cleared (1702).

The Duty of Publick Intercession and Thanksgiving for Princes: A sermon preached before the Honourable House of Commons at St. Margaret's, Westminster, 8 March 170$\frac{3}{4}$ (1704).

The Rule of Doing as we would be Done Unto Explained: A sermon preached before the Queen, 3 November 1704 (1704).

[*D. F.A.'s Vindication of the Bp. of Sarum from being the author of a late printed speech, in a letter to a friend* (1704).]

A Letter from the South, by way of an answer to a late letter from a Northern Divine; giving an account of a very strange Attempt made by Dr. A. (1704).

A Continuation of the Faithful Account in a Fourth Letter (1705).

Of Religious Retirement: A sermon preached before the Queen at St. James's Chapel, 23 March 1704/5 (1705).

A Standing Revelation the best Means of Conviction: A sermon preached before the Queen at St. James's Chapel, 28 October 1705 (1705).

A Sermon preached in the Cathedral Church of St. Paul; at the Funeral of Mr. Tho. Bennet, Aug. 30. MDCCVI (1706).

A Sermon preached in the Guildhall Chapel, London, Septemb. 28. 1706, being the Day of the Election of the . . . *Lord Mayor* (1706).

[*The axe laid to the root of Christianity: or, a specimen of the prophaneness and blasphemy that abounds in some late writings* (1706).]

An Account and Defence of the Protestation made by the Lower House of Convocation, April, 30th. 1707,i n behalf of the Queen's Supremacy (1707).

A Large Vindication of the Doctrine contained in the Sermon preached at the Funeral of Thomas Bennet (1707).

Fourteen Sermons preached on Several Occasions (1708).

Some Proceedings in the Convocation, A.D. 1705. Faithfully represented (1708).

An Acquaintance with God the best Support under Afflictions: A sermon preached before the Queen at St. James's, 31 October 1708 (1708).

Concio ad Clerum Londinensem, Habita, in Ecclesia S. Elphegi, Maij XVII. A.D. MDCCIX (1709).

A Sermon preached before the London-Clergy at Saint Alphage, May the 17th 1709 (1710).

A sermon preached before the Sons of the Clergy at their Anniversary-Meeting (1709).

The Examiner: Nos. 10 and 13 (1710).

[*A Representation of the Present State of Religion* (1711).]

[*Considerations upon the Secret History of the White Staff, humbly addressed to the E--- of O----* (1714).]

The History of the Mitre and the Purse (1714)

English Advice to the Freeholders of England (1714).

[*A true Copy of a Letter from* . . . *Viscount Bolingbroke* (Dover, 27 March 1715). (1715).]

Bishop Atterbury's and Bishop Smalridge's reasons for not signing the declaration, lately put forth by the Abp. of Canterbury and the other bishops (1715).

The speech of the Right Reverend the L--d Bishop of R----- at the election for the high steward at Westminster, Feb. 28, 1715–16 (1716).

An Argument to prove the Affections of the People of England to be the best Security of the Government (1716).

Directions for Confirmation (Rochester, 1716).

The Speech of Francis Late Lord Bishop of Rochester at the Bar of the House of Lords on Saturday the 11th May 1723 (1723).

Sermons and Discourses on Several Subjects and Occasions, 2 vols (1723).

The Bishop of Rochester's Vindication of Bishop Smalridge, Dr. Aldrich, and Himself from the scandalous reflections of Oldmixon (1731).

III. PRIMARY SOURCES IN PRINT

It is not possible to list here the vast number of contemporary sermons and pamphlets. Those specifically cited may be found in the footnotes. This section deals with works containing original material directly bearing on the career of Atterbury. The place of publication is London, unless it is otherwise stated.

The Epistolary Correspondence of the Right Reverend Francis Atterbury, D.D., Lord Bishop of Rochester, ed. J. Nichols (4 vols., second edn., 1789–90); Vol. 5 (1798).

The Stuart Papers, Vol. I [all published]: *Letters of Francis Atterbury . . . to the Chevalier de St. George*, ed. J. H. Glover (1847).

ATTERBURY, Francis, *Sermons on Several Occasions . . . published from the originals by Thomas Moore* (2 vols., 1734).

The Letters and Correspondence of Henry St. John, Lord Viscount Bolingbroke, ed. Gilbert Parke (4 vols., 1798).

BOYER, Abel, *History of the Reign of Queen Anne, digested into Annals* (11 vols., 1703–13).

—, *The Political State of Great Britain* (60 vols., 1711–40).

—, *An Impartial History of the Occasional Conformity and Schism Bills* (1717).

BURNET, Gilbert, *A History of My Own Time*, ed. M. J. Routh (6 vols., Oxford, 1823).

A Supplement to Burnet's History of My Own Time, ed. H. C. Foxcroft (Oxford, 1902).

COBBETT, William, *The Parliamentary History of England* (36 vols., 1806-20).

Reports from Committees of the House of Commons. Vol. I: 1715-1735 (1803).

The Private Diary of William , first Earl Cowper, 1705-1714, ed. E. C. Hawtrey (Roxburghe Club, Eton, 1833).

The Diary of Mary, Countess Cowper, 1714-1720, ed. Spencer Cowper (1865).

COXE, William, *Memoirs of John, Duke of Marlborough, with his original correspondence* (3 vols., 1818).

—, *Memoirs of the Life and Administration of Sir Robert Walpole* (3 vols., 1798).

—, *Memoirs of Horatio, Lord Walpole* (2nd edn., 2 vols., 1808).

DEFOE, Daniel, *The Secret History of the White Staff* (1714); *Part II* (1714); *Part III* (1715).

The Letters of Daniel Defoe, ed. G. H. Healey (Oxford, 1955).

DICKSON, W. K., *The Jacobite Attempt of 1719* (Edinburgh, 1895). [An edition of Ormonde's letters]

Hardwicke State Papers, from 1501-1726, ed. P. Yorke (2 vols., 1778).

Remarks and Collections of Thomas Hearne, Oxford Historical Society (11 vols., Oxford, 1885-1907).

Historical Manuscripts Commission:

First Report (1870), *Trelawny MSS.*

Second Report (1871), *Bromley-Davenport MSS., Baker MSS.*

Fifth Report (1876), *Sutherland MSS.*

Eighth Report (1881), *Marlborough MSS.*

Bath MSS., i-iii.

Carlisle MSS.

Cowper MSS., iii.

Dartmouth MSS., i.

Downshire MSS., I.2.

House of Lords MSS., x-xi.

Onslow MSS.

Polwarth MSS., iii.

Portland MSS., i, iv-v, vii.

Stuart MSS., ii-vii.

HOWELL, T. B., *State Trials*, vol. xvi (1816).

Memoirs of the Life, Travels and Transactions of the Reverend Mr. George Kelly (1736).

KENNETT, White, *The Wisdom of Looking Backward* (1715).

The Parliamentary Diary of Sir Edward Knatchbull, 1722-1730, ed. A. N. Newman (1963).

The Lockhart Papers [ed. A. Aufrere], (2 vols., 1817).

LUTTRELL, Narcissus, *A Brief Historical Relation of State Affairs* (6 vols., Oxford, 1859).

Memoirs of the Secret Services of John Macky, Esq. (Roxburghe Club, 1895).

MACPHERSON, J, *Original Papers; containing the Secret History of Great Britain* (2 vols., 1775).

MANCHESTER, Duke of (ed.), *Court and Society from Elizabeth to Anne* (2 vols., 1864).

Private Correspondence of Sarah, Duchess of Marlborough, ed. [Lord John Russell] (2 vols., 1838).

The Diary of Thomas Naish, ed. Doreen Slatter, Wiltshire Archæological and Natural History Society (1965).

NICHOLS, J., *Illustrations of Literary History,* iii (1818). [Correspondence of George Smalridge.]

NICHOLS, J. G. (ed.), *The letters of Pope to Atterbury when in the Tower of London,* The Camden Miscellany, Vol. iv (1859).

The Epistolary Correspondence of Bishop William Nicolson, ed. J. Nichols (2 vols., 1809).

'The diaries of William Nicolson', ed. Bishop Ware, *Transactions of the Cumberland and Westmorland Antiquarian and Archæological Society,* new series, vols. 1-6 (1901-06); vol. 35, ed. R. G. Collingwood (1935); vols. 46, 50, ed. T. Gray and E. Birley (1946, 1950).

OLDMIXON, John, *The History of England during the Reigns of King William and Queen Mary, Queen Anne, King George I* (1735).

The Orrery Papers, ed. the Countess of Cork and Orrery (2 vols., 1903).

PHILALETHES, pseud., *Memoirs of the Life and Conduct of Dr. Francis Atterbury* (1723).

PITTIS, William, *The Proceedings of both Houses of Parliament in the Years 1702, 1703, 1704, upon the Bill to prevent Occasional Conformity* (1710).

—, *The History of the Present Parliament and Convocation* (1711).

The Correspondence of Alexander Pope, ed. George Sherburn (5 vols., Oxford, 1956).

Letters of Humphrey Prideaux . . . to John Ellis, 1674-1722, ed. E. M. Thomson, Camden Society (1875).

The Tryal of Dr. Henry Sacheverell before the House of Peers (1710).

Debates and Speeches in both Houses of Parliament concerning the Schism-Bill (1715).

SHARP, Thomas, *The Life of John Sharp, D.D., Lord Archbishop of York: collected from his Diary, Letters and other Authentic Testimonies* (2 vols., 1825).

Handlingar rörande Skandinaviens historia (Stockholm, 1822), vol. x. [Correspondence of Baron Sparre with Görtz and Gyllenborg, 1716–1717.]

[*Somers Tracts*]. *A Collection of Scarce and Valuable Tracts*, ed. Sir Walter Scott (13 vols., 1809-15).

The Spectator, ed. D. F. Bond (5 vols, Oxford, 1965).

STACKHOUSE, Thomas, *Memoirs of the Life and Conduct of Dr. Francis Atterbury* (1723), 2nd edn., 1727.

The Correspondence of Jonathan Swift, ed. Harold Williams (5 vols., Oxford, 1963-65).

SWIFT, Jonathan, *Journal to Stella*, ed. Harold Williams (2 vols., Oxford, 1958).

—, *Political Tracts, 1711-1713*, ed. H. Davis (3 vols., Oxford, 1951).

—, *Political Tracts, 1713-1719*, ed. H. Davis and I. Ehrenpreis (Oxford, 1964).

—, *History of the Four Last Years of the Queen*, ed. H. Davis (Oxford, 1951).

TIMBERLAND, Ebenezer, *The History and Proceedings of the House of Lords from 1660 to the present time* (8 vols, 1741-2).

The Wentworth Papers, 1705-1739, ed. James J. Cartwright (1883).

WICKHAM-LEGG, L. G., (ed.), *British Diplomatic Instructions, 1689-1789*, iv: *France, 1721-1727* (1927).

—, 'Extracts from Jacobite Correspondence, 1711-14', *English Historical Review*, xxx (1915), 501.

WILLIAMS, Folkestone, *Memoirs and Correspondence of Francis Atterbury, D.D., Bishop of Rochester* (2 vols., 1869).

The Official Diary of Lieutenant-General Adam Williamson, Deputy-Lieutenant of the Tower of London, 1722-1747, ed. J. C. Fox (1912).

IV. SECONDARY SOURCES

The place of publication is London, unless otherwise stated.

BEDDARD, R. A., 'The Commission for Ecclesiastical Promotions, 1681-84: an instrument of Tory reaction', *The Historical Journal*, x (1967), 11.

BEECHING, H. C., *Francis Atterbury* (1909).

BENNETT, G. V., *White Kennett, 1660-1728, Bishop of Peterborough* (1957).

—, 'King William III and the Episcopate' in *Essays in Modern English Church History in Memory of Norman Sykes*, eds. G. V. Bennett and J. D. Walsh (1966).

—, 'An Unpublished Diary of Archbishop William Wake', in *Studies in Church History*, iii, ed. G. J. Cuming (Leiden, 1966), 258.

—, 'Robert Harley, the Godolphin Ministry and the bishoprics crisis of 1707', *English Historical Review*, lxxxii (1967), 726.

—, 'Conflict in the Church', in *Britain after the Glorious Revolution, 1689-1714*, ed. Geoffrey Holmes (1969).

—, 'The Convocation of 1710: an Anglican Attempt at Counter-Revolution', in *Studies in Church History*, vii, eds. G. J. Cuming and Derek Baker (Cambridge, 1971).

—, 'Patristic Tradition in Anglican Thought, 1660-1900', *Oecumenica: Jahrbuch fur ökumenische Forschung 1971/2* (Gütersloh, 1972).

—, 'Jacobitism and the Rise of Walpole' in *Historical Perspectives: Studies in English Thought and Society in Honour of J. H. Plumb*, ed. Neil McKendrick (1974).

BRUCE, M., 'The Duke of Mar in exile, 1716-1732', *Transactions of the Royal Historical Society* (1937).

CARPENTER, E. F., *Thomas Tenison, Archbishop of Canterbury* (1948).

—, *The Protestant Bishop, being the life of Henry Compton, 1632-1713, Bishop of London* (1956).

CLARKE, T. E. S., and FOXCROFT, H. C., *A Life of Gilbert Burnet, Bishop of Salisbury* (Cambridge, 1907).

CRAGG, G. R., *From Puritanism to the Age of Reason* (Cambridge, 1950).

—, *Reason and Authority in the Eighteenth Century* (Cambridge, 1964).

DICKINSON, H. T., *Bolingbroke* (1970).

—, 'The October Club', *The Huntington Library Quarterly*, xxxiii (Feb., 1970).

D'OYLY, G., *The Life of William Sancroft, Archbishop of Canterbury* (2 vols., 1821).

ELLIS, E. L., 'The Whig Junto in relation to the development of party politics and party organization from its inception to 1714' (Oxford University unpublished D.Phil. thesis, 1962).

EVERY, G., *The High Church Party, 1688-1718* (1956).

EHRENPREIS, Irvin, *Swift: the man, his works and the age* (2 vols., 1962-67).

FOOT, Michael, *The Pen and the Sword* (1957).

FRITZ, Paul S., 'Jacobitism and the English Government, 1717-1731', (Cambridge University unpublished Ph.D. dissertation, 1967).

HART, A. Tindal, *The Life and Times of John Sharp, Archbishop of York* (1949).

HISCOCK, W. G., *Henry Aldrich of Christ Church, 1648-1710* (1960).

HOLMES, Geoffrey, *British Politics in the Age of Anne* (1967).

—, *The Trial of Doctor Sacheverell* (1973).

—, and SPECK, W. A., 'The Fall of Harley in 1708 reconsidered', *English Historical Review*, lxxx (1965), 673.

HORWITZ, Henry, *Revolution Politicks: The career of Daniel Finch Second Earl of Nottingham, 1647-1730* (Cambridge, 1968).

JAMES, F. G., *North Country Bishop* [Nicolson of Carlisle] (New Haven, 1957).

JONES, G. H., *The Mainstream of Jacobitism* (Cambridge, Massachusetts, 1954).

KENYON, J. P., *Robert Spencer, Earl of Sunderland, 1641-1702* (1958).

KETTON-CREMER, R. W., *A Norfolk Gallery* (1948).

KLOPP, Onno, *Der Fall des Hauses Stuart und die Succession des Hauses Hannover* (14 vols, Vienna, 1875-88).

MACAULAY, T. B., 'Francis Atterbury' in *Biographies by Lord Macaulay contributed to the Encyclopaedia Britannica* (Edinburgh, 1840).

—, *The History of England from the Accession of James the Second* (Everyman edn., 1962).

McINNES, Angus, 'The Appointment of Harley in 1704', *The Historical Journal*, xi (1968), 255.

—, *Robert Harley, Puritan Politician* (1970).

MAHON, Lord, *History of England from the Peace of Utrecht* (3 vols., 1836).

MICHAEL, Wolfgang, *England under George I*, Vol. I: *The Beginnings of the Hanoverian Dynasty*, trans. L. B. Namier (1936).

MURRAY, John J., *George I, the Baltic and the Whig Split of 1717* (1969).

PLUMB, J. H., *Sir Robert Walpole* (2 vols., 1956-60).

—, *The Growth of Political Stability in England, 1675-1725* (1967).

REALEY, C. B., *The Early Opposition to Sir Robert Walpole, 1720-1727* (Philadelphia, 1931).

SHENNAN, J. H., and Margaret, 'The Protestant Succession in English Politics, April 1713–September 1715', in *William III and Louis XIV*, ed. R. Hatton and J. S. Bromley (Liverpool, 1968).

SMITH, M. G., 'The administration of the diocese of Exeter during the episcopate of Sir Jonathan Trelawny, 1689-1707' (Oxford University unpublished B.D. thesis, 1964).

SNYDER, H. L., 'Godolphin and Harley: A study of their partnership in politics', *Huntington Library Quarterly*, xxx (1967).

—, 'The defeat of the Occasional Conformity bill and the Tack', *Bulletin of the Institute of Historical Research*, xli (1968), 172.

SPECK, W. A., 'The choice of a Speaker in 1705', *Bulletin of the Institute of Historical Research*, xxxvii (1964), 20.

—, *Tory and Whig: The Struggle in the Constituencies, 1701-15* (1970).

STRAKA, Gerald M., 'The Final Phase of Divine Right Theory in England, 1688-1702', *English Historical Review*, lxxvii (1962), 638.

—, *Anglican Reaction to the Revolution of 1688* (Madison, Wisconsin, 1962).

SYKES, Norman, *Edmund Gibson, Bishop of London* (Oxford, 1926).

—, 'The Cathedral Chapter of Exeter and the General Election of 1705', *English Historical Review*, xlv (1930), 260.

—, 'Benjamin Hoadly', in *The Social and Political Ideas of Some English Thinkers of the Augustan Age*, ed. F. J. C. Hearnshaw (1928).

—, *Church and State in England in the Eighteenth Century* (Cambridge, 1934).

—, 'Queen Anne and the Episcopate', *English Historical Review*, l (1935), 433.

—, *William Wake, Archbishop of Canterbury* (2 vols., Cambridge, 1957).

—, *From Sheldon to Secker: Aspects of English Church History, 1660-1768* (Cambridge, 1959).

THOMAS, R., 'Comprehension and Indulgence', in *From Uniformity to Unity, 1662-1962*, eds. G. F. Nuttall and O. Chadwick (1962).

TURBERVILLE, A. S., *The House of Lords in the XVIIIth Century* (Oxford, 1927).

WARD, W. R., *Georgian Oxford* (1958).

WHITE, R. J., *Dr. Bentley: A Study in Academic Scarlet* (1965).

WILSON, A. McC., *French Foreign Policy during the Administration of Cardinal Fleury, 1726-1743* (Harvard: Cambridge, Massachusetts, 1936).

Index

The abbreviation A. indicates Francis Atterbury